Unlimited Partners

Our American Story

Bob and Elizabeth Dole

*with Richard Norton Smith
and Kerry Tymchuk*

SIMON & SCHUSTER

SIMON & SCHUSTER
Rockefeller Center
1230 Avenue of the Americas
New York, NY 10020

SIMON & SCHUSTER and colophon are registered trademarks
of Simon & Schuster Inc.

Designed by Edith Fowler

Manufactured in the United States of America

10   9   8   7   6   5   4   3   2   1

The Library of Congress has cataloged the 1988 edition as
follows:

Dole, Robert J., 1923–

    The Doles: Unlimited Partners/by Robert and Elizabeth Dole.
p.   cm.
    Includes index.
    1. Dole, Robert J., 1923–   . 2. Dole, Elizabeth Hanford.
3. Legislators—United States—Biography.   4. Cabinet officers
—United States—Biography.   5. United States. Congress.
Senate—Biography.   I. Dole, Elizabeth Hanford.   II Title.
E840.6.D64   1988   87-32032
973.927'092'2—dc19   CIP

ISBN 0-684-83401-4

A portion of this book was originally published by Simon &
Schuster Inc. in hardcover in 1988 under the title The Doles:
Unlimited Partners.

*To Russell, Kansas; Salisbury, North Carolina;
and hometowns across America*

Contents

Prologue

BOB

Anyone who wants to understand me must first understand Russell, Kansas.

It is my home, where my roots lie, and a constant source of strength. It is a wellspring of small-town wisdom, the sort of place where everyone is considered equal in kind, whatever their differences in degree.

My hometown is a classroom of sorts. It teaches by example as well as by maxim. It was in Russell, for instance, where I learned to value doing over talking. My father's view of the world as "stewers versus doers" registered early. From my friends and neighbors, I learned to feel deeply for God, country and family. In Russell, I came to understand there are things worth living for, and, if need be, dying for.

The Russell of my youth was not a place of wealth. Yet it was generous with the values that would shape my outlook and the compassion that would restore life's richness after I had begun to doubt my future following the war. Ever since, I have tried in my own way to give back some of what the town has given me. I have tried to defend and serve the America I learned to love in Russell.

Some debts can never be repaid, but only acknowledged. On March 25, 1996, I returned home to Russell to acknowledge mine. Thanks to a string of primary and caucus victories, most observers agreed that I had secured enough delegates to be the Republican nominee for President. Expected victories the next day in California, Nevada and Washington would erase any lingering doubts. My emotional reaction to all this? Amazement, quite frankly, that a boy from Russell could reach such a goal. So on March 25, there was only one place I wanted to be. And that was home.

Nearly five thousand residents of western Kansas greeted us when Elizabeth, my daughter, Robin, and I walked into the Russell High School gymnasium. One way or another, most of the men and women in that room had played important roles in my life. They and their families put hard-earned quarters in a cigar box to help a wounded World War II veteran get the medical treatment he needed but couldn't afford. Through the years they had always been there, to offer encouragement, friendship and prayers. Now, on a blustery spring day, they had turned out once again to lend support. Surveying the room, my emotions got the best of me when I thought of all the people who weren't there—my mother and father, my brother, Kenny, Huck Boyd, who gave me a start in politics, and others who had helped me in good times and bad.

I went to Russell to celebrate a dream come true. But more important, I told my friends, are the dreams that we have yet to realize; dreams not for me, but for America.

Of course, to much of the world, America itself is a dream. In June 1994, Elizabeth and I journeyed to the place that had played a role in my life second in importance only to Russell— the rugged hills around the Italian village of Castel d'Aiano. There on April 14, 1945, my life changed forever when I felt a sharp sting in my right shoulder. While in the hills of Italy, and later on the beaches of Normandy, Elizabeth and I met and talked with World War II veterans who, with their families, had returned to Europe for activities marking the fiftieth anniversary of D-Day.

For several months prior to my European visit, I had been considering a run for the presidency in 1996. It had become clear to me during the year and a half leading up to my trip that

President Bill Clinton, although well-intentioned, was steering America in the wrong direction. More to the point, I looked at the Clinton presidency and saw sizzle over substance; an Administration where political consultants and public opinion polls decided policy, and glossy rhetoric was all too often confused with genuine leadership. The President's own close adviser, George Stephanopoulos, would admit to *Time* magazine in April 1996 that for Bill Clinton "words are actions."

Yet, many of the President's words contrasted starkly with his actions. Thus, 1996 was already shaping up as a three-way contest between "New Democrat" Bill Clinton, "Old Democrat" Bill Clinton and the Republican nominee.

Could I be that nominee? I could never match Clinton's dazzling verbal skills, to be sure. Indeed, there have been occasions when I have been accused of having a sharp tongue. Better to be yourself, imperfections and all, than pretend to be something you aren't. Better to be guided by the values of Russell, Kansas, than manipulated by electronic focus groups and political handlers. (I've never been very easy to "handle.")

Some people thought all this old-fashioned. But you can be old-fashioned without being outdated. In any event, no matter how far I may have traveled in life, I've never forgotten where I came from. Fortunately, many other Americans shared my perspective, and they flooded my office throughout the first years of the Clinton presidency with flattering calls, letters and promises of support. By the spring of 1994, I sensed that if a decision was not made soon, those who had pledged assistance might start looking at other candidates. Elizabeth said she would support whatever choice I made. My health was fine. (In fact, as *USA Today* reported, my weight is lower, and my blood pressure and cholesterol level better than President Clinton's— but I stand by my promise not to make health an issue in the campaign.)

To be honest, there were times when I wondered if someone with my experience might not be at a disadvantage in an age when distrust of politicians at all levels seems pervasive. To be called a "Washington insider" was the ultimate insult.

Leadership is measured by more than just experience. It requires the right kind of experience. Over the years I've come to think of leadership in Washington as a combination of background and backbone. It's knowing how the political process works and, crucially, how to make it work better. Can you bring together people of diverse views and often clashing priorities, and get them to rise above selfish interest to serve the public interest?

Can you look beyond the next election, to the next generation? Can you tell your pollster that winning an election should not take precedence over preserving Medicaid and Medicare? Can you take on the National Education Association and other lobbyists for the status quo who have saddled the world's brightest kids and teachers with the dumbest bureaucratic process imaginable?

The American people, who for four decades held firm in opposing foreign threats to human liberty, deserve a government that reflects their values. They want a President who will lead by example as well as words, one who is willing to make tough decisions without calculating the effect on his own chances for reelection. They want individuals held responsible for their actions, and institutions held accountable for theirs. They want their anxieties about the future addressed calmly and sensibly, not exploited for short-term political advantage.

This and much more went through my mind as I walked over the Italian landscape with my fellow veterans. I thought of the America we had fought for, the America that subsequently fought and won the Cold War. Our America did the impossible and never paused to boast of it. We overcame the scourge of polio and left our footprints on the moon. And through the civil-rights revolution, our America made good—however belatedly—the promises of opportunity and inclusion that we made to one another at the birth of our nation.

So it was with an ingrained sense of optimism that I thought of the problems confronting today's Americans—an intrusive federal government, deadweight deficits, a tax system that punishes success, a welfare system that traps people in poverty, unsafe streets, inferior schools, and a loss of the timeless values that made America the greatest land in human history.

I knew the challenges were great, but I also knew the American will to overcome was greater. I knew that if words alone could balance the budget, lower our taxes, put people back to work, reform welfare, fix our schools, make our streets safe, truly end the era of big government, and restore American values and leadership to their rightful place, I wouldn't be thinking of running for President. Few people were better at words than Bill Clinton.

But words aren't enough. And I concluded that if our country's future was to be as glorious as its past, then America needed a President who would keep his word . . . a President who knew something about sacrifice . . . a President who didn't consult pollsters before making a decision . . . a President who would provide common-sense answers to complex problems.

I didn't just want to be President, I wanted to be *that kind* of President; one who would never confuse words for deeds; one who wasn't content to feel people's pain—I'd felt enough of my own over the years—but who would seek to cure it, even at the expense of my own political future.

Historians and journalists often speak of "the Nixon goes to China syndrome," meaning that leadership, especially of the historic variety, often takes unpredictable forms. And just as it took Richard Nixon, the hard-line anti-Communist, to make people look beyond the conventional wisdom, so I, with all my experience, would like to be the President who restores trust and public confidence in the American political process.

The decision I made in Europe became official on April 10, 1995, when I announced my candidacy in Topeka, Kansas. The campaign trail was to take its normal—and some not so normal—twists and turns. But within a year of my Topeka announcement, thanks to countless Americans who shared my willingness to sacrifice for the future, I had the nomination in my grasp. And so I went home in March 1996.

As I concluded my remarks in Russell on that very special homecoming day, I posed the question that all candidates seeking America's highest office are asked: Why do I want to be

President? My response was—and is—because I will not permit the country I love so much, the country I sacrificed for, to continue down a road that leads to economic and moral disaster. Because I am convinced that America's finest hour is not in our past, but in our future.

I then asked one more thing of the people who had given me so much. I asked for their prayers.

Throughout my life, my goal has been to honor Russell by being worthy of the men and women who have believed in me. It is a commitment I hope to carry to the White House.

ELIZABETH

What Russell is to Bob, Salisbury is to me. And two weeks after Bob returned to Kansas to claim victory in the race for the Republican presidential nomination, he and I journeyed to North Carolina for a homecoming celebration.

More than 2,700 people were on hand when Bob and I entered Salisbury's Catawba College gymnasium. Front and center were my ninety-four-year-old mother; my brother, John, and his wife, Bunny; my nephew John; my mother's ninety-two-year-old brother, Joe Cathey; and my cousins Anita and Kevin Ryan.

Looking out over the room, I caught sight of lifelong friends and high-school classmates, many of whom had traveled great distances to attend. Bob said everyone had come to see me. But I knew better, because I knew Salisbury—they had also turned out to see Salisbury's favorite adopted son.

When it was my turn to speak, I proudly related the story of the man who I believe has the character, the vision and the values to lead America into the twenty-first century. It was a message I had been sharing across the country on a full-time basis for the better part of six months.

At the time of Bob's announcement on April 10, 1995, I had been president of the American Red Cross for nearly five years—the most challenging and rewarding time of my life. More than a job to me, the Red Cross was a mission—one enabling me to lead an organization bigger than half the companies on the Fortune 500, with the goal not of making a profit, but of making a difference in the lives of those in dire human need.

It is a mission to which I will rededicate myself, no matter the outcome of this November's election. My decision to return to the Red Cross after the campaign was one that made headlines across the country—and it was one that was not made lightly. I knew that every First Lady in American history had been closely scrutinized by the public and the media. Each has placed her own personal imprimatur on the role of First Lady, a position for which there is no job description. Rather it reflects the personal and life experiences of each individual. No one, however, had done what I proposed to do—hold a full-time paying job while serving as First Lady.

My intention to do so, then, broke new ground. Seen in another light, however, by returning to the Red Cross I would be doing just as other First Ladies did before me—filling the role in the way that best fit my personality, interests and life experience.

My experience included working for the American Red Cross—an organization with no agenda other than a humanitarian one. Although my decision to continue at the Red Cross while serving as First Lady would break new ground, I believed the presidency of the Red Cross and the role of First Lady would be a good fit—both in terms of geography—the Red Cross national headquarters building is only one block away from the White House—and responsibility. I knew that if I were to become First Lady, I would devote my time and energy to helping those in need, reaching out to at-risk youth, and encouraging Americans to donate time and money to charitable organizations: in short, to causes that already formed my daily mission at the American Red Cross.

In making my decision, I realized that serving as First Lady and president of the American Red Cross might create some unique and challenging situations. But I was confident that if the Red Cross—an organization that must respond to natural disasters with speed and ingenuity—could not handle these situations, then no one could.

I did not make my decision alone. There were many heart-to-heart talks with Bob, who, as has always been the case throughout our marriage, was completely supportive of my decision. "Just don't ask me to turn my Cabinet meetings into blood drives," he joked.

I also met with my talented Red Cross management staff, and with a number of those on our fifty-member board of governors—including Norm Augustine, the savvy chief of Lockheed Martin, who serves so ably as the board's chairman. I asked if Bob's running for President might lead some to question the independence and nonpartisanship of the Red Cross.

"Correct me if I'm wrong," said Norm, "but you're not running for President of the United States—your husband is." He pointed out that during my entire service at the Red Cross Bob held the very partisan job of Senate Republican Leader, and it had not led to any problems. We had learned long ago to compartmentalize our professional life from our personal life. To avoid any suggestion of partisanship, however, the board and I agreed that when I traveled with Bob on his announcement tour, or on any other campaign trip, I would do so on unpaid leave, and would not discuss political issues.

But as the early primaries drew closer, I knew it was time to hit the campaign trail on a full-time basis, and to speak openly. Like many other Americans, I believed our country was headed in the wrong direction. I had no doubt that the man I loved was precisely the person who would fight for the fundamental change necessary to get America back on track, and I wanted to devote all my energies to sharing that belief with others. And so with the board's approval, I began my leave of absence.

I have not regretted my decision for a minute. Campaigning for and with Bob is a privilege that I cherish each day. I enjoy introducing voters to a man who has been elected six times by his fellow Senators to be Republican Leader—and the Senate is a tough precinct. Bob's colleagues recognize his exceptional leadership skills and revere him as a man whose word is his bond, and who is trusted and respected by Democrats and Republicans alike. I was proud of Bob's courage as he traveled to Hollywood to speak frankly about the role the entertainment industry has played in the coarsening of our culture. I'll always remember the hotel doorman who returned the tip I had given him, saying "Please give this to Senator Dole's campaign." And who wouldn't be moved by the young people who come up to tell me that in Bob they have finally found someone they regard as a hero.

As Bob and I look to the campaign ahead, we take heart in one of our favorite stories told about his hero, Dwight Eisenhower. It is said that one night in 1945 General Eisenhower was walking along the Rhine, thinking of the crossing in which he would lead the Allied Armies. He met a soldier, and asked him why he wasn't sleeping. The young GI, who didn't recognize Ike, said, "I guess I'm just a little nervous."

"So am I," said Eisenhower. "Let's walk together, and perhaps we'll draw strength from one another." For the past twenty years, Bob and I have walked together and drawn strength from each other along the way. And whatever challenges may lie ahead, we will continue to do just that.

CHAPTER ONE

The Doles
of Russell

BOB

Ad astra per aspera:
To the stars through difficulties.

—KANSAS STATE MOTTO

Shortly after my U.S. Senate colleagues elected me Majority
Leader in November 1984, a banker friend from Wichita, Kansas, stopped by the Capitol to offer congratulations. The security people directed him to S-230, part of a handsome suite of
rooms just off the Rotunda. As a fellow Midwesterner, he had
no trouble recognizing earlier Republican Majority Leaders
whose pictures lined the walls. He admired the portraits of
Lincoln and Eisenhower, heroes of mine I had added as a personal touch.

Something about the place touched a common nerve. We
fell silent before a marble fireplace, where we gazed at each
other for a moment. Then a smile crossed my visitor's face.

"Imagine a kid from Russell, Kansas, having an office like
this."

Imagine indeed. Such ambitions would never have occurred
to me as a child, the son of a volunteer fireman, who lived
during Dust Bowl days at the corner of Eleventh and Maple;
who along with my family looked on helplessly as the prairie
blew away; and who later, in my own time of trial, would be

rescued from despair by generous friends and neighbors. I don't get back to my hometown as often as I would like, but when I do I find it crowded with ghosts. So many people I knew as a boy are gone. In their place is a community struggling to adapt to changed conditions on the farm and in the oil fields.

It is often remarked that in politics twenty-four hours can be a lifetime. In the turmoil of Washington, it's good to have some things that don't change. Elizabeth's love and that of my family provide a special kind of strength. The same is true of the memories and values I associate with Russell, Kansas.

Places shape people, Kansas more distinctively than most. The name conjures up a gallery of pictures. Sunflowers and cottonwood trees. Farmland flat as a tabletop. The Old West of Boot Hill and the Pony Express. And, of course, Dorothy Gayle forsaking her black-and-white surroundings for a more colorful neighborhood over the rainbow.

What people tend to forget is that Dorothy spent the rest of the movie trying to get *back* to Kansas.

Like most Kansans, I understand how she felt. It would take someone with a more poetic gift than I possess to convey the lonely majesty of the prairie, broken only by an occasional farmhouse or grain elevator. Few sights can match the reflected gold of a Kansas wheat field. Overhead, hawks swoop low over barns and over windmills drawing water for thirsty cattle. At night a blanket of stars covers the land, casting a glow unknown to city dwellers. With a little imagination, you can see a herd of Texas longhorns bound for Abilene, or a wagon train lumbering along the Oregon Trail.

The sounds of Kansas stir just as many memories for me. In the countryside around Russell, you can catch the hum of an oil rig, and the chime of cottonwood leaves tossed about by a restless wind. Nearby Dodge City lays claim to being the windiest place in America, with a constant speed of fourteen miles per hour. Somewhere between the breezes of Dodge City and Dorothy's tornado, the winds of Kansas have done a great deal to define the American landscape.

"When anything is going to happen in this country, it happens first in Kansas," vowed William Allen White, the homespun editor from Emporia, who combined the better qualities of Ben Franklin, Horace Greeley and Teddy Roosevelt. White wasn't indulging in Chamber of Commerce puffery. Kansas voters chose the first female mayor in America (Argonia, 1887) and the first woman elected to the U.S. Senate in her own right (my colleague Nancy Landon Kassebaum). From the ground-breaking work of Topeka's Menninger Clinic to the record-shattering achievements of runner Jim Ryun and pilot Amelia Earhart and the works of playwright William Inge, Kansans have pushed out the boundaries of individual creativity and social conscience.

We're in the middle of things, geographically. And over the years a picture has been painted of us as a triumph of the ordinary. You know, Lake Wobegone on a grand scale. But there's more to Kansas than white picket fences and porch swings.

Kansas is two states. The first stretches from the Missouri border to the one hundredth meridian. Much of the land is buried under blue stem grass and a rich alluvial soil that is reminiscent of the Mississippi Valley. Here you'll find university towns like Lawrence, and newspaper readers who reach for the *New York Times* as well as the *Kansas City Star*. In the state's southeastern corner, a region whose ethnic diversity won it the nickname "the Balkans," men burrowed into the earth for mineral wealth as their grandfathers did at the turn of the century.

Back then, oil siphoned out of eastern fields was used to grease wagon wheels carrying pioneers to the Pacific Coast. To get there, they had to cross western Kansas, once home to nomadic tribes like the Osage and horse-riding Arapahoes. As white men flooded the plains, they drove out the buffalo the red men relied on. Early explorers dubbed the area the Great American Desert, and some Kansans still call everything west of Salina "out there."

Life in the west was never easy. As a boy, I heard stories of hardship and the stoicism it bred, of men who lived on potato pie and women who covered the walls of sod houses with newspapers. The history of those times reads like a catalog of natural disasters. Fires leapfrogged the tinder-dry prairie, and droughts rendered the earth infertile. Tornados appeared out of nowhere, to do a dance of destruction. In the summer of 1877, grasshoppers came on the wind, so thick they blotted out the sun. From Texas to the Dakotas, they devoured clothes off people's backs. They also changed the shape of Kansas agriculture, by leading farmers to plant less of the vulnerable corn and more wheat.

The same plague inspired Kansas' distinctive brand of humor, part tall tale, part poker-faced witticism. The hoppers ate pigs' noses, it was claimed. This was no more an exaggeration than the boast that cabbage leaves are used for circus tents or that cornstalks are suitable for bridge building. If the Kansas wind steals your hat, it's said, don't bother running after it. The next gust is sure to bring a replacement.

I used to tell out-of-town visitors that on a clear day you can see all the way to Kansas City, 250 miles away. Kansas may be flat, but it isn't *that* flat.

Along with a hint of the absurd, Kansas humor is irreverent. If you can joke about natural disasters, you are not likely to take people too seriously, or to think that those who are put into office are any better or worse than those who put them there. We tolerate anything but snobs. John J. Ingalls found this out for himself during the Populist uprising of the 1890s. For eighteen years, the classically educated Ingalls had represented Kansas in the U.S. Senate, where he made no attempt to conceal his favorable view of himself. When the farmers lost their land, Ingalls lost his seat. As one wag put it:

> Up was he stuck
> And in the upness of his stucktitude
> He fell.

Anyone who wants to understand present-day Kansas, or its politics, needs to know a little bit about the Populists. In January 1886 the state was paralyzed by its worst blizzard ever. The windchill hit minus 100 degrees. Next came a severe drought. Crops failed. Land prices fell. Before long, westward immigration reversed itself, with wagons headed east proclaiming their own version of a state motto: "In God We Trusted, In Kansas We Busted." In the state's Seventh District, a candidate for Congress who had lost a fortune in the Blizzard of '86 accused his Republican opponent of wearing silk stockings and was swept into office. Thus the legend of "Sockless Jerry" Simpson was born. Simpson joined with the Farmers' Alliance, a forerunner of the People's, or Populist, Party, and demanded the nationalization of railroads and a graduated income tax.

When the price of wheat went up, Populist fortunes plummeted. But Simpson and his allies left an insurgent virus in the state's bloodstream. Periodically activated by troubles on the farm, the Populists forced Republicans across the spectrum to soften their hostility to government action. Accustomed as we are to being the state's dominant party of government, the GOP in Kansas must appeal to the widest range of voters to earn its majority status. Perhaps this, along with the compromising spirit required in a state whose eastern and western halves are so different, explains my own brand of conservatism.

Another thing about Kansas: women have always played a significant role in its political dramas. In the late nineteenth century, rural audiences were spellbound by Mrs. Mary Elizabeth Lease, "Lady Orator of the West." When she wasn't warning against government "of Wall Street, by Wall Street, and for Wall Street," Mrs. Lease urged destitute farmers to raise less corn and more hell.

Another woman on the hustings, of even greater influence, was the wife of a Medicine Lodge minister. After her first husband succumbed to alcohol, Carrie Nation launched a one-woman crusade against the stuff in 1873. Members of the Women's Christian Temperance Union, which she founded, prayed in saloons before taking an ax to the bar. Within five years they had persuaded the voters of Kansas to impose prohibition. In 1905 the battleship *Kansas* was christened with spring water instead of champagne. I have a soft spot in my heart for Mrs. Nation. For years, the WCTU was the only union that had anything nice to say about me.

Joseph Talbott of Rising Sun, Indiana, and his wife, Elva, were part of a wide river of humanity which flowed westward in the years after the Civil War and was joined by tributaries from other already settled regions in the old Northwest Territory. Out of Ohio and upstate New York came fresh currents, bearing travelers like Robert and Margaret Dole. The two streams converged around a little crossroads settlement in north-central Kansas. Originally called Fossil Station, in 1871 it changed its name to Russell, in honor of a minor Union Army hero who never visited his namesake.

Others came in his place. German-Russian families from the Ukraine, escaping Czar Alexander II's universal conscription, built rock houses in open range country along the Smoky Hill River and harnessed oxen to plow up the ground. The last of the cattle drives wound through the area, led by cowboys who spent sixteen hours a day in the saddle and relaxed at night to guitar music. But their days were numbered by the spread of another kind of horse, this one made of iron.

By 1870 the Union Pacific had arrived to encourage the civic planners of tiny Fossil Station. A schoolhouse was built. A hotel opened its doors. After an intense dispute with neighboring Bunker Hill which stopped just short of bloodshed, Russell won designation as county seat. When a sizable number of Russian immigrants settled in the area, they imported the methods of cultivation first perfected on the steppes of their homeland. They brought something else as well, a foreign strain of wheat called Turkey Red. Slumbering in the earth during the long winter, ready for harvesting by late June, the new wheat crop ensured that agriculture would reign supreme in this part of the state.

Wheat, milo and alfalfa flourished in the black earth of Russell County. Trees were another story, and wood was so scarce that Russell merchants paid three dollars per cord for post rock, a honey-colored stone left behind by ancient oceans. Soft enough to quarry by hand or cut with a saw, it went into countless rail and fence posts which still dot the countryside around the town.

Before barbed wire, post rock divided one farm from another. Joseph Talbott, my grandfather, lived on such a farm ten miles south of town. He worked the land for what it would yield and also custom-butchered steers and hogs for delivery to local grocers. It was a hard, bloody way to feed his family.

Several miles to the east, Robert and Margaret Dole scratched a living from land they occupied as tenant farmers. Doles and Talbotts shared a common ethic in which work was instinct, idleness a sin. Affection was more often implied than stated. Likewise with praise for work done well.

Yet feelings ran deep and loyalties were for life. Among the latter was an old-fashioned patriotism. It led the Doles' seventeen-year-old son, Doran, to drop out of Russell High School in November 1917. Along with a friend who repaired shoes on the side, Doran Dole lied about his age, hoping to get into uniform and to go Over There. He got only half his wish, spending the last year of World War I at army posts in Texas and Illinois.

Doran returned in 1919 to a thriving village of two thousand people, the sort of place Sinclair Lewis would have recognized, even if he might not appreciate its virtues. An old dream of making Russell a commercial rival to Denver and Kansas City was gone. Still, town fathers were not short of promotable assets. There was a new $40,000 high school, an enlarged flour mill and what the *Russell Record* called "a real live Chamber of Commerce." Summers were enlivened by the tent-show lectures and popular entertainments of Chautauqua. Other times, people created their own diversions. They went to bridge parties, dropped in on friends, attended ice-cream socials and high-school athletic contests.

Home from the service, Doran opened the White Front Café on Main Street. It was there, according to local legend, that the cook prepared a wedding supper for Doran and Bina Talbott in February 1921. Two months short of her eighteenth birthday, Bina was the oldest daughter in a family of twelve. She was a pretty girl, with a gift for homemaking and an inexhaustible supply of energy.

Bina had even more reason than the average bride to rejoice on her wedding day. A freak accident had nearly deprived her of her groom. Doran had agreed to play Santa Claus for children in the nearby Pioneer neighborhood. Reaching behind a tree decorated with burning candles, Santa ignited the sleeve of his red coat. Fortunately, the ground outside was snow covered. The next day, those around the dinner table noticed that young Doran Dole had blisters on his ears. The resulting damage to the youngsters' faith in Saint Nicholas was far worse than any temporary burns sustained by my father. It wasn't the last time a Republican has been accused of killing Santa Claus.

The summer of 1923 was a busy one in Russell. President Warren G. Harding's train passed through twice. The first time was on the harried Chief Executive's way to Alaska, where he hoped to get a respite from the mounting scandals in his Administration. Two weeks later, a black-draped engine re-traced the route, carrying a dead President past grieving crowds back to Washington. Russell closed its shops and held a memo-rial service in the hall usually reserved for Odd Fellows meet-ings.

Also that summer, an outbreak of pink eye was reported in local herds. Two blocks of Main Street were paved over for the first time, with red bricks produced in the county. People were singing a hit song by a University of Kansas student, "Daddy Stole Our Last Clean Sheet and Joined the KKK." Before Wil-liam Allen White drove the Wizards out of the state, mostly by laughing at them, Klan activity briefly threatened both major political parties. A large crowd attended a Klan picnic south of Russell in 1923. Afterward, hometown papers noted that the main address of the day, a three-hour harangue delivered by a Salina preacher, alienated nearly everyone it didn't put to sleep.

By far the most excitement that summer was generated by the prospect of an oil boom. Attention was focused on Fairport, eighteen miles from Russell, where a group of investors jointly dubbed the Lucky Seven were surveying lime formations and preparing to drill at what they called the Carrie Oswald well. The rumors mounted for months. Oil leases and real-estate speculation replaced Kansas City cattle markets in conversa-tions along Main Street.

Doran and Bina Dole paid little attention to all the talk of oil and impending wealth. Doran by then was busy running the

Fairmont Creamery Company and urging readers of the *Russell Record* to buy cows. That way, he insisted, they could produce one cash crop that wouldn't rob the soil.

On July 22 Doran went to work as usual. Before the day was out, he was called home. Home was a three-room house located a stone's throw from the Union Pacific tracks in the town's less fashionable North Side. It had a living room, a bedroom and a lean-to kitchen. Even by the day's standards, it was a modest address.

It was also crowded. A year before, Bina had presented her husband with their first child, a daughter they named Gloria. Now Gloria had a brother. The latest addition to the family was named for his two grandfathers, Robert and Joseph.

Writing about another small Kansas town, Dwight D. Eisenhower said of his boyhood home of Abilene that "it provided both a healthy outdoor existence and a need to work. The same conditions were responsible for . . . a society which, more nearly than any other I have encountered, eliminated prejudices based upon wealth, race or creed . . . any youngster who has the opportunity to spend his early youth in an enlightened rural area has been favored by fortune."

Russell was like that. It shared Abilene's devotion to self-sufficiency, but also thought of itself as an extended family. It had its social distinctions, humorously summed up in the handsome neighborhood south of Wisconsin Street dubbed Quality Hill. It also had a surprising degree of ethnic variety. In the southeast corner of town, German-Russian families clung to their old ways. In the winter they soaked a cloth in oil and applied it to the chest to ward off colds. First-generation immigrants munched on what we called Russian peanuts, or sunflower seeds. They used their teeth to crack open the shell, extract the seed inside and spit out the husk.

Today, as when I was a boy, few of Russell's people think that bloodlines or bank accounts are valid tests of character. The sudden wealth that followed the Thanksgiving Day 1923 discovery of oil at the Carrie Oswald site changed many things in town, but it didn't change Russell's fundamental beliefs.

There was no landed gentry to call the shots, there were few big houses or flashy cars. Bank still lent money to wildcatters or farmers with a handshake for collateral.

Of course, some things were different. Strange faces crowded the porch of the Driscoll Hotel. Aspiring tycoons unable to rent a room were forced to live in tents. And an influx of Democrats from Texas and Oklahoma reduced Republican margins on election day from crushing to merely huge.

Oil meant money and lots of it. It lured outsiders, many of them lonely men with cash in their pockets and time on their hands. Along Highway 40, just outside Russell, the oil boom spawned nightclubs and dance halls. Casinos like the Big Apple or the Wagon Wheel led some residents to fear that their community was becoming a regular little Chicago.

My folks passed up floor shows and slot machines for homelier pleasures. After the brutal heat of the day, a young couple might climb into the family car and drive out to the countryside, where temperatures were cooler than in town. Or they joined in the horseshoe contests at the Happy Hollow, a workingman's retreat on the banks of the Saline River. At the Hollow they could dance in the open air, under strings of electric lights. In between sets of music there was croquet. Some patrons indulged in homemade ice cream. Others preferred illicit 3.2 beer.

More than one Russellite padded his income by selling bootleg whiskey. Like many of his best customers, my father occasionally felt the urge to quench the public's thirst. But it wasn't the refreshments he served that attracted business to his Main Street creamery station or to the grain elevator he managed in later years. It was the fair prices he paid for locally produced milk, cream and eggs and for the cans of sour cream I helped him load onto an eastbound car of the Union Pacific.

But most of those clustering around "Doley's" each morning, talking politics, forecasting the weather or playing the Kansas City futures market, were there because of the proprietor himself. My father was the sort of man who never forgot a name, never went to a doctor and never felt as comfortable in a J. C. Penney suit as in his well-worn, immaculate overalls. He wore Old Spice and called women Sis. He cracked jokes and kept his dignity.

He rarely repeated himself. He didn't have to, because he spoke with such authority the first time that you would never question him. When the alarm clock went off by mistake at three o'clock one morning and he groggily sent me for some milk at the grocery store, I went. I waited outside the closed door for a couple of hours, until Dad realized what had happened and came to get me.

One thing he didn't do much of was relax. My father's proudest boast was having missed just one day of work in forty years. Since his workdays customarily began at six in the morning and rarely ended before sundown, he had little time for self-improvement in the modern sense. He never went to the scrubby pasture on one side of town fixed up as a golf course. To him, golf was a game for loafers. Dad found his recreation in the town ball team, a pitch game or the volunteer fire company he belonged to for fifty-five years. A shopping trip to Kansas City was a cosmopolitan adventure.

My father shared the Kansan's love of the outdoors. He liked to fish and hunt. My brother, Kenny, and I used to walk behind him on frosty autumn mornings as he tracked down jackrabbits. He sometimes let me try my hand at the wheel of our boxy old Whippet, a car that seemed to have more power backing up a hill than going forward.

Dad shared everything with his family except his own troubles. Emotionally self-contained, he could be a man of eloquent silence. All you had to see was his face as he approached the hospital door to know what he thought about what went on behind it, yet when his friends were sick he spent hours at their bedside. Sometimes he stayed at the hospital all night. Friends kept a watch over one another in those days. When a life ended, they put on Sunday suits and with sunburnt hands carried a friend to his grave.

Students of Freud might find repression in Dad's habit of greeting a loved one with a handshake rather than a hug. Not I. Around the Dole house, we were taught that gestures, like words, have an emotional currency, that compliments can be devalued by overuse. So if you mowed the lawn to perfection, on time and with every blade of grass in place, you treasured Dad's "Pretty good."

My father divided the world into two camps. As he put it, "There are doers and there are stewers." If you were on a sinking ship, some people would sit around stewing about the impending disaster, others would get up and do something about it. He didn't have to add that if the doer succeeded in radioing for help, he needn't expect a ticker-tape parade when he returned to port. Why make a fuss over doing your duty?

Yet if my father was sparing with his praise, he gave generously from a storehouse of wit. He couldn't even take a family argument too seriously. When tempers flared up, as they do sooner or later in most households, he would slip out the front door, a half-smile on his face. An hour later he'd be back, having put the time to good use by raking the lawn or clearing the sidewalk.

I'm not certain any boy can do justice to his mother. My own had a phrase she used to repeat. "Can't never could do anything," she told us. Obviously, my father had married a doer, not a stewer. If Dad laughed at the world, Mom set out to conquer it. Formal discipline was left to her. In fact, her whole life was an exercise in self-discipline. She was a perfectionist when it came to appearance and almost everything else. She even insisted on waxing the little wooden porch at Eleventh and Maple, the house I was born in and where I lived until I was nine, when we moved just down the street.

By then, Gloria and I had not only a brother, Kenny, but a sister, Norma Jean. We all shared one room, a bike, a pair of roller skates. Our home was humble, but it was always spic-and-span. Mom saw to that. Gloria still has the set of dining-room chairs we sat on as kids, hitching our legs up so they wouldn't touch the floor Mom had just washed and waxed. It was a long wait for that floor to dry. It was also a lesson in self-control.

Some people around town suspected Mom of washing Dad's overalls when he went home for lunch every day. I know that every night she washed the corduroy outfits Kenny and I wore to school. My mother made most of our clothes. And since she seemed able to make almost anything on a sewing machine, it wasn't long before she began a career as a sales-woman and a sewing instructor. During the week she sold Singer products door to door, and on Saturday mornings she conducted sewing classes for the women of Russell in a little shop downtown. I can still see her lugging those bulky old sewing machines and vacuum cleaners. In the afternoon we'd come home from school to find food she had left out for us. We didn't know it then, but we were latchkey children. Long before the term became fashionable, the Doles were a two-career fam-ily. We had no choice.

My mother's strength nurtured us through the same hard times experienced throughout America's Farm Belt in those days. But in her eyes it wasn't enough just to get by. She wanted us to get ahead. Never having finished high school, she was determined that we would do better. I'm sure that I owe much of whatever success I've achieved to her example.

I don't want to leave the impression that she was a task-master. She adored her family, doted later on her grandchildren, and delighted in decorating our house weeks in advance of Christmas. When a neighbor died, she was the one who knocked on doors to collect money for flowers. During the war, she invited servicemen from a nearby airbase into her home for weekends, capped by a Sunday chicken dinner she cooked herself.

Sacrificing her own comfort for others was a habit she never lost. For my sixtieth birthday, I flew out to Kansas to spend the day in Russell. Mom was up at five o'clock that morning, laying out the ingredients for my favorite meal, fried chicken and gravy. Over the years, I've probably eaten more chicken than Colonel Sanders—the fate of anyone who spends time on the political-dinner circuit—but none ever tasted better to me than the chickens prepared in the little kitchen at 1035 Maple.

Neither of my parents was politically active. Both were Republicans until an American Legion buddy of Dad's named Cliff Holland ran for Congress as a Democrat. Not until my own race for county attorney did they change their voter registration back to Republican. Mom always got mad when people wrote letters to the editor criticizing her son's performance. She was particularly outraged when the county Democratic chairman plastered a Main Street storefront with signs reading "Vote for Bob Dole and Twenty-five Cent Wheat."

It was all politics, I told her. Nothing more.

No matter how great her pride in my accomplishments, she was always one of my closest, and most helpful, critics. Following my vice-presidential nomination in August 1976, I delivered an acceptance speech before the convention in Kansas City in which I thanked delegates for their support and unleashed a few one-liners at the opposition's expense. Afterward I returned to the holding room just off the speakers' platform.

"How did I do?" I asked my mother.

"You usually do better."

His own family may have been poor, said President Eisenhower, "but the glory of America is that we didn't know it." In Russell as elsewhere, the depression that gripped agricultural America throughout the 1930s exerted its own leveling influence. Thanks to the chickens my father brought home and the cream my mother made into butter, we lived comparatively well. Other families traded chickens for groceries. A dozen eggs paid the doctor for the removal of a child's tonsils.

On Saturday mornings, I watched as farmers hauled sour cream into my father's store. The few dollars they were paid was a week's spending money. As usual in a farm economy, products in the greatest supply earned the smallest return. Wheat sold for a pittance, oil for a quarter a barrel.

Merchants borrowed money to pay their taxes. Housewives made rag rugs. Yet, even with their own hardships, people still paid attention to the plight of others. If you had your field plowed ahead of schedule, you helped your neighbor prepare his land for planting. When hoboes came through town, on rail or by foot, rarely were they turned away without something to eat. They too were seen as victims of forces beyond their control or understanding.

Even the weather turned hostile. Back in the days of the First World War, Washington had persuaded farmers to plow up their pastures and plant wheat. Food would win the war. At the time no one anticipated a drought. But that's exactly what happened after 1933. When the rains failed to come, the earth became powder dry. Soon there was nothing to prevent the wind from carrying off once rich topsoil.

Anyone who lived through those times remembers the first sighting of an ominous cloud, leading to hopes of rain. The clouds were real, but they contained dirt instead of water. Dust storms blotted out the noonday sun and made the air taste of grit. Kids raced home from school to stuff wet towels and rags under doors and windowsills. Some people lost their way, and there were stories of trains being derailed in the black blizzards. Standing on Main Street in Russell, unable to see the marquee of the Dream Theater fifty feet away, I wondered whether whole towns might disappear under the grimy film left by the storm. No wonder we called the Dust Bowl decade the Dirty Thirties.

During one of these storms, I got pretty dirty myself delivering copies of the *Salina Journal*. It wasn't my first job. My brother and I had been washing cars and delivering handbills since grade school. At the age of twelve I went to work at Dawson's Drugstore, a few steps down Main Street from my father's business. For a dollar a day I whipped up chocolate malteds behind the soda fountain, and gave curb service on weekends. I picked up the comic style of the Dawson brothers, who enjoyed a local renown for their tart one-liners. I also developed an appetite for ice cream that would horrify nutritionists. In my first two weeks on the job, I put on nine pounds.

Dawson's was the most popular watering hole in town. Sports figured heavily in the conversations that went on there. In later years, one side of the place was decorated in the purple and white colors of Kansas State University, the other in the red and blue of rival University of Kansas. Farmers would stop by after dumping their grain at the nearby elevator. On Saturday night, cars parked out front as families came into town to do their weekly grocery shopping. Stores along Main Street stayed open late then, and the drugstore itself rarely closed before eleven. The one exception was Sunday evening, when Chet Dawson hurried home in time to catch that week's broadcast of *Amos 'n' Andy.*

For me, Dawson's was a place to make friends, a marvelous listening post and a source of income, all rolled into one. Men who dropped by for coffee stayed to talk politics. In between their Bromo-Seltzer and cigars, they compared notes on Franklin D. Roosevelt's latest fireside chat. The debated Henry Wallace's controversial policies to limit agricultural production and thereby drive up prices. They calculated our Governor Alfred M. Landon's chances of unseating FDR in the 1936 presidential contest.

Spending so much time around the drugstore, I was bound to come into contact with medical men. A frequent visitor was Dr. Koerber, our family doctor, whose office was over the pool hall on Main Street. Another physician for whom I developed enormous respect was Fagan White. I can't think of anyone who contributed more to the life of the community than Koerber and White. It was a short step from admiring doctors to wanting to be one myself.

The hard times of the Depression were fertile breeding grounds for political extremists, some of them richly entertaining. As regular listeners to radio station KFKB ("Kansas First, Kansas Best"), my family heard the spoutings of a quack doctor (and would-be governor) named John R. Brinkley. "Goat Gland" Brinkley had earned his nickname promoting what he claimed was a restorative for male virility. By the early thirties he was a mainstay of Midwest airwaves, dispensing advice worth what it cost on his program, *The Medical Question Box of the Air.* Doc Brinkley was an early media star.

For less ephemeral values I visited my grandparents' farms outside Russell. Grandpa Talbott made regular delivery trips into town in a Model T with side curtains and lap robes. My brother, Kenny, and I often went along. If we were lucky, the grocer to whom we were delivering freshly butchered meat might generously hand us a nickel sack of candy. Grandpa Talbott sometimes came out with a stick of bologna and a loaf of store-bought bread. Then we were content to sit on the front step and watch the world pass in review as the old man completed his business inside.

My grandfather had little, materially speaking. But he shared whatever he had. The same was true of my Dole grandparents, whom we often visited after Sunday school and church. Grandmother Dole could make a chicken that had been scratching in the yard an hour before taste like ambrosia. Meat was a rarity in that house, refrigerators unheard of. The Doles had big crocks in which they covered fried-down sausage in warm grease for preservation. For Kenny and me, no visit was complete until we fished out a piece of sausage. After that we went outside to feed the chickens, gather eggs and help milk cows.

My Dole grandparents enforced a strict code of courtesy, honesty and personal integrity. Any youngster who slipped into slang or called an elder by his first name instead of Mister was sure to be reprimanded. And, like the Talbotts, like virtually everyone I knew in Russell and the surrounding countryside, Robert and Margaret Dole believed in self-reliance.

Farmers live out a paradox. Their way of making a living by working the soil often borders on the heroic, yet their survival largely depends on factors beyond their control, including, but not limited to, climate and government action. With so much riding on chance, it hardly seems fair to brand them personal failures when things don't go their way. Yet it happens.

In my experience, people can stand the loss of a house, however shattering, better than the loss of their self-respect. So while the residents of Russell believed in the individual work ethic, they were also reluctant to define personal worth with a dollar sign. Over the years, much of the town's economy has been based on agriculture and oil. The volatility of each is seen in how many may have been down on their luck at one time or another, only to scramble back at the next turn of the economic cycle.

Not everyone was so fortunate. When I was county attorney in the 1950s, it was part of the job each month to sign papers approving welfare benefits for my Dole grandparents, among others. Things were rough on farm people back then, roughest of all on their pride. For my grandparents, a lifetime of toil and sacrifice hadn't been enough to gain financial security for their final years. They weren't alone in their plight.

To the casual observer, Russell probably looks just like a hundred other Kansas towns. It is laid out on a familiar geometric grid, around a red-brick business block. Its streets have numbers for names. It's a product of the railroad, which comes by less frequently now than when I was a boy.

Once a year there was the Russell County Fair. On Memorial Day, which we then called Decoration Day, an ancient Civil War colonel named F. S. Ames led a parade down Main Street. When it was over, half the town crowded into Dawson's for banana splits. Five weeks later came the Fourth of July, one of those days when it would have been 105 degrees in the shade had there been any. That evening, when it had cooled off enough to raise the window shutters, Dad would bring home a big chunk of ice and a case of soda pop. The ice was placed in front of an electric fan while my father and his friends shot off fireworks.

The Doles were not globetrotters. In my first twenty years I went no farther east than Kansas City. One week when I was twelve or so, Kenny and I went with Dad to a friend's cabin in Estes Park, a couple hundred miles west of the Colorado line. We fished in mountain streams and reenacted Indian raids among piles of boulders.

Such exposure as we had to the larger world came mostly from the silver screen. Once a week, Russell's Dream Theater staged the Owl Show, a late-night performance which cost a dime. And children with good school attendance records received a free pass for a Saturday matinee of Hoot Gibson. At home, we gathered around a big old Philco radio placed outside on the porch so that neighbors could also hear Fibber McGee and Fred Allen. Sometimes at night I crept close to the set, turned the sound down low to avoid detection and listened to postbedtime treats like *The Shadow*.

Education came in many forms. Aunt Mildred Dole offered twenty-five cents for a perfectly spelled paper. I accepted the bribe, and remain a stickler on the subject to this day. My schoolteachers did their best to draw out a rather bashful boy. I was more interested in history than in math, and the study of Latin verbs seemed pretty pale stuff beside the shoot-'em-up heroics of Bleeding Kansas and the farm revolt of Populist days. But my teachers persevered. Spurred on by my teachers' faith and my mother's encouragement, I was selected for the National Honor Society. As a regular at the local Methodist church, I was also elected president of a young Christian organization called Hi-Y.

I didn't go out for debating, being preoccupied with physical contests rather than verbal ones. I lifted homemade barbells made from concrete blocks and lead pipe. In those parts and in those days, if you breathed and walked and weighed eighty pounds you were a candidate for the football squad. And if you lived in our part of town, it was only a question of time before you joined the North Side Gang for some vigorous sandlot contests.

I played alongside friends like Phil Ruppenthal, the son of a local judge. Phil was the backyard genius who read every book in the town library before going off to Harvard. Maybe my closest friend was Bud Smith, a teammate on the Russell High School football team, the Broncos. Bud was killed when his plane went down in the South Pacific in the spring of 1945. News of his death reached Russell while I was on an Italian battlefield half a world away.

As a competitor in the 440 and the 880, I gave Glenn Cunningham no cause to worry about his place in the record books. Whatever I lacked in natural athletic gifts, I tried to compensate for with willpower. When that failed, my teammates and I invented unorthodox ways to psych ourselves for a big game. We played Glenn Miller's "In the Mood" before taking to the basketball court and drank a sugary liquid called Glyco Elixir before positioning ourselves in the starting blocks.

Most of the time, the only formula for victory was that old, unglamorous one of work. After two hours of football practice I would run a mile around the track in uniform, often with my friend Warren Cooksey. As a powerful middle-distance runner,

Warren was a mainstay of the Russell track squad that won the
Class A regional competition during my senior year.

He was also black, a fact which ensured second-class treatment in some towns on the track circuit. I was impressed by
Warren's quiet dignity in the face of affronts. I was also angered
at what seemed a blatant contradiction. If a man could be accepted on the running track for his talent alone, how could he
be denied equal treatment in the race of life? I've never understood how anyone could cheer for a black man on the basketball court but feel uncomfortable sitting beside him at a lunch
counter.

In June 1941, graduating seniors of Russell High School
heard a Lutheran minister preach the Biblical injunction "Narrow is the gate and strait the way that leads into life."

I seemed pointed in the direction of Lawrence, on the other
side of the state, and the hilly, shaded campus of the University
of Kansas. Without a college degree I knew my ambition for a
medical career was only a daydream. All that stood in my way
was family finances. Times were so tough that it hadn't been
long ago when all six Doles were living in the basement of our
small house. Continuing hard times had forced my father to
rent the upstairs to an oil prospector.

George Deines, a local banker, came to my aid, lending me
three hundred dollars and giving me some advice. Wear a hat,
he told me. He even offered to buy me one. To him, I guess, it
was a sign of maturity.

It would have taken more than a hat to instill seriousness
into four thousand youngsters who gathered in Lawrence that
fall. Much of the world was at war, but Europe's conflict occupied little space in the newspapers, still less in our thoughts.
Like other communities in the American heartland, Russell was
glad to be left alone. So were most university students. The siege
of Leningrad was less important to us than getting through
Rush Week or surviving a fraternity pledge court.

Most of us danced our way blindly through those last pre-
Pearl Harbor months. As more of an athlete than a ladies' man,
I was drawn to the basketball court before the dance floor.

Although I was enrolled in pre-med courses, the instructor who made the biggest impression on me was the legendary coach "Phog" Allen, regarded by many as the father of modern basketball. I was only on Allen's freshman team, so I definitely didn't spend all of my time practicing jump shots. With the war edging closer, farewell parties were frequent occurrences. And I didn't want to appear unsociable.

To a generation raised on *Animal House,* the Kappa Sigma fraternity to which I belonged would seem awfully tame. We suffered our share of paddling. But instead of toga parties we had lessons in dinner-table etiquette, conducted by dignified house mothers. Waiting on tables in the fraternity house, I received $12.50 a month and all I could eat. I was too busy to sow wild oats even if I had been so inclined. Besides waiting on tables, I had a milk route that had me out on the streets of Lawrence at five every Saturday morning.

By mixing me in with all sorts of people, living in a frat house was good preparation for what lay ahead. That's where I was on December 7, 1941. My brothers and I knew almost nothing about Pacific geography. We didn't have to, to grasp the enormity of the day's events and their implications for our futures. After December 7 we began to pay more attention to our studies and to the radio reports from exotic locations I had never seen on the Dream Theater's screen. However, this newfound seriousness didn't show up in my grades, which hovered stubbornly around the gentleman's C.

In the months following Pearl Harbor, the military draft reached into millions of Midwestern homes. Few males of athletic build and conventional patriotism were likely to escape its clutches. In December 1942, twenty-five years after my father joined the Army in hopes of seeing the world, I signed up for the Army's Enlisted Reserve Corps. I was nineteen years old, and eager to look life in the face.

CHAPTER TWO

The Hanfords
of Salisbury

ELIZABETH

In the spring of 1986, as part of its centennial festivities, the Charlotte, North Carolina, *Observer* held a public forum and invited me to speak.

For me, a native of nearby Salisbury, it was something of a homecoming. While I was growing up, the *Observer* had been a morning ritual in the Hanford household, like breakfast ham and grits. And in the summer of 1958, fresh out of Duke University, I had my first job interview at the paper. As the winner of Salisbury's annual fire-prevention essay contest and a silver loving cup handed out by the United Daughters of the Confederacy, I thought my journalistic credentials were self-evident. The editors thought otherwise.

Since then I've held many jobs, few of which were thought of as suitable for women back in the starchy fifties. This includes my positions as Secretary of Transportation and Secretary of Labor. Selling railroads, pressing Congress for trucking deregulation, mine safety, and repetitive motion injuries—here is the stuff of a dozen speeches.

But they hadn't asked me to give a public-policy speech. I hoped instead to keep things on a personal level, to describe some of the experiences and people that had helped to shape my values. In preparing my remarks, I came across some words written half a century earlier by North Carolina's literary favorite son, Thomas Wolfe:

The unity that binds us all together, that makes this earth a family, and men brothers and the sons of God, is love. That love can take many forms. There is the love of one human being for another, the love which cements our attachment to a place of memory, the love of work and the sense of mission which must of necessity replace purely individual ambition if that work is to be truly fulfilling.

To love, to remember, and to work with a higher purpose in mind: Wolfe's words reflected the ways of Salisbury. And they brought back a host of memories of the state whose motto is: "To be, rather than to seem."

The first white settlers of Rowan County, in the hilly Piedmont region of North Carolina, were greeted with many demands and few promises. Their original plan was for a settlement of continental proportions, extending west to the South Seas. Salisbury, established as the county seat in 1753, was laid out on a more modest scale. It has always been called a "main-line" town, a distinction originally earned as an outpost on the fringe of a pathway known to colonials as the Great Wagon Road, a former Indian trail. A century later, Salisbury became a genuine hub of transport with the arrival of the Western Carolina Railroad en route to Asheville. As a girl, my mother rode the twenty-six miles from Salisbury to Statesville in a horse and buggy. The round-trip journey took most of a day.

Transport aside, Salisbury boasts a rich history. Twenty years before the Revolution the courthouse on the town square was the westernmost in America. Daniel Boone used Salisbury as a jumping-off point to explore the wilds of Kentucky. Another kind of trail-blazing pitted area residents against the British crown in a direct challenge. The people of Rowan County and neighboring Mecklenburg County were the first colonists to boycott British goods in protest of British tyranny. By passing the Rowan Resolves calling for "an indissoluble union" of the thirteen colonies in the spring of 1775, they anticipated by over a year the men of Philadelphia and their more formal Declaration of Independence. Aides accompanying the British commander Lord Cornwallis in his 1780 invasion of the Piedmont pronounced Rowan and Mecklenburg the most rebellious counties in America.

Nine miles south of Salisbury stands an old Presbyterian church once called Cathey Meetinghouse. As a girl, I learned its history from my Cathey grandmother. We kids were always told that pirates were buried in the adjoining churchyard. President James K. Polk's ancestors lie there. So do those of my distant relation, former Vice President Alben W. Barkley. A personal favorite is George Cathey, who as a signer of the Rowan Resolves was one of the first of my forebears to make a habit out of challenging the status quo. I also have a special affinity for Francis Locke, who, elected United States senator in 1814, turned back before ever reaching Washington, complaining that the roads to the capital were inadequate.

After the Revolution, a fresh wave of settlers passed through the area. Most were like the Catheys, of Scotch-Irish descent. Clannishness and frugality set the local tone, along with fierce independence and deep religious conviction. The latter were combined in a prayer attributed to early settlers of the Piedmont: "Lord, grant that I may always be right, for Thou knowest that I am hard to turn."

Salisbury needed such qualities, for it suffered badly in the Civil War and its aftermath. In her girlhood my mother was told stories of postwar hardship that followed in the wake of retreating soldiers, of cotton crops that failed, of grain substituted for coffee and honey used in place of sugar. My own generation would pay less attention to such tales and to the Confederate monument in front of the Lutheran church.

After Appomattox, Salisbury evolved a diversified economy. Less dependent than other Carolina towns on textiles or tobacco, it played host instead to shopkeepers and small farmers. In 1879, Livingstone College opened its doors as a coeducational school designed to prepare black youths for a place in what its founders hoped would be a racially enlightened South. Later, Catawba College was established as a church-sponsored institution of higher learning.

Local residents nurtured a distinctly Southern ambience.

The pace of life was a little slower here, the greeting extended to a stranger a little warmer, than in Northern cities. Salisbury is still the kind of place where people on the street tip their hat in welcome, and where conversations start with a friendly "Hey." You don't need a holiday as an excuse to fly the flag. And families mean a lot, in part for their own camaraderie, but also for the foundation they lay for other relationships.

Religion exerts a powerful hold. In a world where so little seems permanent, we draw strength from eternal truths, expressed in customs handed on like fine family silver from one generation to the next.

All this may seem provincial to some. But to me such values show a pride of place and a perspective that transcends conventional wisdom. Instead of narrowing one's range of vision, they expand it and point up what is truly important. In an age when roots are shallow and purposes confused, they provide a distinct sense of who you are and why you are here.

Washington is full of excitement and professional challenges. But Salisbury is home. It is my personal Rock of Gibraltar.

The twentieth century was still young when Doles and Hanfords crossed paths for the first time. At almost the same time Robert and Margaret Dole decided to leave Ohio for Kansas, my grandfather John Wilbur Hanford headed east from Colorado.

As a young man Hanford had run a mercantile store in Carbondale, Illinois, where neighbors drafted him to serve on the local board of aldermen; newspapers still on file there show his contributions to the business and civic life of the city. He had next bought a Colorado fruit ranch, but his greatest pleasure came from the roses and other flowers he raised as a hobby. In 1905, a green thumb inspired him to change his address and his career. Because of his wife's delicate health, he sought out a new home at a lower altitude.

Both Hanfords loved music. On reading an article in a musical journal about North Carolina, "land of the sky," my grandfather was seized with an enthusiasm that never left him.

Since Charlotte and Greensboro already had floral businesses, he split the difference and settled on Salisbury. After his wife and their only child, also named John, joined him, they helped him in the business. Young John, my dad, emulated his father's interest in music. He organized the Salisbury municipal band and for many years served as its conductor. In his handsome uniform with gold braid and buttons to match, he cut a distinguished figure.

Certainly my mother thought so. Mary Cathey first caught sight of her future husband on one of the electric trolleys that plied the streets of Salisbury in the early decades of the twentieth century. They shared a musical bond. Mary's mother wanted her to become a professional music instructor. Mary devoted herself to practice and performance, spending much of her youth at the keyboard of a pipe organ in the Second Presbyterian Church. To lighten the church's somewhat gloomy atmosphere, she often opened a stained-glass window. One day when she did so, she spotted a familiar face below. It was young John Hanford, working in a carnation bed. She called down to him and he responded, beginning a conversation that turned into a lifelong romance.

Some time later, Mary's parents proposed the next step in her musical training. The elder Catheys planned a trip north, including a stop in New York City to look at the famous Juilliard School. But John knew enough to fear the outcome of a prolonged separation.

"If you go," he told Mary, "someone else will come along and that will be the end of us."

He must have been a persuasive suitor, because Mary Cathey dropped her career plans and became John Hanford's bride. After their wedding, they moved into a house on South Fulton Street with John's parents. The elder Hanfords lived on the first floor, the newlyweds upstairs in what they called the love nest. This arrangement worked fine until the birth of a baby boy, also named John.

Thirteen years passed before John had a sister. A new medical facility, Rowan County Memorial Hospital, was due to open at the start of August 1936. My mother hoped to be among its first patients. I had my own schedule, however, and was born instead in a sprawling sanitarium called Whitehead-Stokes. We weren't there long. Three days later I was loaded into an ambulance for a ride to Rowan Memorial. Mother went along. So did Mrs. Snowdie Bean, a doting nurse who conducted us across town to the strains of a gift music box.

Selecting a name for the newest Hanford raised unforeseen complications. The morning after my birth, my father sent flowers to Whitehead-Stokes. Attached was a card: "With love from Big John to Big Mary." It was his whimsical way of lobbying for another Mary in the family. Mother liked the flowers more than the idea. In fact, she had already settled on Elizabeth Alexander, in honor of her grandmother. Besides, "Big Mary" reminded her of an elephant by that name, part of a circus that wintered in Salisbury. But when she saw how much it meant to her menfolk, Mother yielded. On Easter Sunday, 1937, I was christened Mary Elizabeth Alexander. A year later, I upset everyone's plans by giving myself the name Liddy. It stuck throughout my childhood; Mary didn't.

I had my first accident at the age of three months. At the time, Mother was so engrossed in the just-published *Gone With the Wind* that she didn't notice the squirming infant headed for the edge of her bed. That little tumble stands out as the only recorded instance of neglect in the Hanford household.

Truth be told, I can't imagine a more loving environment in which to raise a child than the one at 712 South Fulton Street. There is the house itself, where Mother still resides, built of brick and stucco in the English manner. Inside is a formal entrance hall, with a spiral staircase connecting the floors. An attic room nestled under the eaves of the roof was a perfect rainy-day retreat for us youngsters. Off the living room is a side terrace, which was easily converted into a stage for childhood productions. A lovely old magnolia tree shades a yard spacious enough to have served as a pet cemetery for numerous small creatures, none of whom went to their Maker without such funeral rites as a small child could devise.

My brother, John, was too old to be a partner in such activities, but he was a major influence nonetheless. He combined the patience of Job with the deadpan humor of Jack Benny. When not jogging around the house on his shoulders, I found other ways to get in his hair. I was all of three when he had some schoolfriends over for dinner one evening. I insisted on serving the rolls, with more enthusiasm than efficiency. "Most families have skeletons in the closet," Johnny told his guests, "but we can't keep ours *in* the closet."

In a household filled with role models, my brother stood out. He was a gifted musician and presided over the National Honor Society. At Duke he was president of his fraternity, Kappa Alpha, and a mainstay in the group of highly regarded campus leaders called Red Friars. In later years John added his personal creativity to the family business, helping it grow to worldwide scope. I put him on a pedestal as a child. As far as I'm concerned, he's still there. And John's wife, Bunny, his able business partner, is like a sister, always there physically and emotionally.

I used to kid my father by telling him he looked like Harry Truman. He had the same build, the same spectacles, the same Midwestern precision in his voice. He also had a similar gift for directing people with the fewest words possible. I discovered this for myself after covering the walls of my nursery with thirteen comic Valentines. Dad's approach was typically direct.

"Who put these up?" he asked me.

I blamed it on my imaginary playmate, Denaw.

"No," he said, "he hasn't been here today."

"Johnny did it."

"No, Johnny would have put them way up high."

This went on until I had to say, "Liddy did it." After each admission I was given a few pats with a broomstraw switch. They hurt much less than the thought of having disappointed this man whom I loved so much.

My dad liked work and plenty of it. Buddies who tried and failed to lure him on a fishing or hunting expedition finally persuaded him to try his hand at golf. Mother was delighted by the news. After he was gone most of an afternoon, she thought that at last her husband had found himself a hobby. She ought to have known better.

"I played two games," Dad informed her when he returned from the links. "My first and my last. Mary," he went on, "if you ever see me hitting a little white ball around and running after it, I want you to make a reservation for me at Morganton."

Morganton was the state mental hospital.

One thing Dad didn't share with Mr. Truman was voting habits. He had visited Weimar Germany during the peak of hyperinflation there, and the sight of desperate people transporting their money in wheelbarrows was seared into his memory. My father was characteristically outspoken on the subject of Franklin D. Roosevelt and inflationary spending. For years a nominal Democrat, he kept his party registration so that he could vote in the primary, which, in those days, settled elections in North Carolina. When Dwight Eisenhower came along, Dad switched his affiliation to reflect his true beliefs. Meanwhile, I was twelve years old before I learned there *were* two political parties.

My dad was an exemplary manager of any and all affairs in which he was involved, including, of course, his business. His judgment almost always proved to be right. He was a man of integrity, analytical skills, thoroughness and industriousness. This combination earned for him true respect from his employees, some of whom worked with him more than fifty years. After his death in 1981, I had to visit a number of apartment buildings he owned, whose construction he had supervised. In talking with their occupants, I discovered that their rents had been kept extraordinarily low. I also learned why. Some of the residents were widowed and most of them would have to move if rents were raised. At least that's what my father feared. So that their lives wouldn't be disrupted, he simply carried them on his books. It was Dad's expression of a practical faith that regarded every man as his brother's keeper.

My mother is my best friend. She combines traditional graciousness with a genuine interest in everyone who crosses her path. Having abandoned her own career pursuit early on, she poured all the more love and energy into the lives of her children.

During the busy days leading up to Easter, Mother often lent a hand in the family business. She also chaperoned student-government trips to Myrtle Beach, South Carolina, and drove young Methodists to a camp at Lake Junaluska, in the mountains of western North Carolina. And when some of my church friends and I went on a hayride, Mary Hanford, with other mothers, was right behind in a car with the headlights turned up to discourage what Southerners of her generation called bundling.

Faith ranks beside family on her list of devotions. When I was a girl, she told me proudly of Francis Asbury, yet another blood relation, who helped John Wesley spread the Methodist gospel through frontier America. Like many women of her generation, Mother has never received a paycheck, but she has worked tirelessly with church committees, the P.T.A. and such organizations as the Colonial Dames.

Anticipating the historic-preservation movement, Mother joined with other local women to establish a museum and to rescue Salisbury's gaslights and grillwork. Each year for over three decades, they have staged a big antique show, the proceeds of which contribute to the restoration of Colonial and Victorian-era structures in and around Salisbury.

Whether she's reclaiming a neighborhood or whipping up a batch of persimmon pudding, Mother has never tackled anything without giving it her all. It was a quality she transmitted to those around her.

No less important to me were my mother's parents, who lived just two doors down South Fulton Street. I attribute Mother's affability to Grandfather Cathey. He was a large man with an equally big heart that made him a soft touch for any salesman and a friend to nearly everyone he met. As proprietor of the Cathey Buggy Company, he sold surreys, wagons and harnesses. He was an old Southern gentleman in the truest sense, valuing kindliness far more than worldly things.

Pop Cathey was the first to introduce Guernsey cows to the area around Salisbury, bringing them in from Pennsylvania Dutch country, where his natural warmth quickly thawed the suspicion most members of that reclusive community felt toward strangers. Pop never stayed a stranger to anyone for long.

As a true son of the South, he formed his political loyalties early. "Pop," my mother once said to him, "I think you would check the Democratic ticket and let them put the names in later."

"Yes, daughter," he replied, "you know, I believe I would."

My grandmother was more than a role model. Through her example, I was encouraged to have a vital, living faith. Mom Cathey, as we called her, was a continuous reader of the Bible. Next to her bed was a radio that was always tuned to religious broadcasts. In her eyes, we were each pilgrims on the road to grace. Yet it was a joyous faith she practiced. It had none of the smug or solemn piety that can sometimes frighten a child. Laughter came as naturally to her lips as prayer.

On Sunday afternoons, I sat with my cousin Anita Cathey and other children in my grandmother's living room, munching on cookies and drinking lemonade as she told us stories from Scripture. In middle age she lost a son, just out of college, to a drunk driver on a rain-slicked highway. Before he died, he had asked, "Lord, be with those I leave behind and guide me safe across the great divide." My grandmother was not a wealthy woman, but because she was concerned that Vernon never had the chance to make his contribution in life, she took the money from his life insurance and built a new wing for a mission hospital in far-off Pakistan.

Mom Cathey lived to within two weeks of her hundredth birthday. I can't remember an unkind word escaping her lips or an ungracious deed marring her path. When it became necessary for her to enter a nursing home, she thought only of what she could do for others.

"There might be some people there who don't know the Lord," she told us. "And I can read the Bible to them."

The Depression of the 1930s affected Salisbury less dramatically than it did the Kansas Dust Bowl. Or maybe it seemed that way to a child whose family, thanks to Dad's business, was largely insulated from the economic shocks that hit so many. Still, a share-and-share-alike philosophy was imparted by Mom Cathey and others.

I once billed twelve dollars' worth of dime comic books to

my parents' account at a local drugstore. When had I found the time to read so many funnybooks? they asked incredulously.

"I didn't read them all," I said. "Each day on the way home from school, I stopped in to get one and got some for all the friends with me. And you don't even have to pay for them. All you do is say 'Charge it.' "

Time was considered a precious commodity on South Fulton Street. If I had any to spare, Mom Cathey or my mother would suggest something. Once Mom said I should write an essay about my sixth-grade teacher. The result was a gold key and a certificate from a Chicago radio program called *Quiz Kids*.

Another teacher, Helen Jenkins, inspired me to write another paper. Each year, the United Daughters of the Confederacy sponsored a literary contest among Salisbury schoolchildren. First prize was a silver loving cup. For two years running, the cup had been won by the Wiley School, which I attended. I set out to retire the trophy by making it three in a row. An uncle told me about the General, a wood-burning locomotive that plied the tracks between Atlanta and Chattanooga during antebellum days. The train had a rich history, culminating in a daring wartime raid carried out by blue-coated guerrillas in the spring of 1862. For weeks, I corresponded with Chicago rail officials who opened their files and typed responses to my scrawled inquiries. In the end, Wiley extended its winning streak, and I was asked to read my essay on radio station WSTP.

I was a serious child, and eager to please. When my second-grade teacher sent me home to fetch a forgotten book, I considered myself such a total failure that I cried all the way down South Fulton Street. Books played a large part in my youth, both for the joy they brought and as a way of getting straight A's. Animals were another source of pleasure, from an old alley cat named Beauty to Penny the Chihuahua, whose death unleashed another flood of tears.

Mom Cathey liked to point out bluejays and cardinals in our backyard, and I guess you could say that even then I was interested in things that flew. The first political office I was elected to was the presidency of the third-grade bird club. A few years later, I resorted to less democratic methods when selecting the slate of officers for a junior-high book club I started. I simply declared myself president. It seemed a fair reward after a summer spent reading forty books.

I learned a strong work ethic on South Fulton Street. Self-improvement was a measure of personal growth. It was also a way to satisfy my goal-oriented parents. Piano lessons stretched into ten years of spring recitals and accompaniment for the men's Bible class of the Methodist church. My dance career was comparatively short-lived. As the curtain fell on one performance, Dad turned to Mother and said, "Mary, why in the world did you encourage her to take ballet? She doesn't have a single curve!"

As ringleader of neighborhood children, I was a precocious organizer. During the somber days following the Japanese attack on Pearl Harbor, I had little understanding of the war, even less of the battlefronts on which it was fought. This didn't keep me from joining forces with Miss Fanny Funderburke of the Girl Scouts in supervising what the *Salisbury Post* called the town's youngest defense group. We collected used postage stamps, tinfoil, wastepaper. Mother pitched in on wartime drives and greeted boys in uniform when they passed through town on their way to Fort Bragg. Everyone made do with rationed sugar and shoes.

However ignorant I was of the war's larger implications, I found it a continuing lesson in sensitivity to the feelings of others. It was one thing, for example, to adjust to three gallons of gasoline per week; it was something else entirely to go to bed each night uncertain whether your son was alive. With Johnny off in the Pacific somewhere, assigned to the carrier U.S.S. *Saratoga*, Mother wore a path to the mailbox. Thinking she simply wanted more mail, I wrote home at least once a day from the camp on the Outer Banks where I spent the summer of 1944. Her trial was made painfully vivid for me on Johnny's twenty-first birthday. That day florist trucks that had been repainted to read "J. Van Hanford and Son" appeared on the streets of Salisbury. When Mother first saw one, she pulled her car over to the side of the road and wept. Dad, without telling anyone, had used the occasion to make the family business a partnership. Mother just wanted to make sure her son lived to see it.

Anticipation of Johnny's return overshadowed another news bulletin, delivered on a warm afternoon in April 1945. I was riding my bicycle that day through Salisbury streets that seemed more than usually quiet. The stillness was broken by a voice telling me of the death of President Roosevelt. Months later, Johnny came home for good.

Postwar turbulence did little to disturb the peace of Rowan County. The Cold War found its way into the *Salisbury Post*. So did Chambers and Hiss, Korea, Joe McCarthy and the first, tentative stirrings of the civil-rights revolution. But townspeople generally went about their business as usual. The daily patterns of small-town life gave most people the reassurance they were denied in the headlines.

The Hanfords were no different. On our farm outside town we had a cabin, with a grove of tall pines that sang a gentle lullaby in the night breezes. We had our cabin parties and Fourth of July fireworks. We also took to the American road. Throughout the 1950s I accompanied my parents on rail journeys to the walls of old Quebec and the falls at Niagara. We climbed the Rockies and gazed out over Puget Sound. Somewhere in those years, I developed a wanderlust that has never left me.

When I ran for Boyden High School president, a job pretty much off limits to girls, my campaign manager linked my candidacy to another Elizabeth, Britain's newly crowned monarch. "More and more," she contended, "the modern world is giving women a big part to play. Boyden must keep pace in this world."

Boyden turned down the invitation. Instead I was given a lesson in how to lose, something no one likes but from which most of us can benefit.

That same year, the high-school drama society at Boyden presented a one-act comedy, "If Women Worked as Men Do." Few women in those days expected to work. We were taught the traditional patterns at school. Shop class was required of all boys, home economics for young women. Indeed, it was alleged that no girl could hope to graduate from Boyden unless she could sew a button or attach a zipper.

Whether such rumors were true or not, they were enough to strike fear in me and my classmates. When I was having trouble putting a zipper in a green cotton skirt—after seven tries—I took it to my friend Virginia Bibb's house, where her mother guided me through a final successful attempt. Wyndham Robertson, another close friend, was struggling to master cheese croquettes, and worried that her diploma would be withheld if the mayonnaise in a beet salad turned pink. Wyndham went on to become a distinguished journalist and later a vice president of the University of North Carolina.

Although my mother is an excellent cook, the kitchen was not my natural habitat. Neither was the playing field. In those days, women's athletics were relatively neglected, denying many like me the opportunity to test ourselves. Wearing glasses was no help on the baseball diamond, and my disdain for the American Game (perhaps brought on by embarrassment over line drives dropped) prompted me to stay home from school once or twice.

One thing that was definitely expected of both sexes was a driver's license, which in my case almost didn't happen. On one trial run in the family car, I stepped on the accelerator instead of the brake and ran over a neighbor's dogwood tree. My profuse apologies did nothing to ease the pained expression on the owner's face. Of course I told her that I would gladly replace the tree if it died.

"Oh, I'm sorry," she informed me, "but you couldn't replace it. My poor dead husband planted that tree."

At that moment, the mangled dogwood looked more robust than Mother, slinking down in the seat beside me.

In the spring of 1954, we held our senior prom. "Around the World or Bust" was probably suggested by a creative classmate named Betty Dan Nicholas. Everyone was supposed to come dressed as their fantasy persona. There wasn't a Southern belle in the place. Editors of the class yearbook predicted that I would spend my life as "a French interpreter in an airport."

A more immediate concern was college. I applied to only one school, Duke, for the simple reason that my brother had gone there. That fall I checked into Room 304 of Alspaugh House, on Duke's East Campus. In my first letter home I told my parents I was "crazy" about the place. I also told them I was thinking of majoring in political science, adding, "I think it would be fascinating to learn about American government, history in the making."

At 712 South Fulton, my announcement caused a ripple of concern. Mother's secret wish was that I study home economics. She thought this would be a natural prelude to marriage and life next door. Armed with my letter, she sought counsel from a professor at the University of North Carolina.

"Let her take political science," said the professor. "We need women in government. And anyway," he added, "they all get married eventually."

CHAPTER THREE

Hills and Valleys

BOB

Learn to make the most use of what you have.
Don't worry about what you've lost.

—Dr. Hampar Kelikian

On December 14, 1942, I joined the Army's Enlisted Reserve Corps. Up until then, my primary concerns in life were catching a football and outrunning competitors in the quarter-mile dash. Whatever leadership skills I possessed had never been tested off the playing field. At the University of Kansas I contributed more to the social life of my frat house than to the intellectual life on campus.

Before enlisting that December, I had never flown in an airplane or ridden in a bus. Of course I had never been shot at either. Except for the last part, I liked just about everything military life offered. There was a camaraderie in uniform that reminded me of what I'd known on the football fields and basketball courts of Russell and Lawrence. On the battlefield, men shared everything as if their lives depended on it. Often they did.

Any military organization is a structural pyramid. What could be more hierarchical than the Army? Yet it was also a family, and highly democratic at that. The only privilege given to rank was proximity to the front line, where survival involved split-second timing and character was forged in the heat of battle. It was the work ethic raised to the highest degree.

In June 1943 I was stationed at Camp Barkley, a few miles outside Abilene, Texas. For the next few months I trained to be part of the Army Medical Corps. After a brief reunion with my brother, Kenny, who had joined up also and would go on from Texas to the South Pacific, I was shifted to an engineering class at New York's Brooklyn College.

Brooklyn itself was an education. Back in Russell I had known only a sprinkling of black or Jewish families. Now every time I rode the subway or walked the streets around the college I was exposed to the world in miniature. Surrounded by such a mix of cultures and accents, I thought to myself, This is the real glamor. Flatbush Avenue held more fascination than Park Avenue.

In the spring of 1944 I left Brooklyn for Camp Polk, Louisiana, and then for training as an antitank gunner at Camp Breckenridge, in Kentucky's bluegrass country. Two months after applying for officer candidate school, I enrolled in Class 360 at Georgia's Fort Benning. The Benning School for Boys, as it was popularly known, was mass-producing officers for an Army that was rapidly losing its leadership stocks.

I arrived at Benning a corporal and left a second lieutenant. In between, I experienced the Army's version of Southern hospitality. This meant strenuous days packed with marches and combat practices, classroom lectures on the use of mortars and machine guns, field instruction on how to hurl a hand grenade and how to operate an antiaircraft gun.

After every exercise there was an intensive round of questioning.

"What did you learn from the march you just completed?"

You learned to adjust the backpack you carried on your shoulder, for one thing, since even a slight change could make a big difference over twenty miles. You also learned how to shift your weight while covering the red-clay roads of southern Georgia in a half-trot.

Field operations came under the same scrutiny.

"What did you experience?"

"What do you think?"

"What do you know?"

At the end of the OCS assembly line was a class of ninety-day wonders, with a question of their own: What next?

My answer came in December 1944, when I was put on board a troopship headed for Italy. The next two weeks convinced me that Kansans are born without sea legs; they also gave the words "green soldier" a whole new meaning. I arrived in Naples Harbor a few days before Christmas and was assigned to the 24th Replacement Depot, stationed near Rome.

The battle for Italy, the long campaign that started in Sicily and dragged on for nearly six hundred days before coming to its victorious conclusion, was already a year and a half old by the time I joined it. It had originated in the fertile imagination of Winston Churchill, whose gift for strategic thinking usually matched his penchant for memorable phrases—but the great statesman's love of vivid language betrayed him on the subject of Italy. As early as the Casablanca Conference of November 1942, Churchill had set out to persuade his reluctant allies that here was the Axis' "soft underbelly." Putting aside their own doubts, Roosevelt and Stalin went along with an Italian offensive, just so long as it did not divert forces from a cross-Channel invasion of Hitler's European bastion.

In July 1943, separate contingents from the U.S. Fifth and British Eighth Armies had stormed the beaches of Sicily. Their occupation of the big island paved the way for Mussolini's downfall. Allied flags were flying over Naples by October 1. Thereafter, the resistance stiffened as Hitler annexed his former ally. Berlin ordered that Italian soil should be defended with the last drop of German blood. The "soft underbelly" proved anything but.

Little of the war's grand strategies filtered down to the average GI. We knew only what we read in *Stars and Stripes* and what we heard from the scuttlebutt of rumor common to any army in the field. In the third week of February 1945 my perspective changed abruptly when I was sent to the front lines to plug a vacancy in Company I, Third Battalion, 85th Mountain Regiment.

The 85th was part of a larger unit, the Tenth Mountain

Division, whose origins lay in an earlier conflict, the 1939–40 border war between Soviet Russia and tiny Finland. Impressed with the gallant resistance put up by Finnish troops on skis, Charles Minot "Minnie" Dole (no relation) and others in the National Ski Patrol urged the War Department in Washington to create a similar force. In the fall of 1941 the National Ski Association began recruiting applicants, who were required to submit letters testifying to their athletic ability. The result was a division with a highly unusual profile. Side by side with forest rangers and cowboys, over half its members were men with doctorates, many from the Ivy League. The youthful captain of Dartmouth's ski team, Charles McLane, belonged to the Tenth. So did Torger Tokle, the world's premier ski jumper, and American Olympic coach Friedl Pfeiffer.

The Tenth had a crack commander. He was Major General George P. Hays, a polo-playing hero whose exploits during the Second Battle of the Marne in the First World War had earned him the Congressional Medal of Honor. Hays and his men were offered first to General Eisenhower for use in his sweep across Fortress Europe. But Ike declined, and the division wound up spearheading an assault against the Germans' heavily fortified Gothic Line, a 120-mile barrier stretching across the lofty Apennine Mountains north of Florence and guarding the entrance to Italy's Po Valley. The key that would unlock the valley was Bologna, an ancient university town nestled in the shadow of 3,500-foot Monte Belvedere.

On a map of Italy, you can see that it is only fifty-six miles from Florence to Bologna. Yet the fighting along this largely forgotten front was so savage that it took Allied armies a full six months to cover the distance. Like a stopper in a bottle, the hills around Belvedere prevented entry into the valley beyond.

On the night of February 18, members of the Tenth moved to break the logjam. In sheer daring, their assault on 1,500-foot Riva Ridge compares with the Union Army's sweep up Lookout Mountain and far surpasses Teddy Roosevelt's attack on San Juan Hill. Within twenty-four hours, they had dislodged the entrenched Germans from the mountain itself and then held their ground against seven furious counterattacks.

By the morning of February 25, when I arrived to take up my new assignment, Monte Belvedere was securely in Allied hands. At first I felt a little out of place in the Tenth. This had nothing to do with the fact that Kansans don't get much practice on the ski slopes; the division had long since dropped its stringent requirements on that score. But it was still a top-drawer outfit, proud of its record and emotionally bonded with the blood of fallen comrades. My own company's commander, an All-American from Nebraska named Butch Luther, had been killed just days before my arrival. And now here I was, a second lieutenant straight out of Fort Benning, dropping in on everyone else's party.

As a platoon leader, I was responsible for three rifle squads and a machine gun unit, nearly fifty men in all. My chief task was finding ways to keep everyone busy: cleaning weapons, doing calisthenics, going on patrol. Most of our patrolling came after dark, and on one such foray, the night of March 18, I had my first taste of battle.

We were sent out against German snipers holed up in a nearby farmhouse. As we approached the enemy, there was a brief exchange of gunfire. I took a grenade in hand, pulled the pin, and tossed it in the direction of the farmhouse. It wasn't a very good pitch (remember, I was used to catching passes, not throwing them). In the darkness, the grenade must have struck a tree and bounced off. It exploded nearby, sending a sliver of metal into my leg—the sort of injury the Army patched up with Mercurochrome and a Purple Heart.

For the next few weeks, the Tenth Mountain Division tried to pick the lock barring entrance to the Po Valley. We didn't get very far. Roads in the area were more easily covered on mule than by a modern, mechanized army. A single dynamite blast to an exposed bridge or roadway could halt traffic for miles. And with the winter now on us, even a dusting of snow was enough to hide enemy minefields from view.

March can be pretty cold in the Apennine Range of northern Italy. Digging trenches was one way to stay warm. Dodging sniper bullets was another. Like soldiers everywhere, we killed more time than anything else. We waited for mail from home.

We sweated out news from the front. Men lay flat on their bellies for hours, peering through a twenty-power scope at enemy soldiers on a nearby ridge.

In the face of pervasive boredom and uncertainty, nerves frayed easily. Artillery fire punctured an uneasy calm, making sleep all but impossible and keeping men emotionally off balance. I learned this for myself one morning when I talked with a young private who had been wounded in the assault on Monte Belvedere. The kid had left the platoon for ten days, receiving treatment for his injuries. Now he was back, with a leg healing faster than his psyche. While he was away, memories of earlier combat and premonitions of future fighting had combined to weaken his confidence. In fact, he told me, he thought he was a coward. He was anything but. Like the rest of us, he was tired, far from home, and nervous about rumors of an impending breakout for Bologna. What he needed most was a receptive ear.

After that morning, he no longer talked of cowardice, real or imagined. Small as it was, the incident taught me that listening can be a form of leadership.

By the first week of April 1945, it was obvious that Hitler's thousand-year Reich was on the brink of collapse. How much longer could it hold out? The question had life-and-death importance to me and my buddies. While we wagered over the date of Germany's surrender, our commanders were formulating battle plans to bring the war to a quick end.

Operation Craftsman was one. Beginning in the rugged hills around the village of Castel d'Aiano, forces spearheaded by the Tenth Mountain Division would leapfrog the mountainous spine of central Italy. If all went well, Bologna would be snared and the Po Valley secured, clearing the way for Mark Clark's Fifth Army to chase the retreating Germans to—and perhaps beyond—the Brenner Pass.

Enemy soldiers were well dug in around Castel d'Aiano. No one thought they would be easily dislodged. To help tip the scales, planners of Operation Craftsman enlisted unprecedented outside firepower. On the morning of the attack, tentatively scheduled for April 12, waves of fighter bombers would leave their fields around Pisa to soften up German defenses in the hills to our north. In addition there would be hundreds of artillery pieces shelling from the ground.

With so much riding on air support, the attack was held hostage to the weather. On April 12, due to fog and low overcast, it was put off for twenty-four hours. Similar conditions the next day led to a second postponement. In the meantime, soldiers in the field were jolted by news of Franklin Roosevelt's death at Warm Springs.

Like most of my buddies, I shed tears over the loss of our Commander in Chief. The fighting in Europe would end soon, maybe in days. For FDR, time had run out. Few men on the eve of battle cared to ponder the implications of such a cruel fate. No one wanted to be the last casualty of World War II.

I'm often asked to describe what happened to me on April 14, 1945. To be honest, I've always thought that telling old war stories is like showing slides of the family vacation. You had to be there. Other than that, I'm not the first person to avoid unpleasant memories. Most of us who have left something of ourselves on a foreign battlefield are reluctant to talk about it. Fewer still use stock expressions like "the glory of war."

Certainly there is heroism in the line of fire. And there is courage in the soldier's willingness to risk his life for the sake of others. When men who have been pushed to the brink of endurance discover hidden emotional reserves, there's inspiration in that. But when all is said and done, war is infinitely more wasteful than glorious.

Pins stuck in a field map hardly do justice to the organized chaos of battle. Vision is blocked and distance distorted, until, for the average foot soldier, the whole war shrinks to a few hundred yards of unfamiliar terrain. Survival takes precedence over grand strategy. If you can find your way into a protective shellhole, the fifteen miles to Bologna will take care of itself. When it's over, you carry away only pieces of a memory puzzle. Old soldiers hold reunions to try to put them together.

April 14 was a long day for me, but a short battle. At its start, the 85th Regiment occupied the left flank of a two-mile front along the slope of Monte della Spe. Directly opposite was a ridge of hills held by enemy gunners. Separating Company I's staging area from the flat-topped summit of Hill 913 were a thousand yards and a shallow valley called Pra del Bianco. Dotting the sides of Hill 913 was an intricate system of bunkers and gun emplacements manned by German defenders. Minefields added to their security and our danger.

Early that morning air attacks were launched against the entire enemy line. Smoke filled the air, and our ears were still ringing when, shortly after ten o'clock, I Company started down into the green basin of Pra del Bianco. We were headed in the direction of a stone wall and some hedgerows, beyond which lay a clearing and the gradual incline of 913. A sweeping flank movement brought us into an exposed position, where my platoon was pinned down by sniper and small arms fire.

At that, we were comparatively lucky. Others made it over the wall, only to step on land mines called "Bouncing Betties." Such an innocent name for so lethal a weapon. Adding to the carnage were a couple of machine guns off to our left, raking the field and cutting down attack forces near the foot of the hill. Pulling my men back to such cover as I could find, I chose a small squad to help find a less deadly passage up the slope. According to Technical Sergeant Frank Carafa, I altered the original orders, which called for him to lead a party into the clearing while I remained behind.

I don't remember the exact sequence myself. Everything happened so fast. All around me, men were being hit. A combination of raw anger and protective instinct for my buddies took over. We resumed our flanking movement, this time approaching the farmhouse from which German machine gun fire was coming. I tossed a grenade at the target and hastily took cover as our little squad was detected and a fresh barrage opened up. The field was pitted with holes as a result of the morning's aerial bombardment; I dived into one of them. From where I crouched, I could see my platoon's radio man go down. I crawled out to retrieve him, but it was too late to do much.

After pulling his lifeless form into the foxhole, I scrambled back out again. As I did, I felt a sharp sting in my upper right back. Exactly what caused it remains a matter of guesswork. Most likely, an exploding shell had ripped into my body, smashing the right shoulder and scattering metal fragments along its path. Whatever it was, it crushed my collarbone, punctured a lung and damaged vertebrae, leaving me paralyzed from the neck down.

I lay face down in the dirt. Unable to see or to move my arms, I thought they were missing. In fact they were stretched out above my head, until Frank Carafa made his way across forty yards of scarred earth to drag me to safety and cross them over my chest.

Other men disobeyed orders to leave the wounded to medics. Not many medics were going to survive this battle. My second in command, Platoon Sergeant Stan Kuschik, gave me a shot of morphine. Kuschik then dipped his finger into blood and made a cross on my forehead. It was an old battlefield precaution, used to alert any medics who happened by and keep them from administering a second, fatal dose of the powerful drug.

The rest of the day was a fever dream of pain and confusion. Nine hours passed from the time I was hit to my arrival at the Fifteenth Evacuation Hospital. During those hours I wondered about my injuries, and wandered back in time. It was like watching a movie of my life. I saw Russell and kids I had played with, and my parents at the dinner table. I remembered Spitzy, a little white dog we had when I was a child. Maybe it was the morphine, or the strange sense of release that attends utter helplessness. All I know is that I knew almost nothing. That is, I had no idea where I was or where anyone else might be. So I went home.

From the field hospital I was transferred to a larger facility in Pistola, near Naples. For weeks I couldn't move my legs. Feeling was slower still returning to my arms. The letters I wrote home at the time—or, rather, that the Red Cross wrote for me —spoke of restlessness and "a little trouble with my right arm."

I was getting better every day, I informed my parents at the end of April, "and there isn't any reason why I shouldn't be as good as new before long." I believed it, because I wanted to. I went on believing it when I was loaded onto a hospital plane, like furniture in a crate, bound for Miami by way of Casablanca. Under the circumstances, Miami seemed like the Promised Land. I was back on American soil; nothing before or since has ever felt quite so good. The first thing I did was call my folks back in Russell. Someone held the receiver for me as I assured them that I would soon be home. And home meant recovery.

By the twelfth of June, when I checked into Topeka's Winter General Army Hospital, it was harder to deny what had happened. I arrived in a plaster cast that went from my ears to my hips, and with a persistent fever that doctors couldn't figure out.

Meanwhile, my wounds were hardly more terrifying than telling my mother I had taken up smoking—a habit I have long since abandoned, but in those days a godsend for me. I couldn't light my own cigarette, so someone else would have to come and light it for me. That meant a chance to talk, maybe to laugh, and a break from the monotony of hospital life. My mother detested cigarettes, but, sitting there at Winter General by my bedside, she held them for me and pretended the smoke didn't bother her.

Mom moved to Topeka to be with me around the clock. She was there early in July when my temperature reached 108.7 (axillary) and Dad was summoned from Russell. They looked on as doctors wrapped me in a rubber sheet and packed me in ice. It was touch and go for a while, but I survived the night, and on July 11, my right kidney was removed.

The immediate crisis past, my thoughts turned to the future. I was going to live; I never doubted that for a moment. But what kind of life would it be? In moments of self-pity, I saw myself going through life unmarried, selling pencils on street corners and living off a disability pension. My dream of being a star athlete and perhaps a doctor was shattered along with my body.

For nearly a year I couldn't feed myself. It took longer still to reach the point where I could get dressed unassisted. Six months went by before I was back on my feet. Even this modest accomplishment was overshadowed when the attendants helped me out of bed and I saw myself in the bathroom mirror. It was the first good look I'd had at myself since April 14. Back then I had weighed a strapping 194 pounds. Now I was down to 122. The shock of recognition made me go weak in the knees.

I didn't walk that day, nor for a long time after that. Truth be told, I still have trouble looking in the mirror.

In November 1945 I left Topeka. My home for most of the next two and a half years was Percy Jones Army Medical Center in Battle Creek, Michigan. Opened the summer after Pearl Harbor, by V-J Day it had over eleven thousand patients. The hospital specialized in orthopedics, neurosurgery and X-ray therapy. It was also the Army's leading amputee center.

I arrived in my by now familiar suit of plaster, with my right hand strapped to a device that looked like a tennis racket and was intended to stretch splayed fingers back into shape. As it happened, a deformed hand was soon the least of my concerns. A few days before Christmas, I woke with pains in my chest. Doctors traced the problem to a "pulmonary infarct" and prescribed dicumarol to dissolve blood clots.

This latest crisis interrupted my family's holiday plans. In Topeka my mother had practically lived at my bedside. Now Dad took the train from Russell, standing up most of the way in a car crowded with servicemen, so that he could spend Christmas with me.

At Percy Jones I had my second brush with death since returning from Italy. To guard against possible blood clotting, doctors prescribed total inactivity. They came by constantly to stick needles into my veins and monitor the dosage of the blood-thinning drug. Seven weeks after it was started, the dicumarol was stopped. My temperature soared again, this time to 106 degrees. Despite massive doses of penicillin, the infection persisted. As a last resort, doctors suggested an experimental drug originally developed in the fight against tuberculosis. It was called streptomycin.

Still in the early stages of testing, the drug could not be administered without a consent form signed by a patient's next of kin. My parents gave their consent, and I became one of a handful of patients in the country cleared to receive the medication.

The wonder drug lived up to its name. By early March 1946, I was even out of bed for short periods of time. Thereafter, my physical health improved steadily.

What still had to be fought was a quiet battle against the emotional ravages of war. Much of it was played out in a brightly lit ward on the fourth floor of the main hospital building, in a whitewashed room, maybe twenty by forty feet, that housed a dozen other young men. Most of them had spinal injuries of one sort or another. Philip A. Hart, whose name today graces the building in which I have my Senate office, was in that same ward with me. In another ward at Percy Jones was Daniel K. Inouye, now a Senate colleague from Hawaii.

One day a young Air Force captain named Bill Fitz arrived in our ward. He had been seriously injured in a plane crash, and his spirits seemed more broken than his body. As the days passed and Billy received no visitors or mail, the rest of us took him on as a special project. We tried to get him to talk, to laugh, to show some interest in anything.

When someone heard a song on the radio called "Nancy with the Laughing Face," we immediately adopted it as our standard. It was fresh and positive, qualities sorely needed on the fourth floor. Any infantry officer worth his salt is a natural-born scrounger. It's part of his unofficial job description. I managed to scrounge up the record, and a big old Stromberg-Carlson set on which to play it. From then on you couldn't walk past our ward without hearing the honey-on-toast baritone of Frank Sinatra, singing about his good-natured Nancy.

It did us all a lot of good, all but Billy Fitz, who remained mute and immobile. Late one night we heard a noise from his corner of the ward, a sort of quick, shallow gasp. Men surrounded his bed across from me. We summoned a nurse, but it was too late. The next few days were pretty grim on the fourth floor.

As doctors in our area of the hospital tried to ward off osteopathic deterioration, patients battled decay of another kind, one that destroys the spirit before it takes the body. Fighting back, we took emotional inventory of whatever spiritual and mental resources we could find. If you were in pain, the doctors would give you morphine and Demerol. I didn't want that forever. Yet thinking about how much you hurt makes you hurt more. So you tried not to think about it. There was a choice: spend your time complaining about needles and bedsores or open your eyes to the suffering around you and decide to become useful.

I said a lot of silent prayers in those days, at least some of them tinged with initial bitterness. Why me, I demanded—why hadn't someone been watching out for me? In time, I came to realize that someone *was* watching out for me, and had been from the morning of April 14. Maybe it was all part of a plan, a test of endurance and strength and, above all, of faith.

There were still times when I became angry at a body that was my enemy. In order to restore the feeling and the strength to my lifeless hands, I was given muscle-relaxing baths and hot-wax treatments by therapists who pulled clawlike fingers apart. Some days I spent hours trying to close two fingers of my right hand.

It was like starting life over again, in a second childhood of unknown length and without one's original physical attributes. But when I saw men around me who had lost their arms or legs or sight, it had a way of putting my own condition into perspective.

One late-winter morning when I sat out in a hospital parking lot, waiting to be shuttled between sections of the medical complex, I struck up a conversation with a patient beside me.

"Don't your feet get cold out here?" I asked.

He pointed down and tapped his artificial legs with his cane. After that I stopped asking "Why me?"

I began to look beyond external appearances in judging a person. At first glance, the guy in the next bed or the room down the hall might seem fine. Physically whole, not a scratch or a scar on him. But then you saw doctors making regular visits, and you knew he was suffering from something much worse than not being able to move his fingers or walk on two legs. My only phobia from the years when I lay flat on my back is a fear of fire. When staying in hotels, I prefer the ground floor. I'd have a pretty tough time letting myself down from a burning building on a bedsheet.

Meanwhile, I learned to hide my feelings behind a wisecrack. Laughter really was a medicine. At least, that's what hospital officials seemed to believe. They started wheeling me around to wards where morale was low.

I spent my early months at Percy Jones in traction. Later I was able to sit in a wheelchair. Unable to roll it myself, I relied on others to push me around. Physical helplessness changes the way you see yourself. It demolishes conventional views of time and distance. Like everything else at Percy Jones, regaining the use of my legs was an exercise in patience. From wiggling a toe to bending a knee, the slightest sign of movement was a cause for celebration. With a right arm in a cast and a left of not much greater use, crutches were out of the question. So I took slow, wobbly steps, baby steps at first. I got up and walked around my bed, then around the ward. I rested awhile, read awhile, and started the process all over again. Unless leg tremors set in.

Sometimes I fell. When that happened, I tried to pick myself up without assistance. I didn't want to depend on others for more than essential help. Even today, I don't like to ask Elizabeth to help me put on formal evening wear, except for the tie and those little tux shirt buttons that drive most men crazy.

All this was like athletic training on a field no longer than a hospital corridor. But at least I began to see progress, more so than in the agonizingly slow attempt to regain the use of my hands. After several months, I could reach the second-floor dayroom on my own and join in bridge games by the hour. Someone else shuffled and dealt the cards.

I began experimenting with Velcro jackets and shirts with snaps or zippers, anything to get around the buttons that were my nemesis. I wore clip-on ties and laceless shoes. A couple of times each day I had therapy to strengthen my arms and legs and speed the laborious process of becoming mobile. To help their patients pass the time, the nurses organized birthday parties, with favorite dishes supplied by the hospital dietitian. We watched movies, played chess, ransacked the local libraries.

I conducted a little business on the side. Auto production was just starting to crank up again after the restrictions of wartime, and disabled veterans were given priority. I sold cars to fellow patients—at 6 percent commission—until the authorities put a stop to it. Subsequently, thanks to a generous government, I got a specially designed model that I could drive with my left hand.

I also used much of my hospital time to go back to school, figuratively speaking. Fellow patient George Radulescu and I began a personal survey course of sorts, rooted in our wartime experiences. Conceding to the Germans good field command and armaments capacities, we decided that our own victory must have resulted from the individual character of Allied soldiers. Working back from this premise, we traced the history of warfare and the organization of armies. From Alexander the Great to Lee and Grant, we analyzed tactics and pursued the essentials of leadership. We studied societies as well as individuals. We read Plato (I thought his ideal society much too regimented) and subjected the Ten Commandments to our relentless quest for positive thinking.

Reading on through the Renaissance and English common law, we eventually came to the foundations of the American republic. I liked George Washington better than Benjamin Franklin. Washington appealed to my interest in practical organization. Franklin, by contrast, seemed just a tinkerer. Lincoln was my hero, the voice and symbol of American democracy. His humble origins inspired me. So did the way personal tragedy only deepened his sensitivity.

In a different context, I admired Dwight Eisenhower, himself a product of small-town Kansas who had gone on to forge history's greatest alliance. This was no small undertaking. Anyone who could work harmoniously with Bernard Law Montgomery, George Patton and Charles de Gaulle had to be some kind of genius.

At about ten o'clock most nights, the nurse came around to announce, "School's out, Lieutenant." That was the signal to go across the street to the Hart Hotel, a brick hostelry with a coffee shop that served grilled-cheese sandwiches until two in the morning. Since the elevator near our ward was an unpredictable relic, getting to the Hart called for a certain resourcefulness. More than once, George and I slipped out disguised in an outlandish costume of oversized trench coats scrounged from the supply closet. Safely across the street, we could rehash our theories until closing time. Then we retraced our steps, whispering all the way to avoid detection by the powers that be.

Eventually, I was well enough to escape the hospital walls for longer periods. I got leave to visit Russell, where I moved into my parents' old room and worked out in a little exercise area my dad set up in the backyard. I squeezed a rubber ball to build up the strength in my left hand. It was already good enough to hold a hand of playing cards for hours, as friends dropped by and my family rearranged their schedules to spend time with me. Mom would come back late from selling sewing machines and sometimes do a load of wash at midnight while the card games went on around her.

On one of those visits, I went to see my old friends at Dawson's Drugstore. Walking down Main Street that first time was the hardest thing in the world. Thinking the eyes of the entire town were on me, I felt that my disability was an embarrassment. My mood in those days was summed up in the tunes I played over and over on Dawson's jukebox. "Laughing on the Outside, Crying on the Inside" was one. "You'll Never Walk Alone" was another. One day, someone called me a hero to my face. I disagreed. I had come home; the real heroes hadn't.

By now I had made as much progress as seemed possible at Percy Jones. When I went back in early 1947, it no longer seemed a premier orthopedic center, much less a miracle factory. Miracles were in short supply just then, but that didn't keep me from wanting one.

That's when I ran into Hampar Kelikian.

His friends called him Dr. K. He was a short man, but a giant in the operating room. As a boy Kelikian had escaped the blood-spattered landscape of his native Armenia. Three of his sisters were less fortunate; a fourth sibling, a brother, was killed in Italy during World War II. Hampar arrived in Chicago in 1920 with two dollars in his pocket and a rug from his homeland under one arm. He got a job on a farm, where he impressed his employer into paying his way through college. The young immigrant went on to medical school and an apprenticeship at Cook County Hospital.

When war broke out again in Europe in 1939, Dr. K shared

his talent with his adopted country. He was a pioneer in the surgical restoration of otherwise useless limbs. For his contributions to military medicine, Harry Truman gave him a medal. Those whom he rescued gave him their love.

I first heard about Kelikian from Lamont Jahn, an uncle of mine who had served in the Medical Corps with the Armenian-born physician whose special interest was wounded GI's. When I went to see Dr. K in Chicago early in 1947, I was still looking for a miracle.

My definition of recovery was simple. It meant being put back the way I was before April 14. Any good surgeon should be able to restore my ability to shoot baskets and catch passes. In my search for such guarantees, I had already consulted doctors in Wichita, Kansas City and Denver. They talked about nerve damage and impaired functions, but none of them did anything to discourage my search for a magical scalpel.

Now Dr. K sat me down and administered the verbal equivalent of a slap in the face. There would be no miracles, he told me. He would do all he could to give me back as much use of my arm and hands as possible, but after that it was up to me to make the most of what I had. What he was really saying was, accept the situation and get on with the business of life.

Kelikian reserved an operating room for June 1947. For this first procedure, and for a half dozen that followed, he refused to take a penny. But there were still hospital bills to pay. So Chet Dawson and my high-school buddy Phil Ruppenthal joined with VFW Chapter 6240 and started the Bob Dole Fund.

It began with a few paper bills tossed into an old cigar box —a box I still have in my Senate desk. Local banks volunteered to handle contributions. Free publicity was given by the *Russell Record*. From thirty cents to a hundred dollars, dozens of my neighbors dug into their pockets to give whatever they could. One man brought in a live duck. In the end, the contributions added up to around eighteen hundred dollars. I can never repay the people of Russell. When I needed them, they were there. Their gifts were not limited to money. A friend named Adolph Reissig spent hours designing and building a special lead weight, covered in felt, to help me straighten my arm.

Dr. Kelikian strained his own ingenuity to the limit, first

removing the head of the humerus bone, then replacing the damaged ball and socket by drilling a hole in the humerus. Taking a piece of muscle sheathing from my left leg, he re-attached the arm as if threading a needle. When Kelikian was through, my right arm was two and a half inches shorter than my left. The arm couldn't be rotated, and Dr. K's efforts to implant tendons in the right hand were largely unsuccessful.

Today I am unable to grasp objects with my right hand or carry anything heavier than a pen. Limited sensation in the fingers of my left hand makes it impossible for me to tell the difference between a quarter and a dime with my eyes closed. Getting dressed each morning is a time-consuming process, and I rarely loosen my tie in public, given the effort it requires to knot it back again.

Yet none of this detracts from Dr. Kelikian's medical achievement or personal influence. Even if he couldn't restore my right arm, he gave me something much more important: an example to live by, and a philosophy of making the most of what you have.

"The mechanical part of surgery," he once explained, "is like carpentry. Anyone can learn that. The important thing is to be able to suffer with the patient, to see if they are in pain."

Whether economic or physical, suffering can do one of two things to someone. It can toughen him or it can harden him. It can make him more, or less, sensitive to the needs of those around him. He can say to himself, "I overcame this, the tough-est challenge of my life. And if I did, then everyone else ought to be able to do the same thing."

Or he can develop a special bond with other sufferers, seeing the world through their eyes and combating the smug belief that physical wholeness is an accurate gauge of a person's abilities. I've known victims of physical disability who, in their emotional and mental depth, go far beyond people with conven-tional appearance and mobility. Today this sounds so obvious as to barely require stating. But it was a different story in 1947, when disabilities were still kept in the closet.

When Dr. K died, in the summer of 1983, I took the un-usual step of quoting poetry on the floor of the Senate. The words came from Robert Frost:

Nature's first green is gold,
Her hardest hue to hold.
Her early leaf's a flower,
But only so an hour.
Then leaf subsides to leaf,
So Eden sank to grief.
So dawn goes down to day,
Nothing gold can stay.

Hampar Kelikian was pure gold.

In November 1947, I returned to Percy Jones for extensive therapy on my rebuilt arm. Within a few months I gained another kind of right arm, one that would be invaluable in the painstaking process of emotional and professional reentry. Phyllis Holden was a pretty brunette, originally from New Hampshire, where her parents were active in conservative Republican politics. She was working as an occupational therapist at Percy Jones. As she tells it, she was having coffee with a couple of other nurses one day when I walked by.

"There goes that poor Bob Dole," declared one of her companions. "He's not supposed to live."

Actually, by the fall of 1947 I was well on the way to recovery. Expressions like "poor Bob Dole" were exactly the opposite of what I wished to hear. Phyllis understood this, and behaved accordingly. I think maybe that was what first made me think she was special. We met formally at a dance for patients. She was in charge of decorating around the theme of heaven (the dance floor) and hell (the bar). I arrived with a friend who had originally been admitted to the hospital with two broken legs. Before the evening was over, he was jitterbugging. And Phyllis and I were dancing close. That was the only way we *could* dance, since I couldn't extend my right arm.

Three months after I asked her for a date at the hospital coffee shop, we were married in St. Paul's Cathedral in Concord, New Hampshire. Among the notes of congratulation we received was a wire from Dr. Kelikian. He said he hoped I would make loving use of the arm he had gone to such length to restore.

Up to this time, I hadn't expected to walk down the aisle with any woman. As I explained to my family, I didn't think I had a right to impose on a wife the burdens that would accompany marriage to someone in my physical condition. Phyllis made me forget my injuries. She helped me think, not in terms of disability, but of ability. She treated me like everyone else.

As my nervous system came back to life, I experienced occasional tremors in my arms and legs. They made me shakier than usual, and more self-conscious than ever. One hot summer day in Russell we were all sitting around the dinner table. I was holding a glass of iced tea somewhat unsteadily in one hand and suddenly it slipped out of my grasp and shattered on the floor.

"Can't you hold anything?" Phyllis said in a jocular voice. She was thinking only that the glass was moist, and was determined to laugh the accident off. The rest of my family was a little shocked. They were used to treating me as a fragile object, like the glass on the floor. But Phyllis was right.

By the time we were married, in June 1948, I was out of Percy Jones for good. Thanks to the GI Bill, I was about to pick up on the college education so rudely interrupted by the war. The doctors in Battle Creek urged me to go to Arizona for its warm winters and dry climate, so I enrolled at the University of Arizona for a year. In between classes, I ran in the hills around Tucson. Except for a brief recurrence of lung problems which put me back in the hospital for a week, my recovery was uneventful.

Phyllis went with me to my classes, taking notes and writing exam papers from my dictation. Later on, I got a tape recorder, a primitive machine the size of a breadbox that I hooked up beside the professor. Nights were given over to transcribing the lectures in my left-handed scrawl. It was pretty slow going.

In the fall of 1949 I began lugging my tape recorder to class at Topeka's Washburn University, where I enrolled in a joint program for an undergraduate degree in history and a graduate degree in law. Phyllis meanwhile worked at the Topeka State Hospital and at the State Rehabilitation Center for the Blind. We lived in a small complex called the Senate Apartments, where I wore a hole in the living-room carpet pacing around with a book in my hand, reciting the day's lessons. Phyllis told me I didn't have to work so hard. Not every grade had to be an A.

"I don't know how to study for a C or B's worth," I told her. That's what I had done in my prewar days at the University of Kansas. A lot had changed since then, including my study habits. From now on, the only way I could study a subject was to master it.

The classrooms of Washburn were filled with older students, many of them beneficiaries of the GI Bill. Some were married, with small children. Not only had the war consumed their youth, it had also burned away frivolous notions. Remaining were a seriousness and an almost desperate wish to find meaning in the recent past. It was a class taught by some first-rate professors who challenged us to live up to all our noble-sounding precepts.

Perhaps the most influential politically was Beth Bowers, the law librarian, who was only a couple years older than I, and a registered Democrat to boot. Miss Bowers encouraged my classmates and me to take an active interest in politics. Having just fought a war for the survival of democracy, she explained, we might presume to hold a franchise on the democratic process. When Bowers suggested I run for the Kansas state legislature in the fall of 1950, I cocked an attentive ear.

It was a time for taking stock. I was never going to play football or wear a surgeon's gown. New ambitions sprang up in their place. It might take extra effort to achieve them, but that was no excuse to go home, rock on a porch and collect disability checks for the rest of my life.

Politics was a natural substitute for athletics. Knocking on a stranger's door, looking him in the eye and asking for his vote was a way to overcome my disability without denying it. Public service was also a way for me to give back a little of what had been showered on me by a generous community.

I had a more optimistic view of the human race than those who had stamped the GOP with a sour face and a country-club image. Having benefited from an extraordinary outpouring of affection and support, how could I feel otherwise?

It wasn't just my neighbors in Russell. In Topeka, Roy and Inez Finney, parents of Herb Finney, a Kappa Sigma brother of mine who had been killed in the war, became virtually a second set of parents, inviting me into their home and taking me around to spend time with their friends. There was M. C. Shell, who ran a Phillips gas station near our apartment. One of his employees was a guy named Shorty who would do anything for me, from fixing my car to getting it started on cold winter mornings. And, of course, there was Dr. K, who helped me begin again, with a fresh outlook, seeing possibilities where others saw only problems.

I've said many times how much I regret losing four years out of my life, and being determined to make up the loss by living each day as if it were my last. Actually, my years of hospitalization gave me more than they took away. Before the war I'm not sure what kind of career I had in store. Being injured narrowed my options, but it broadened my outlook.

Beginning the morning of April 14, 1945, I learned the value of adversity. A handicap can become an asset, I've since discovered, if it increases your sensitivity to others and gives you the resolve to tap whatever inner resources you have.

Something else I learned, surrounded by so many survivors. Courage is mental as well as physical. It is the resistance to fear rather than the absence of fear.

Much of my life since April 1945 has been an exercise in compensation. Doors have been closed but windows opened. Maybe I couldn't use my hand, I told myself, but I could develop my mind. If unable to greet voters with my right hand, I could always reach out with my left.

Physical limitations teach perseverance and humility. Since I have trouble enough lining up shirt buttons with the proper holes, breaking a fingernail can be a minor crisis. That's when a buttonhook comes in handy. I've long since gotten over my early feelings of embarrassment. Often these days I write to youngsters who are themselves disabled. Every time I sign my name I'm reminded of my mother's old maxim, "Can't never could do anything."

CHAPTER FOUR

Against the Grain

ELIZABETH

In the fall of 1954 I entered Duke University, a great research institution that at times resembled a finishing school. A freshman handbook set forth the prevailing criteria for academic success: "A Duchess should have the tact and good judgment to know when the occasion requires her to be serious and when to be gay, when to dress up and when to be casual. Everything she does is in good taste and up to the highest standards."

Incoming students were given a long list of the established dos and don'ts. Eat breakfast every day. Wear hats and hosiery to church. Go down receiving lines at dances. Write thank-you notes to your date and your hostess. Avoid blue jeans.

Early in its history, Duke separated the sexes, first with screens dividing the classroom, later by painting over dorm windows so that young women couldn't look out at passing boys. In the 1950s the university continued to play the role of surrogate parent, requiring every freshman to take religious studies, and prohibiting young ladies from staying out later than ten-thirty at night. Alcohol was off limits to both sexes. To enforce the Eighteenth Amendment at Duke there was a semi-official watchdog, the Delta Patrol in undergraduate parlance.

Contrary to later portrayals of a Silent Generation, my classmates were neither frivolous nor irresponsible. A more accurate reading of the class of '58 was that its values were fixed in a simpler time, when a college degree meant different things for men and women.

There might have been a moat surrounding the Duke Forest, so insulated was our world. Back then students found relief from their studies at Harvey's Cafeteria and the Blue Light. We drank Coke at the Devil's Den. If you wanted dancing with dinner, there was the Saddle Club over at Chapel Hill, fifteen minutes away if you kept a heavy foot on the pedal. More than one Saturday night, my date rounded the corner leading into the Duke campus on two wheels to beat curfew.

Student customs dictated student calendars. In November 1954 I joined Delta Delta Delta, which since its formation at Boston University nearly seventy years earlier had emphasized service projects like raising scholarship funds to aid needy young women. Later that fall the Blue Devil football squad generated excitement on its way to a nationally televised game in Miami's Orange Bowl.

At Christmastime, Duchesses were reminded to leave gifts for the maids and to attend parties for the underprivileged children of Durham. A winter cotillion featured name performers like Louis Armstrong and Perry Como. In the spring we had Joe College Weekend, highlighted by a parade, Les Brown's dance band, and a dramatic performance from the Hoof 'n Horn Club. Glossy boxwood scented the air around Carr Gymnasium, where classmates liked to sunbathe. As the days lengthened, so did the lines to get to nearby Grandma's Lake. Religious Emphasis Week preceded Easter. Mother-Daughter Weekend followed close behind.

It was social convention that got me to a debutante ball in Raleigh, an evening I vaguely remember as a haze of satin and chiffon. As an international-affairs major, I was more interested in writing a paper examining the decision-making process leading up to America's use of the first atomic bomb.

I plunged into student government, and found it almost as instructive as my textbooks. In the fall of my freshman year I ran for class representative. Encouraging classmates to take a more active interest in campus politics, I did the unpolitic thing of comparing them to Rip Van Winkle.

"Then let us show that we're alive," I declared in somewhat overwrought language, "and strain and strive, that we may say at set of sun, 'So much to do, but something done.' "

Rip Van Winkle woke up long enough to defeat my candidacy.

There weren't many feminine-support systems in those days. I was tapped for White Duchy, a semisecretive honor society which paralleled my brother, John's, Red Friars and served as a primitive sort of old girls' network. At the time of my appointment as Secretary of Transportation in 1983, I received many messages of support and encouragement, but none meant more than six white carnations from the other women who had been selected for membership in White Duchy that spring of 1957.

Among the most influential figures in Durham was the dean of East Campus, a professor of English literature named Florence Brinkley. Miss Brinkley was a tall, stately woman whose surface reserve masked an almost maternal warmth. She taught her students to think for themselves, and to think hard. It is not going too far to describe the Women's College at Duke as her lengthened shadow.

One of the regular events on our calendar was Sunday-afternoon tea at Dean Brinkley's home, located behind Giles House. It was close enough to Giles for her to hear the sounds of undergraduate partying the night before, but the dean never called to complain. She always looked the other way when walking through the Giles parking lot at night. As a token of sisterhood, undergraduate admirers once gave her a pair of red tennis shoes.

I had a number of opportunities to work with this remarkable woman after my March 1957 election as student government president. (This time around I had avoided Rip Van Winkle in my campaign speeches.) With Dean Brinkley's permission, I shuffled my academic schedule, dropping a couple of courses to accommodate my new responsibilities, and making them up by attending summer school at the University of Colorado.

The mountains of Colorado only whetted my appetite for

exotic scenery and experiences. One by-product of that Western summer was the discovery that I wasn't a total athletic klutz. Members of the Pacific Coast championship team, led by a very handsome blond, had me water-skiing on one ski by the end of an afternoon.

That's not all I learned. At the end of my junior year I had been criticized by Fred Sheheen, editor of the campus paper, *The Chronicle,* who said that my command of parliamentary procedure was a little shaky. Spurred on by his comments, I pored over *Robert's Rules of Order.* Come September and the start of a new school year, I could have held my own with the legislature at Raleigh. Meanwhile, a series of student town meetings furnished their own training in mediating, presiding and public speaking.

Returning to Durham in the fall of 1957, we launched a series of raids against campus tradition. Heading the list of reforms was establishment of a university-wide honor code. East and West Campuses had different views on the subject, however, and the idea died aborning. Not so with dorm hours: by the time we were through, Saturday-night curfew was pushed back to one o'clock Sunday morning.

With help from Duke administrators, including Dean Brinkley, a leadership-training program for women was established and a variety of speakers were imported from around the country. We set up a permanent foreign-student fund and raised money to bring a Danish girl to Durham. One evening, E. E. Cummings read his modernistic verses before an only slightly puzzled East Campus audience. More traditional rites led up to the selection of a May Queen. On a Friday night in May 1958, Duke president A. Hollis Edens put a crown on my head, a few weeks before he placed a diploma in my hand.

A diploma is not a compass, and the end of my college days found me groping for direction. My brother, John, offered to tailor a job in the family business to fit my interests. As he explained it, I would be free to write a newsletter or become a buyer, traveling to the Orient and other corners of the globe where the Hanford name was a familiar one among floral suppliers. A typically thoughtful gesture, John's proposal fell victim to my own restlessness and uncertainty.

That summer after graduation was spent pounding local pavements in search of I didn't really know what. During an interview at the *Charlotte Observer,* I learned something that had nothing to do with journalism. I went in assuming that if you wore the right dress and nodded at appropriate moments your credentials would speak for you. But I soon discovered the hard way that if you couldn't, or wouldn't, make the case for why you should get the job, you could hardly expect a prospective boss to make it for you. It was a mistake I would not repeat.

In my imagination I caught the rhythm of a different drummer. It beat a cadence familiar since childhood. Life was more than a spectator sport, and I couldn't settle for observer status. For the moment, however, I was like that old standard "I'm Just an In-Between." So were a lot of other women in the transitional 1950s.

Around East Campus it had been said, somewhat cynically, that there were girls with dates and girls with data. My own priorities were less restrictive. I was pinned to a young man from nearby Davidson College, and though I cared for him very much, I simply was not ready for marriage. Not yet anyway.

It wasn't as if I had a carefully drawn blueprint for the future. Women in that era rarely had one; you might take a job, almost by accident, only to discover ten years out that it had turned into a career. Meanwhile there were so many things I wanted to do, like attending graduate school and sampling the broad, eventful world that lay beyond Salisbury and Durham.

My first steps toward a career grew out of my old curiosity about remote places and lifestyles. According to the mapmakers, less than seven hundred miles separate Salisbury's courthouse square from Harvard Yard in Cambridge, Massachusetts. However, the two are in many ways worlds apart.

In the fall of 1958 I took a job in the Harvard Law School library, and all of New England became a classroom without walls. For a girl from Salisbury, there was something almost magical in the salt air of Marblehead and the icy perfume of a winter's morning in Vermont. I took to the ski slopes like a duck to water. When friends or family came north, I delighted in showing them around Harvard or pointing out the historic sites of Boston, Lexington and Concord.

The next summer was another course of study-in-travel, undertaken at the suggestion of Dean Brinkley. My old friend advised me to sample the glories of Oxford University, where many years earlier she had fallen under the spell of Milton and other giants of seventeenth-century literature. I had first been to Europe two years earlier, visiting châteaus and art museums with a group that included my best friend from Salisbury, Jean Stanback. More memorable than Versailles or the Swiss Alps was the day in Rome when Jean and I escaped from our group long enough to be driven around the Eternal City by a couple of Italian boys on motorcycles.

I approached Oxford in similarly adventurous spirit. Ostensibly there to study English history and government from 1870 to the present, I had no intention of limiting my education to the classroom. C. S. Lewis had just left Magdalen for Cambridge, but his departure had done nothing to lessen the majesty of Evensong under the vaulted roof of Christ Church. At other times, I rode my bicycle out to the Trout, or went to the Mitre Hotel for tea and crumpets. On weekends I rambled through Welsh coal-mining valleys and attended the Edinburgh Arts Festival.

If rules are meant to be broken, then walls are perfect for hurdling. Such was the reasoning of a twenty-three-year-old eager to experience everything possible in that city of dreaming spires. One night I deliberately stayed out late, until the gates of Exeter College were closed. Then I climbed a ladder to the top of the wall, jumped over and landed in the don's garden. I had barely enough time to scamper to my room without the housemaster identifying the intruder in his yard.

My Oxford sojourn was a brief one. From the land of Milton to the false utopia of Marx: I suddenly got a hankering to visit the Soviet Union. Maybe it was all those newspaper stories about Sputnik and spy planes that sparked my curiosity. Certainly it had nothing to do with any political illusions about the men in Moscow. To me, it was one more challenge, a chance to go where few Americans had been.

My father had built one of Salisbury's more elaborate bomb shelters, which showed how he felt about the Iron Curtain and the leaders operating behind it. Mother shared his feelings. I had tipped them off by letter about my planned trip, so when the long-distance operator alerted them one night to a call from Oxford they were both ready. They shook hands at the bottom of the staircase before taking up battle stations at separate phones.

It was tempting fate, Dad told me, to be in the USSR at the same time Soviet leader Nikita Khrushchev was touring America. What if someone took a shot at Khrushchev in New York? The Russians would lock up every American they could get their hands on. Fortunately, I was prepared. Before placing my call I had covered a legal pad with arguments to convince my folks that the trip's dangers were far outweighed by its educational benefits.

Besides the family debate preceding it, what stands out about the journey isn't Red Square, the vast GUM department store or the artistic treasures stuffed inside Leningrad's Hermitage. Instead, I remember a badly infected foot that was swollen to twice its normal size, and which landed me in a People's Clinic for a night I'll never forget. In the ambulance on the way there I used sign language to have a conversation of sorts with the first average Russians I had encountered on the trip.

I didn't want to go home having seen no more than the sanitized version of Soviet life you get through the Intourist guides. When a Russian emigrant stepped out of the hotel crowd that surrounded me as I was placed in the ambulance, I saw my chance. He identified himself as a member of my tour group and said I shouldn't be afraid. He was in Moscow for a short time to visit his mother. With typical audacity, I asked if later I could tag along with him.

My new friend hesitated, but I persisted, and he agreed to ask his mother. The next night we went to one of the cold gray apartment complexes that give the Soviet capital such an impersonal character. If his mother was at all reluctant to host such an unusual gathering, she didn't show it. After a few minutes of spirited conversation, I noticed that she kept her radio on, its volume turned up to frustrate would-be eavesdroppers. That simple gesture taught me a lot about a claustrophobic society. It made my homecoming especially joyous.

Back in Cambridge, I hedged my bets. In September 1959 I

enrolled in a joint-degree program that combined the study of government with the occupation of teaching. The first was my emerging passion, the second a vocational insurance policy.

As far as instructional techniques were concerned, I was green as Boston Common. No matter; Harvard believed that the best way to learn the art of teaching was to teach. It was sink or swim, with the students of suburban Melrose conducting the swimming lessons. I remembered from my own school days the difference between a creative teacher and one who taught literally by the book. The one might fan a spark of student curiosity; the other could just as easily smother the fire before it was ever lighted.

My assignment was to teach history to a class of eleventh graders. Determined to avoid the dull, numbing recital of kings and battles and treaties that can drain life from the past, I hoped to show how front-page events had affected earlier generations —how it felt to be making history before the historians made it over.

At first glance, the Boston police strike of 1919 seemed as distant as the Punic Wars. Then I spent an afternoon in the Police Department archives, combing through records buried in forty years of dust. In the process, I unearthed a surviving member of the striking force, and after tracking him down, recorded his memories on tape. He was such a hit with my class that they insisted he come in person and tell his dramatic account of the labor dispute that had paralyzed post World War I Boston and, coincidentally, elevated Calvin Coolidge to national prominence.

Next we turned to the Prohibition era of flappers and speakeasies and the rise of organized crime. How could one make so remote an age come alive to a class of seventeen-year-olds? I went back to the library and researched the national commission appointed by President Hoover to investigate and pass judgment on the dry decade. Sifting through contemporary accounts of its work, I kept stumbling over the same name.

Roscoe Pound.

But I *know* Roscoe Pound, I thought, confusing the occasional glimpse I'd had around Harvard of this legendary scholar and law school dean with a firsthand acquaintance. I figured that all it would take to close the gap was a little initiative, or a lot of nerve. Lacking neither, I tapped on Dean Pound's office door in the law school's Langdell Hall one afternoon. Inside I found an elderly man with a green eyeshade, alone in a room full of books and a life's worth of memories, both of which he willingly shared. As a matter of fact, Pound told me, he had the complete minutes from the commission meetings. Would I like to look at them? Perhaps take them to school with me?

At that moment, I couldn't have been happier had I discovered DNA.

Not all my efforts were aimed at transporting students to a distant past. One day I met a Buddhist monk in Harvard Square. He became part of a curriculum designed to open kids' eyes to a culture far removed from the manicured comforts of suburban Boston. Such experiences showed me what a noble profession teaching is. When professors at the School of Education urged me to pursue it as a career, I was flattered, but the lure of government outstripped the satisfactions of the classroom.

It was a time of awakening for America's youth. Public policy was being made in Southern streets and department stores. Early in 1960, four black college freshmen refused to accept Jim Crow treatment at a Greensboro, North Carolina, lunch counter. They joined a lengthening procession that had begun with a Birmingham housewife named Rosa Parks. They insisted that promises of legal and social justice which had been delayed for a hundred years could no longer be put off. In Salisbury, the civil-rights revolution was peaceful. Thanks to moderating influences on both sides, no one afterward could recall precisely when racial barriers came down in the balcony of the local movie theater or the bus station waiting room.

During the summer of 1960, I worked on Capitol Hill as a secretary in the office of North Carolina's B. Everett Jordan. Jordan was a Senator from the old school, a courtly figure who was unfailingly kind to staff and youngsters like myself. Although I had known his niece Elizabeth at Duke, I got the job by appearing in the doorway one day and announcing that I wanted to work there. For the next few weeks I did exactly that, all the while envying Suzanne Rodgers, a receptionist who was later a housemate of mine. Suzanne had a front-row seat at the legislative parade, while I was lucky to sit in the bleachers.

Before 1960, my most vivid memory of Washington was a childhood stay at the old Willard Hotel on Pennsylvania Avenue. My friend Jean Stanback and I said our nightly prayers in a room overlooking the floodlit Washington Monument. Now it was as if those prayers had been answered. When not staring at senators, gaping at Statuary Hall or climbing to the top of the Capitol Dome, I sought out prominent women in government for professional guidance.

Topping my list was Margaret Chase Smith, a Maine Republican who was one of only two women in the upper chamber. Known affectionately as "the lady from Skowhegan," the feisty, thoroughly independent Mrs. Smith was regarded by many as the conscience of the Senate.

When I walked into her private office, Senator Smith was wearing her trademark rose. She spoke briskly, with the clipped Yankee accent of Down East. Mrs. Smith recommended that I bolster my education with a law degree. That way, I would bring more to a public-policy job than aptitude or an M.A.

I don't know how many busy legislators would share an hour with a total stranger seeking advice. The incident impressed me deeply, so much so that whenever a young woman calls my office with a similar request, I make time to see her. It's my way of repaying a debt to the lady from Skowhegan.

Nineteen sixty was a presidential-campaign year. It was also my introduction to national politics. Suzanne Rodgers revealed plans for an old-fashioned whistle-stop tour of the South by Democratic vice-presidential nominee Lyndon B. Johnson. Senator Jordan's administrative assistant, Bill Cochran, offered to help me get on board. Added to all that, there was a handsome advance man on the train. With him, Suzanne and a prospective Vice President of the United States along for the ride, how could I resist?

As a dedicated Republican, my father didn't think much of his daughter riding Lyndon Johnson's campaign train through the heart of downtown Salisbury. Deep down, he was probably drawing a line through all my activities of recent years and extending it to the logical conclusion—a full-time career in government.

"Now, Dad," I said, "it will be perfectly all right. It's just a learning experience. It doesn't mean anything."

Secretly, I think, he was rather proud to have me riding on the Johnson train. The next few days were a blur of cheering crowds, rear-platform speechmaking and trackside renditions of "The Eyes of Texas Are Upon You." As befitted a candidate from the Lone Star State, there were enough yellow roses handed up from the throngs to impress even a florist's daughter.

Through her warmth and vivacity, Lady Bird Johnson endeared herself to everyone on the LBJ Express. But if she had a calming presence, her husband swept through the train like a Texas tornado. At the first sight of Lyndon Johnson's towering figure, staffers made themselves scarce. From engine room to caboose, doors could be heard slamming as orders were barked out.

I returned to Cambridge in September 1960 and resumed work at Harvard Law. During each of the next two summers, I forsook the library of Langdell Hall for New York, drawn to the Big Apple for the sheer challenge of living there and in hopes of getting a job at the United Nations. Admittedly, I had been told that UN employment required a two-year commitment and the ability to speak five languages. But whenever anyone says, "It can't be done," I have a way of double-checking, just to be sure.

I made my way to the UN placement office overlooking the East River and told them I had a yen to work for the international organization; I couldn't stay for more than three months; I'd have to return to Cambridge in the fall. A few days later I was taking tour groups through the UN complex as a $162-a-week employee of the Public Information Section.

The next summer I lived with other UN interns at Riverside House in the Morningside Heights section of Manhattan. Being assigned to the General Secretariat provided a worm's-eye view of international diplomacy. I also stumbled onto some cloak-and-dagger stuff. I had casually gotten to know some of the members of the Russian delegation. Because he knew I'd been to Russia, it seemed perfectly natural for one of the Soviet diplomats to invite me to dinner. Before saying yes, I checked with my superior, who assured me there was nothing improper about dining out with a Russian envoy. She came along anyway.

The next thing I knew, the FBI asked me to meet some agents in a nearby parking lot. The upshot was a request to let federal investigators know should my Russian friend call me for another dinner date. I was willing. Apparently he wasn't. At least, I never heard from him again.

Meanwhile, there was no shortage of other social opportunities in that exuberant city. My chief interest at the time centered around a fellow North Carolinian, a young doctor whose friendship dated back to my Oxford summer. He was probably the most brilliant person I've ever known. He was also the most intense, with a pale, nearly ghostlike complexion, the result of too much studying and not enough sunshine. Because of his grueling schedule, he had suggested we get better acquainted by taking the train home together the previous Christmas.

I probably should have been flattered that he broke away from Harvard Medical School long enough to visit me in New York that summer. Instead, we quarreled, leading up to a scene worthy of a Woody Allen movie. We were at Grant's Tomb, and I was rambling on about the UN and all the fascinating people I had met there. My friend was less impressed by the global village than I was. Loving music and philosophy, in his cerebral way he wished always to be surrounded by the very best. But the best as defined by his narrow code.

"You are totally out of touch with the common man," I told him.

"I have no desire to be in touch with the common man." It was an honest answer; but one can be honestly wrong.

"You just go live in your test tube," I said, "because that's not the life for me."

"You're a political animal," he replied, "and that's not my cup of tea."

Inscribed over the portal of Grant's Tomb is the Civil War hero's famous admonition "Let us have peace." There and then, we decided to take his advice and go our separate ways.

The future began to press in on me. In May 1962, as queen of the First Naval District's "Space Age Frolics," I was photographed with the Red Sox pitching staff. Baseball players have short careers, but so do women who wear cardboard crowns. I was getting a little old for this sort of thing. But was the space age ready for women with more substantive ambitions?

My Langdell Hall mentors, librarians Earl Borgeson and Vaclav Mostecky, thought it was. They urged me to apply to the law school. So did others.

"Submit the application," one said. "There's no harm in submitting an application."

My brother thought I was making a mistake.

"Here you are, in the golden years of youth," he reminded me. "Do you really want to bury yourself in a monastery for three years?"

But it wasn't going to be like that at all, I assured John. Since I had no intention of going on to Wall Street, I was under no pressure to make A's. I would apply myself as usual, but not at the cost of enjoying the experience. This time out, I would lead a more balanced life. Rationalizing law school as an experiment, I concluded that even a year at Harvard Law would be excellent training and background. So I told myself. So I told John.

Neither one of us really believed I would be there only one year.

And why should I? Listening to my dates from the law and business schools discuss their cases and papers, I had a strong sense of being able to hold my own academically. My grades were as good as or better than many, and I already had an M.A. from Harvard's Graduate School of Education. Why not go forward like all the men around me? Why did I have to take a backseat?

My parents saw it a little differently. I broke the news to them at the end of a long day of sightseeing in New Hampshire. Mother's reaction was less one of opposition than of puzzlement.

"Don't you want to be a wife, and a mother, and a hostess for your husband?" she asked.

I told them I wanted to be all those things. In time. But

just then I had other aspirations. As usual, Mother and Dad understood. Even though law school wasn't something they would have chosen for me, they would stand behind me. After all, it was my life, my little red wagon.

Later that night I was awakened by sounds of distress coming from the adjoining bathroom. Mother had lost her dinner. No doubt she thought she was losing her daughter.

I was embarked on another pioneer experience. There were 550 members of the class of '65 at Harvard Law School, only two dozen of them women. (Today, by contrast, the female contingent at HLS is almost 40 percent.)

On the first day of classes a male student approached me in Langdell Hall Library. "Elizabeth, what are you doing here?" he demanded, in tones of moral outrage. "Don't you realize that there are *men* who would give their right arm to be in this law school, men who would *use* their legal education?"

Such insensitivity thrived on both sides of the lecture podium. That first year I took a course in property, taught by an august personage named Leach. Among the class's 150 members were five women, none of whom was ever called upon. We did our reading and analyzed our cases, we held up our end of the Socratic bargain, but it wasn't enough. As far as Professor Leach was concerned, we simply didn't exist. The only exception was an annual display known as Professor Leach's Ladies' Day, when the women in property were summoned to the front of the room to read a poem of their own composition. Once this ritual was over, Professor Leach, seated with the male students, would pelt us with questions. Charles W. Kingsfield at his most perverse could not have devised a more public humiliation.

All this added up to the academic equivalent of boot camp. Friends turned a deaf ear to the inevitable complaints. As one put it, "You *worked* at Harvard. You saw for yourself the agony of first year. But you went into it anyway. How could you?"

In fact, I was less prepared for my first year of law school than I thought. There was nothing at Duke or the School of Education that compared with the impossible hours or beady-eyed competition of Harvard Law. None of my prior classmates had ever torn pages out of a textbook in order to deny them to rivals, as was sometimes done at HLS.

Studying fifteen hours at a stretch during exams, pausing only for a can of soup eaten directly from the saucepan: this was a far cry from the Devil's Den and Durham's tobacco-mulched lawns. First-year students had the added insecurity of not knowing whether they were candidates for law review or in danger of flunking out, because there was no full-scale exam until June. Then we filed into a stifling hot room for a four-hour test. The first question alone filled twelve pages.

Outside the classroom, student-teacher interaction was sporadic and perfunctory. A few years after graduation, I happened to sit next to the school's former dean, Erwin Griswold, at a Washington dinner party. By that time he was Lyndon Johnson's Solicitor General. (His old job at the law school had been filled by a youthful reformer named Derek Bok, who a few years later would become Harvard's president.) I greatly admired Dean Griswold and his wife, but I couldn't resist pouring out three years' worth of pent-up frustrations. Did law school have to be so thoroughly unpleasant? I asked. Did students (among them some of my own classmates) have to come close to nervous breakdowns trying to cope with Harvard? Why couldn't there have been a sense of community as well as classroom excellence? Although Dean Griswold accepted my assault in good humor, he stood his ground. No minds were changed that evening.

Bob likes to say I'm never content to ask what time it is. I want to know how the clock was made. While I've always had a healthy appetite for information and a disciplined approach to work of any kind, Harvard reinforced these traits. At the same time, it has taken me years to see that you don't *have* to always strive for perfection, that "perfection" itself can become a kind of social tyranny, and that there is most definitely a point of diminishing returns.

Author and critic Marya Mannes has summed this up, memorably, in describing the different set of expectations governing male and female conduct: "Nobody objects to a woman being a good writer or sculptor or geneticist if, at the same time, she manages to be a good wife, a good mother, good-looking, good-tempered, well-dressed, well-groomed, and unaggressive."

In the legal fraternity of 1962, perfection, as defined by Miss Mannes, was not so appealing on the social front. Jean Eberhart, later a justice of the Colorado Supreme Court, was a roommate of mine. We sat on our beds one afternoon convincing ourselves we were on the fringe of spinsterhood. Finally I put into words the question plaguing us both: "Do you think that *anyone* will take us out, once they learn we're Harvard Law students?"

Most of my dates were with men from the Business School on the other side of the Charles River. Not only were they closer to my age, but they also didn't discuss cases over candlelight and wine, nor were they so blinded by torts and contracts that they lost sight of the real world.

On the afternoon of November 22, 1963, I was studying in the international-law library when someone blurted out the news that shots had been fired at President Kennedy's motorcade in Dallas. Harvard suspended classes and grieved with special poignance over its most famous alumnus. For the next few days the young man I was dating and I sat glued to the television screen, mesmerized like the rest of America by the public rituals of farewell.

It was no accident that I was in the international-law library that tragic afternoon. As a break from my corporate-law classes, I liked nothing better than courses in Russian and Chinese law, international codes, diplomatic statutes. In the fall of 1963, like-minded classmates elected me president of the international-law club named for John Marshall. (I also consented to run for class secretary, thinking that it was only a five-year term. More than twenty years later, I am still sending out those gossipy class newsletters.)

The women of HLS have made the most of their legal educations. Today Patricia Schroeder is a well-known congresswoman from Colorado. A generation ago she was a fellow law student, first encountered one morning when my unoccupied car rolled down the driveway and slammed into hers. In the course of clearing it all up, we became friends. It still helps to have that common point of reference these days, when we often find ourselves on opposite sides of the political street.

Pat and I were not the only ones to disprove the chauvinistic view that only men could properly utilize a legal education. Jane Roth, wife of Delaware Senator William V. Roth, Jr., is another former member of our class. She sits on the bench in Delaware. Other women from the class of '65 are law school instructors, judges, and influential members of the bar.

Like legal students everywhere, I spent my final year sifting options. Wall Street held no allure, and Washington law firms were nearly as reluctant as their New York counterparts to recruit women to their ranks. Teaching belonged to my past; marriage was part of a still dim future. One thing held immediate and continuing appeal: the governing process.

Under John F. Kennedy, Harvard had come to be known, only half in jest, as the fourth branch of American government. While there, I had gotten caught up in the enthusiasm for public service that flavored the early sixties. One summer it had led me to a personnel job in the Peace Corps's Washington headquarters. The agency reflected a missionary impulse as old as America and as youthful as the operatives who were sent in her name to sixty countries. They were the best of the best and brightest.

Twenty years later, I would accompany UN Ambassador Jeane J. Kirkpatrick on a visit to the African nations of Senegal, Togo, Rwanda and Burundi. Wherever we went, we met tribesmen whose lives had materially improved thanks to the Peace Corps and its seat-of-the-pants diplomacy. The trip confirmed my respect for a generation whose desire to serve made its members our most valuable export.

In 1965 the White House Fellows program was created as an apprenticeship matching would-be public servants with Cabinet officers and high-ranking members of the White House staff. Three thousand candidates applied for fifteen slots. Among the final panel of judges were David Rockefeller, John B. Oakes of the *New York Times* and John W. Macy, Jr., chairman of the old Civil Service Commission that was precursor to the Office of Personnel Management.

Several months of essay writing and preliminary interviews led up to a regional competition in Atlanta. After making that cut, I found myself competing with two other women and forty-two men at Virginia's Airlie House. While the other finalists were enjoying themselves around a swimming pool, I indulged my tendency to overprepare. It did me in. Staying inside, reviewing notes for the next round of interviews, I missed out on a critical piece of information. One of the judges happened by the pool and dropped the hint that he and his colleagues were looking for people who would apply what they would learn in Washington to their own backyard.

I could honestly have told the judges, "I love North Carolina, and may go back and run for office there someday." Or I could have said that Washington looked irresistible. I chose the second. More rankling than not winning the fellowship was the realization that I'd blown an opportunity that was unlikely to come again.

The game of "If only" is a form of torture invented by and for second-guessers, control seekers, and perfectionists of every stripe. As a disease of ego, it is something that can take a lifetime to overcome. In the meantime, the best medicine is the ability to laugh at yourself—something Bob prescribes in large doses.

Opening the 1965 Harvard commencement where I received my law degree, university president Nathan M. Pusey delivered the traditional greeting to graduating seniors, welcoming them into "the fellowship of educated men." As usual, words trailed behind deeds. Even then, Harvard's sexual caste system was crumbling. Take it from an old hand at leaping walls.

CHAPTER FIVE

Through the Ranks

BOB

> *Politics are almost as exciting as war, and quite*
> *as dangerous. In war you can only be killed*
> *once, but in politics many times.*

—Winston Churchill

War has many by-products. For the victorious side, there are peace treaties, ticker-tape parades and candidates for public office. An old soldier's political philosophy matters less to voters than the number of stars on his cap or ribbons on his jersey. If you've been shot up and lived to tell about it, odds are that some slate-maker will ask you to run for office.

That's exactly what Clifford Holland, Sr., an old family friend from Russell, did in the spring of 1950. Holland was a lawyer widely known in the state and a major figure in Kansas Democratic politics. Cliff hoped he could sign me up as a card-carrying Democrat.

More persuasive was John Woelk, a former Navy pilot and current Russell County attorney who thought I was a natural-born Republican. Woelk urged me to run that fall for the state legislature. The honor of legislative service in those days far exceeded the financial reward. Lawmakers received a daily wage of five dollars (to a maximum of $350) plus seven dollars expense money for each day of the biennial legislative session.

Since many would-be legislators were reluctant to forgo a business or a law practice and drive two hundred miles to Topeka, my own proximity to the seat of government was of no small advantage.

Washburn's law school already served state departments as a kind of think tank and employment agency. Many of the Kansas Supreme Court's law clerks were Washburn trained, and the legislative galleries on the third floor of the Capitol building were regularly filled with my classmates. John Woelk laid out the reasons for my running in practical terms. "Just remember, Bob," he said, "there are hundreds more Republicans in this county than Democrats." A pretty persuasive argument.

Notwithstanding those registration figures, there was nothing assured about my first campaign.

To win a place on the floor of the House, I had to defeat an incumbent legislator from nearby Dorrance named Elmo J. Mahoney. Mahoney was a tough-talking self-styled populist, considerably older than myself. Name a problem, he had a solution—a verbal one, anyway. Discontented farmers were his natural constituency.

To be honest, there weren't many issues dividing the local electorate. Legislative candidates were graded on how many homes they visited, how many pairs of shoes they wore out. Campaign funds in that part of Kansas were scarce as sea gulls, so I served as my own ad agency, speechwriter and press agent, calling editors and hand-delivering newspaper ads.

I'm not sure who suffered more through my early speeches, the audience or me. Gradually, I got over my stage fright. I also began a habit that has stayed with me ever since, of leaving head tables and mingling with those out front. At first it was just a way of avoiding the embarrassment of asking someone next to me to cut whatever was on my dinner plate, but I soon found I preferred chatting with people in the crowd to staring down at them from a raised platform.

Nineteen fifty was a Republican year. Kansans chose 105 Republicans and 20 Democrats to serve in their lower house. And Russell County voters made me their youngest legislator ever. A few days after the election, a reporter for the *Topeka*

Capitol came by to do a human-interest story. He asked me whether I had a legislative agenda.

"I'm going to sit and watch for a couple of days," I told him, "and then I'll stand up for what I think is right."

Brave talk, coming from a twenty-seven-year-old back-bencher.

The legislature that took office in January 1951 had a new governor to work with, Edward F. Arn. As Kansas' attorney general, Ed Arn had carried out a series of raids under the state's prohibition laws. These forays showed how difficult it was to enforce a law so widely laughed at. They paved the way for a 1948 referendum repealing the ban on alcohol sales in the state, sixty years after an outraged Carrie Nation first wielded an ax against a Kansas saloon.

The 1951 legislative session was marked by evasion, confusion and occasional bursts of inspiration. A right-to-work law was bottled up in the state Senate. Plans to reorganize state government by creating a "little Hoover Commission" were sidetracked with the Governor's acquiescence. The House endorsed voting rights for eighteen-year-olds one day, but reversed itself the next.

Most of the time, lawmakers did what they always do— spend money. And in 1951 we ought to have been counting our change. Revenue windfalls derived from wartime taxes were all but exhausted. A new conflict in Korea promised a fresh round of inflation. The decade-long agricultural prosperity couldn't last forever.

But legislators are more predictable than the weather; and few things are more permanent than a temporary tax. So a provisional levy on gasoline was extended, and a sales tax originally earmarked for educational and welfare programs was stretched to finance hospital construction.

One argument that spring featured a proposed Fair Employment Practices Commission. The bill as introduced in the House was mild enough. It would establish a state FEPC whose mandate was to educate Kansas employers on the virtues of color-blind hiring. However meager its budget and staff, the FEPC would make an important statement, a declaration of intent consistent with Kansas history and Republican politics. I was part of the House majority that voted on March 16, 1951, to pass the bill. The Senate was another kettle of fish. There it took two years and the personal involvement of Lieutenant Governor Fred Hall to override the opposition of commercial interests and to force a public roll call. In the end, it was Hall who cast the deciding vote to create the commission.

The legislature did not meet in 1952. My only visit to the House chamber that year was in the spring, when I took my bar exams there. A few weeks later, when Dwight D. Eisenhower returned to Abilene to launch his late-blooming campaign for the Republican presidential nomination, I was in the crowd of rain-soaked admirers on hand to greet him. Kansans of both parties were intensely proud to see one of our own achieve international fame and the highest honors a nation could bestow.

My ambitions were humble by comparison. Eric "Doc" Smith, a young lawyer recently established in Russell County, reassured me that my physical disability needn't interfere with a legal career. Smith didn't stop there. As soon as I finished my legal studies and passed the bar, he told me, I could count on a place in his office. That same year I took him up on his offer. To formalize our partnership I moved a battered old desk into an empty room over L. Banker's mercantile establishment at the corner of Eighth and Main in Russell. In a fit of extravagance I went out and bought a handsome leather chair to go with the enormous desk. Someone said my new chair looked like a hundred-dollar saddle on a ten-dollar horse.

Like most small-town lawyers, Doc and I took just about any case that came through the door. This was oil country, so title matters were our bread and butter, a diet offset by the usual probate and family disputes. In June 1952, I announced my candidacy for Russell County attorney. Looking back, some have interpreted my race that year as a logical step on the road from Russell to Washington. At the time my sights were fixed on more immediate concerns. Like earning a living. With the legal contacts developed over a couple of terms as county attorney, I hoped to build a Russell law practice that would sustain my family for the rest of our lives.

Politics at the grass-roots level is almost always personal. The smaller the town, the fewer the secrets and the greater the importance placed on personal connections. To many voters, the chief function of the county attorney was springing their friends nabbed on traffic charges. On primary day I scored a narrow win over Dean Ostrum, a Yale-educated lawyer whose professional credentials probably counted less than the local voters' sympathy for a banged-up veteran. November was much easier, as Kansans trooped to the polls to ratify Dwight Eisenhower's candidacy and almost incidentally vote in the rest of the Republican slate.

My new position paid $248 a month, four dollars less than the salary of the custodian who swept the courthouse. Maintaining a private practice on the side, in what passed for spare time I sought out the classic unpaid advertising of small-town lawyers everywhere. There were meetings of the Elks and the Masons to attend, 4-H fairs to patronize, the county Red Cross to chair. I taught Sunday school at the Methodist church. After October 18, 1954, I had a fresh incentive to keep the courthouse lights burning late. That was when Phyllis presented me with a baby daughter, whom we named Robin. Life was full, and full of promise.

As county attorney I was forced, on a couple of occasions, to step in and take abused children away from their parents. Aside from this, my official duties were not burdensome. There was the usual run of traffic and liquor violations, some bad checks, an occasional burglary. The attempted bribery of a city commissioner enlivened front pages for a season. Probably my biggest day in court came when a majority of the Kansas Supreme Court agreed with me on technical grounds that a one percent severance tax on oil and gas production was unconstitutional.

By the late 1950s, I was all ears when my old hospital buddy Phil Hart, by then a United States senator from Michigan (and a Democrat, at that), urged me to take a look at a political career. The House seat in question was very much occupied by Wint Smith, a Republican who had spoken for Kansas' Sixth Congressional District since 1946. At six feet five inches and three hundred pounds, Wint cut a memorable figure whether in

Washington or Mankato. In style and philosophy he combined the country squire's love of tradition with the combative instincts of the brigadier general he'd been in World War II. Before that, as director of the Kansas Highway Patrol, Smith had fought his own private wars against rural bank robbers he liked to take off the hands of local law enforcement officials and transport back to Topeka in chains.

His approach to politics was just as blunt. The New Deal appalled Smith. But he was hardly less offended by so-called "modern Republicans" who had willingly accepted much of Franklin Roosevelt's emergency-generated safety net. In 1952, when Republicans nationally were choosing sides between Robert A. Taft and Dwight Eisenhower, Wint got himself a big button that said "MacArthur." His congressional newsletter was a forum for attacks on foreign aid in general and the Marshall Plan in particular. Sooner or later, he argued, Americans would pay dearly for making wartime enemies into industrial competitors.

As Smith readily acknowledged, he was frozen in opposition to trends he could neither halt nor compromise with.

"I was all right until we elected a Republican President," he remarked to a friend soon after Eisenhower's 1952 triumph, "but now there are things I can't go along with. Any man who can be elected President of the United States can't go along with some of my positions and I'm not about to change."

In 1958, the Congressman from Mankato had been challenged in the GOP primary by Keith G. Sebelius, a young state senator from Norton. Wint interpreted his 51-vote victory margin as handwriting on the wall. Not long after, he appeared in the Phillipsburg, Kansas, newspaper office of McDill "Huck" Boyd and told Huck that after a cold-blooded appraisal of his chances in a 1960 rematch he had decided to write his own political obituary.

The conversation turned to possible successors. Sebelius was one of a half-dozen people mentioned. I was another. Wint said he doubted he could "pick ships in a primary by endorsing one candidate over another." But the heat of a campaign can easily melt resolves made in the political off season. Privately,

Smith made it clear that he hadn't forgotten the help I'd given him in the 1958 contest and he expected his conservative supporters to repay the favor in 1960.

Smith's theory was quickly put to the test. I went to see Dane Hansen, a staunch Smith ally and a power broker in his own right, whose influence and connections stretched from the crossroads villages of northwest Kansas to the Governor's Mansion in Topeka. Hansen lived according to an unorthodox schedule. He began his workday around the supper hour. Then he held court with visiting politicos or businessmen, often until dawn broke over the boundless prairie.

It took only one postmidnight visit to Logan, Kansas, to convince Hansen that I was ideologically trustworthy. As Hansen put it later, "Hell, I knew he was a fiscal conservative. The tires on his car were threadbare."

No one in rock-ribbed Kansas seriously doubted that the state would go with Republican candidate Richard M. Nixon over John F. Kennedy in the 1960 presidential race. We were still a lot closer to Oz than to Camelot. But beneath the surface flowed currents of dissatisfaction, even within GOP circles. In the Sixth District, Keith Sebelius' strong showing against Wint Smith in the congressional primary two years earlier had served notice of a desire for change among the party rank and file.

For all the signs of restlessness, however, one ritual never varied. Each January on the anniversary of Kansas' statehood, Republicans flocked to Topeka's venerable Jayhawk Hotel. Few of those jammed into the Jayhawk's public rooms for Kansas Day, 1960, to trade gossip and float balloons had ever heard of Bob Dole. Fewer still were prepared for the hoopla designed to change that.

Ordinarily, such gatherings were pretty sedate affairs— county barons like Dane Hansen, J. Harm Voss and Harry Darby holed up in smoke-filled rooms. In the evening, everyone donned uncomfortable clothes and ate in the hotel ballroom, where an out-of-state luminary expounded the party gospel. The routine was as fixed, and the effect as predictable, as a Buckingham Palace garden party.

So when a rough-and-tumble caravan of Dole supporters from Russell County rolled into town on Friday, January 29, 1960, it bordered on the subversive. Out of nowhere appeared twenty pretty girls dressed in identical red felt skirts and matching handbags. They were accompanied by a quartet of "Bob-O-Links," led by a ukulele-playing songstress. In their wake trailed a football player riding a tricycle, a middle-aged farmer wearing an elephant's head, and a group of pallbearers transporting a mock coffin containing the Frankenstein monster, who held a placard reading: "You Have Nothing to Fear with Dole."

There was method to our madness. At the beginning of the campaign I faced a special problem of name identification. It wasn't only that Keith Sebelius was already a familiar figure throughout the district and I was not. What really complicated things was a third candidate on the ballot, a state senator named Phillip J. Doyle. I was less worried about Doyle's appeal to the farm vote than about the confusion that was sure to arise from the similarity of our names.

What I needed was a means of distinguishing between us, a gimmick that people would remember. The Kennedys were famous for their kaffeeklatsches. Why couldn't the Doles serve —pineapple juice?

"Roll with Dole" was my 1960 campaign slogan. Soon we had it emblazoned across a mock Conestoga wagon, which became a familiar sight on the streets of communities like Colby, Ellsworth and Hoxie. So did a bevy of volunteers adorned in campaign outfits designed and stitched by Phyllis and friends from Russell.

We developed an unvarying routine. The wagon team set up cardboard tables in the local square, its members began distributing cups of pineapple juice, and I went off to stalk voters in barbershops and five-and-dimes. Or I worked a parade crowd while a dozen campaign workers passed out enough pineapple juice to float a battleship.

Hungry campaigners said I refused to let them go to dinner until I'd met every single voter lingering on Main Street. Even six-year-old Robin became part of our road show. She wore a skirt announcing, "I'm for Robin's Daddy."

One morning, my daughter wished me luck in winning

what she called the "collection." Given the state of our finances, I could only hope she was right. After Wint Smith changed his mind about a public endorsement and flooded the district with five thousand letters in my behalf, some editors printed letters of their own that linked me to "grain barons" and "millionaire oilmen." The allegations were quickly disposed of, since our largest contribution was under two hundred dollars.

The entire campaign cost less than $20,000. Even so, long before November we were forced to take out a mortgage on the family's five-room house. With the help of the mortgage money, we managed to patch together some primitive TV spots. Add to that the free media coverage, plenty of shoe leather and the ubiquitous cups of pineapple juice, and I got my message across.

I drove over forty thousand miles during that campaign. If I saw a farmhouse light burning I took it as an invitation to drop in and make my case. All the candidates agreed about the dangers of selling grain to the Russians and the need to keep America's military defenses up. Most of our time was spent on homelier concerns: repeal of an excise tax on phone calls; support for a third federal judgeship, to be located in Salina; money from Washington to help pay the cost of educating the children of military personnel on area bases.

For weeks, our basement served as a central command post, a place where friends could hand-letter placards or make phone calls to uncommitted voters. On primary night, it looked more like a bunker fortified against defeat. Early reports from Sebelius strongholds in Salina and Norton County were discouraging. But the race began narrowing as outlying communities weighed in. By dawn it was virtually a dead heat. It wasn't until early Wednesday afternoon, however, after UPI announced it had erred in transposing Russell County votes for Dole and Doyle, that the deadlock was broken.

By a scant one thousand votes, I was the Republican candidate in a district whose traditional party loyalties all but ensured victory in November. When it was over, a good-natured Keith Sebelius gave me his explanation of what had happened.

It was quite simple, he said. "You drowned me in pineapple juice."

· · ·

As a very junior member of the Eighty-seventh Congress, I was invited to a White House reception and spent much of the evening gawking at famous faces in the East Room. As the Marine Band struck up "Hail to the Chief," Phyllis and I drew back for the ceremonial entrance of President and Mrs. Kennedy. Later we were introduced to the youthful President and his elegant First Lady. Although impressed by the surroundings, I wasn't swept off my feet. All glory is fleeting, as I reminded Rose Mary McVey, the wife of another freshman in the Kansas congressional delegation.

"Live it up while you can, Rose Mary," I told her. "Just remember, we're in a ten-minute parking zone."

I arrived in Washington a marked man. As a result of the 1960 census, Kansas was due to lose one of her six House seats. That meant there would likely be a merging of my district with neighboring territory represented by Democrat J. Floyd Breeding. Job insecurity cast a pall over my early years on Capitol Hill. It also placed strains on the Doles' family life.

Given the centrifugal forces of a political career, I sometimes think that anyone who would marry a politician should have his/her head examined. (If you're reading this, Elizabeth, I'm only kidding.) The hardest thing for a politician to do is say no. It becomes virtually impossible when he knows he's facing a strong challenge at the polls and the folks back home are counting on him to open a supermarket or address the local Rotary. Before you know it, you're on a plane bound west every Friday night, mending fences in the district, which often means neglecting your own family back in Washington. It's awfully tough to sustain a marriage when one partner is usually in the office fourteen hours a day and spends most weekends on the road.

I am happy to report that my daughter, Robin, grew up to be completely unaffected by the Washington limelight. (She has never held a federal job, for instance.) Her mother insisted on it, and it no doubt helped that Robin inherited the family sense of humor. When she was a teenager and wanted our permission to pierce her ears, she researched and wrote a decision memo similar to one a congressional staffer might prepare for his boss. At the bottom of the memo were two option boxes, one marked

"Yes," the other "No." The next morning Robin woke to find the memo slipped under her door, with a third option scribbled in by her father: "Maybe."

One thing about teenagers: just being around them is a constant education in popular culture. I'm afraid I missed out on a few lessons. After hearing Robin go into raptures over a British rock band that was planning a visit to the U.S., I wrote to the British Embassy asking them whether they could get the band to surprise her and play at her high school. Unfortunately, embassy officials replied, the Beatles would be unable to accommodate Miss Dole and her classmates on their forthcoming American tour.

Meanwhile, I discovered that a congressman gets a lot of invitations on his own. Speaking on the mashed-potato circuit is a bit like KP in the Army—it's part of the job. At the same time, anything that keeps a politician humble is good for democracy. Certainly that was the case with a visit I made to a small town in Indiana. The name Bob Dole had little marquee value in 1961, so the GOP dinner committee had to hype the box office. When I arrived in town, I was whisked off to the local radio station, where the announcer was supposed to give people some incentives to boost attendance. He began with a more or less accurate rendition of my résumé.

"The guest at this evening's dinner," he said, "will be Congressman Bob Doyle [*sic*]. He will speak at the American Legion Hall. Tickets have been slashed from three dollars to one dollar. A color television set will be given away. You must be present to win, and we're not going to draw till Congressman Doyle gets through talking.

"Doyle was born in Kansas, raised in Kansas, educated at the University of Kansas. Prior to World War II, he was a premedical student. He fought in Italy, where he suffered a serious head injury. Then he went into politics."

As president of the GOP's freshman class in the House, I came to the attention of Gerald R. Ford, a genial six-term veteran from Grand Rapids. Jerry Ford's relaxed manner did nothing to conceal his competitive instincts or his fierce partisan loyalties. I also struck up close friendships with Robert P. Griffin and Donald Rumsfeld after they arrived on the scene—both fellow Midwesterners who later served in Ford's White House Cabinet and his informal Kitchen Cabinet. Perhaps my closest friend from those days is Bob Ellsworth, who was sent to the House from Lawrence the same year I was elected, and who would play a significant role in Richard Nixon's successful 1968 campaign for the presidency.

I was practically invisible to the Democratic side of the House. I'm not sure whether Speaker Sam Rayburn of Texas or John W. McCormack, his white-haired successor from South Boston, ever knew I was there. In the House of 1961, seniority was the password to power. Young men in a hurry, especially those who belonged to a seemingly permanent minority, were thought of as party crashers.

It's a popular lament that in this mediagenic age statesmanship often runs a poor second to showmanship. In fact there is nothing new about congressmen playing the role of watchdog to bring them attention. By presenting a 1962 resolution to investigate the dealings of Billy Sol Estes, I did a little barking of my own. Estes' manipulation of government-owned agricultural stockpiles was sufficiently scandalous to land him—and me— on the front page of the *New York Times*. Taking a jab at Estes' White House connections, I made up some acerbic buttons for the occasion: "S.O.B." they read, for Save Our Billy.

This illustrates the first and riskiest avenue to success in the House: playing to the outside audience. A second is accepting the institutional ethic, mastering a few subjects and allowing time and the seniority system to work their will. A third path, one heavily traveled by freshmen, is to forgo most larger issues in favor of diligent casework and constituent services.

But even this brand of micropolitics strained available resources. Office staffs were small in the sixties, which meant long hours and professional versatility. Administrative assistants mimeographed newsletters. Office managers doubled as caseworkers. I read every letter that came in the mail, and dictated personal responses to most. I also played tour guide. More than once I went down to the White House to plead personally for tour passes for visiting constituents.

Visibility was pursued like the Holy Grail. I sent all graduating high-school seniors in the Sixth District a certificate to mark their commencement. No bride walked down the aisle without a copy of *The Congressional Cookbook*. I once mistakenly extended congratulations on the birth of a baby to a couple observing their golden wedding anniversary. So many pictures of myself with visiting Kansans appeared in local papers that I was accused of not having an office and conducting my business on the Capitol steps.

My voting record faithfully reflected district sentiments: in favor of rural electrification, soil conservation and economy in government; against foreign aid and most of Lyndon Johnson's Great Society programs. When the Supreme Court handed down its famous one-man, one-vote ruling, it was a body blow to western Kansas, whose population was less concentrated than in the more urbanized east. I proposed to take the sting out of the decision with a constitutional amendment allowing states to consider factors other than population in apportioning at least one house of their legislature.

On the subject of grain sales to the Soviet Union and Red China, my initial preference was to give the surplus wheat to America's friends rather than sell it to her enemies. Anything else, I thought, would put us in the position of fighting Communists with one hand while feeding them with the other.

But the world economy was changing. Global interdependence and our own abundant harvests harmonized in the Food for Peace program, which built upon an Eisenhower Administration initiative to distribute U.S. agricultural surpluses to underdeveloped nations. I supported the program (which had been revised by JFK to stress nutrition and to target specific foreign needs) after amending it to send U.S. farmers overseas as agricultural technicians and advisers. Though hunger was nonideological, it was often exploited for ideological purposes, especially by antidemocratic forces who would trade personal freedoms for a bowl of rice. Here was a chance for the United States to exert moral leadership rather than military might, to share her expertise as well as her surpluses.

• • •

I met up with Huck Boyd in the spring of 1960. Driving through Russell around ten o'clock one night, Boyd noticed lights on at the courthouse. They aroused his journalistic curiosity. He found me inside the county attorney's office poring over card files, spadework for that year's race to succeed Wint Smith in Congress.

My late hours impressed Huck more than my sense of humor. Early in my House career he informed me, "We don't need a Jack Benny in Washington."

I wasn't laughing in the spring of 1962, when I asked Huck to take the organizational reins of what was going to be a tough reelection campaign. I hired a campaign manager; I got a mentor. Huck Boyd's political experience dated to the summer of 1936, when he had sat spellbound at the feet of Alf Landon's presidential-campaign strategists. For twenty years, with the help of his wife, Marie, Huck represented Kansas on the Republican National Committee. Although his was a familiar face around Republican White Houses and on Capitol Hill, the publisher of the *Phillips County Review* never felt as happy on Pennsylvania Avenue as he did on the main street of Phillipsburg, Kansas.

From the start, Huck and I knew we had our work cut out for us. With fifty-eight counties sprawling over nearly half the state, Kansas' new First District—known locally as the Big First—was geographically the largest in America. My opponent was Democrat J. Floyd Breeding, a farmer who had stepped down from his tractor in 1958 to run for Congress in what had been a Democratic year. Breeding was better known than I and had been in Congress longer. And he already represented a majority of the new district's population.

To overcome these obstacles, I set out on a campaign to convince normally conservative voters of the basic differences between Breeding and myself. He was a strong supporter of John F. Kennedy's New Frontier. While I admired Kennedy personally, I disagreed with much of his program. Breeding believed in more federal control of agriculture. I preferred a voluntary approach which would let market forces operate to the greatest extent possible.

Like any contest, this one had its unexpected twists. *Time* magazine caused bipartisan laughter by running a picture of some of my opponent's campaign workers outside a storefront. Over their heads was a sign that read: "BREEDING HEADQUARTERS." Breeding himself was less amused when I dramatized the differences in our congressional attendance by sending him tongue-in-cheek reminders of all the votes he was missing— messages like "Dear Floyd: While you were in Ness City today, dedicating a new post office, I was in Washington, voting to help the wheat growers."

I was just as aggressive in challenging the *Hutchinson Daily News,* which, under the fire-breathing editorship of John McCormally, was openly pro-Breeding. When McCormally's preference spilled over from his editorial page to the paper's news columns, I began calling his paper "the prairie *Pravda."* It was the start of a long-running feud, since ended.

In November 1962 I defeated Breeding by 21,000 votes. Two years later I faced an even stiffer test. As one of forty-three House members who were charter supporters of Arizona Senator Barry Goldwater for the 1964 Republican presidential nomination, I spent most of that summer and fall defending our nominee against charges that he was a pistol-packing, bomb-dropping relic of the Old West. As Ronald Reagan's success would demonstrate, Goldwater was actually a man ahead of his time. Few politicians outlive their enemies, but Barry has had the much greater satisfaction of seeing his ideas vindicated.

For me, the fall of 1964 was notable in another respect. Richard Nixon swooped into Pratt, Kansas, that October on a political rescue mission in my behalf. He stood on some hay bales and delivered one of the best speeches I've ever heard. Without a note. It was the first time I witnessed up close Nixon's mastery of issues. Neither then nor later did he ever find it necessary to halt in midsentence and look over his shoulder to have an "expert" brief him on his position.

From Pratt, the former Vice President flew east to attend funeral services for Herbert Hoover. I rode with him partway. Politics dominated our conversation, as it would every time Nixon and I talked. He wanted to know how old I was, and the age of Kansas' senior Senator, Frank Carlson. What about the rest of the state's congressional delegation? Who excelled on the campaign trail? Who was most comfortable in a committee room? Before I had given it much thought, Nixon was sizing me up as a possible successor to Carlson in 1968.

I survived another close call that fall, despite the best—or worst—efforts of the *Hutchinson Daily News.* Back in Washington, the 1964 election had decimated Republican ranks on Capitol Hill. In Congress, as everywhere else, the party seemed dead in the water, a victim of internal divisions and intellectual malnutrition.

So when Jerry Ford, the forty-nine-year-old chairman of the House Republican Conference, announced he would challenge Minority Leader Charles A. Halleck, I quickly added my name to the Young Turks who were supporting him. We were part of a restless minority, tired of simply reacting to Democratic legislative proposals and eager for more aggressive leadership.

I watched Ford during my early years on the Hill and was impressed by his intelligence, industry and capacity for growth. Before the GOP caucus met on January 4, 1965, I had a talk with other members of the Kansas delegation, three of whom followed me into the Ford camp. We gave the new Minority Leader his margin of victory.

Ford more than lived up to my expectations. He never abandoned his essential conservatism, but he wanted to restrain government, not dismantle it. As anxious as LBJ to attack poverty in America, Ford was convinced that government alone would fail in the effort, and that only the private sector could create jobs with a future. Ford's commitment to civil rights reflected a Midwestern concern for fair play and the politics of inclusion.

In the 1964 Civil Rights Act, Congress struck down racial barriers in the workplace and public accommodations. With the 1965 Voting Rights Act, it moved to enfranchise millions of blacks. I supported both measures. I did so for sound conservative reasons. If American conservatism stands for anything, it is the protection of individuals in all their rights, the right to vote being the most basic in any democracy.

President Eisenhower once said that if the only thing the American people wanted was security, they could find plenty of that in jail. Conservatives believe in the economic and social benefits that come with competition. Life is a contest, with rewards in proportion to the risks taken. But to be valid, the contest must be open to all equally, and the same set of rules must be applied to everyone.

Conservatives abhor waste, whether it's measured in dollars or in human lives. But until 1964 the plain truth was that millions of Americans were prevented from developing God-given talents because of restrictions imposed by manmade laws. In denying our heritage, we were endangering our posterity.

Two years later, President Johnson requested that I visit India to see firsthand that country's chronic food shortage. Johnson was under heavy pressure to increase U.S. grain shipments to the subcontinent. He responded with a shrewd reading of domestic politics combined with a long-range vision for which he was rarely credited.

When he was a young man fresh out of college, Johnson's first job had been teaching students in what residents of sun-baked Cotulla, Texas, called "the Mexican school." At his best, LBJ retained the educator's passion for knowledge, along with his capacity for changing minds. Before long, he had taught himself everything there was to know about rain patterns in the Ganges Valley and the amount of wheat leaving Wichita granaries for Bombay. Armed with such details, he tried to enlist other countries' help in preventing mass starvation in India. At the same time Johnson hoped to prod the Indians themselves toward future self-reliance. Finally, he saw a chance to blunt congressional opposition to foreign aid by sending Farm Belt congressmen to witness India's agony for themselves.

In India, we went from official dinners in our honor to Calcutta slums teeming with homeless people, beggars and flies. Hunger stalked every city street. Outside the urban areas, barren fields showed the severity of a drought brought on by unusually light monsoon rains. I visited rural-electrification projects, met with Prime Minister Indira Gandhi, and slept under mosquito netting in a government guest house while lizards crawled over the ceiling.

When we returned, the delegation advised President Johnson to send 1.8 million bushels of grain immediately to the desperate country. Congress readily went along with the President's request. Ultimately, American farmers shipped one fifth of their 1967 harvest to Indian ports. For me the experience was a learning one. No doubt that's exactly what the old teacher from Cotulla, Texas, had in mind.

Frank Carlson was an authentic Kansas institution. The son of Swedish immigrants who settled in Cloud County in the 1880s, he was also that rarest breed of political animal, one who by refusing to court power and popularity assures himself of both.

Carlson began his career in public service in 1928, when he was approached in a Concordia wheat field by four local businessmen who were looking for a state legislative candidate. Carlson turned them down. He would be too busy shucking corn for cattle feed to spend the first three months of the year in Topeka.

"Don't worry," one of the men told him. "You won't win anyway."

Carlson's supporters wore buttons that fall with the slogan "I'd Rather Be Farming." Voters disagreed. In November 1928 they launched Carlson on a trajectory that would take him from the Topeka legislature to the governor's office and both houses of Congress. As governor in the late 1940s, Carlson was a road-builder and a ground-breaker. He instituted workmen's compensation and hatched initiatives in education and medicine. In 1950 Kansas sent him to the Senate, where he served on a committee investigating the anti-Communist activities of Joseph R. McCarthy and later voted to censure the Senator from Wisconsin. Carlson also played a leading role in drafting his fellow Kansan Dwight Eisenhower in 1952.

Soon after taking office, Ike expressed a familiar presidential lament. "Frank," he said, "this is the loneliest house I've ever been in. What can I do?"

Carlson responded by inviting Eisenhower to meet with a small senatorial prayer group. In 1953 Eisenhower attended the National Prayer Breakfast which Carlson had helped initiate. And Presidents have been doing so ever since.

In the first week of January 1968, the man who forty years

earlier declared his preference for farming bowed out gracefully from the Senate. Carlson had told me his decision in advance, and within twenty-four hours I jumped into the race to succeed him. For the next eleven months, I stumped Kansas in a '68 Oldsmobile driven by Bill Frazier, one of the best friends I ever had. We first met when Bill was a student in a Sunday school class I taught in Russell. He came from a family that loved politics, and in time he became what you might call my Bebe Rebozo—a delightful companion whom I could trust completely and who desired nothing for himself except mutual friendship. His death in 1982 at the age of forty-one was a heavy blow.

Running for a statewide office gave me a chance to discuss more than agriculture. I talked about law enforcement and drug prevention and an early proposal to repackage federal education money in the form of block grants that would be used as state and local officials saw fit.

Traveling across the state, I saw just how far the Republican Party had come in attracting fresh blood since we burst onto the scene at Kansas Day, 1960. There were plenty of volunteers to spread the word. The press was friendly. Kansas' largest paper, the *Wichita Eagle,* noted my "growing concern about the problems of the underprivileged at home and the underfed abroad." More surprising were some carefully measured words of praise from my old nemesis the *Hutchinson Daily News.*

In the August primary, I defeated my good friend former Governor William H. Avery. By carrying all but two of the state's 105 counties, I put to rest lingering doubts about whether I could expand my agricultural base into urban areas and the Kansas City suburbs.

That fall Republican candidates everywhere were bolstered by disenchantment over Vietnam and the Johnson Administration. My Democratic opponent for Carlson's Senate seat was William Robinson, a highly regarded Wichita lawyer. On election day, just over 60 percent of Kansas' voters put a check beside my name.

Two months later, I sat down and wrote a very special message.

Dear Robin:

Today is a most important day in my life, and I trust in yours. The days and months ahead will be hectic, exciting ones, but my one hope is that I can share more time with you and your mother. In future years, as you look back, you might recall that my first letter after taking the oath as a United States Senator on January 3, 1969, was written to you.

In the rush of today's activities, just remember that I always appreciate, more than you know or I can express, your patience, understanding, and devotion.

Love,
Dad

Politics has many rewards. But it can also make demands, on no one more than your loved ones.

In the spring of 1969, for the first time in eight years, there was a Republican President in the White House. Implicit in Richard Nixon's election was a popular rebuff to liberal dogmas that had been unchallenged since the early days of the New Deal. Americans were emotionally spent by Vietnam and the cultural strains of the 1960s, and they wanted a period of healing. The President-elect took note of this in his inaugural address.

"We have endured a long night of the American spirit," said Nixon, "but let us not curse the remaining dark. Let us gather the light."

Along with the new President's chance to "bring us together," his party was given a golden opportunity to pursue lasting political realignment through policies of conservative innovation. Whatever the history books may say about the Nixon years, they shouldn't forget such domestic advances as revenue sharing, pension reform, clean air and water legislation, energy conservation, the first steps toward meaningful welfare reform—and the last balanced budget of the twentieth century.

While voters may have seen Nixon's election as a mandate for change, their message was all but lost in the partisan fog of Capitol Hill. Nixon was the first newly elected President to confront hostile majorities in both houses of Congress since

Zachary Taylor in 1848. Democrats controlled the Senate 57 to 43. Their dominance was psychological as well as numerical. Only a handful of Republican senators could recall being in the majority, and few were Nixon loyalists. Their allegiance was to the Senate itself.

One of Washington's wisest observers likes to describe a particular senatorial pretension he calls the "I Have Been Chosen" Syndrome. Chance and not choice, he argues, is the biggest factor in getting to the Senate. An incumbent decides not to run again, or falls victim to a presidential landslide for the opposition party, or becomes tainted by questions about his finances or the company he keeps. If you are the beneficiary of his demise, you suddenly find yourself in a chamber whose illustrious ghosts include the likes of Webster, Clay and Calhoun. You grow to like the historical company. Reelection confirms your sense of personal destiny. You have been chosen, so the theory goes, and it's only a matter of time before you decide you should return the favor by offering your services to the voters in a much higher capacity, such as the presidency.

The early years of the Nixon Administration confirmed the theory. Democrats who regarded Nixon's election as a fluke turned the Senate into a launch pad for their own 1972 aspirations. It got to the point where I urged the presiding officer to set aside sixty minutes each day for the Senate Presidential Hour, during which senators who thought they were President, senators who thought they should have been President, senators who thought they wanted to be President and senators who were willing to settle for being Vice President could express themselves.

It was customary in those days to regard first-termers as children to be seen and not heard. Three and a half months passed before I made my first floor speech, an appeal for experimental housing for the handicapped. Over time, I became closely identified with the disabled and their legislative agenda. I also supported a constitutional amendment giving eighteen-year-olds the vote, proposed legislation to help economically depressed rural America and opposed court-ordered busing and abortion.

The unexpected death that September of Senate Minority

Leader Everett M. Dirksen deprived the Nixon Administration of a forceful and vastly experienced Capitol Hill advocate. There was much more to Ev Dirksen than the tousle-haired Wizard of Ooze depicted by cartoonists. He was a partisan who loved the Republican Party second only to his country, and whose loyalty to both country and party never came into conflict.

Similar qualities distinguished Howard Baker of Tennessee, who as Dirksen's son-in-law inherited both the old man's well-traveled De Soto and a gift for reconciling legislative differences. Howard came to the Senate two years before I did, as part of a large, unusually prominent freshman class that included Edward W. Brooke of Massachusetts, Michigan's Bob Griffin, and Mark O. Hatfield of Oregon. The fact that most of them were to my left philosophically didn't prevent us from working together for the day when Republicans would control the levers of congressional power as well as the White House.

So it was only logical that when Howard threw his hat into the ring for the Minority Leader's position, I supported him enthusiastically. Baker was narrowly defeated by Hugh Scott, a sixty-nine-year-old former congressman from Philadelphia's suburbs whose owlish appearance and ever present pipe complemented his scholarly interest in Chinese porcelains. Politically, Scott was a Rockefeller man, a fact sure to increase friction with White House staffers who were openly contemptuous of Congress and its untidy methods of operation.

Personally, I thought the Pennsylvanian was far more conservative than Nixon detractors like Clifford P. Case of New Jersey or New York's Charles E. Goodell. It's just that Scott liked the Senate well enough to want to stay in it. A reading of home-state politics may have influenced his opposition to Nixon's choice of South Carolina appeals judge Clement Haynesworth to fill the Supreme Court vacancy left by the resignation of Abe Fortas. On November 21, 1969, after a long campaign by labor and civil-rights groups to discredit Haynesworth's record, Scott and sixteen other Senate Republicans voted with the majority to reject the nomination. Even more humiliating for the White House was the subsequent defeat of Fifth District appeals judge G. Harrold Carswell, a Floridian named to replace the ill-fated Haynesworth.

I voted for both men. In retrospect, I was right on Haynesworth, wrong on Carswell. As I saw it, Haynesworth had been unfairly victimized by headlines over minor stock holdings and alleged conflicts of interest. (Carswell was another story, a man who probably would never have been nominated except in the heat of presidential anger at senators who had denied Nixon his Southerner on the Court.) "You've got guts," South Carolina's Ernest F. "Fritz" Hollings remarked to me at the height of the controversy. It was his way of thanking me for standing by an earlier commitment to support the judge from Greenville. Fritz and I have been friends ever since.

On the heels of the Carswell fiasco, Nixon faced more dissension from Senate Republicans over an antiballistic-missile system and production of a U.S. supersonic plane to compete with Europe's Concorde. His Administration struggled to unite GOP lawmakers behind Vietnamization, Nixon's attempt to extricate America from the Southeast Asian tar pit by turning battlefield responsibilities over to the South Vietnamese.

Politics, like nature, abhors a vacuum. Since freshmen had relatively little influence on committees, I began spending a lot of time on the floor reminding colleagues just who had won the 1968 election. I didn't have much company. Sometimes there were so few Republicans in the chamber that the Democrats could have stolen the furniture and no one would have complained. Barry Goldwater, at least, seemed appreciative. Barry was no more than his usual frank self when he described me as "the first fellow we've had around here in a long time who can grab 'em by the hair and haul 'em down the aisle."

There's nothing wrong with partisanship as long as it's constructive and doesn't descend to the level of personalities. Adlai E. Stevenson, a Democrat noted for his bipartisan appeal, went so far as to label it "the lifeblood of democracy." By cloaking his loyalties in elegant phrases and self-mocking wit, Stevenson earned plaudits for civility. Take a less polished—or less orthodox—approach, you're liable to be called a gunslinger.

In truth, as the Haynesworth nomination showed, there

was a lot of political hardball played in the Senate back then. Most of it originated on the Democratic side of the aisle, as senators who had dutifully backed Lyndon Johnson's conduct of the Vietnam War turned on Nixon with all the fervor of converts. But Nixon had been elected to bring the conflict to the earliest honorable conclusion. "Honorable" was the key word. I couldn't see any honor in congressionally imposed deadlines for troop withdrawal or funding cutoffs for field operations.

In the first months of 1970, U.S. ground forces in Vietnam were reduced from 543,000 to 340,000. Nixon assured the country that another 60,000 boys would be coming home by May 1. But at the Paris peace talks, the North Vietnamese negotiators dug in their heels, confident that American war-weariness would give them what twenty years of combat had not.

On April 30, the President went on television to announce a military thrust into the Parrot's Beak area of neighboring Cambodia, thought to be a nerve center of Vietcong activities for the entire region. The action ignited a firestorm of protest on America's campuses and in the halls of Congress. Nixon said he intended to withdraw the invading force from Cambodian territory by June 30, and I plunged into a fight to stop Senate doves from pulling the plug before that date.

For seven weeks, the Senate was tied up in knots. By the time they were unsnarled, Nixon's self-imposed deadline was at hand. And I had stolen a march on one of the war's most outspoken critics, Foreign Relations Committee Chairman J. William Fulbright. My call for repeal of the 1964 Tonkin Gulf Resolution, the measure repeatedly cited by Lyndon Johnson in justifying his undeclared war in Southeast Asia, both astonished and angered Fulbright. He had wanted to present such a motion himself. What I had done, claimed Fulbright, was like stealing another man's cow. I didn't want to steal his cow, I replied. All I wanted to do was milk it a little.

The 1970 midterm elections fell far short of what political analyst Kevin Phillips called "the emerging Republican majority." The two seats gained in the Senate were more than offset by losses in the House and among state governorships. Strident rhetoric from Nixon, Vice President Spiro T. Agnew and others about law and order and student unrest failed to galvanize voters who were chiefly worried about the war, inflation and 6 percent unemployment.

Almost immediately, steps were taken to prevent a repeat performance in the presidential year of 1972. Agnew was effectively muzzled. President Nixon, whose standing in the polls suffered from a campaign that had him, in Attorney General John Mitchell's phrase, running for sheriff, was distanced from day-to-day political management. At the same time, Rogers C. B. Morton left his job as Republican National Committee chairman to become Nixon's Secretary of the Interior.

Washington was rife that fall with rumors of prospective replacements for Morton as chairman. Most of those mentioned were reluctant to take a job that had lost much of the prestige it had enjoyed in the days of strong party structures independent of the White House. Modern Presidents were less willing than their predecessors to entrust their political fortunes to a James A. Farley or a Leonard W. Hall. As a result, party chairmen have become media point men instead of back-room strategists.

I understood this, and was willing to accept the limitations that the job entailed in exchange for the opportunity to reach some groups previously neglected by the GOP. I was especially eager to expand Republican appeal among farmers, young people, veterans and minorities, and to take our case into neighborhoods where traditional liberalism had failed.

John Mitchell told me in the first days of January 1971 that the job was mine. Or it would be, following the National Committee's regular midwinter meeting a few days later in Washington, Mitchell said. No sooner had I passed along the good news about the offer to friends in Kansas and on Capitol Hill than it was withdrawn.

White House chief of staff H. R. Haldeman once said, "Every President needs an S.O.B. and I'm Nixon's." The night before the National Committee was to ratify my selection, Haldeman lived up to his own billing. He called me from the Western White House in San Clemente, California, to tell me that Nixon had changed his mind. He was sorry, said Haldeman, if the President's abrupt volte-face caused me any trouble back home. He said Nixon had concluded after thinking it over that the business of the Senate was too pressing for me to serve as a full-time chairman.

Haldeman didn't say so at the time, but later the same night I found out whom the palace guard preferred. Thomas B. Evans was a favorite of the party's money men. A Delaware native, he had distinguished himself as a Southern coordinator in Nixon's 1968 campaign. Tom was an impressive guy, and in time we became good friends. But just then I had no intention of quietly folding my tent. Bond lawyer or no bond lawyer, John Mitchell was enough of a politician to know that in this business your word is your bond. And I had Mitchell's word on the chairmanship.

There had to be some reason why, in just twenty-four hours, both Nixon and Mitchell had changed their minds. There was: they had been warned of the consequences of having a national chairman who might be too independent or irreverent for the White House's tastes. It wasn't hard to trace such reports to the Senate Minority Leader's office, and to Ohio's maverick Senator William Saxbe in particular. Bill Saxbe hadn't forgotten my earlier support of Howard Baker over Scott, as he demonstrated by telling reporters that as the so-called "Sheriff of the Senate" I'd have trouble selling beer on a troopship.

Hugh Scott, with his own sense of institutional protocol, could hardly have relished the thought of a Senate newcomer like myself being out front as a party spokesman. (Ironically, as a young congressman Scott himself had once held the chairmanship. In 1948 presidential nominee Thomas E. Dewey had relegated the Pennsylvanian to a sidelines role. Maybe Scott wanted to spare me a similar fate; in any event, we drew much closer in later years, swapping stories of all the hot coals tossed in the direction of any national chairman.)

The next few hours were a whirlwind of intense negotiation between Capitol Hill, the RNC and San Clemente. Around midnight, Rog Morton telephoned Bryce Harlow at home. Harlow headed the White House congressional-relations staff during Nixon's first two years in office. Until his death, in February 1987, he was one of Washington's most esteemed Wise Men.

("If judgment were oil" was the way columnist Mark Shields put it, "then all by himself, Bryce Harlow would be OPEC.")

Harlow's talent for damage control made him indispensable. Of course, had people listened to his advice in the first place, they probably wouldn't have had to call on him later to pull their chestnuts out of the fire. This was one scrimmage Bryce would just as soon stay out of. It was late at night, he had put a log on the fire, and the streets outside were glazed with the residue of a violent ice storm.

"You're out of your mind," he told Morton. "I couldn't get there from here if I wanted to. Which I don't."

Refusing to be put off, Morton sent a car to pick up Harlow and bring him to party headquarters at 310 First Street. Harlow arrived to find the mood grim. For months I had carried water by the bucket for the Administration. Yet it wasn't enough to get Haldeman or others in the West Wing Mafia to return my phone calls.

I remember saying to Harlow in the heat of the moment, "If this is the way you're treated as a loyal Republican senator, after all I've done for the President, all the battles I've fought on the floor, all the heat I've taken in the press—well, I'm not so sure I want to be a senator."

Harlow told me to dismiss any such thought. He didn't begrudge me my anger, however. Even with Bryce's ingrained loyalty to the party and the President, he could hardly contain his resentment of a White House staff that wanted only a chairman subservient to them.

The lights on First Street burned late that night. By three in the morning, when Harlow finally escaped RNC headquarters, he had negotiated the outlines of an acceptable deal. I would become chairman, in fact was well as title. Tom Evans would become my deputy, in charge of administrative and financial oversight. (Subsequently I named Anne Armstrong of Texas as deputy chairman, the first time the title had been bestowed on a woman.)

A final hurdle remained. It took Huck Boyd's intervention as chairman of the official nominating committee to prevent a rules change that would have led to separate elections for myself and Evans. As Huck explained it later, the White House wanted this unprecedented step to show publicly that the new chairman's power was to be shared. Thanks to Huck, Nixon's men couldn't get anyone on the nominating committee to approve the scheme.

And I wasn't about to budge from my position.

"I'll be pleased to appoint Evans," I told Rog, "but there can be only one chairman."

On the morning of the vote, I was roused from a short night's sleep by another call, this time from Nixon himself. Whatever his true feelings, on the phone the President managed a more or less convincing note of satisfaction.

Our contacts thereafter were sporadic. Signals got mixed, as when I insisted in a San Diego press conference in August 1971 that the Nixon Administration would never accept wage and price controls. When I got back to my hotel room, White House staffers called to tell me that the President was about to make a speech that would knock my economic predictions into a cocked hat.

Occasionally, I was invited to sit in on a Cabinet meeting and give a short briefing on my political travels. Nixon didn't need anyone to give him a report. He knew more about politics than anyone in Washington. He also knew what he wanted. Though generally removed from RNC operations, Nixon took a hands-on approach when he personally ruled out a strong Republican challenge to Alabama Senator James B. Allen. Besides personal affection for Allen, Nixon felt gratitude for his pro-Administration voting record. Having concluded that an ideological majority was better than no majority, Nixon could easily be forgiven for wishing that his own party's leaders would support his programs as much as an unreconstructed Democrat from Dixie. In the meantime, he made clear to me that Allen was to have a free ride.

There's never a perfect package. In office, Richard Nixon combined visionary statecraft with a surprising grasp of detail. But he was a man haunted by the past, unable to escape the shadow of defeat at the hands of John F. Kennedy. Kennedy hovered over the Nixon entourage like Banquo's ghost. It was as if, ten years after the fact, Nixon couldn't forget the cavalier, even cruel judgment supposedly pronounced on him by JFK during their 1960 campaign: "No class."

I wish he could have. As far as I was concerned, Nixon had every reason to be proud of his origins and the determination that enabled him to overcome the hardships of his youth and a lack of social connections to reach the highest office in the land. Quite simply, he had worked harder than anyone else, studied longer, become more knowledgeable. He had taught himself the minutiae of precinct organization and the intricacies of super-power relations. In many ways Nixon's was a classic American success story. Out of his own will to succeed, he could identify with millions of people—the so-called Silent Majority—whose values were his values, but who for years had been taken for granted or laughed at by the sophisticates of Georgetown.

As part of our party-building activities at the RNC, we tried to capitalize on Nixon's appeal among voter groups not often receptive to Republicans, particularly ethnics and blue-collar workers. The door to the chairman's office was literally removed from its hinges. In a similar spirit of openness, we organized the Black Council and began other programs to reach Hispanics and voters of Eastern European descent. Under Secretary of Labor Arthur Fletcher, an old Kansas friend and the ranking black in Nixon's Administration, addressed an RNC meeting in Denver in May 1971. His success there spurred more invitations, including a major speech to a gathering of Southern Republicans in Memphis.

Working through communications director Lyn Nofziger and others, we introduced state-of-the-art television and radio facilities. We conducted a series of field schools to help recruit strong candidates and train campaign managers. Tom Evans did a superb job of broadening our financial base, until it included thousands of small contributors giving ten, twenty-five or fifty dollars. The RNC itself channeled more money to more local candidates than ever before. And it was a rare night when I wasn't attending some party function which might be hundreds of miles from Washington.

All of this took a personal toll. For some time before we divorced in 1972, Phyllis and I had been drifting apart. I was caught up in one life, whose demands were escalating, she in another. While Robin was still young she helped keep us together, but it wasn't a happy time for either of us. I had been raised to believe that anyone who couldn't make his marriage work was a failure. It was a lesson my mother, among others, didn't hesitate to remind me of.

Before going ahead with the divorce, I went to see Nixon in the White House and offered to quit the chairmanship if it would spare him and the party any embarrassment. He turned the offer aside, later sending me a copy of Lord Blake's biography of Benjamin Disraeli to underline his message that public and private lives are to be judged separately.

Mine was not the first or, sadly, the last marriage to founder on the political rocks. Fortunately, Phyllis and I remained friends—if not always political soulmates. When President Ford asked me to be his running mate in 1976, Phyllis, by then remarried to a Kansas banker and rancher, expressed her relief at having escaped the intense media scrutiny and round-the-clock campaign duties inflicted on modern political wives. A strong Reagan backer, she reacted to the news of my selection with typical candor. As she put it, Ford had chosen the second-best conservative for the job.

The 1972 campaign was notable for the tensions it spawned between the Republican National Committee and the Committee to Re-Elect the President (CREEP). Privately I told John Mitchell and others at CREEP how unhappy I was over their failure to develop a strategy for translating Nixon's personal popularity into support for other GOP candidates. Their caution reached absurd proportions when campaign officials refused to allow a public presentation of a sweater with an elephant on it to Mrs. Nixon.

"We have to appeal to donkeys," one CREEP official informed me.

"I'll give her a donkey sweater next week," I said.

Sorry. Elephants were out of fashion.

CREEP's indifference was matched by an almost excessive interference in our work by some of Nixon's own staff. One

White House office sent us cartoons for *First Monday,* the RNC's monthly periodical. One showed Democratic hopeful George McGovern in a Vietcong uniform. A second, to be mailed out on plain stationery, suggested that former Vice President Hubert H. Humphrey, another Democratic contender, had a drinking problem. After Alabama Governor George Wallace was gunned down by a would-be assassin in May 1972, the same office dispatched a list of pre- and post-shooting comments by Senator Edward M. Kennedy and other leading Democrats. Underneath was the caption "What a Difference a Bullet Makes."

Tom Evans, who later described these "bombshells" to me, made sure none of them saw the light of day. In the meantime, I had my own run-in with the human bottleneck surrounding the President. Nixon wanted the 1972 Republican convention to be held in San Diego. The selection of San Diego, a short helicopter ride from his San Clemente residence, would not only be a convenience to him but would also acknowledge California's growing clout in presidential politics. RNC legal counsel Fred Scribner discovered that among the convention's financial guarantors in San Diego was a host hotel owned by ITT, the conglomerate that had an antitrust dispute pending before the Justice Department. Scribner said he was concerned about the possible appearance of conflict of interest. When San Diego failed to come up with a replacement guarantor, the convention was shifted to Miami Beach. Such independence didn't go over well with the West Wing crowd. They had long memories.

On June 17, 1972, five middle-aged men looking for documents were arrested in the Watergate offices of the Democratic National Committee. Their captain was E. Howard Hunt, sometime spy novelist and CIA operative. Hunt's links to the White House were soon revealed. Prior to that, my own reaction had been to dismiss Hunt and his band of Cuban emigrés as the Gang That Couldn't Shoot Straight. Besides, the break-in at the DNC occurred on my night off.

More seriously, it made no sense to spy on an opposition that was headed over the cliff. At the time of the break-in,

Nixon was far ahead of George McGovern, his probable Democratic rival, in the polls. McGovern was badly out of step with popular attitudes on practically every important issue. The antiwar movement that had made him its champion seemed openly contemptuous of millions of regular Democrats for whom a distant war was less threatening than a perceived assault on traditional values of work, faith and family. With all this going for us, why engage in acts of criminal stupidity to run up the score?

At a White House meeting a few days after the break-in, I raised the subject and, along with it, the eyebrows of everyone present.

"Out on the road I'm getting some questions about Watergate," I remarked. "Do you think we should clear the air, just to put people's minds at ease?"

Bryce Harlow predicted the story would have a short life, because, as he put it, it had "no legs." Nixon brushed the subject aside without comment.

That was the only time before the election I heard the word "Watergate" used around the Oval Office. Not that I was there that often. At public events I'd go up to the President and suggest that as national chairman I wanted to see him. Nixon would be perfectly agreeable, but it was often impossible to penetrate the little circle that was rapidly becoming a noose around the President's neck.

When I was asked embarrassing questions about this arm's-length treatment, I described an imaginary call to Haldeman:

"Bob, I'm the national chairman and I need to see the President."

"You want to see the President? Fine. Tune in Channel Nine tomorrow night at ten o'clock."

Less easily laughed off was the growing alienation of National Committee members and party activists who were also excluded from campaign involvement. Money is one measure of political status. The RNC's budget for 1972 was $4 million. CREEP, by spending ten times as much, showed what can happen when money floods the normal channels of political communication. No matter what Mae West said, too much of a good thing is *not* wonderful. An organization that can afford computer banks, tracking polls and other devices of modern, high-tech campaigning is often tempted to put its faith in flow charts and focus groups and overlook human emotions and intellectual substance. Telephone banks don't drive people to the polls; their convictions do. Anyone who forgets that fact is in danger of undermining the political process, whether or not he violates formal campaign law.

Nixon campaigned as if he were above the fray that fall, emphasizing his peacemaking journeys to Beijing and Moscow and leaving a small army of surrogates in charge of answering opposition charges. For most of the campaign, I played the loyal soldier, assailing McGovern's platform for its isolationist strain and calling the Democratic candidate "a left-leaning big spender." One day I was handed a speech draft declaring that the *Washington Post*'s Watergate coverage—admittedly intense and often partisan—was based on the alleged personal hatred publisher Katharine Graham felt for Nixon.

"I'm not saying this stuff," I responded. "I don't care where it comes from. Unless you can confirm the source, I won't make any charge."

That November Nixon won by the expected landslide. What should have been a joyous election night party at the Shoreham Hotel was instead a bittersweet moment. In his victory speech, Nixon neglected to mention any of the regular Republican organizations that had contributed to the sweep. Within days, rumors of an imminent shakeup at the National Committee began circulating.

With a reelection fight of my own coming up in 1974, I had already decided to leave the chairman's job and the arduous travel schedule that went with it. The White House staff reached the same decision, only they had a different timetable.

Two weeks after the election, I joined Attorney General Richard G. Kleindienst for a helicopter ride to the presidential retreat at Camp David in the Maryland mountains outside Washington. If he's going up for the hanging, I thought, they're probably going to hang me too.

"Did you bring enough rope for us both?" I asked Kleindienst.

When the time came, I was ushered into Aspen Lodge for

an awkward conversation. Nixon began by telling me I'd done a hell of a job. "I'm proud of you, Bob." He autographed a map charting the hundreds of thousands of miles I had traveled as national chairman, and presented it to me with a Camp David jacket.

Then came the hangman's noose.

"I know after all this you probably want to move on to something else," Nixon said.

"Well, I sure don't want to be chairman till '74," I told him. "But I would like to leave later on. You know, stick around for a little while and have some fun with the job."

Haldeman entered the room, and I felt like the condemned man facing his executioner. Talk turned to 1974. Nixon wanted to help me get reelected. Fresh hints were dropped. Finally, I was asked for names of a potential successor. On my way out, Nixon suggested that I drop in at a nearby cabin and greet his friend Bebe Rebozo.

It took a few more days for me to realize that though I hadn't been the victim of a hanging, I had been pushed off the mountain. At John Mitchell's urging, I went to New York early in December to sound out United Nations Ambassador George Bush about the chairmanship. I'd heard that Bush wanted to be number one somewhere, a desire that couldn't be accommodated at the Pentagon or anywhere else in the Nixon Cabinet. The only alternative was the National Committee.

So I was out, Bush was in, and Nixon was presumably mollified.

The more I thought about it, the more prearranged the whole thing seemed. I had nothing against Bush. What angered me was the callousness of a White House staff that demanded loyalty but failed to return it. Regarding their handling of the whole transition as shabby, I resolved to go quietly—but on my own terms.

Again I turned to Bryce Harlow. My trusted friend and broker drew up a parting agreement under which the President pledged to campaign for my 1974 reelection and assist in raising campaign funds. Like so much else in the unhappy days that followed, time rendered the document and the promises it contained inoperative.

Traditionally, a victorious party chairman occupies a prominent spot in the festivities surrounding a presidential inauguration. In the old days, he used to have a place in the inaugural parade right behind the winning candidate. Not so on January 20, 1973. That day, Robin and I rode down Pennsylvania Avenue in just about the last car in the parade. George McGovern was probably ahead of me. It was a final, intentional snub from CREEP's Jeb Magruder and his boys.

By the spring of 1974, the sands were running out on Richard Nixon's presidency. Impeachment talk was rife on Capitol Hill. Public revulsion over abuses of power lumped together under the umbrella of Watergate threatened disaster for Republicans in the upcoming midterm elections.

Kansas Democrats had not elected one of their own to the United States Senate since the Depression year of 1932. William R. Roy hoped to break the jinx. A forty-six-year-old doctor from Topeka, Bill Roy had every reason to feel optimistic. He had knocked off three-term House member Chester Mize in 1970, turning himself overnight into a force to reckon with in Kansas politics. Roy enhanced his standing two years later when he withstood the Nixon landslide and won a second term with 61 percent of the vote.

By concentrating his energies on broadly popular issues like public health and the environment, Roy impressed many voters as a thoughtful, nondoctrinaire liberal. The politics of antipolitics was his stock in trade. It was a popular stance to take, especially amidst the continuing fallout from Watergate.

My own problem that year went beyond the Nixon scandals and the guilt-by-association tactics used by the opposition. Even without Watergate, the headlines were doing nothing to bolster Republican prospects. The first Arab oil embargo was sending shock waves through the American economy, and agriculture was being particularly hard hit. Inflation was a topic of popular conversation, along with gasoline allotments and rising unemployment. A mood of national frustration bordering on helplessness, the first forerunner of what Jimmy Carter would later call malaise, was eroding public confidence and traditional voter allegiances.

All this would have a much greater effect on elected officials than we knew at the time. Both the Senate and politics generally were rapidly changing. What had once been a genuinely deliberative body, almost an American House of Lords, was being dragged kicking and screaming into the modern era. Doors were coming off committee rooms and private offices. Television increased the visibility of senators and, with it, the demands for direct contact with the voters. Gone was the day when a Frank Carlson could survive politically by going back home only a couple of times each year. In its place was a more representative democracy, the exact opposite of the secretive mentality that had given rise to Watergate.

Campaigning had also become more expensive. Most candidates will tell you that the only thing they dislike more than spending campaign funds is raising them. But this was also part of the new politics. By the middle of January 1974, I was forced to raise a $250,000 war chest. By November I'd have to spend more than all my previous campaigns combined had cost.

Nineteen seventy-four was the first Dole campaign in which we had a paid, professional campaign manager and staff as well as consultants, pollsters and ad men. The overhead was substantial. Worse, volunteer workers were being turned off by the out-of-state professionals who, for all their technical and organizational skill, couldn't match the Kansans' knowledge of or sensitivity to the local electorate.

The campaign went into a tailspin. Polls taken in August showed me trailing Roy by thirteen points. We were $100,000 in debt, and new bills were coming in daily. Roy's broadcast offensive was exactly that—offensive. "Dr. Bill Roy, a *respected* voice for Kansas," it intoned in coded allusion to Watergate. Roy said that, as national party chairman, I either had known about the break-in before it happened or should have. He stuck to this line even after Senate Watergate Committee Chairman Sam Ervin went out of his way at a Washington press conference to exonerate both me and the Republican National Committee of any Watergate involvement.

On August 8, 1974, Richard Nixon resigned the presidency to make way for Gerald Ford. The new President entered office on an almost euphoric tide of national goodwill. It was a mood that quickly dissipated. Less than a month after Ford's inauguration, his pardon of Nixon touched off a storm of protest. A snap poll of Kansas voters showed opinion running 52–40 percent against the pardon, a margin that widened over the next week.

Ford's move was as courageous as it was politically risky. One immediate effect was to lessen the new President's effectiveness on the 1974 campaign trail. Inadvertently, he set off a fresh round of Watergate innuendo that endangered Republican candidates everywhere.

In the middle of this supercharged atmosphere, I decided to switch campaign managers late in August, giving Kansas Lieutenant Governor Dave Owen overall responsibility for my campaign. Owen's first priority was to counter Roy's negative television spots, which before August we had left unanswered. Roy's strategists had combed *The Congressional Record* and sifted through hundreds of legislative tallies. Isolating votes for their maximum potential damage, they fashioned a series of specific charges. Bob Dole voted against farmers. Or the handicapped. Or the elderly. If I had believed what was in Roy's ads, I'd have voted against me, too.

Owen was unhappy with the advertising we were running, and, on his own initiative, he went to a Kansas City television station and hired an announcer whose voice dripped sarcasm. The announcer sat on a stool, turned full face to the camera and detailed Roy's liberal voting record and his reliance on campaign contributions from organized labor. With the tape in hand, Owen telephoned the Boston-based ad agency that had been brought in during the campaign's late stages and told them what he wanted to do. They begged him to delay for twenty-four hours the airing of the homemade spot.

The next day a special-delivery package arrived at campaign headquarters. Inside was a tape of a proposed commercial. It featured my face, gradually obliterated by graffiti—or mud—while a voice-over detailed and then refuted Roy's allegations. "All of which makes Bob Dole look pretty good," ran the tag line. "All of which makes Bill Roy a liar."

Owen exploded with anger at the last phrase. Within minutes he was on the phone to Washington, where he tracked me down on the Senate floor and read the ad copy to me. It was my turn to hit the ceiling. I was already suspicious of television's distorting power and wasn't thrilled about repeating Roy's charges, even in self-defense. Nor did I like the idea of my video image being spattered with mud. And the word "liar" was out of the question in describing my opponent.

But we were behind, and Roy *had* repeatedly stepped over the line between legitimate criticism and dirty pool. I let the spot run but insisted that the last line be changed to read: "All of which makes Bill Roy look like just another old politician."

The effect of the ad was felt instantaneously. Tracking polls showed a surge in my favor. Caught off guard, Roy made his Watergate references still more explicit, which only compounded his problem. By the closing days of the campaign he was caught in his own trap.

There were other charges, regarding the issue of abortion. Just a little more than a year before, the Supreme Court had issued its landmark ruling in *Roe* v. *Wade* legalizing abortion during the first three months of pregnancy. The issue was on many minds, and deservedly so. As an obstetrician, Roy had delivered over five thousand infants. Belatedly he acknowledged having performed a few abortions as well. Roy claimed he personally opposed the procedure, justifying it only when the mother's life would be endangered by carrying a pregnancy to term.

In the closing days of the campaign, pamphlets were passed around some Topeka neighborhoods denouncing Roy and showing graphic depictions of what their authors said was infanticide. Roy's advisers tried to link the grisly literature to my campaign, but failed, simply because no connection existed. But by making such an accusation the Congressman did, quite accidentally, add to the doubts in the minds of many voters, for whom his earlier, nonpolitical image was by now badly tarnished.

The night before the election, I sat in a Topeka hotel room thinking how much harder it would be to pay off a $50,000 campaign debt if I lost. But Kansas voters dispelled my fears while reaffirming my belief in their fairmindedness. Election night was a long one, though. At three in the morning we called every county clerk in the state, routing some of them out of bed, to confirm our vote count against their official tallies. Only then would I go down to the ballroom of the Ramada Inn with my parents and Robin to claim victory.

The final margin was less than fourteen thousand votes. Slender as it was, I took it as personal vindication. I also thought back to my visit to Camp David two years earlier. In handing me my head, Nixon's palace guard may have saved my hide.

I can hardly close this account of campaigning without mentioning the most important campaign of my life. Elizabeth tells the story of our courtship better than I, so let's just say that on December 6, 1975, we were married. Long before that date, friends knew that something was in the offing. According to staffers on the Hill, they could tell by the way I whistled around the office, and the way I refrained from calling them with work assignments each weekend.

It's true that it took me several months to work up the nerve to ask Elizabeth out. But it wasn't that long before I saw in her a genuineness and a sensitivity to others that are rare in power-hungry Washington.

When I asked her about Salisbury, she described it as "a small town of twenty-two thousand."

"You haven't seen a small town until you've seen Russell, Kansas," I told her. And we agreed right then that the day you forget where you come from is the day you should retire from public service.

Elizabeth comes from a family of perfectionists, so she has a natural tendency to dwell on what she sees as her own imperfections. Over the years I've tried to convince her that life is too short to worry about yesterday, and perfection is an impossible standard. Returning the favor, Elizabeth has shown by example the value of intellectual and organizational discipline that tightly grabs hold of a problem and won't let it go until it's resolved.

Like many men of my generation and background, I've

always tended to internalize my feelings. She's just the opposite. Her emotions are more apparent, and no doubt that too has had a beneficial effect on me.

As we got to know each other better, we found that we had enough in common and enough that was different to sustain a lifelong partnership of equals. She's the early bird, up early most mornings to open her Bible or other devotional reading; if it's still dark outside, I figure it's the middle of the night. She's the culture buff; my way of keeping in touch with opera and theater is driving past the Kennedy Center each day. She likes to rehearse a speech, believing that delivery is an important part of the whole effort; I sometimes give a speech only once.

Elizabeth will read everything she can get her hands on, which led me to joke that if something should ever happen to me, the only book I want her opening at my funeral is a hymnal. She keeps notepads all around the house, and not just next to the telephone. I once asked whether she takes notes on wrong-number calls.

I guess if you look only at our public roles, at the hours we keep and the crazy travel schedules that have us waving to each other in airports en route to the latest road swing, our marriage may appear a bit unusual. On the other hand, as countless professional couples will tell you, our two careers enrich our marriage and make the time we have together all the more meaningful. We speak the same language. We share the same passion for public service.

None of this would matter if we didn't love each other very much. In my case, love is mingled with profound gratitude. Coming off a divorce, living alone and being unhappy with a bachelor's life, many men would be vulnerable to impulsive judgment and a mistaken second marriage. I was saved from all that the day Elizabeth appeared in my office. God was looking out for me then, as He has so often. Through all the years since, she has cheerfully accepted the demands of politics, and I have rejoiced in her graces. I'd say I got the better of the deal.

CHAPTER SIX

Courtrooms, Courtship

ELIZABETH

After three years at Harvard Law School, I spent the fall of 1965 in the equally exotic culture of the Orient. Instead of returning to Salisbury or Cambridge, I settled into an eighteenth-century house in the Georgetown neighborhood of Washington, D.C. In the evening, my guests took off their shoes and sat on pillows around a low table in the dining room while I served teriyaki and sukiyaki to Japanese koto music. During the day, I left the kitchen and looked for a job through government employment offices.

I soon landed a position at the Department of Health, Education and Welfare. While Bob Dole was voting against the Great Society, I was working for it. Actually, I was not much more than a footnote to its organizational chart. At HEW there were the Secretary, the Assistant Secretary, a deputy assistant secretary—and me. A low General Services rating didn't keep me from stopping Secretary John W. Gardner in the hallway outside his office and asking him questions about Washington and the department's agenda, which he graciously answered.

The job gave me a chance to use some of the skills picked up in my education courses at Harvard, and to act on my growing interest in the rights and potential contributions of disabled Americans. HEW assigned me to plan a conference on education of the deaf, the first of its kind held under government auspices. There were a site to choose, a roster of speakers to

135

organize, and the publication of conference reports to oversee. In the spring of 1967, several hundred participants assembled at Colorado Springs' Broadmoor Hotel.

When the conference ended, so did my HEW responsibilities. I decided to take a month between jobs to learn my way around the courtroom, since I hadn't taken trial practice at Harvard. This would prepare me to handle cases for local indigents, I thought, and do some socially useful volunteer work.

With that goal in mind, I walked into a D.C. night court that had recently been established to handle a bloated docket. Presiding over the arraignment proceedings was a black-robed Captain Ahab named Edward "Buddy" Beard. Outspoken and highly unorthodox, Judge Beard inspired fear among young lawyers. He once invited a courtroom audience to vote on whether it believed a defendant's plea of innocent. At other times Beard asked defendants to define the binomial theorem or to identify the author of the poem "Ozymandias."

"Who are you?" Beard abruptly asked one night, pointing his finger in my direction.

"Elizabeth Hanford."

"What are you doing here? I've seen you here the last three nights."

"I'm observing the proceedings, Your Honor, so that I can take cases."

"Are you a member of the D.C. bar?"

"I am."

"Come up here. I have a case for you."

I couldn't possibly comply with his request, I informed Judge Beard. I wasn't ready. I was still observing.

Judge Beard didn't make requests, he issued commands. "If you're a member of the D.C. bar, Miss Hanford, you are ready to take this case. Come up here."

I looked around for the nearest exit, but then reconsidered. I'm going to have to practice before this judge sometime, I figured. If I'm serious about defending indigents, I can't afford to alienate him. Besides, I might pick up some valuable legal training from this whole crazy venture.

Reluctantly, I approached the bench. Beard handed me the information slip for my very first case in the courts of Washington. What followed could have come straight out of a TV sitcom.

My client was a Greek national who was accused of petting, and thereby annoying, a lion at the National Zoo. I was taken to a cell block under the courtroom where the defendant was locked up. It was an iron cage, filled with inmates hanging on the bars. From the way these men greeted me, it was clear they weren't used to seeing female lawyers (this was 1967, remember).

"Hey, man, she's your lawyer," someone called out. As the catcalls continued, I made my way to the opposite end of the cell block and met my client, Mr. Marino.

"Now, Mr. Marino," I told him, "this is not the most serious crime. I think I can get you out tonight. But you'll have to come back and stand trial in about three weeks."

Mr. Marino didn't know what I was talking about. He understood just enough English to protest vehemently that he was going to New York and was never coming back, trial or no trial. As I attempted to dissuade him, the court marshal informed me that Judge Beard was ready for me.

"Well, I'm not ready for Judge Beard. Can't you see? We're still trying to communicate."

The marshal told me to come anyway. No one kept Judge Beard waiting.

As I stepped out of the elevator, I was surrounded by a group of strangers who seemed curious about the case and how I would try it.

"It's ridiculous to keep a man locked up on a charge like annoying and petting a lion in the zoo," I said. "If I get him out he's not coming back. So we're going to trial tonight. Even though I've never seen a trial except on *Perry Mason*."

Everyone around me was scribbling in a notepad.

"You're not court personnel," I gasped. "You're press."

Reporters from the *Post,* the *Star* and the *Evening News* kept on writing.

"Don't you dare print what I just said."

By now, the courtroom was packed with two hundred people clamoring for a show. As I took my place at the defense table I glanced over at my adversary from the U.S. Attorney's

Office. It was my classmate Lee Freeman, editor of the *Harvard Law Review*, 1965.

When the proceeding finally got under way, I argued that without the lion as a witness there was no way to know whether he had been "annoyed or teased." Freeman advised the judge not to release my client, who a few weeks earlier had climbed into an antelope case. Beard looked to the defense team. He wanted Marino's word of honor that he would steer clear of the National Zoo. "Say yes," I whispered in Marino's ear, while punching him in the ribs. "Say yes."

By the grace of God, I won the case. "If this ever gets back to the *Harvard Law Record*," Lee Freeman said between clenched teeth, "I'll know how it got there." I assured him I had no intention of telling anyone at Harvard about that night's judicial burlesque.

The next day's papers noted the valiant lady lawyer whose novel defense had snatched victory from the jaws of defeat. Judge Beard passed me in the hallway outside his courtroom. "Not bad for the first time out of the box," he said.

That was the beginning of a year that was sometimes hilarious, more often heartrending, but never dull. I didn't make any money, but I wouldn't trade the experience for all the gold in Fort Knox. I know on that first night I must have looked like a delicate Southern flower to the onlookers in Judge Beard's courtroom. Beard later warned me that I would see a lot of the underside of urban life in his court. To prove it, he then sent me to the cell block below, where a young man was writhing in the anguish of drug withdrawal. My blood went cold.

Before long, I was defending alleged drug addicts and armed-robbery suspects. I look back now and marvel at the chances I took prowling around some of Washington's meanest streets looking for witnesses. I often met characters like Racehorse Mitchell, a courthouse legend straight out of Damon Runyon. I also ran into other attorneys—Fifth Street Lawyers, we called them—whose specialty seemed to be cynicism. They laughed at my naiveté and couldn't understand why I continued to counsel my clients to believe that people could change if only they were given a chance.

I will admit that what I didn't know would have filled

several issues of *True Detective*. One night, just as I began the
defense of a streetwalker, the judge recognized my client. "Take
off your wig," he directed her. When my client did what the
judge ordered, I realized I was defending a female impersonator.
I turned every shade of the rainbow. The judge took it all in
stride. Nothing surprised him. I guess he was used to this sort
of thing.

As chairman of the United States Civil Service Commission,
John Macy operated as Uncle Sam's chief headhunter. First appointed by John F. Kennedy, Macy became Lyndon Johnson's
presidential talent scout, with a computerized file of twenty
thousand prospective jobholders. His commitment to public
service was infectious. Determined to knock down the stereo-
type of federal employees as a clock-punching army, he was just
as committed to advancing women and minorities in the federal
workforce.

Macy had served as a juror on the 1965 White House
Fellows panel that turned me down. Now, two years later, I
took him up on his invitation to drop by the Civil Service Commission.

Someone on Macy's staff told me about "a great job" in
the White House Office of Consumer Affairs. This was a logical
extension of my year in private practice. It was also a chance to
get in on the ground floor of an issue that was sure to excite
public and legislative interest for years to come.

The job was literally too good to be true. Because of budgetary pressures, the only way I could fill this particular opening
was by convincing another agency to pick up the tab, to fund it
out of a payroll separate from the Executive Office of the President. In bureaucratic jargon, that meant I had to find a slot
before I could fill it.

Then I remembered that Food and Drug Administrator
James Goddard (whom I had gotten to know at HEW) had
encouraged me to get involved in the consumer movement.
Goddard quickly agreed to put me on the FDA payroll, and a
few days later I marched into the White House to announce, "I
come with a slot!"

I reported for work at the Old Executive Office Building,

just across the street from the White House, in April 1968. Hubert Humphrey's vice-presidential office was down the hall. From time to time I saw Humphrey, a gregarious man whose natural ebullience seemed dimmed by the angry emotions of the time.

Normally, no season is more glorious than springtime in Washington. Crocuses perfume the air, and a southern breeze carries with it hints of gentler days to come. There was nothing gentle about the spring of 1968, however. In one week, Lyndon Johnson stunned the nation by withdrawing from the presidential race and Martin Luther King was murdered on the balcony of a Memphis motel. In the wake of King's shooting, a spasm of violence spread across urban America. Johnson was forced to call out National Guard troops to quell riots just a dozen blocks from the White House. When Robert Kennedy was assassinated two months later, many Americans feared that their society was coming apart.

Under the circumstances, Washington's social circuit was less inclined than usual to buzz over primary results and campaign scenarios. Most of what I heard in those crowded, tragic days came secondhand. As deputy assistant for legislative affairs, I spent most of my time shuttling between the EOB and Capitol Hill. My boss was Betty Furness, perhaps best known then for a series of television commercials in which she opened refrigerator doors. By 1968, Furness was opening doors on behalf of millions of American consumers. Most important of all, she made certain the door to Lyndon Johnson's Oval Office was open.

That November the federal government changed hands when Hubert Humphrey was defeated by Richard Nixon. After the votes were counted, Betty left and so did her chief assistant, Les Dix. The rest of us stayed on, a crew without a captain, unsure of our place in the newly commissioned fleet.

Several weeks after the election, two men who identified themselves as members of the Nixon transition team dropped by our EOB quarters. One was Bob Ellsworth, Bob Dole's friend and the future best man at our wedding. Ellsworth clutched a massive volume describing the form and functions of the entire executive branch. His demeanor was serious, a bit accusatory.

"What is this office?" he asked, leafing through the book. "What exactly is it that you do?"

I had a second chance to explain what we did a few days later when I was summoned to meet with Harry Flemming of the White House staff. I half expected to be tossed out of the office. Instead, I got a pleasant surprise. The Nixon Administration was aware of political realities. It had come to power during the heyday of consumerism. By the spring of 1969 twenty-three states had their own consumer protection offices, and together they coordinated over four hundred programs designed to replace the outmoded and socially irresponsible notion of caveat emptor.

Our operation was spared, even though its title would soon change, and, by implication, its standing in the executive pecking order. We became the President's Committee on Consumer Interests, under the guidance of Virginia Knauer, a former Philadelphia city councilor-at-large and director of Pennsylvania's consumer protection bureau whom President Nixon appointed in March 1969.

Because she had very little Washington experience, Virginia kept most of the existing staff. One change she made was to jump me two grades and move me into an office next to hers as her deputy. So began a very special relationship between myself and a woman who would become both mentor and surrogate mother.

Virginia had and has a kind of balance that is rare in Washington. She is a gifted artist and a pioneer in historic preservation; along with her husband, Bill, she restored and opened as a museum a Colonial-era tavern in Philadelphia's Society Hill neighborhood. She has never allowed her love of public life to crowd out her family or her friends, yet, make no mistake about it, Virginia is a great politician. As one of the first Republican women to hold office in heavily Democratic Philadelphia, she was unabashed in her partisanship, but she was thoroughly professional. In Washington she refused to check her conscience at the door—even at the door to the White House. She could be as feisty in arguing consumer interests before Richard Nixon's Domestic Policy Council as she had been in opposing the Democratic juggernaut in Philadelphia's City Hall. She kept her dissents out of the press. And she extended her loyalty to subordinates no less than to the man in the Oval Office.

Virginia wanted me to share in all her experiences. Among other things, that meant hitting the road to sell Administration policies and serving as Virginia's backup on the Cost of Living Council and the Task Force on Product Liability. We attended an international conference of consumer organizations in Vienna and domestic business gatherings coast to coast.

I made my first public speech before a Prairie Village, Kansas, seminar on women and financial credit. Still thinking of myself as a private citizen who just happened to work at the White House, I was surprised when a knot of reporters at the airport bombarded me with questions about legislation I supported making credit available regardless of gender.

The first presidential statement devoted exclusively to consumer issues was published during Richard Nixon's administration. Noted nutritionist and educator Jean Mayer chaired a White House Conference on Food, Nutrition and Health—another first. Joining forces with Dr. Mayer to promote a 30 percent ceiling on fat in hot dogs got us into as much hot water as the hot dogs themselves. The President sided with his consumer advisers against his very agitated Agriculture Secretary, Clifford M. Hardin. "I'll calm Hardin down," Nixon promised Virginia. "You just keep doing what you're doing."

Strictly speaking, our office had no actual regulatory function. Each month we forwarded approximately four thousand complaints to agencies like the Federal Trade Commission or the Consumer Product Safety Commission, or directly to the companies involved. The mail contained a depressing litany of deceptive packaging, shoddy workmanship, and warranties not worth the paper they were printed on.

Both inspired and angered by what we read, Virginia and I sought common ground between the consuming public and product manufacturers. We established a series of Consumer Action Panels in an effort to mediate consumer complaints against industries ranging from furniture and appliances to automobiles and carpets. These early mediation panels, supported by industry as a form of self-regulation, paved the way for current third-party mechanisms to resolve conflicts in the marketplace.

Virginia and I worked hard to convince businesses that responsiveness to consumer needs and complaints would carry commercial rewards. Unit pricing was a typical case. At first chain store executives resisted spelling out for supermarket customers the comparative cost of twelve ounces of detergent. Faced with already thin profit margins, they were concerned about the expense of figuring and posting such information. It took time, but eventually we convinced a few of the largest chains that the cost was small for the consumer goodwill to be gained. Once firms like Safeway and Jewel came around, smaller stores quickly fell into line.

We persuaded manufacturers to date supermarket items for their freshness and to identify the source of fats and oils in their products. Cosmetic firms agreed to list on the label of creams and lotions the full ingredients, including any substances that might cause allergic reactions.

A simple philosophy guided us. For consumers to make wise choices, they must have access to all relevant information. Our advice to the President led to the creation, by executive order, of the Consumer Information Center, based in Pueblo, Colorado, and designed as a clearinghouse for government publications on health, safety, housing and money management. We launched the newsletter *Consumer News* (which cost a dollar a year) and packed it with useful tips culled from federal agencies and the pages of *The Federal Register.*

"Suggested Guidelines for Consumer Education," a curriculum for young people from kindergarten through the twelfth grade, was created under the guidance of our consumer education director, a former Cambridge housemate and a longtime friend named Doris Sasser. I traveled around the country urging that students be taught how to obtain insurance, personal credit, and home mortgages. On college campuses and at law schools I promoted courses in consumer law.

What began as just a job soon turned into something of a personal crusade. Underdogs have always appealed to me. As a public-interest lawyer I had already seen how fraud or deception can victimize the elderly and others too young or impoverished to fight back.

I even experienced a bit of consumer woe myself when furnishing my apartment. General Sherman reached the sea faster than two rolls of carpet ordered from an Atlanta store arrived at my front door. When finally laid down, the carpeting was too small for my carefully measured rooms. Next came two beds, one more than I had ordered. And to top it all off, the store's computer kept sending me someone else's bill.

My experience with the carpet and the beds might easily be dismissed as a comedy of errors, but unfortunately it was being repeated in thousands of other American homes. Few of their owners were laughing.

I had joined the White House staff at a time when consumerism was still an exotic subject in some policy-making circles. At about the same time, I became involved in two other movements with profound implications for the future. One was economic deregulation, a largely uncharted field whose potential was first glimpsed in our office by a young, brainy and obviously prophetic member of Virginia's staff named Jack Pierce. Because Jack wasn't the kind of person who would raise the office's emotional temperature for no reason, everyone paid attention when he said that deregulation was an idea whose time had come. *We* paid attention, anyway. It would take a while yet for Congress to open its windows to the winds of economic change blowing across the American landscape.

Another major change was already under way, challenging the sexual stereotyping that begins at birth, when a pink blanket is used to identify a girl and simultaneously limit the range of opportunities open to her when she grows up.

The women's movement didn't happen overnight, much less in a vacuum. Thirty years earlier, during World War II, women left their kitchens and worked in munitions plants. A largely female workforce built the B-52 bomber. When the war ended and the planes returned to earth, most of their construction crews traded in their overalls for more conventional feminine garb. The new working woman of the early 1970s was no Rosie the Riveter. Instead of patriotism, she had internal drives that propelled her into the workforce to excel and wield power. Women who waited longer than their mothers to marry sought the same professional fulfillment as men. And millions more worked out of simple economic necessity.

By 1970, more than 23 million American women were employed full time. Eight million more held down part-time jobs. Forty percent of the female workforce was married. A third had children under eighteen at home. Meanwhile, a rising divorce rate was expanding the number of single-headed households, and the vast majority of them were supported by women.

What all this added up to was nothing less than a quiet revolution. Notwithstanding all the economic and demographic trends, however, America's organizational culture remained predominantly male. In the early 1960s, Margaret Chase Smith wittily summed up the difficulty for women in entering politics, when a group of female journalists asked her how she would respond if she ever woke up one morning and found herself in the White House.

"The first thing I'd do is go straightaway to the President's wife and apologize," she said. "Then I'd go home."

We have come a long way in the years since. But even as a fairly high-ranking woman in the Nixon Administration, I still encountered lingering resentment among those who saw women only as envelope stuffers. Oh, sure, we could type position papers, but having those papers ever reflect *our own* positions as candidates and officeholders was the sort of utopian vision best left to a party platform.

The first time Virginia Knauer testified before a congressional committee, I went with her. So did our very able general counsel, Tillie Fowler, who has remained a close friend of Bob's and mine, and who currently represents the Jacksonville, Florida, area in the United States Congress.

"Mrs. Knauer," my boss was asked in a senatorial baritone, "do you have anything against men in your office?"

Another time Virginia had to leave midway through some testimony before the House Appropriations Committee and its imperious chairman, Representative Daniel J. Flood. When I stepped forward to complete the statement and take questions as prearranged, Flood called a recess. Only he forgot to turn off his microphone.

"Are we going to let this kid take over the hearing?" he was heard to ask.

Most unsettling was the day I hurried to the Metropolitan Club on I Street for a business meeting with a senior partner of the Cleveland law firm of Jones, Day. The doorman stopped me at the entrance.

"You can't go in there," he said.

"I beg your pardon."

"Women are not permitted in the club."

"I'm sorry. I don't think you understand. My name is Elizabeth Hanford, and I'm here to meet with some attorneys from Cleveland. We have an appointment."

"I'm sorry, ma'am. If you were Queen Elizabeth I couldn't let you into the Metropolitan Club."

After a few minutes, the man I was supposed to meet appeared at the door.

"I had no idea," he said, apologizing.

"You can take your choice," I told him, knowing all along that he didn't really have a choice. "I can go back to the office and send over some man. But I can tell you now that he won't be prepared, and I've spent the weekend getting ready for this meeting."

The meeting went on—without me. Joe Dawson, our press spokesman, wanted to put the story out on the news wires, but I convinced him that a front-page dust-up with a bastion of Washington chauvinism would do no good for either my work or Virginia's.

In the summer of 1973, a vacancy opened up on the Federal Trade Commission. Virginia Knauer proposed me as replacement for retiring Commissioner Mary Gardner Jones.

"Hey," she said that July, "you're just the one for this."

Consumer advocates outside the White House were surprised by her suggestion, especially the chairman of the Senate Commerce Committee, Washington State's Warren Magnuson. "Maggie," as he was popularly known, seemed to be a permanent part of the Washington scene, like the Capitol Dome or August heat waves. It was Magnuson's committee that would pass on any presidential selection for the FTC.

In the spring of 1973, Magnuson and other senators had reluctantly confirmed the FTC nomination of Texas lawyer Mayo Thompson. At the time, an implicit deal was made to assure Magnuson that the next FTC commissioner would have more obvious consumer credentials. Enforcing the deal from Magnuson's end of Pennsylvania Avenue was Michael Pertschuk, the Commerce Committee's chief counsel and staff director. Mike was a friend of mine, but he didn't let that color his opposition to Virginia's idea. He told me frankly that groups like the giant Consumer Federation of America and the National Consumer League would see the nomination of any White House insider as a broken promise. He backed his assertion with a laundry list of people and organizations that would have to be won over.

It was a formidable challenge. Virginia suggested that I take a swing around the consumer circuit, beginning with an appearance before the annual convention of the Consumer Federation of America. I should confront issues head on, she told me, even if that meant detailing internal differences between our office and those around the President.

I had my doubts about the propriety, and wisdom, of taking a roomful of strangers into my confidence, many of them openly hostile to the Nixon Administration, but Virginia insisted.

"It's the only thing to do," she said. "Don't worry about me. Just make sure the meeting is off the record. Once you have that assurance, state your views. They may disagree with you, but they'll respect your honesty." Hers was a selflessness rare in Washington.

Walking into the CFA's meeting room in Milwaukee felt a bit like that first night in Judge Beard's courtroom, except that this time I was no novice. There was no real grilling; the meeting was cordial enough. It showed me that communication can often begin in a simple gesture. Even if the walls dividing us were not leveled, they were breached.

I also called consumer advocate Esther Petersen and syndicated columnist Sidney Margolis. These conversations—like discussions with other consumer advocates—were spirited, what diplomats call "frank and constructive dialogue." Soon I was able to give Mike Pertschuk a list of my own.

"Now, Mike," I began, "let me try this out on you." Then I went down my list. It included over two dozen state attorneys general, journalists and organization leaders. When I reached the bottom, there was silence on the other end of the line. But only for a moment.

"You got it," Mike said. Magnuson was going out of town for a few days, and a hearing would be scheduled promptly. According to Mike, there would be no problems.

Being confirmed was relatively simple. Getting sworn into office was another matter. One of my final assignments as Virginia's deputy was a speech in New Jersey just across the river from Manhattan. Coming out of the Holland Tunnel, a drunk driver rear-ended the police car in which I was riding. I suffered a ruptured disc which put me into Georgetown Hospital for a month in traction.

Accident or no accident, FTC Chairman Lewis Engman expected me to carry my load. Fine, I told him, come on out to the hospital and swear me in there. On December 3, 1973, Engman appeared in the doorway of my hospital room, accompanied by other commissioners and staff members.

I took the oath from my bed. We celebrated with quiche and tossed salad, and champagne chilled in a bedpan. Two hours later, everyone else made his way back to the office. I remained in the hospital for another two weeks, enjoying Chesapeake Bay crabs and a full Italian meal. I also boned up on the FTC caseload. It wasn't restful. But it was good preparation for what lay ahead of me.

Virginia Knauer was a natural-born matchmaker. In the spring of 1972 she had asked me to help her get a consumer plank into that year's GOP platform. She arranged for us to make a pitch to Bob Dole, the Kansas Senator who was also Republican Party chairman.

This was the first time I met Bob. When a side door of his

office opened to reveal a tall, dark stranger, I thought he was awfully attractive. He claims he wrote my name on his blotter right after that. Maybe so. But I didn't hear from him for several months.

Other suitors were less bashful. About this time I was dating a fellow Southerner. Like the rest of football-mad Washington, he was devoted to the Washington Redskins. It was a passion I didn't share, as he discovered the day he called to tell me he had somehow wangled tickets on the fifty-yard line.

"Thanks," I replied. "It's nice of you to invite me, but I've got so much to do. I'm getting an advance copy of the new Nader report to read this weekend."

My date was aghast. He could go along with Nader six days a week, but the seventh unquestionably belonged to George Allen and Billy Kilmer. Eventually, I agreed to meet him at RFK Stadium. On Sunday he arrived early to load up on hot dogs, programs and other essentials. As the opening kickoff approached, he looked at his watch and scanned the rapidly filling stands for signs of his reluctant date.

He finally spotted me slowly advancing through the crowd. His smile did a vanishing act when he saw the briefcase I was carrying. For the next two hours, I glanced through the Nader report and basked in the sun. I thought it was a pretty good afternoon. He thought it was a pretty poor date.

"I said I would *go* to the game," I told him. "I didn't say I would *watch* it."

I ran into Bob Dole a second time when he and Tricia Nixon opened GOP campaign headquarters a block from the White House. And our paths crossed again at the Miami convention, when we both attended a party thrown by insurance magnate Clement Stone. Not long after that, Bob called me. We talked for forty minutes or so, long enough to discover how many interests and friends we had in common.

A few weeks later I got a second call. We covered new ground, and Bob said it might be nice to go out some evening.

It certainly would, I replied, waiting for him to suggest a time and place. But he didn't.

Third time never fails. After another long conversation, he

finally invited me to dinner at the Watergate restaurant. Later Bob told me he had delayed asking me out because he had been concerned about the thirteen-year difference in our ages. And he was a little shy. I liked that. It contrasted nicely with the image some have of Washington as a town full of ladies' men.

He was also straightforward and absolutely honest. On a visit to my parents in Salisbury, he appeared one morning in the kitchen with a towel draped over his right shoulder.

"Mrs. Hanford," he told my mother, "I think you ought to see my problem."

"That's not a problem, Bob," she told him. "That's a badge of honor."

Even today, Bob kids me about forgetting his physical disability. "How am I supposed to hold the nail and hammer it?" he'll say with a smile when I ask him to hang a picture. Someone with his energy and stamina makes you forget that he's limited in any way.

From the first time I met him, I was impressed by his way with people. On one of those trips to Salisbury, Bob invited Mother and a group of her friends to lunch at a local club. He sat at the head of the table surrounded by twenty gray-haired ladies who laughed at his jokes and decided on the spot that I'd be foolish not to marry this man. Bob has always been good at building coalitions.

The Federal Trade Commission is one of the oldest of Uncle Sam's consumer watchdogs. It grew out of the fertile mind of Louis D. Brandeis, the famous "people's lawyer" from Boston who convinced Woodrow Wilson of the dangers of business monopoly. The FTC was chartered in 1914 to probe alleged violations of federal antitrust laws and to issue cease-and-desist orders against corporations found guilty of engaging in unfair methods of competition.

Like so much of Wilson's New Freedom, the FTC was intended to be a bulwark against bigness. It began with the premise that economic concentration could be carried to such extremes as to endanger democracy itself. In the 1930s this assumption led the commission to side with small business against food giants like A&P. Yet the commission's fervor ebbed over time, until critics derided Brandeis' once vigorous agency as "the Little Old Lady of Pennsylvania Avenue."

About the time I arrived on the scene, things were changing again, and for the better, as consumer groups and the organized bar prodded the commission to take a more aggressive stance. In 1974 Congress passed the Magnuson-Moss Act, which dramatically increased the FTC's power by authorizing it to write rules affecting entire industries instead of determining unfair trade practices one company at a time.

My early months on the job were notable for Chairman Lewis Engman's oft-asked question "How much will it cost?" Federal regulators back then weren't accustomed to such inquiries, but Engman wouldn't be put off. An old friend from Harvard Law days, Lew was an effective chairman whose willingness to apply fresh schools of thought to the regulatory field came as no surprise to me. It was Engman, for instance, who institutionalized "cost-benefit analysis" as an FTC policy-making tool. By utilizing the talents of economists, statisticians and others, it was possible to gauge the benefits of government action against their social and economic costs to society at large. Properly conducted, cost-benefit analysis could serve as a check on the long arm of federal regulators.

Additional innovations followed as the FTC became the first agency in Washington to raise the banner of deregulation. The agenda of increased competition and lower consumer prices that I would pursue as Secretary of Transportation had its genesis in my days as an FTC commissioner. Before arguing for more head-to-head competition at agencies like the Interstate Commerce Commission and the Civil Aeronautics Board, we had to get our own house in order. So the FTC launched an exhaustive review, which led to the rescinding of 145 of our rules, some of which regulated industries no longer in existence.

On the surface, such issues may sound dry. From my vantage point, they were anything but. Rather, they were a logical extension of my earlier work on behalf of individuals victimized by discrimination or economic abuse. One early case involved a group of West Coast travel agencies that were taking advantage of distraught people by making false claims on behalf of Philippine doctors. The travel firms proposed to fly desperately ill people five thousand miles and back, to be treated by so-called "psychic surgeons" who removed diseased organs with their bare hands. The FTC quickly put an end to the scheme.

Likewise with owners of a Montana uranium mine offering to transport those suffering from arthritis, bursitis, asthma—you name it—to the bottom of a shaft to inhale radon gas, a substance claimed to have beneficial effects on the nervous system.

Not all my time was spent fighting quack cures. The FTC took an active role in enforcing the Equal Credit Opportunity Act. Women were especially vulnerable; divorce or separation could be a kind of fiscal death. Without a credit record of their own, women were often denied credit of any kind, while the income of working women was commonly discounted by mortgage lenders and insurance companies.

To help women know their rights under the law, we developed imaginative public-service spots which in turn were vigorously promoted by American Women in Radio and Television. One of these ads dramatized the effect on a family when a breadwinner disappears—vanishing from the picture on the screen and leaving a gap in any woman's future. We convened FTC workshops on women in business, and I invited female colleagues at the FTC to regular "networking" sessions in my office.

Another priority was the elderly. I never forgot the excellent care my Grandmother Cathey received in a North Carolina rest home. From visits I made to her, it was a short step to arguing the need to investigate complaints against other, less reliable facilities. The result was a grim education in deceptive claims regarding nursing-home services and contractual disclaimers relieving the homes of responsibility for patients' health, safety or property.

And there were reports of some nursing homes receiving kickbacks from pharmaceutical and other suppliers and mishandling patients' money and valuables. Surprisingly, the commission staff showed little initial interest in pursuing an investigation of such reports. When I called in the director of the Bureau of Consumer Protection for "a little talk," the staff's attitude underwent a sudden and welcome change. More important, the stage was set for changes in the nursing-home industry.

Generally speaking, I saw the commission as a chance to bring about lower prices for consumers, to ensure better-quality goods and services, and to expand the choices available in a free, competitive marketplace. One of my proudest moments came in leading the charge to overturn an old common-law rule that posed dangers to consumers who bought on credit, and especially to the poor and disadvantaged. The so-called "holder-in-due-course" doctrine took away their only remedy against schlock merchants who refused to honor their contracts.

Under the old rule, when the consumer purchased an item on credit, the merchant was allowed to sell the customer's note of indebtedness to someone else, making it impossible for the consumer to withhold payment in the event the product failed to work. The seller had no incentive to honor the warranty or resolve the problem. Our decision changed all that by requiring finance agreements to include a written statement preserving consumers' rights against the original seller.

There were times—and the change in this old doctrine was one of them—when service on the commission satisfied a deeper need, which I tried to communicate to college audiences wherever I went. In an age of massive, overpowering institutions—big business, big labor, big government—it was essential to let the individual know that his voice still counted, that there was an alternative to the apathy or cynicism that inspired many Americans to turn inward during what Tom Wolfe labeled "the Me Decade."

I believe now what I believed then. Perhaps no one in our society is more unjustly maligned than the bureaucrat. Even the phrase has become a pejorative. Taxpayers don't like the way their money is collected. Local officials and individual recipients are critical of the way government returns their money. And almost everyone has something unkind to say about mail delivery.

Woodrow Wilson used to say that government had to borrow all the brains it could get. It still does. Now more than ever, we need the energy, the drive and, most of all, the idealism of young Americans. I tell youthful audiences they can find no higher calling in life than that of public service. They may not get rich, but they'll enrich the lives of countless others. Along the way, they can raise society's sights and elevate its standards. And when the time comes to look back, as inevitably it will, they can take pride in having been an active part of the struggle of their times. Because of them, the world is a little better.

August 8, 1974, was wet and dreary in Washington. On this final day of Richard Nixon's presidency, my mother looked out my FTC window at rain-slicked Pennsylvania Avenue and said, "All of Washington is crying today."

My thoughts were with Bob, whose reelection campaign might easily be damaged by Nixon's downfall. We had grown much closer in the two years since our first meeting. I admired Bob's strength of character, his intellect, his incisive mind and, of course, his sense of humor. He was someone I could look up to but also be a peer to.

We had so much in common, not least of all careers that were distinct but in some ways overlapping. Clearly, I was never going to be the kind of wife who worried about my husband being home in time for dinner. Luckily, Bob didn't want that. Now, as then, one measure of our love is the freedom we give each other to pursue professional interests, without jealousy or competition. (Of course, he says I steal his best jokes. And he keeps threatening to give my recipe for pie crust to the Federal Highway Administration.)

By the summer and early fall of 1974, I was leaving my phone on when I turned in for the night. At one or two in the morning Bob would call me long distance. After fifteen hours on the campaign trail, with another day like it soon to begin, hearing my voice gave him something to look forward to each day, he said.

That October I was invited to join a group of young American political leaders on a trip to Japan for three weeks. When I told Bob, he said I should take advantage of what sounded like a great opportunity. "You'll probably learn a lot," he added.

Only later did it dawn on him that I would be away beginning the day after the election. That night he called from Topeka. "I'm looking forward to celebrating with you when I get back to Washington," he said.

"Don't you remember?" I told him. "I'm leaving for Japan tomorrow!"

"What?"

When I arrived home from the trip and found a bottle of champagne and a dozen red roses, I knew that things were getting serious. Bob said he had just wanted to make sure he had a job before he popped the question. He never got down on his knees. Come to think of it, I don't even remember a formal proposal. We just gradually began to think of the future as something we wanted to share. We were happier together than apart.

We were out walking one day when a friend of mine approached us and expressed the hope that I would keep my own name after our marriage. She went on at length about my having worked long and hard to develop a career and a professional identity. Surely I didn't want to give all that up, she continued.

"I think we want to have the same name," Bob shot back. "I don't care if it's Bob Hanford or Elizabeth Dole, we want the same name."

Our wedding was scheduled around the congressional calendar. We settled on a Saturday in December 1975. Since Bob and I each had an ailing father, we decided to have a small, private ceremony, followed by a large reception at the Washington Club on Dupont Circle. I looked at several churches before choosing the Washington Cathedral's Bethlehem Chapel. It is the oldest part of a church that had been under construction since 1907 and originally intended as an American Westminster Abbey. Woodrow Wilson had been entombed in a crypt under the chapel floor, as had other statesmen and heroes. I was less concerned with its historic associations than with the Gothic chapel's intimacy. I fell in love with it, and have gone back often.

President Ford would be in China on December 6, so he entertained us at the White House a few days before. Richard Nixon called to invite Bob and me out to San Clemente for a cup of tea. Consumer Product Safety Commissioner Barbara Franklin told me I could call her if I ever needed advice on safe cribs or toys.

A Washington astrologer took one look at my palm lines and announced, "To have a successful marriage you will have to be a lamb in politics and a lion at home. You are both romantics with strong minds and you ought to rule the home and he the rest." My horoscope for December 6 urged me to pay special attention to "public relations, legal affairs, cooperative efforts, marriage."

At a wedding breakfast at the F Street Club, there was a reproduction of *The Congressional Record* on each guest's plate. Included in the "Extension of Remarks" was a suggestion already made by my colleagues at the FTC: "I move to amend the Robinson-Patman Act to render the Dole-Hanford merger a combination in the public interest, and not in undue restraint of trade."

A few minutes before 6 P.M., I stood outside the Bethlehem Chapel, reading over my marriage vows. Bob decided to wing it. The ceremony was delayed for a few minutes by the cathedral's organist, who seemed determined to perform a concert instead of just playing the Wedding March. As soon as Dr. Elson, the Senate chaplain, stemmed the flow of music, the fifteen-minute service began. At the first ministerial pause in the vows, Bob jumped in with a hearty, if premature, "I do."

Our honeymoon was cut short by the sudden death of Bob's dad, who had stayed on in our Watergate apartment. I felt cheated of the years I could have enjoyed with a man whose warmth and kindness had deeply impressed me.

A month later, I had a chance to test Kansans' response to their newest adopted daughter. I needn't have worried. Three hundred and fifty people came out in zero temperature to greet Bob and me one evening in Hays. They confirmed what Bob had already told me: Kansas isn't a place on the map. It's a state of mind.

CHAPTER SEVEN

Ramrod and Rainbow

BOB

Finality is not the language of politics.

—BENJAMIN DISRAELI

There's an old rule in American politics that says you don't run for Vice President. Neither do you run away from the job if it's offered. Franklin Roosevelt's first Vice President, John Nance Garner, once described the job as not worth a pitcher of warm spit, but it has long since ceased to be a national joke. By 1975 there was even an official residence for the nation's second-highest office. Alexander Throttlebottom, the hapless Veep of musical comedy, wouldn't recognize the rambling, turreted structure perched high on a hill overlooking Washington's Embassy Row.

Gerald Ford's Vice President, Nelson A. Rockefeller, disliked the place, preferring his elegant Foxhall Road mansion. He helped with the refurnishing of the house, but he refused to spend more than a few nights in it.

Accommodations were the least of Rockefeller's disappointments in a job he had rejected at least once before Ford called in August 1974 and persuaded him to take it. It seemed at first to be a perfect match: Rockefeller's international experience and administrative background balancing the down-home appeal of a former Michigan congressman untested in the global arena. The two men admired each other; each wanted their political partnership to be successful.

Despite all the changes that have transformed the modern vice presidency, the office remains a hostage to fortune. No one who occupies it can do more than a President desires or the rest of the executive branch will allow. Rockefeller wanted to break that historic mold. As head of the White House Domestic Council, he expected to be a key policy-maker, implementing an ambitious agenda drawn up by his personal secretariat.

It didn't work out that way. The Council of Economic Advisers and the Office of Management and Budget thought Rockefeller's ideas were too expensive for a conservative Administration trying to patch a hemorrhaging federal budget. Politics submerged policy-making. For twenty years Rockefeller had battled the Republican right, and his name had become synonymous with an Eastern establishment that was distrusted by grass-root Republicans in the South and the West. Fairly or not, by 1975 New York's four-term Governor was seen as a political liability in the very regions where the GOP staked its future.

That November, Rockefeller took himself out of the running for 1976. Prior to his announcement, the Vice President had let it be known that the only way he would stay on in the job was if his responsibilities were broadened to include those of White House chief of staff. He would serve in a second Ford term, Rockefeller made clear, only as a kind of deputy president. That way he could finesse White House organization charts.

Rockefeller's departure was not enough to prevent a stiff challenge to Ford's presidency from the right. On March 2, 1976, the President chalked up a narrow victory over Ronald Reagan in the New Hampshire primary. A week later he won in Florida, and on March 16 he took Illinois' big delegation by a decisive margin. Anticipating an early end to Reagan's insurgency, Ford got a severe jolt on March 23. North Carolina Republicans rallied to the former California Governor, whose bristling rhetoric appealed to their suspicions of Secretary of State Henry A. Kissinger, détente with the Soviet Union, and proposed treaties that would relinquish U.S. control of the Panama Canal.

The Reagan campaign, energized by its North Carolina victory and by a series of televised attacks on Ford's foreign policy, was able to shake off defeats in New York, Wisconsin and Pennsylvania. On May 1, Reagan swept all of Texas' one hundred delegates, setting the stage for a protracted round of trench warfare leading up to the August convention.

When Kansas held its state convention in May, friends advised me to stay away. I had been mentioned as a possible running mate, and they were afraid I would alienate partisans in both camps, dooming whatever slight chance I might have of being on the ticket. But there are times when silence is not golden, just yellow. As I told the delegates in Topeka, one reason the people of Kansas had voted for me in the past was that I never reneged on a commitment. I wasn't about to start now. On the first ballot, Kansas would be with Ford.

On July 26, Pennsylvania's moderate Republican Senator Richard S. Schweiker sent shock waves through the party when he accepted Reagan's offer to be his running mate. Schweiker's announcement shook delegate loyalties, but not the way Reagan strategists had envisioned. Within twenty-four hours former Texas Governor John Connally got off the fence and publicly endorsed Ford, as did Mississippi's Clarke Reed, whose support was crucial to winning that state's thirty delegates. Schweiker's home state held firm in its commitment to Ford.

Ford and his managers had spent so much time on the fight with Reagan for the nomination, they had given little thought to putting together an organization for the fall campaign against the Democratic nominee, Jimmy Carter, or to selecting a vice-presidential running mate. A couple of weeks before the convention, I was asked, along with a dozen other candidates, to send financial and medical records to the White House. When we got to the convention in Kansas City, I spoke to a few strategically placed opinion-makers like former Defense Secretary Melvin R. Laird. I asked Laird whether he would do me a favor by raising my name in press speculation—I might run for reelection in Kansas someday and it would sound impressive back home.

I also talked with my old friend Lyn Nofziger, then working

as Reagan's press secretary. I knew that Ford and Reagan had agreed to meet as soon as the presidential balloting was concluded. If Ford won, he was sure to ask Reagan who he thought should be his Vice President. Could Reagan say something nice if my name came up? Lyn jokingly offered me the job, saying that all I had to do was jump ship and board the Reagan campaign.

Monday, August 16, was opening day in Kansas City's Kemper Arena. As temporary chairman, I welcomed delegates with a verbal blast at Jimmy Carter, who was asking voters to elect him on trust alone. The speech was well received by delegates who agreed on little else. It also appealed to Ford's personal combativeness.

Several factors were coming together to influence the vice-presidential selection. Ford was well aware of the Midwestern farmers' resentment over the 1975 embargo on grain sales to the Soviet Union. Carter was strong in the South, and his running mate, Senator Walter F. Mondale of Minnesota, was there to hold wavering liberals in line. Ford knew that the Farm Belt was essential if he was going to win the 270 electoral votes he needed in November. I had the good fortune of having been born in Kansas, and I could talk the language of farmers whose daily existence depended on faith, hope and parity.

Ford wanted a running mate with whom he was philosophically and personally compatible, someone who would be able to discuss a wide array of issues knowledgeably and who could heal wounds left by the divisive primary contest with Reagan.

On the eve of the convention, presidential advisers urged boldness, but polling data modified this counsel. If Ford chose John Connally, for instance, he would make a bold grab for Texas, but he might also turn off voters who were suspicious of Connally's big-business image. Another Texan, Anne Armstrong, who was now ambassador to Great Britain, would dramatically shuffle the deck. She would certainly throw Carter off stride. But Ford pollsters had found resistance, especially among Republican women, to the idea of a woman on the ticket.

According to their numbers, Howard Baker would add less Southern strength than might be expected from his Tennessee roots. Treasury Secretary William E. Simon was too much of a

Washington insider. Former Deputy Attorney General William D. Ruckelshaus had no clearly discernible political base. Besides, his name would never fit on a campaign button.

On the convention's second night, delegates defeated a Reagan-sponsored rules change that would have compelled Ford to name his running mate before Wednesday night's presidential balloting. With that, the die was cast for the President's first-ballot nomination twenty-four hours later. As soon as his victory was official, Ford and a few advisers went to Reagan's Alameda Plaza hotel suite for their prearranged meeting. Ford threw out half a dozen vice-presidential possibilities. Reagan responded favorably to my name.

Elsewhere around Kansas City, Reagan diehards were trying to force their man on the ticket despite his protests. Their predawn rebellion dramatized the party's internal divisions and raised the pressure on Ford to select a running mate acceptable to the right.

At ten-thirty Thursday morning, the phone rang in our hotel suite. A White House operator was on the other end.

"Hello, Bob. This is Jerry Ford."

"Nice to hear from you, Mr. President."

"Bob, I've given it a lot of thought and I'd like you to be my running mate. We've known each other for a long time. You know the Midwest and the Farm Belt. You can hit the ground running. You've got the experience to be President. We've got a way to go, but I know we can do it. What do you think?"

I thought it over for about a second. "If you think I can help. Certainly, Mr. President."

There was a brief visit to the Fords at their hotel, which included a quick, cautionary warning about my occasionally caustic humor. There was nothing wrong with having a little fun, Ford assured me. "Just be careful what you say."

ELIZABETH

The Federal Trade Commission is a semijudicial body, so it has a calendar of oral arguments and weekly conferences where cases are decided. By July, commissioners are in the middle of round-the-clock opinion writing, interspersed with budget meetings for the coming year. August is a vacation month, and a welcome escape from the heavy early-summer workload and Washington's brutal heat.

August 1976 was going to be different. How different I had no way of knowing when Bob and I arrived in Kansas City. If we could just get through convention week, I told myself, we could go away and collapse on a beach somewhere.

Gerald Ford had other plans. Bob has given you his version of that frenetic morning; let me give you mine. In Kansas City we stayed on the seventeenth floor of the Muehlbach Hotel, where Harry Truman had sweated out election night 1948. John and Nellie Connally were next door. Early Thursday morning, August 19, while the rest of the city rubbed sleep from its eyes, reporters gathered in the corridor outside our door.

"Bob," I said, "I hear people out in the hall. I'll bet it's the press."

"What?"

"There's a crowd outside the door. I think they're reporters."

"Elizabeth, put your ear up against the door. See if you can hear what they're saying."

At first I could make out only a low, indistinct babble. Then I heard Bob's name. Someone else repeated it.

The phone rang. It was ABC's Bob Clark, wanting Bob to verify the news.

"What news?" Bob asked.

"Come on, Senator. Are you kidding me? I've been told that you're Ford's pick."

Ford's pick. The words barely registered. Just enough to send alarms out in all directions. My emotions were definitely mixed. Of course I was proud of Bob and happy about his achievement, but I also felt that a distinct change was about to occur for a couple only recently married. The honeymoon was over.

Within minutes, a group of Secret Service agents came to our room to slip a protective cordon around us and bestow official names. For the next ten and a half weeks, we were Ramrod and

Rainbow. Thoughts of a tropical beach were dropped for more immediate concerns. Who would place Bob's name in nomination? Who would second it? Where could we find someone to translate his speech for hearing-impaired viewers?

Reporters had some questions of their own. "I think my own career is a pretty good testament to my belief that women should be able to develop their full potential," I told them. "Above all, they should be able to *choose,* whether it's a career, or the role of homemaker and mother, or both. Choice is what it's all about."

Early in our relationship, Bob had encouraged me to continue my career. Now outside forces threatened to take matters out of our hands. Briefly, it appeared as though I might be forced to resign from the FTC. Deputy White House counsel Ed Schmults did some hasty research and reported back that a leave of absence would satisfy legal requirements under the Hatch Act. I wrote a letter to the commission that same day, returning my post–August 19 salary to the Treasury to be applied to the national debt.

I tried unsuccessfully to reach my family in Salisbury. Newsmen had more luck. By midafternoon they were traipsing through the backyard at 712 South Fulton Street and snapping pictures inside the house. Finally I got through to my brother in Charlotte. He was all ready to head to Salisbury and protect our elderly parents from the demands of instant celebrity.

"You know," I told him, "they've never been through anything like this before." Neither had I.

That night the bands playing and the roar of the crowd made me forget for a moment polls showing us thirty-three points behind the opposition. They were enough to make me dismiss the Democrats' five-week head start and GOP organizational unpreparedness caused by a divisive primary fight. Maybe we *could* pull off the biggest upset in the history of American politics. The mood carried over into the next day. Ford decided to launch his campaign immediately in Bob's hometown of Russell, Kansas. It was a symbolic way of reassuring farmers that the President meant what he said when he promised no future grain embargoes.

It was also one of the emotional highlights of my life. The logistics of mounting a presidential visit on twenty-four hours' notice are daunting, especially when the nearest airport capable of handling Air Force One is seventy miles from the scene of the rally. Somehow, everything came together.

There were ten thousand people packed tightly on the courthouse lawn when we arrived a few minutes after noon. The Russell High School band played "It's a Grand Old Flag." Volunteers handed out hot dogs, and supporters waved homemade signs welcoming the first President to visit Russell since Theodore Roosevelt stopped off at the train depot one day in 1905. Elderly people sat in lawn chairs down front, and farmers in pickup trucks completed a scene straight out of a Norman Rockwell poster.

August 19 would have been Doran Dole's seventy-sixth birthday. This made the occasion all the more poignant. Bob began his speech by describing the telephone call from the President and how he had weighed his response "for about one minute." He recalled his county attorney days, and an even more distant era when Russell rallied around him when he most needed help.

"I am proof that a person today can come from a small town and doesn't need wealth and material things to move ahead," he said. Looking out over the crowd, he saw familiar faces from an earlier time. They touched something deep inside him, something he could not hold back.

"If I have had any success," he told his audience, "it is because of the people here. I can think of all the times the people of Russell helped me when I needed help." He paused, and put one hand to his forehead. Tears rolled down his face. When he spoke again, it was in a near-whisper.

"That was a long time ago, and I thank you for it."

I had a catch in my own throat as I sat ten feet away, wanting to go to him. Glancing over at President Ford, I saw him almost imperceptibly shake his head. But an instant later Ford himself rose to his feet, leading ten thousand people in a spontaneous ovation.

The moment passed as quickly as it came. But from then

on, observers began to describe what they called "a new Bob Dole." He was the same man I had known for four years.

After the rally, Bob's mother invited the President to her house for some refreshment before the Fords went on to Vail. Someone had taken visitors through the house earlier in the day and had forgotten to put Bina's spare key back in its usual place. After a frantic search, I found the missing key behind a drainpipe, but not before a crowd of onlookers gathered to see the President of the United States locked out of the house whose doormat read, "Welcome to the Home of the Doles."

BOB

Russell's pleasure was not universally shared. Tom Wicker described me in the *New York Times* as "the most distinguished Republican vice presidential nominee since William E. Miller." The *Washington Post* said I was "Ronald Reagan's gift to the party." Considering how much conservatives longed for the vanquished challenger, the *Post*'s observation was more complimentary than critical.

Post columnist Mary McGrory was typical of Washington pundits who expressed "shock and dismay" over my selection. Others reacted in their own way. Minnesota GOP Chairman Chuck Slocum thought I was a combination of Bob Taft and Don Rickles.

"We've got righteous Jimmy, dull Walter and stuffy Jerry," said Slocum. "At least Bob Dole will add some zip to the campaign."

Carter pleaded indifference to my nomination, telling reporters in Plains, Georgia, on August 20, that he would let Walter Mondale or his press secretary, Jody Powell, respond to any charges I might make. Having established his above-the-battle stance, Carter unsheathed a silk-covered stiletto. He would not make an issue out of Watergate, because, he said, the American people were well aware which party was responsible for the scandal.

One reporter asked Carter whether he was being fair in his

constant referrals to "the Nixon-Ford Administration." Wasn't that only an attempt to link the incumbent with "an unsavory name"?

"It's not my fault that Nixon's unsavory," Carter retorted.

In the same press conference, Carter said that in my 1974 campaign against Bill Roy I had called Roy an "abortionist." (This was news to me.) "But I don't begrudge Senator Dole or any other candidate the right to be combative and aggressive and to raise issues that might be politically advantageous to them."

Carter's performance that day was typically adroit. Democratic rivals had spent a frustrating primary season trying to put a glove on the Georgian who placed emphasis on the atmospherics of trust to the exclusion of substantive policy discussions. Now it was my turn to shell a few peanuts, to see whether Carter could catch hardball as well as he pitched.

Ford spelled this out on August 26, when I went to Vail for a series of strategy sessions. He and his top advisers had decided that the incumbent should stay in the White House Rose Garden for as much of the campaign as possible and that I would be sent out into the briar patch, to rally Republicans, placate farmers, and poach on Carter preserves in the South and border states.

"You're going to be the tough guy," Ford said.

There were only sixty-seven days until November 2, and I had no campaign organization in place, no staff, no schedulers. The latest Harris Poll said we had to convert 350,000 voters a day in order to win. The first step was to reassemble a Republican Party shattered by Watergate. Fortunately, there were plenty of issues to draw on. Carter was pledged to carry out the Humphrey-Hawkins Act, a legislative witches' brew that committed the federal government to tax and spend whatever was necessary to get the jobless rate down to 3 percent. By contrast, the Republican platform called for an end to deficit spending and proposed tax cuts to stimulate private investment and job formation. Democrats demanded a comprehensive, federally funded program of national health insurance; we favored catastrophic insurance extended through private companies.

The most striking differences were over defense. Carter-Mondale wanted an immediate cut of five to seven billion dollars in the Pentagon budget. At a time when the Kremlin was in the midst of a massive military buildup, we believed that would send the worst possible signal to the men in Moscow.

One day after Carter spoke to American Legion convention delegates in Seattle, I gave them a very different message. Better to spend billions for defense, I told the Legionnaires, than to lose one life on a foreign battlefield. On the highly charged issue of what to do with Vietnam draft evaders and deserters, I contrasted Carter's offer to issue a blanket pardon with Ford's conditional amnesty in which draft evaders would perform public-service jobs in order to regain U.S. citizenship.

Later that week, I dogged Carter's trail again, catching him in a flip-flop on grain embargoes at the Iowa State Fair. I tried to dent the Georgian's hold on his home region by linking him to the Democratic platform and to big-spending Democrats in Congress, his running mate included. Walter Mondale's 1975 rating of 94 percent from Americans for Democratic Action gave me plenty to talk about in Dixie.

Mondale and I had served together on the Senate Finance Committee. Our differences in committee as well as on the floor made us one pair of senators who could be absent for months and never be missed; in most cases when I voted yes, he voted no, and vice versa. Mondale's opposition to military spending was as reflexive as his support for domestic programs like Humphrey-Hawkins and court-ordered busing. He had voted against the antiballistic-missile system, the B-1 bomber, the Trident submarine and the cruise missile.

Meanwhile, I was busy putting together a campaign organization. Before leaving Kansas City, I had reached out to the Reagan camp. Lyn Nofziger accepted an invitation to go on the road with me. "We won't win," he told a friend at the time, "but we'll have a lot of fun." Larry Speakes came over from the White House, where he had been press secretary Ron Nessen's deputy, to handle the journalistic road show. Noel Koch, a deputy assistant secretary of defense and Nixon speechwriter, took on writing chores. Besides Nofziger, old Reagan hands like

Charles Black and Paul Russo pitched in. So did Tully Plesser, a New York–based pollster who had helped out in my 1974 Senate race.

There's a simple formula for national campaigning: up before dawn each day, into a motorcade to catch an airplane waiting to whisk you to three media-market cities, more motorcades and flashing lights—anything to get a cameraman to snap your picture or a network anchorman to put you on the evening news for ten seconds.

Nothing about the 1976 campaign was simple. Things were done on short notice, like turning the plane around in midair one day and heading for Denver, where Ronald Reagan and I had a pleasant if unexceptional meeting. I was willing to go the extra mile—in this case about five hundred extra miles —to get Reagan and his followers to support the ticket more actively.

Politics is not a job for insecure people. On the night of my nomination, half of America didn't know my name. The other half thought I was something to drink. On the campaign trail I was variously called Bob Doyle, Bob Dale and Bob Daley. I spent an hour one morning stranded at a horse farm in Lexington, Kentucky. I like horses, but they don't vote. In Boston the press bus got stuck coming out of a tunnel. Later that same day I was scheduled to visit a carnival in Trenton, New Jersey.

At Trenton the plan called for me to ride in a car escorted by an American Legion honor guard around an oval track next door to where the carnival had set up shop. Advance men disappeared behind the stadium stands to rustle up a crowd. They came back discouraged. Everyone was having too much fun at the carnival and no one wanted to stop throwing money into bottles to listen to some politician. By the time I got to the stadium it was practically deserted, so I rode around waving at empty bleachers for ten minutes. The one good thing about the event was that it came too late in the day to make the network news broadcasts.

At the Southern 500 stock-car race in Darlington, South Carolina, I maneuvered myself next to Jimmy Carter, who was also there that day. "I'm more of a stock-car fan than I was yesterday," I assured the huge crowd. Big deal. Carter one-upped me by promising to invite all the drivers to the White House.

"It's going to be a busy place," I remarked.

Early in September, we got our first real break: Carter's famous interview with *Playboy* magazine in which he said he had "lusted in his heart" and in which he also harshly criticized Lyndon Johnson. Johnson was still revered in Texas, and polls showed Carter's once commanding lead in the West and the border South melting away.

Just when the campaign was shifting our way, a mid-September flap arose over press reports that I had received an illegal 1970 campaign contribution from Gulf Oil lobbyist Claude Wild, Jr. To back up my denials of any illegality, I invited the *Washington Post*'s Walter Pincus to review my past campaign records. Pincus spent two days poring over papers on Capitol Hill. The story collapsed. But in the meantime I had suffered through a week of intensely critical reporting.

Nelson Rockefeller offered some friendly counsel. "I never read anything about myself in the papers," he told me during a swing through upstate New York. "My advice to you is to do the same. Otherwise you'll spend half the day reading the criticism and the other half reacting."

Rockefeller gave me more than advice. The Vice President sent Jerry Waters from his staff to smooth out a ragged scheduling operation. This freed me to concentrate on Carter, Mondale, the Farm Belt and discontented Republicans. On September 18 I met with Ford and his campaign manager, Jim Baker, at the White House. The President wanted me to take the gloves off and really go after Carter. He wasn't the only one. That same week, *Time* assessed my performance so far as surprisingly tame. Instead of "a tabby cat," said *Time,* voters expected a display of slashing partisanship. When were they going to see it?

If I'd had my way, the answer would have been no time soon. My near-defeat in 1974 had led me to some soul-searching. Ideally, 1976 should have been an affirmative campaign, a party-building exercise taking advantage of the national optimism surrounding the Bicentennial and Ford's restoration of trust to a tarnished presidency. I would have liked to make more appearances in urban neighborhoods, on college campuses and among audiences rarely reached by Republicans. But the first principle of campaign scheduling is that you go where the ducks are, particularly when you're far behind.

Occasionally, there were times when everything clicked and the campaign soared to emotional heights. I'll never forget the day in late September when I visited with disabled members of what I called "my community" in Hollywood, Florida. I referred to myself in terms similar to the ones used at the Democratic convention by Barbara Jordan, whose spellbinding oratory and articulate performance on the House Judiciary Committee that voted Richard Nixon's impeachment had thrust her onto the national stage.

According to Jordan, the greatest thing about the convention that nominated Carter-Mondale was her own highly visible leadership position. She had come full cycle; black America had come full cycle.

"And I would like to think," I told the group in Florida, "that when I stood up in Kansas City I might have given hope to someone, some person or group of persons, who had reservations about whether anyone with a handicap could succeed. If you can use me in the next six weeks, use me. If you can use me in the next four years, that would be even better."

ELIZABETH

Bob had commented that our life together would never be dull, but there was no way he or anyone else could have prepared me for the fall of 1976.

Members of the Federal Trade Commission were supposed to be apolitical. Joining the FTC was like taking the veil. The first inkling that all this would change for me came in Seattle a few days after the convention. While Bob addressed the American Legion convention, I visited the FTC's regional office, where I stood out like a fifth ace in the pack. According to the commis-

sion's scrupulous code, I was no longer a government professional. As of August 19, I was the wife of the Republican
candidate for Vice President.

There was nothing in my past experience to ground me in
politics. I had never given a political speech. And with so many
demands over the previous weeks, with a staff to hire and a
schedule to arrange, the last thing in the world anyone had
thought about was what the candidate's wife should say.

I wasn't presumptuous enough to think the voters were
electing me, any more than they were deciding between Betty
Ford and Rosalynn Carter. They wanted to know what Ford
and Carter would do for America, not what I thought about the
Humphrey-Hawkins Act or the Angolan resistance. But as an
independent career woman, and an FTC commissioner with ten
years of government experience, I wasn't going to spend the
whole campaign answering reporters' questions with a demure
"I don't do issues." *I did do issues.* Six days a week. The genie
couldn't be put back into the bottle.

It was an awkward situation all the way around. Bob jokingly referred to me as his Southern strategy. But for the first
week or so after the convention I pretty much played the traditional political wife, standing at my husband's side and smiling
for the cameras.

I was caught between conflicting emotions. Bob wanted me
to campaign with him. Hoping to give whatever moral support
I could at what was bound to be a difficult time, I didn't want
to leave the side of the man to whom I'd been married less
than a year. But I also agreed with campaign veterans who
downplayed media interest in candidates' wives and families.
At the same time, I was under pressure from women at the
Republican National Committee and elsewhere whose political
activism predated my own. The best way to help Bob, they
argued, was to carve out a separate campaign schedule and
cover as much territory as possible. My instincts told me they
were right, so Bob and I attempted a compromise. We went to
the same cities, split off on separate agendas and joined up
again in the evening.

One thing about a campaign. You cherish more than ever

the rare moments you have together. When the door of your hotel room closes behind you, you kick off your shoes and savor the exquisite feeling that for the next few hours your life is your own. And certainly, after sixteen hours of speechmaking and press interviews, you are not going to review the intricacies of Bob's farm policy.

Instead, I listened to his speeches closely for a few days, got the gist of what he was saying and where he was putting his emphasis. Finally I told everyone that the time had come for me to go out on my own. Bob thought it was worth a try. But he also gently warned me not to expect too much media attention.

One of my earliest stops was Baton Rouge, Louisiana. I'll never forget it. Bob was due to pass through town the very next day. When he arrived, he was handed a local newspaper whose front page featured four pictures of his wife—with news stories discussing the issues. Real issues.

"Well," I asked him that night, "what do you think now?"

"Why aren't you headed for the airport?" he said.

Not all my events were headline-makers. I fed peanuts to an elephant in Huntsville, Alabama, joined a kazoo band in Edwardsville, Illinois, went to a Bohemian mushroom festival in a Chicago suburb and later that same day marched in Newark's Columbus Day parade. It was like a civics lesson you can't possibly get in the classroom or in Washington.

Politics blends high drama with low comedy. In Houston, Nellie Connally told me of having been struck by camera equipment as eager newsmen rushed to tape her husband for the evening news. She had once been left behind in a strange city when the Connally campaign express roared off without her.

That has never happened to me, but I have had my share of mishaps. I don't like surprises. I want to prepare for things, to organize and, if possible, to manage a situation. Controlling a national political campaign, especially one put together as hastily as Ford-Dole in 1976, is out of the question. It's like riding a tiger. You hold on for dear life or else you get devoured.

You learn to improvise. Once, asked to deliver a speech to a West Palm Beach, Florida, chamber of commerce, I discovered that I was booked instead into a joint appearance with Jimmy

Carter's son Jack. I had thirty seconds—the amount of time it took to escort me to the podium—to adjust to the change in format.

On another day in Florida I covered five cities, giving speeches and press conferences and visiting senior citizens and Republican women's groups. Everywhere I assured my audience that win, lose or draw in November, I had no intention of living off a dole. By this time I had taken up Bob's habit of skipping meals to circulate through the crowd and thank people for coming. At lunch that day, a woman took my hand and asked me where in the world I got the energy to do what I was doing.

"I get it from you," I told her.

It was true. Something about a campaign sweeps you up on an emotional current and hurtles you from one situation to the next. That something is the high-voltage support that charges a live audience and inspires a candidate. I hope the day never comes when television substitutes for face-to-face contact with the voters.

The televised debate has become a standard of modern presidential campaigns. More citizens watch these encounters in a single evening than turn out to see a candidate in six months of whistle-stopping, which explained the Ford camp's eagerness to lock horns with Jimmy Carter. Coming out of Kansas City so far behind, White House strategists hoped the debates would level the field of competition overnight. They viewed a one-on-one debate as Ford's best shot at making Carter the issue.

Also, 1976 was the first time vice-presidential candidates debated each other on television. Ford suggested it within twenty-four hours of Bob's nomination, and Bob agreed. But as the October 15 confrontation in Houston drew near, it seemed to me that too little time had been set aside for preparation. We had originally planned to prepare one afternoon a week, but that had gone by the boards because of increasingly heavy travel schedules. Bob was inundated with briefing books detailing Mondale's Senate voting record. I doubted whether anyone could master a foot and a half of paper while campaigning all day and half the night.

Three days before the debate, Bob flew to Marysville, Tennessee, to keep a campaign commitment to an old friend, Howard Baker. On the way back to Washington, I was determined that Bob would have a little peace and quiet in which to work. I didn't want him badgered by a whole lot of people with magic formulas for victory in Houston. But they wouldn't leave him alone. So I did something I had thought about doing for a long while: I blew my stack and ordered everyone out of Bob's private compartment. Unfortunately, there was nothing I could do about the bad cold Bob had picked up in Tennessee, or the briefing books that continued to arrive.

BOB

Since Vice Presidents don't make policy, vice-presidential candidates have to be careful how they make news. I discovered this for myself after telling an audience at an agricultural event in Mankato, Minnesota, that if Ford was reelected he would raise farm price supports. Later, the President informed me in unmistakable terms that from then on he would make any such announcements himself.

As far as the debate went, I didn't expect the seventy-five-minute clash with Mondale in Houston's Alley Theater to generate many headlines. I knew it would be a chance to score some points with groups crucial to Republican success. I went in with a simple strategy: to appeal to conservatives by criticizing Mondale's voting record and going after Carter as a litmus liberal whose promises would add a hundred billion dollars to the federal budget, forcing higher taxes while short-changing military preparedness.

Shortly before eight-thirty, Mondale and I shook hands and took up our places at lecterns precisely seven and a half feet apart. Unlike the earlier debates between Carter and Ford, the Houston ground rules allowed for a freewheeling exchange on any number of topics. In my opening statement, I set the tone of the evening by praising Ford's proven leadership, raising doubts about Carter's qualifications and labeling Mondale a big spender on everything but national defense.

Mondale, besides promoting the usual Democratic shopping list of federal programs, promised to play a major role in government reorganization. I responded by saying that I hoped his government shake-up wouldn't be patterned on Jimmy Carter's reorganization of Georgia's executive branch, in which the state Agriculture Department had been reorganized right out of existence.

The early stages of the debate seemed to drag. Mondale looked nervous, and I should have smiled more. (At least, that's what the campaign consultants said afterward.) But I felt pretty good about the way it was going. I hammered away at Carter's spending plans and the renewed inflation that was sure to ravage low-income Americans if even half the Democratic platform was enacted. I suggested that Carter needed three presidential debates so that he could state his three positions on each issue.

But I tripped up badly later on. In briefing books from the Republican National Committee there were references to the GOP as the party of peace. I had used the line many times in the past. Out in Kansas, and all through the Midwest, Democrats like to accuse Republicans of causing depressions, and Republicans respond by pointing out the wars we've gotten into under Democratic administrations. This is treacherous ground. I should have been more careful in approaching it at all, but I resented the fact that Carter and Mondale were scoring points by referring to "the Nixon-Ford Administration." They also blamed Nixon and Ford for Vietnam, which is at the least a highly novel interpretation of history. I should have kept the two issues separate. But I jumbled them together, arguing that Republicans generally were no more to blame for the excesses of Nixon and his courtiers than Democrats were to blame for the 1.6 million American lives lost in twentieth-century warfare.

As a result, I left the impression that I thought both World Wars, Korea and Vietnam were "Democrat wars." Mondale jumped at the chance to label me a hatchet man. For good measure he tossed in a jab at Ford's pardon of Nixon, and said I had "probably the worst record" in the Senate on tax loopholes.

I don't know how many people Mondale and I kept away

from the Friday-night football game, but no one said we put them to sleep. When the debate ended, the President called me. "Your performance was superb," Ford said. "You hit hard but fair." Nelson Rockefeller phoned with similar words. So did Mel Laird and others who were not usually my staunchest admirers.

Bob Healy, writing in the *Boston Globe,* said I had been assigned Jimmy Carter as a target and had "chewed him up." Polls taken immediately after the Houston confrontation showed a 6 percent surge of support for Ford-Dole among the voter audiences we had targeted. Everywhere I went, the crowds were noticeably larger and more enthusiastic than before. Yet to this day all that some voters remember about my 1976 campaign is a single remark, a poorly phrased argument that canceled out ten weeks of constructive campaigning and overshadowed the thirty-one points we made up in the polls. Given television's power to form instant identities, I had no reason to expect anything different. I was in the big leagues now and would be held accountable for whatever I said, just as Jimmy Carter would be for his reference to "ethnic purity" and Jerry Ford was for asserting that Eastern Europe was free of Soviet domination.

The only way to justify a mistake is by learning enough to avoid its repetition. Win, lose or draw, the 1976 vice-presidential debate taught me to think twice before saying something that might appear insensitive or call into question the patriotism of any American. There is nothing partisan about war or the sacrifice that attends it.

I saw Ronald Reagan again during the first week of October in New Haven, Connecticut, where he was visiting his son at Yale. Reagan's Secret Service agents were gone, and in place of the dozens of newsmen who a few weeks earlier had hung on every word he said there was a single local reporter. It was a poignant reminder that power in a republic is a temporary thing.

In the campaign's closing weeks, I concentrated on the agricultural Midwest and South, where polls showed us gaining fast. After telling farmers that the original grain embargo had been caused in part by labor leader George Meany's endorsement of longshoremen's demands to utilize U.S. shipping capacity, I added that if Carter was elected the White House would have two hot lines—one to Moscow, the other to AFL-CIO headquarters.

The stretch run to the election was frenzied. A typical day began with a walking tour of Sioux City stockyards in a snowstorm. Lunch was in Corpus Christi, dinner in Louisiana's bayou country. In a voice cracking with fatigue, I reminded voters that our candidate's name wasn't Ford-Nixon; it was Jerry Ford.

Everywhere I cited Ford's accomplishments: cutting inflation in half, reducing unemployment, maintaining a trade balance with foreign nations in the black, and, most important of all, restoring public trust in government. Jimmy Carter talked trust; Jerry Ford had earned it.

Airport for airport, rally for rally, Ford matched my pace, visiting seventeen states during the campaign's last ten days. On the Thursday before election day, he called me at 5 A.M. Mountain Standard Time with news too good to put off. A new Gallup Poll that showed us in the lead for the first time all year would be published that weekend. The one-point margin was as thin as December ice, and other surveys by Harris and Roper continued to show Carter clinging to a slim advantage.

Still, the momentum was with us. "I know you must be exhausted," Ford told me. "But we're going to make it, Bob. You're doing a great job. Keep it up, and I'll see you back here on Tuesday."

On Monday, the first of November, I campaigned in five Midwestern states. It was a fitting climax to a ten-week odyssey covering forty-four states and 62,000 miles. As I flew back over the eastern half of the United States, the skies were cloudless. I wanted to believe that Gallup was right—but there were other, less encouraging numbers that weekend.

Government statistics released in the campaign's closing days suggested at least a pause in the economic recovery. Inflation appeared to be reheating, and unemployment hovered stubbornly close to 8 percent. The new reports could not have come at a worse time. According to Lou Harris, the percentage of voters who credited Ford with pulling the country out of recession slipped to 47–41 negative that last weekend. We also took a pounding on the Nixon pardon. In a single week, public disapproval of Ford's action had widened from 55–34 to 57–32. That might not seem like much, but in such a close race the slightest shift could make the difference in key states of the industrial Midwest and the border South.

On the morning of November 2, a Secret Service agent confidently said, "You're going to win. You're never going to drive a car again." Publicly, I predicted a sharp drop in the price of peanut butter and a corresponding rise in pineapple futures. But I had been through too many campaigns to feel as optimistic as I sounded.

ELIZABETH

We spent election night with the Fords at the White House. Bob detected trouble early on. Carter's sweep of the South sealed our fate, and sent us on our way home long before the result was official.

Hope dies hard, however. As late as Wednesday afternoon, Bob asked me to call Bryce Harlow about voting irregularities. He wanted Harlow's opinion about doing a recount that might reverse Carter's razor-thin margins in Ohio, Missouri and Hawaii. Ford scotched the idea.

That afternoon Bob got up from a sickbed (he had finally given in to a bad case of flu) to host a party for reporters who had covered the campaign. He was interviewed by Barbara Walters, who boldly inquired whether he thought he was responsible for Ford's defeat. Bob answered her with more restraint than I would have been able to muster.

"Elizabeth," he told me a few days later, "I couldn't have gotten through this without you. We gave it our best shot. That's all that counts. Now there's just one thing for me to do, and that's go back and be the best United States senator I can."

As usual, my husband looked forward, not back. There was no depression, no second-guessing. He must have felt an ache to come so far and finish so close, but he concealed it with a stoicism rooted in his hospital days and the buttoned-down emotions of Kansas.

BOB

If you want to find out who your friends are, lose an election. For the first few days after November 2, I was consoled by sympathetic messages. But as it dawned on people just how close we had come to winning, they needed to blame someone. Barbara Walters wasn't the only one to assign me responsibility for the loss. It's said that when you're the cutting edge of a campaign, *somebody* has to get cut. I tried to make a joke out of that saying, telling people that I had been told to go for the jugular and I did—my own.

One day I was alone in the Senate dining room when Hubert Humphrey sat down at my table. "How are you doing, Bob?"

"Fine, Hubert. I'm hanging in there."

"Bob, I've been where you are," Humphrey said. "I know what you're going through. Some people around this town have awfully short memories. They forget how much ground you made up in the polls. All they can say is, 'Why didn't you carry Ohio?' Well, you did everything they wanted you to. They assigned you the Farm Belt, and you carried it for them. You did one hell of a job."

Humphrey's old antagonist, Richard Nixon, called with a similar message. "It's scapegoating time," he said. As if I needed reminding. Nixon told me to forget about the Monday-morning quarterbacks and the temptation to dwell on what might have been. Move on: that was Nixon's message. Before hanging up he reminded me that I had an obligation to support the man who would be President after January 20, 1977.

During the campaign, I had been pretty rough on Jimmy Carter. Over the next four years I wouldn't shy away from criticizing the Carter Administration's handling of economic and foreign policy. For all his talents, and they included a formidable intellect, Carter seemed oddly miscast in an office that demanded inspiration even more than administration.

Carter scattered his energies, trying to do too much on too many fronts. I also think he misread public disenchantment with the so-called imperial presidency. Walking down Pennsylvania Avenue on Inauguration Day, selling the presidential yacht *Sequoia,* carrying his own bags, wearing a cardigan sweater for a nationally televised address—these were all minor bits of political theater, but as image-making they trivialized the most powerful office in the world. Presidents from Franklin Roosevelt to Ronald Reagan have demonstrated that the American people have a hard time accepting the leader of the free world as one of the boys.

I prefer Harry Truman's view. Truman never forgot where he came from. But no matter what those around him thought of Harry S. Truman of Independence, Missouri, he never let them forget that the office he held deserved their respect.

Carter's failure to adopt the folkways of Capitol Hill was less crippling than his philosophical isolation from the Democratic Old Guard. Elected without a strong ideological base, he put all his eggs into the basket of competence. This made him doubly vulnerable when events slipped out of control and the early promise of Carter's leadership gave way to presidential complaints about a national malaise.

History will credit Carter handsomely for his peacemaking efforts in the Middle East. And if Democrats break free of the New Deal's grip and pursue more centrist policies, Carter may yet be seen as a man ahead of his time.

My personal contacts with Carter were limited. Early in the Senate debate over ratification of the Panama Canal treaties which would turn over control of the canal to the Panamanians in the year 2000, he phoned me with a message of thanks for the Ford-Dole ticket's support of the treaties.

"Mr. President," I said, "I don't recall taking a stand."

"Would you like me to send up the Joint Chiefs to brief you?"

"Oh, I'm not that important."

"Oh yes you are," Carter insisted.

His call was premature. When I failed to get what I thought were necessary guarantees of U.S. military and shipping rights through the canal, I opposed the treaties.

Travel can be as broadening for politicians as for other tourists. In the late seventies I was on the road more than Charles Kuralt.

In Jerusalem, I reassured Prime Minister Menachem Begin and Golda Meir that the United States would never pressure Israel to negotiate with the Palestinian Liberation Organization until the PLO renounced terrorism and accepted Israel's right of existence. After replacing New York Senator James L. Buckley on a commission overseeing compliance with the human-rights provisions of the Helsinki Accords, I gained fresh, painful insight into the anguish of Soviet Jews, intellectual dissidents and other victims of official persecution in a society where anti-Semitism is rampant and the only religion tolerated is orthodox Marxism. When the Carter Administration campaigned against human-rights violations in the Third World, I sponsored amendments blocking international lending assistance to the notorious Marxist regimes in Vietnam, Cambodia and Cuba.

I was just as active at home. As the ranking Republican on the Senate's Nutrition and Human Needs Committee, I fought for food stamps, Meals on Wheels, and women and children's nutrition programs. I criticized Carter's energy policies as unduly harsh on the poor, proposed a catastrophic-health-insurance program and introduced a plan to help American families save for a child's college education with the help of federal tax credits.

"Republicans need to make the extra effort to erase the lingering image of our party as the cadre of the elite, the wealthy, the insensitive," I told an Atlanta gathering of black Republicans. "Our job now is to demonstrate our concern to blacks and others who doubt our sincerity."

Long before Ronald Reagan proclaimed his "New Beginning" in January 1981, I was part of congressional efforts to rewrite the tax code. In 1978 we enacted a major cut in capital-gains taxes. A year later, Colorado freshman William L. Armstrong joined me in proposing a law requiring a balanced federal budget. In losing, we started a dialogue that continues to this day.

I went a step further and introduced a constitutional amendment mandating a balanced budget except during wartime or a congressionally designated emergency. Year after year, it gained greater support as the American economy slowed and middle- and low-income workers suffered the biggest drop in purchasing power since the end of World War II.

Subsequently I tried to amend a bill raising the national debt ceiling with a provision to tie personal-tax rates to changes in the cost-of-living index. Other members of Congress had proposed this most fundamental of tax reforms; Ed Brooke, Jim Buckley and Bob Griffin had all done so before me. But now they were gone. Congress needed to be told that it couldn't go on forever practicing pickpocket government and that's exactly what indexation was meant to halt.

The idea came from economist Milton Friedman, who objected to a tax code that in effect punished workers who received a cost-of-living adjustment or a merit raise. If a raise kicked them into a higher bracket, they found that instead of getting ahead they were lucky just to keep their heads above water. By letting inflation and "bracket creep" do their dirty work, Congress was able to count on a cool $10 billion in extra revenues each year to spend to its heart's content. Barely offsetting this were periodic "tax cuts," usually timed to coincide with election campaigns. These were as fraudulent as they were politically attractive.

Although indexation lacked a Senate majority at the time, the political dialogue was beginning to reflect ideas Ronald Reagan would implement during his presidency. By 1985, tax indexation would be law, and the tax code itself would be poised for massive overhaul. Words once banned from Washington's polite conversation, words like "profit" and "incentive," would guide Congress' reform efforts.

By then, too, I had begun to construct working alliances with my colleagues on both sides of the aisle, putting into practice the lessons of twenty years in Congress. Hubert Humphrey and I became sparring partners on the Senate Agriculture Committee. We also became close friends. Whether it was words or federal dollars, Hubert was never stingy. One morning in committee, when he was well into a stem-winder on how much we needed higher dairy price supports, I pulled a glass of milk from under my desk.

"Here, Hubert, wet your whistle," I said.

For once, even Hubert was speechless.

But not for long. After we had settled on a support price that was less generous than he wanted, Hubert promised me he was going out to his place at Waverly, Minnesota, to tell his cows what Bob Dole had done to them that day in committee.

By the middle of 1977, Hubert was spending less time in Washington and Waverly and more in New York's Memorial Sloan-Kettering Cancer Center. I often talked with him on the phone during his stays there. Some people say the Senate is like a club, but at its best it's more an extended family. It certainly was throughout Hubert's long illness. He had the courage of a prizefighter, and I marveled at the way his spirits never drooped. Before he entered the hospital for the last time, I introduced legislation naming the new Department of Health and Human Services building on the Mall for him.

And when I spoke at the annual Gridiron Dinner in January 1978, I couldn't leave the podium without paying tribute to the happiest warrior in American politics. "He died January thirteenth," I said, "but we don't have to believe that if we don't want to. His legacy ennobles us, teaching us that nothing is so temporary as political animosities, nothing so cleansing as forgiveness, and nothing so vital to the proper governance of this great people as a capacity for laughter and a loving heart. That's really what it's all about."

ELIZABETH

In 1977, the Federal Trade Commission, to which I returned after the election, got a new chairman—not Bella Abzug, as had been rumored, but Mike Pertschuk from the Senate

Commerce Committee. The scrappy, outspoken Pertschuk had something in mind to offend practically everyone from advertisers to used-car dealers. When one FTC antitrust ruling threatened to disrupt long-established patterns of bottling and distribution in the soft-drink business, industry representatives asked Congress to review our decision. I wrote the opinion in the case. Bob was part of the Senate majority voting to overturn it.

That June, just prior to a Senate vote on the matter, Bob and I laid out our differences over a proposed consumer-protection agency before the American Advertising Federation. I thought such an agency would consolidate the overlapping work of twenty-six separate consumer offices, and serve as a permanent advocate for economic deregulation inside the federal establishment. He dismissed the CPA as overly intrusive and costly. I couldn't resist a gentle tweaking of my husband's strong pro-business stand. Bob had been delayed, I told the crowd, because he had to stop by the Chamber of Commerce to pick up his speech.

A few days later we repeated our public disagreement on ABC's *Good Morning America.* As I was listing the reasons why an agency should be established, Bob interrupted.

"If I could just get a word in," he said.

"But I'm trying to make my point," I countered.

I clocked it later, to see whether I really hogged most of the time. (I didn't.) For about twelve minutes the program's host looked on as we went at it. We got a flood of mail after that show. One lady wrote Bob that if he ever wanted to get anywhere in politics, he had better get his wife to shut her mouth. Others praised my courage and endorsed my position. One viewer expressed hope that our "marital differences could be resolved."

Over the next year, Bob moved closer to announcing his candidacy for the presidency in 1980. As he did so, my professional status became the subject of intense debate. Before I resigned from the FTC in March 1979, Bob and I talked it over at length. He exerted no pressure, unlike some of my women friends who thought I was mistakenly putting my own career on hold for his presidential ambitions.

I didn't see it that way. A career is more than a paycheck: it's a series of learning opportunities. A national political campaign, with all its potential for growth as I discussed issues across the country with the press and the public, would be an unparalleled learning opportunity. I didn't rush to judgment. But I had no trouble making up my mind either.

BOB

On May 14, 1979, when I went home to Russell to announce my candidacy for President, four thousand people filled the streets around City Hall. On the fringe of the crowd were a few members of the American Agricultural Movement. AAM was used to being on the fringe. Earlier that year it had staged a highly publicized "tractorcade" in Washington to dramatize the plight of farmers and to pressure Congress into giving them immediate relief.

That morning in Russell, AAM posted a pair of signs on tractors parked near the courthouse lawn. "Where Was Bob in Washington?" they read.

It was an ironic complaint. Being in Washington *was* the problem in my 1980 campaign. Part of it, anyway. In truth, it was Ronald Reagan's year. In the meantime I was busy with work on the Finance Committee, while also keeping an eye cocked on home-state politics, where the calendar forced me to weigh running for reelection to the Senate against a long-shot bid for the White House.

Sometimes I think I never really ran for President in 1980. Certainly few people seemed aware of my candidacy at the time. There was a lot of talk about the five M's: money, manpower, management, media and momentum. While my campaign wasn't broke, it was on the verge of qualifying for food stamps, and I was too occupied with Senate business to pay much attention to campaign management. Although I was ranked third in New Hampshire (behind Ronald Reagan and Howard Baker) in the fall of 1979, any momentum I had soon dissolved in the media attention focused on George Bush after he upset Reagan in the Iowa caucuses.

My one hope was to pick up Reagan's supporters if he faltered. Friends questioned the realism of that scenario. Looking back I can see why. In any event, with me in Washington plugging away on legislation, the brunt of the campaigning fell on Elizabeth.

ELIZABETH

One story sums up some of the frustration of the 1980 campaign. Bob was scheduled to speak to a gathering in a key farm state, but at the last minute he was unable to leave the Senate, where he was heavily involved in efforts to repeal the carryover-basis provisions. The language was arcane but the effect of repeal would be to save farmers and small-business owners from paying massive additional taxes.

I offered to speak in his place. Sorry, they wanted Bob Dole or nobody. Wives didn't count. I reminded them that carryover basis was their organization's top legislative priority. "Where would you like him to be?" I bluntly asked one of the group's officials. "Here or in Washington?"

"In Washington, of course."

"Then why can't I take five minutes to describe his farm program and his twenty-seven years of support for farmers on the House and Senate Agriculture Committees?"

"I'm sorry, Mrs. Dole. The rule is no surrogates."

That night Bob flew out, to receive passing mention at a dinner sponsored by the farm group. Before dessert was served he was on his way back to Washington, where he arrived at two in the morning. A few hours later he was on the Senate floor.

BOB

I pulled out of the 1980 presidential contest at about the time Elizabeth passed me in the polls. My Senate race was looming. For a few weeks I toyed with the idea of leaving politics altogether. I imagined my name on the door of some Washington law firm. Nine-to-five days. Weekends around the house. I didn't have to be a senator.

I did want to be a player, though. Back in the Finance Committee that fall, the opening rounds of the Carter-Reagan bout reminded me just how much I would be missing if I walked away from Capitol Hill on the eve of a Republican restoration. After committee members approved a 10 percent personal-tax cut in line with the GOP platform, the Democratic leadership (and the Carter White House) made sure the bill never made it to the Senate floor.

Following Ronald Reagan's nomination at the Detroit convention, I concentrated on my Senate reelection fight. Elizabeth joined the Reagan campaign as head of Voter Groups for Reagan-Bush and traveled extensively as part of a GOP Truth Squad taking aim at Jimmy Carter's record. On the night of November 4, Reagan's landslide showed up early. The same was true of my own win among the voters of Kansas.

The real election drama in 1980 centered on an unexpected race for control of the Senate. For Howard Baker to replace Democrat Robert Byrd of West Virginia as Majority Leader, Republicans had to pick up eight new seats. Before that Tuesday, almost no one in Washington expected a shift of such magnitude. But as the night went on, and one incumbent Democrat after another tumbled in the Reagan onslaught, the improbable became the inevitable.

Around two in the morning, Baker called me.

"I've been checking races around the country," he said, "and if current trends hold, there's going to be a Republican Senate next January. And you're going to be chairman of the Finance Committee, Bob."

"That's great news, Howard. One thing, though—who's going to tell Russell Long?"

On Wednesday morning, I met the press in Topeka. Reporters expecting an ebullient performance were disappointed. One even complained that I hadn't cracked a single joke. Why?

"All of a sudden," I told him, "I realize that we're going to have to deliver. And it's a lot harder to deliver than it is to criticize."

The campaigning wasn't over yet. Between election day and the inaugural, Reagan had a Cabinet to choose, and a government to staff. Senators were generous with advice. One Western colleague of mine suggested names for eight Cabinet positions. Asked by the Reagan transition team which of his candidates was the most important, he replied, "All eight."

I had a contender of my own. He was John R. Block, a hog farmer who doubled as director of the Illinois Department of Agriculture. I thought it would be a welcome change to have a farmer with dirt on his hands running federal farm programs. Elizabeth had brought Block to my attention. She had come to know him during the Reagan campaign as an articulate spokesman for free-market farm policies.

Several weeks went by, and one slot after another was filled. Treasury went to a Wall Streeter named Donald T. Regan, State to Alexander M. Haig, Commerce to a Connecticut CEO named Malcolm Baldrige, Defense and Justice to Californians who were also longtime associates of the new President. The Reagan Administration was beginning to look positively bicoastal.

I took a map of the United States and drew a big red circle around the middle. I sent it to my colleague Paul Laxalt, a close friend of Reagan's who was helping with the Cabinet selections. The map was accompanied by a note that said, "Paul, that blank space is what's referred to as the Midwest."

A few days later John Block was named Secretary of Agriculture.

CHAPTER EIGHT

Team Players

BOB

*At first I intended to become a student of the
Senate rules and I did learn much about them,
but I soon found that the Senate had but one
fixed rule . . . which was to the effect that the
Senate would do anything it wanted to do
whenever it wanted to do it. When I had
learned that, I did not waste much time on the
other rules, because they were so seldom
applied.*

—CALVIN COOLIDGE

In January 1981, Republicans took control of the Senate
for the first time in a quarter century. For me and others in the
new majority it meant a chance to show that we could deliver
more than speeches. Instead of railing against government, we
were the government. When you're in the minority, you have
the option of standing on the sidelines; when in doubt, you can
always vote no and put out a press release. This may be enough
to stay in office, but it isn't leadership.

Part of the challenge we faced was to make the creaky,
tradition-encrusted Senate respond to the conservative mandate
of 1980. It wouldn't be easy, since Senate rules are hand-tailored

for obstruction and delay. It's easier to keep something from happening there than to make it happen. And for all the speech-making and debate on the floor, most of the real discussion takes place off the floor. Outside forces tend to set our agenda, forcing members to react more than they anticipate. If the Senate ever resembled a club, those days are past. Elizabeth has pointed out that members' wives are probably closer to one another than are their husbands. Partisanship and ambition can frustrate collegiality, and it's tough to find time in which to nurture close friendships.

Some senators choose to observe the political process more than they participate in it. Some are reflexive presidential supporters, taking their cue from the West Wing of the White House. Some are themselves potential Presidents. Nearly all are dedicated men and women, required to master subjects of enormous complexity under intense pressure and constant deadlines. Seniority is far less important today for a senator's advancement than is plain hard work. To make your mark, you have to know what you're talking about, be honest with your colleagues and live up to your commitments. In the Senate as anywhere else, you become a leader by knowing where you want to go, and by persuading others to follow you.

Ronald Reagan came to Washington with that kind of personal vision, as well as the leadership skills to implement it. His presidency would be a turning point in public policy and in public attitudes toward conservatism. Before January 1981, American conservatives were caricatured as little old ladies in tennis sneakers looking for Communists under their beds and fluoride in their water. Or we were lampooned as overstuffed men in batwing collars who never did anything for the first time and who were afraid to look at a new moon out of respect for the old.

Reagan changed all that. His conservatism was an instrument for reform, a dynamic substitute for government that measured compassion by what it spent and not by what it bought. Reagan understood that voters didn't want an economist in the White House. They sought leadership to inspire a common effort for the common good. Government is about hope, not budget formulas, aircraft carriers or UDAG grants. Hope had run out for those who were weary of Jimmy Carter's malaise and misery index. Their rejection of the status quo paved the way for the Reagan Revolution.

They had to start the revolution without me. I was out of commission for a few weeks in February and March 1981, recovering from an operation to remove a kidney stone. One day the new President helicoptered out to Walter Reed Army Hospital for a visit and a little missionary work. Reagan brought with him George Gilder's book *Wealth and Poverty*, a provocative history of capitalism that held a place in the library of supply-side economists beside Arthur Laffer's napkins.

I didn't tell Reagan, but I was already reading Gilder's book in my hospital room. I didn't *have* to tell him of my personal loyalty or of my gratitude at being part of a congressional majority for the first time in my career.

Reagan and I had a lot in common. We both grew up in small towns in the Midwest. We preferred straight talk to bureaucratic mumbo-jumbo. We liked a good joke. And we found it hard to stomach the feeling of self-importance that thrives inside the Capital Beltway and regards the rest of America—the real America—as if it were a suburb of Washington, D.C.

I made it clear to Reagan that day at Walter Reed that I would be his ball carrier on the Senate Finance Committee. I might not always be able to run straight downfield. Sometimes I would have to change course a little, follow my own pattern. That was a matter of tactics. What counted was that we were both on the same team.

Nevertheless, I had my doubts about supply-side economics, which seemed to vary depending on who was describing it. Mathematicians aren't the only ones who would like to square the circle. If there was a magic formula that would give us lower taxes, all the benefits voters clamor for and every weapons system on the military's wish list, politicians would have figured it out years ago. The reality is otherwise.

As the new chairman of the Finance Committee, I faced my

own reality. Replacing a legendary figure like Russell Long was a bit intimidating. Long had dominated the most powerful committee in the Senate for fourteen years, wielding a gavel as if he had been born to it. In a way he had been: Russell was the son of Louisiana's famous Kingfish, Huey P. Long.

Russell's resourcefulness had led to all sorts of Senate folk tales. There was his 1965 race for majority whip, for example, in which he needed a vote from South Carolina's Olin Johnston. Johnston coveted Russell's Senate desk, which long before Huey owned it had been the property of the Southern firebrand John C. Calhoun. Long casually remarked to Johnston that maybe he would like to have this little piece of history. The desk switched hands; Long won the election. Afterward, someone asked him what Huey would have thought of his tactics. "He would have understood," said Long.

No one understood the Senate better than Russell Long. Scheduling legislative markups, often late at night and close to deadline, was a Long forte. Once, during final consideration of a 1978 tax bill, a junior committee member asked for explanation of the pending roll call. "If everyone knew what they're voting on," Russell cracked, "we'd never get out of here."

He had a point. The Finance Committee oversees roughly half the federal budget. No other arm of Congress touches as many lives or has the potential to ruffle as many feathers. Because members deal with such high-visibility issues as taxes, Medicare, Social Security and trade, getting a quorum is seldom a problem. Long had a reputation for making his committee work on a reasonably bipartisan basis. Filibustering was unheard of, in part due to committee rules that gave the chairman the power to decide when debate had run its course.

Watching Long operate was an education in itself. Some chairmen call meetings; others orchestrate them. Russell was of the latter school. The ability to conciliate differing viewpoints is at least as important for success on Finance as knowledge of the federal tax code. For all the power granted him by formal rules, a chairman leads by consensus, not command. Those were lessons I intended to put to use during my own term in the chairman's seat.

The house where I was born, on July 22, 1923, during the Dust Bowl Depression days that hit families hard all across Kansas.

In the fall of 1941, I entered the University of Kansas at Lawrence. With a little talent and a lot of perseverance, I was able to break the tape at a quarter mile.

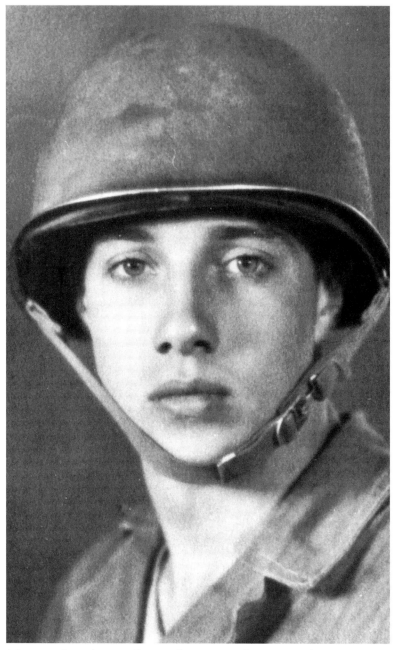

After Pearl Harbor, millions of American boys were drawn into the armed forces. By the end of 1942, I was one of them.

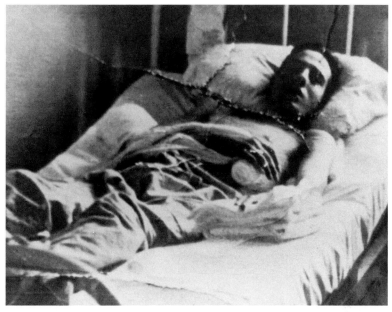

Life changed forever on April 14, 1945. In the months that followed my wounding on an Italian battlefield, my weight dropped from 194 to 122 pounds.

My dad and my grand-father help me out of the house on leave from the hospital.

The two greatest people I ever knew: my mother and father.

My dad wore his overalls to work nearly every day for forty years.

The man who played a role in my early life that was second only to my family's was Dr. Hampar Kelikian, an Armenian-born surgeon who performed numerous operations on my arms and helped restore a sense of purpose to my postwar years.

One way or another, I've spent most of my life looking up to my brother, John. Here's an early instance of our seeing eye to eye, when I was mascot at his high school graduation.

Bob and I were married on December 6, 1975, in Washington Cathedral. Bob said life would never be dull. (*U.S. Senate Photograph*)

Barely eight months after the wedding I was plunged into a crash course in American politics when Gerald Ford tapped Bob to be his 1976 running mate. One of the campaign's emotional high points came early, when President Ford accompanied Bob and me to a Russell homecoming.

At my Secretary of Transportation confirmation hearings, Bob introduced me by likening himself to Nathan Hale, saying he regretted that he had only one wife to give to his country's infrastructure.
(*U.S. Senate Photograph*)

Two of the most genuine and gracious people I know: my mother and President Ronald Reagan.

One of the best presents of the 1989 Christmas season was the settlement of the bitter labor dispute between Pittston Coal Company and the United Mine Workers. Joining me in my Department of Labor office to announce the resolution were (from left to right) Paul Douglas, then CEO of Pittston; Supermediator Bill Usery; and Rich Trumka, then president of the United Mine Workers, and now Secretary-Treasurer of the AFL-CIO. (© 1990 Focused Images—ARR)

Walking from the shipyards of Gdansk with Lech Walesa was an experience I'll always remember.

Our schnauzer, Leader, would love to be First Dog. Here I am with the proud father and one of a litter of puppies that had a Capitol Hill pedigree—the mother was a schnauzer belonging to Senator Strom Thurmond. (*U.S. Senate Photograph*)

A Thanksgiving prayer with President and Mrs. Bush, congressional leaders and the courageous forces of Operation Desert Storm. (*White House Photograph*)

This is what a balanced budget is all about: our children.
(*U.S. Senate Photograph*)

Elizabeth and I traveled to the beaches of Normandy to mark the fiftieth anniversary of D-Day in June 1994. Talking with my fellow veterans helped inspire me to take on one more mission.

Joking with David Letterman in 1995. One of my "Top 7 Ways to Balance the Budget" was to save government ink by replacing the lengthy William Jefferson Clinton signature with the much shorter Bob Dole signature. (*Photo by Alan Singer*)

In Russell with Elizabeth and Robin at the end of my presidential announcement tour on April 14, 1995—fifty years to the day after I was wounded in Italy. (*Kansas VFW*)

BOB DOLE

MAJORITY LEADER, U.S. SENATE
CHARTER MEMBER, VFW POST 6240
RUSSELL, KANSAS

DEDICATED ON THE 50TH ANNIVERSARY
OF WOUNDS HE SUSTAINED IN WWII

APRIL 14, 1995

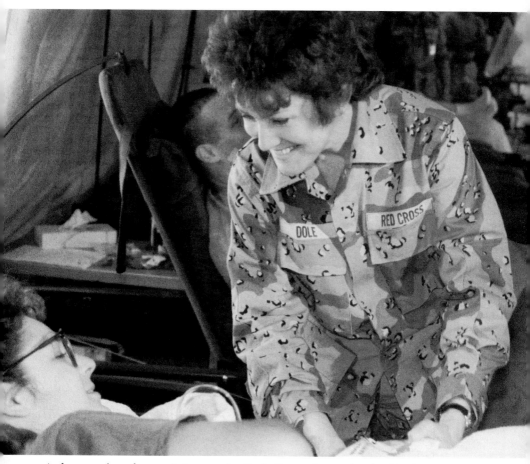

A few weeks after arriving at the Red Cross, I was in the Persian Gulf, visiting wounded American soldiers. (*American Red Cross Photograph*)

In Somalia in December 1992. This is when the horror of starvation becomes real—when you can touch it. (*American Red Cross Photograph*)

In Zaire in July 1994 with some of the 25,000 children separated from their families. The fate of these children haunts me still. (*American Red Cross Photograph*)

Surveying the devastating Midwest floods in the summer of 1993.
(*American Red Cross Photograph*)

One of the best parts of campaigning in New Hampshire was the chance to hit the slopes. I also managed to get in a little advertising for Bob! (© *Tim S. McGough*)

In the early weeks of the Reagan presidency, the committee's eleven Republicans resembled a theatrical cast on opening night—a little nervous and not quite sure of their lines. Our first vote was on Don Regan's nomination to be Secretary of the Treasury. By custom, when the committee staff director runs down the list of members for their votes he calls for the chairman's vote last. This time, Russell Long voted twice—once when his name was read and again when he heard the words "Mr. Chairman."

Realizing his mistake, Long joined in the laughter. "I not only vote with my chairman," he quipped, "I vote for my chairman."

My Senate predecessor, Frank Carlson, once told me about the time he received two telephone calls from the same chamber of commerce within an hour. In the first, someone demanded economy in government; in the second, someone demanded Carlson's support for a federally funded water project. Carlson chuckled over the story and what it said about human nature. David A. Stockman would have missed the humor.

A congressman from a safe district in Michigan when Reagan named him director of the Office of Management and Budget, Dave Stockman was a thirty-four-year-old closet zealot in a Prince Valiant haircut who saw the Reagan Revolution as a national means test. Like nearly everyone who dealt with Stockman, I was impressed by his intellect and numbers-crunching skills. As if he didn't know already, the budget director soon had plenty of evidence to confirm that one man's boondoggle is another's sacred cow, and that it's easier to eliminate waste, fraud and abuse in speeches than in the federal budget-making process.

The White House had decided that its first priority would be reductions in spending. Assuming that Congress went along with nearly $50 billion in proposed budget cuts, the Administration could fulfill its promise to lower personal-tax rates and make it easier for business to write off capital investment.

One of the real heroes of that momentous session was Budget Committee Chairman Pete V. Domenici. Even before

Domenici's colleagues formally took up the Reagan budget, storm signals were flying on the House side of Capitol Hill. Representative Jack Kemp of New York and other supply-siders claimed that their 30 percent tax cut would generate enough economic activity to pay for itself. Kemp predicted that any significant effort to reduce federal spending would lead to blood on the floors of Congress.

Kemp was right about one thing. The proposed spending cuts—most of which weren't cuts at all, but merely reductions in planned increases—touched off a public outcry. Some of the most fervent protests came from old friends and allies. The Veterans of Foreign Wars sent me a stiff letter about belt-tightening in veterans' programs and reminding me of the group's support in prior campaigns.

As a life member of the VFW, I have tremendous respect for its members and leadership. Even so, I could hardly conceal my surprise and disappointment when an organization whose members had distinguished themselves by service to their country in the past failed to see the importance of the current battle. My own duty was to control the growth of federal spending. Things finally became so confrontational that I decided it was best to return the VFW's 1980 campaign contribution—five hundred dollars, as I recall.

We made history on a daily, almost an hourly, basis in 1981. One afternoon in May, I excused myself from a discussion of food stamps in the Agriculture Committee to run over to Finance. "We've got a little package of budget cuts to consider," I explained. The "little package" covered twenty-four single-spaced legal-size pages. It sliced $22 billion from federal spending over the next two years, exceeding the White House's own request by a billion dollars.

Cutting taxes should be easier than cutting programs. But when the Finance Committee took up the original White House proposal, the only consensus on supply-side theory was negative. There was widespread agreement on the need to boost personal savings and encourage investment. The same was true of curtailing estate and gift taxes and applying tax indexing to safeguard workers' incomes against inflation.

There was the rub. Even with the budget cuts, there

wouldn't be enough money in the pot to pay for all these specifically targeted incentives and still afford Roth-Kemp in its
most generous form. Across the Hill, the House Ways and
Means Committee also had a new chairman. Tough as nails and
tested in Richard J. Daley's Chicago, where no prisoners are
taken and no quarter given, Democrat Dan Rostenkowski had
as much to prove to his troops as I did to mine.

After weeks of jousting, I knew Rosty might go along with
a two-year, 20 percent tax cut, something I mentioned in a
White House meeting with the President, his chief of staff,
James A. Baker III, and Baker's pragmatic second, Richard Dar-
man. I was barely back in my office when a White House mes-
senger delivered a note from the President ruling out any such
measure.

I told Reagan there was no way I could marshal eleven
votes in the Finance Committee for his original version. To
break the impasse, the President suggested that committee staff
members get together with their counterparts at Treasury and
try to work something out. A weekend of round-the-clock negotiations produced a modified tax cut of 25 percent, to be phased
in over three installments starting on October 1, 1981. The plan
was next broached to conservative Democrats in the House,
self-proclaimed Boll Weevils, who along with Republicans were
looking for ways to frustrate efforts by the House Democratic
leadership to delay, reduce and restructure the Reagan tax cuts.
By the time I went public with the new formula at the end of
May, it had already been embraced by Reagan loyalists in both
houses.

The ground was laid for congressional acceptance of a bill
to the White House's liking, despite a last-minute bidding war
with Rostenkowski, House Speaker Thomas P. "Tip" O'Neill
and others. On July 23, 1981, the House voted to cut personal
taxes by 25 percent. A final package that emerged from conference included individual retirement accounts and some generous ornaments that real-estate and other business interests
could hang on their Christmas trees. Only later would anyone
ask out loud whether the Economic Recovery Tax Act of 1981
was too much of a good thing.

After the vote, Reagan called me from Air Force One en

route to the West Coast. The President asked whether there was anything he could do to thank me for my work in committee and on the floor. I said there was. He could telephone my mother, who was in the hospital. Reagan placed the call within an hour. It was a characteristic gesture from one whose political instincts were equaled by his personal thoughtfulness.

ELIZABETH

In December 1980, Jim Baker asked me to become head of the White House Office of Public Liaison.

OPL was descended from an earlier Office of Public Affairs, which had been created during the Nixon Administration by White House counselor Bryce Harlow to tap the energy of organized Americans. As post–New Deal government took on the appearance of a broker state, Harlow saw the possibilities that modern communications offered for mobilizing grass-roots support behind a President's policies. At the press of a button in a Washington office, an avalanche of mailgrams or telephone calls from interested citizens could be directed at members of Congress. Subsequent administrations built on Harlow's original idea.

By Jimmy Carter's time, the Office of Public Affairs had become a mirror of the Democratic coalition, with separate operations addressing issues of concern to women, blacks, Hispanics, labor, business and consumers. Each one had an equal place at the bargaining table where public policy was crafted and past loyalties were rewarded. Under such a setup, White House staffers tended to become caseworkers for the groups they represented. Jim Baker had something else in mind. In Baker's view, we shouldn't be playing divide and conquer—let alone divide and be conquered *by*. Because economic reforms would dominate Ronald Reagan's first year in office, it was essential that Public Liaison rally the organized public around *our* agenda.

My staff would be half as large as that of my Carter Administration predecessor, Anne Wexler. What we lacked in numbers we would make up in versatility. For example, I asked Morton Blackwell to come on board to work with religious organizations and the defense community. As the youngest delegate supporting Barry Goldwater at the 1964 GOP convention, Blackwell had gilt-edged conservative credentials. But as a friendly emissary to right-to-work groups, Morton didn't always see eye to eye with Bob Bonitati, our labor liaison, who had been a leader in the professional Airline Pilots Association (AFL-CIO) before joining Public Liaison.

I was fortunate to land Red Cavaney as my deputy. Red had been connected with the White House since the early 1970s, when he helped with Richard Nixon's travels and directed Gerald Ford's advance office. His later forays into issue work brought Cavaney to the attention of Jim Baker, who in turn recommended him to me. Red and I hit it off from our first meeting. Not the least of his professional assets was a range of contacts, developed over his earlier White House stints, that made him a walking Rolodex.

One of my associates once remarked that the atmosphere around the White House was like the men's locker room at Burning Tree Country Club. There is a jackets-off, loose-tie informality that goes with the long hours, the high pressure and the slangy irreverence of the political fraternity. The language is politician's shorthand—colorful and to the point.

One morning at the regular eight o'clock staff meeting in the Roosevelt Room, I took a head count. There were thirty-two men in the room. And me. From grade school through the FTC, I had gotten used to firsts, but this was the first time in my career I ever felt sensitive to being "the woman" in a government setting.

Truth be told, my gender was less an obstacle than my marriage. In those early weeks, a lot of people inside and out of 1600 Pennsylvania Avenue shook their heads in disbelief when they were told that Bob and I didn't regularly exchange strategic information over dinner. After all, they reasoned, he was writing tax laws and I was promoting them as the Administration's number-one priority.

Bob laughed it off, bragging that he got more calls from

the White House than anyone on Capitol Hill, even if most of them were from his wife telling him what to put on the stove for dinner.

With me it was different. Business lobbyists would call my office hoping to get me to put in a word on their behalf with the Finance chairman. I had a stock reply: Call the Hill yourself.

I initially hoped to discuss in depth with Bob his work and its implications for the Reagan program. At Jim Baker's request I passed on an occasional message from the West Wing. But I discovered soon enough that Bob didn't want to talk shop extensively at home. He got plenty of that during the day. Just as quickly, I came to share his desire for an oasis from the job, one neutral zone that was more or less off limits to tax-leasing and the latest budget battle with OMB.

An exception occurred in the fall of 1981, when the Reagan Administration was backed against a wall over a controversial multibillion-dollar arms deal with Saudi Arabia. The dispute centered around five sophisticated early-warning planes known as AWACS. Around seven one evening, Red Cavaney, business liaison Wayne Valis and I were parceling out the names of undecided lawmakers, among whom Bob Dole's was prominent. The session came to an abrupt end when I said I was going home to cook dinner.

"Gee, that sounds nice," said Valis.

As a matter of fact, I told them, I planned a thick steak, candlelight—the whole nine yards.

"That's great, Elizabeth," said Valis. "Sounds really romantic. But isn't this a bit early for you to be going home? Don't you want to finish targeting these senators?"

"Wayne," I said, "you don't seem to understand. Tonight, Bob Dole is my target."

When I accepted Public Liaison, I didn't know much about the office or its functions. Today I still think very few people understand what it does, or fully appreciate its vital role in building support for a President's programs.

From prior experience, I had some definite ideas about how I wanted the office organized. You can rush from meeting to

meeting at the White House, confusing activity with achievement. I didn't want to fall into that trap, so I asked my staffers
for regular written reports, in part to ensure accountability but,
more important, to force everyone to think strategically as well
as tactically. The reports, in turn, were the basis for what we
called Red Flag Warnings. Each week, I collected red flags—
prospective political problems—and passed them on to Jim
Baker. The system gave us a chance to anticipate trouble and
hopefully to avoid it altogether. "There is no better way of
solving a problem," I told my staff, "than learning of it early
rather than late."

If the White House were a business, Public Liaison would
be the marketing and sales division. Our job was to make sure
the West Wing's ivory-tower types stayed in contact with the
world beyond the gates, that organized groups had their views
heard and considered, and that once official policy was determined it was supported. Failing this, we hoped to neutralize
opposition at the grass-roots level.

We did our market research by bringing in groups from
outside, often to meet with the President. In a typical day these
might include the Hispanic Chamber of Commerce, the International Longshoreman's Union, the VFW, Hadassah and the
Business Roundtable.

Success at OPL can be measured with two yardsticks. The
positive one gauges close legislative victories in which your efforts may have made the difference. Everyone understands winning. The other, less obvious, method is to list all the things that
could have gone wrong but didn't, thanks to your efforts. It's
like holding your finger in the dike: after two thousand meetings
that we set up in the White House, no one has embarrassed the
President with an unguarded comment or an outright attack.
It's sticking to a script, but allowing enough spontaneity for a
genuine two-way communication between the man in the Oval
Office and the millions who put him there.

There's something about the White House—what with the
marine in formal dress who salutes arriving visitors, the presidential seal over the West Wing entrance, the Secret Service
agents and the historical objects lining the hallways leading to

the Oval Office—that inspires reverence. It's the closest thing we have to a royal residence.

I was always struck that people who beat their breast in my office would fall into an awed silence the moment they were ushered into Ronald Reagan's presence.

I remember an industrialist who, outside of presidential earshot, voiced stinging criticism of certain budget proposals.

"But that's not what you told the President when you saw him earlier this afternoon," I said.

"Don't be silly, Elizabeth, I wasn't going to say anything *to the President.*"

Sometimes it was hard to get visitors to say anything at all. At one of the first meetings we arranged, the President pointed a finger at a visitor sitting a few feet away and said, "I'd like to hear your views. Tell me what's on your mind." The man went white as a sheet.

Ordinarily, President Reagan had an almost magical way of putting people at ease. I once brought in a white-haired Alabamian named Billy Stimson who represented the National Forest Products Association. Like the President, Stimson had been part of a World War II cavalry unit.

"Mr. President," said Stimson, "as one old cavalryman to another, I just want you to know that our cart has gone off the road and into a ditch. And we are here to ask for your help in putting our poor spavined horse back on his feet."

Stimson's appeal for tax relief and lower interest rates summed up what we were working for in the spring and summer of 1981. From the start, Public Liaison's schedule was dominated by the Reagan economic program. Coincidentally this meant that Bob and I were both coalition-building: while he was seeking fifty-one votes for the Reagan package on Capitol Hill, I was organizing popular support through OPL's far-flung network.

It takes a lot of work to arrange for a paper rainfall to hit Capitol Hill. And timing is essential. The whole effort—sending a message from the White House through trade associations and companies and finally to families and neighbors—takes off and you cross your fingers in hopes it returns to Capitol Hill at just the right moment in Congress' schedule. Fortunately, we had good intelligence sources on the Hill.

By the summer of 1981, Congress was considering the Reagan budget and tax cuts. With the President's superb ability to elicit public support, OPL was able to muster the combined resources of over a thousand trade associations, companies and citizen organizations. In order to test our developing coalition, word was passed that Jim Baker and I would like to see copies of specific legislative alerts being sent to grass-roots America. Then Jim and I followed through with random phone calls to thank organization and business leaders for their help. In no time at all, the Washington underground was carrying the message: Dole and Baker are taking names and want to see your homework.

When the Great Communicator turned up the heat on Congress, we were ready. Organizations like the U.S. Chamber of Commerce, the National Association of Manufacturers and the National Association of Wholesale Distributors blitzed Capitol Hill with mailgrams and postcards timed to coincide with each televised presidential appeal. The National Federation of Independent Business alone spent $175,000 per onslaught.

Dozens of companies included endorsements of the Reagan tax cut in their dividend envelopes. There was no way investors could miss the connection between Ronald Reagan's agenda and future prosperity.

Not everything was smooth sailing. One day OPL sponsored an event addressed by the Reverend Leon Sullivan, a Philadelphia minister who would later enlist corporate America to help end racial exploitation of South African workers. A big man with a voice to match, Sullivan is a shrewd idealist, well versed in how the political game is played. At a Roosevelt Room meeting attended by reporters, he expressed concern over the possible impact of Administration budget cuts on the poor. Yet he also promised to cooperate with White House efforts to plug holes in the social-safety net by utilizing private-sector resources. Sullivan was perfectly sincere, unlike some who said one thing in the Oval Office and another a half hour later on the White House driveway. He didn't mean for his comments to be takea as criticism. But he had no more control over press reaction than I had over the *New York Times* Op Ed page.

Long before Donald Regan invented the White House Shovel Brigade, I oversaw the West Wing Fire Patrol. We put out brushfires before they turned into infernos. Ronald Reagan was our fire chief. I'll never forget the afternoon he dropped by a Rose Garden event with a grin on his face, for our third encounter of that day.

"Elizabeth," he said, "we've got to stop meeting like this."

Day after day, in ceremonial sessions like this one, at substantive meetings on the issues and through behind-the-scenes persuasion, we fashioned a popular mandate for change.

The final test came in July 1981. Three days before the vote, President Reagan went on television with a last-minute call to arms. Over the next seventy-two hours, more than a million messages demanding enactment of the President's three-year, 25 percent tax cut inundated Capitol Hill.

Outflanked, outgunned and outmaneuvered, Tip O'Neill called it "a telephone blitz like this nation has never seen." Another member of O'Neill's leadership team marveled at the orchestration of public opinion. "The deals we could withstand," he told the *Washington Star,* "but not that damn Alexander Graham Bell."

BOB

Practical politics consists of ignoring the facts.

—Henry Adams

For the Reagan Administration, 1982 was a time of testing. Economic recession pushed unemployment to a postwar record. Night after night, television beamed pictures of soup lines and shuttered factory gates into millions of homes. Not since the electronic eye made Vietnam America's first living-room war had viewers seen such a barrage of highly emotional images.

The problem went deeper than that, of course. Financial

markets that were made skittish by the rising federal deficit weren't about to reduce interest rates. Resurgent Democrats talked about annulling the 1980 election. It wasn't an idle boast. Unless the economy improved by November 1982, the Democrats might regain control of the Senate, scuttling the third year of the Reagan tax cut and throwing into doubt the rebuilding of America's defenses after a decade of neglect.

All this was on my mind during the winter of 1981–82. Oddly enough, it seemed that whenever I spoke out against the deficit, somebody criticized me for lacking vision. I was called a latter-day Hoover, a green-eyeshade conservative who had attended too many chicken dinners and delivered too many austerity lectures to appreciate the new economics.

If the old-time religion says you can't endlessly spend more than you take in, then old-time religion is good enough for me. The real lack of vision was in those who buried their heads in the sand by refusing to confront the deficit. Their thoughts seemed fixed on the next election when they ought to have been thinking about the next generation, including seventy million or so baby-boomers who will have to wear the financial straitjacket fitted by elected officials addicted to credit-card government.

It was as if Washington had a new beatitude: Blessed are the young, for they shall inherit the national debt.

Real vision tries to reconcile people of seemingly opposite views, whatever the obstacles or the political risks. Yet early in 1982 politicians of both parties appeared determined to validate Henry Adams' cynical maxim by ignoring the economic facts of life. The White House understandably didn't want to tinker with a tax cut that was just beginning to take effect. Congressional Democrats, still smarting from their losses the previous summer, were in no mood to cooperate on a deficit-reduction package that included further spending cuts.

There was a vehicle for responsible action in Congress' own budget resolution, which called for spending reductions of $280 billion over a three-year period, and nearly $100 billion in new revenue. New revenue didn't have to mean new taxes, much less a reversal of the personal-tax cuts enacted the previous summer. Before doing anything else, I thought, we ought to collect what was already due. So Iowa's Charles E. Grassley and I introduced a package of tax-compliance measures designed to retrieve a large chunk of the estimated $100 billion that was owed annually but that went unreported to the IRS. In doing so, Chuck Grassley and I foreshadowed the sweeping tax-reform program of 1986 that put an end to the abuse of tax shelters while directing investment toward more productive channels.

What followed was a predictable game of chicken. Members of Congress, after all, are only human. They prefer handing out benefits to enforcing fiscal discipline. Revenue bills are supposed to originate in the House, but Dan Rostenkowski preferred to let the Senate Republicans take the heat on this one. He'd wait to see what we came up with before committing himself. Russell Long told me bluntly not to expect help from Finance Committee Democrats unless Republicans put together a plan that would pass muster with the White House.

Knowing that our ability to govern was being tested, I invited other Republicans on the committee to an economic conclave in a second-floor hearing room of the Dirksen Senate Office Building. Over the next three days and nights a rare team spirit grew up among Rockefeller Republicans like Rhode Island's John Chafee and New Right activists like Idaho's Steve Symms. There wasn't a single leak from our meetings, despite a near-suffocating mob of reporters and lobbyists in the hall outside.

While I was walking down the corridor one evening, someone remarked that every one of the $200-an-hour lobbyists camping outside our door was wearing Gucci shoes.

"They'll be barefoot in the morning," I replied.

A deliberately informal atmosphere inside the hearing room didn't mask the difficulties confronting us. Unlike the situation in the summer of 1981, we faced choices much harder than how much money to give away.

As far as the original three-year tax cut was concerned, I wouldn't consider repealing it, delaying it or rewriting it. Instead, we removed a few ornaments from the 1981 Christmas tree. We cut back on some generous provisions dealing with business depreciation. We also restrained an accountant's dream called safe-harbor leasing that cost the Treasury $22 billion. The provision allowed profitable companies to reduce their tax bills, sometimes to the vanishing point, by purchasing investment tax credits from money-losers. It may have been a great deal for someone like General Electric or Occidental Petroleum, but it wasn't so hot for the average taxpayer.

Will Rogers used to say that the American tax code produced more liars than anything but golf. Jimmy Carter called it a scandal. Anyone who truly cared about fairness would object to a system so riddled with loopholes that it looked like Swiss cheese and smelled like Limburger.

The result of our work, the Tax Equity and Fiscal Responsibility Act of 1982 (TEFRA), brought the deficit down by nearly $100 billion, with barely 10 percent of the money coming from new taxes. The rest resulted from closing some of the more offensive loopholes and enforcing compliance with existing taxes. One of the smallest revenue sources in TEFRA caused us the biggest headache. The White House, having said no to a gasoline tax, sent Finance Committee Republicans scurrying to embrace an idea straight out of the Administration's own budget proposals. Withholding 10 percent of interest and dividend income was a concept initially broached by Don Regan's Treasury Department. The President himself signified his approval in calls to committee members, pointing out that withholding could be worth as much as three or four billion dollars a year.

Such numbers carried little weight compared with the popular uproar generated by angry bankers. Needing eleven votes on the committee to pass withholding, I finally convinced Hawaii Democrat Spark M. Matsunaga to side with Republicans (all except John Chafee, who had already printed 1982 campaign brochures boasting of his earlier opposition to tax withholding). Inexplicably, Treasury balked at granting a minor tax break to the Hawaiian sugar industry; I balked back at Treasury.

Withholding secured, the White House signed on with us for the whole TEFRA bill after receiving assurances that spending cuts would predominate in the final package. The President afterward complained that he didn't get three dollars in budget reductions for every dollar of new revenue. As far as the Finance Committee was concerned, we reduced spending on programs within our jurisdiction in line with the three-for-one formula. Other major areas of the budget, including defense and federal pay, also met White House targets. As later estimated by the Congressional Budget Office, the Administration itself could have achieved the majority of the savings without congressional action, mostly through managerial reforms and reduced interest on the debt.

Throughout June and July of 1982, I was shelled from all sides. Democrats wouldn't accept a tax-reform package that bore a Republican imprint. The Guccis were out in full force, and so were supply-siders quick to accuse me of betraying the Reagan Revolution. They called me a closet liberal. I was certainly no liberal. Nor was I a lemming.

A dramatic confrontation occurred late on the night of July 22. Senators adopted by a lopsided margin Arkansas Democrat David Pryor's amendment striking out part of TEFRA requiring restaurants to report waiters' tips up to 7 percent of gross sales. Weary but happy, the Guccis went home to celebrate. I had anticipated something like this happening, and had asked Finance Committee staffers to draw up a list of "dogs and cats" —revenue raisers we could add on the spot. It was after two o'clock in the morning when I struck back with my amendment to replace $2.8 billion by cutting in half the deductibility of business-entertainment expenses.

For years liberals had been denouncing the three-martini lunch. Here was a chance for them to put up or shut up. It was a revealing debate. Ted Kennedy suggested that another way to make up the lost revenue was to do away with the third year of the Reagan tax cut. But Kennedy was in the minority, and the three-martini-lunch amendment carried the day, 57–40. Once the sun came up over Washington, Gucci jubilation turned to alarm. By the time the bill reached conference, restaurateurs were offering to report tips up to 8 percent of gross sales in exchange for restoration of the status quo on entertainment expenses. I was more than happy to accept their offer.

The final showdown over TEFRA involved North Carolina Senators Jesse A. Helms and John P. East, both Republicans. Accepting an increase in cigarette taxes was no way for either of them to win votes in the nation's number-one tobacco state. Helms softened the political impact by limiting the tax hike to three years. He then promised to support the final bill if his vote meant the difference between victory and defeat.

Despite Reagan's personal intervention and a round of last-minute phone calls from the White House, Howard Baker was still trying desperately to plug holes in Administration ranks. In the predawn hours of July 23, Baker stood at the entrance to the Republican cloakroom, reminding Helms of his pledge.

"Jesse, we need your vote."

"I can't do it, Howard."

"We need your vote, Jesse."

"It's political suicide, Howard."

"We need your vote now, Jesse."

Silently, Helms made his way onto the floor. At the call of his name, he responded "Aye." So did John East. Together they made the difference, as TEFRA passed, 50–47. Not one Democrat broke party ranks to vote for the bill.

That same week the stock market took off, soaring over three hundred points by the end of the year and launching the great bull market that took it to unprecedented heights over the next five years. Interest rates headed south. The recession bottomed out in November and began reversing itself the next month. Voters, reassured that the deficit was being addressed, returned to office the same number of Republican senators we had going into the election. And GOP losses in the House were far less severe than might be expected. Of even greater importance over the long haul was the fact that TEFRA helped the Republican Party retain its historic reputation for fiscal integrity. To lose that would be a body blow.

Another heated debate taking place simultaneously with TEFRA involved extension of the 1965 Voting Rights Act. Civil-rights groups argued that electoral results were enough to show violations of the original statute, by excluding minorities from office. Opponents, including Attorney General William

French Smith, insisted that legal action must be based on evidence of a deliberate intent to discriminate.

For weeks those of us on the Senate Judiciary Committee tried to decide between "results" and "intent." As one of a handful of uncommitted members, I was ideally positioned to play the honest broker's role. Beyond attempts at compromise, I had my own obligations to consider. Kansans have a special view toward human rights, one rooted in the agonies preceding statehood in 1861, when opposing bands of Free State Jayhawkers and pro-slavery Bushwackers made "Bleeding Kansas" a dress rehearsal for the American Civil War. After the war, the state welcomed tens of thousands of black "Exodusters" from the impoverished South. It led the Union in approving a constitutional amendment giving blacks the vote.

From a practical standpoint, there was no way the President could refuse to sign an extension when it reached his desk. Here, then, was a chance for me to allay conservative fears about quotas and to strengthen the bill. Along the way Republicans might also win some credit from traditionally suspicious blacks and Hispanics.

With the help of Chuck Grassley and others in the conservative mainstream, on May 3 the Judiciary Committee adopted my amendment that accepted results as a valid criteria for legal action while specifically ruling out proportional representation as a remedy for voter discrimination. The 14–4 margin was large enough to prevent opposing lawmakers from burying the bill in oratory. That same day, Reagan hailed the action and pledged his own support for a twenty-five-year extension of the Voting Rights Act.

Actions like this led to speculation about "the new Bob Dole." According to popular theory, Elizabeth was responsible for my sudden mellowing. Armchair psychologists reversed the old adage to suggest that "bedfellows make strange politics."

With all due respect to Elizabeth, it would be unusual if age and experience hadn't broadened my perspective. In truth, most of those who talked about a new Bob Dole hadn't known the old one very well. What had changed was not my character or my personality but my role in the Senate, where success is impossible to achieve unless you have the votes on your side. In

January 1981 I became part of a majority, in position to put forward a constructive program and to line up the votes for its enactment.

Something else. Shuttling between the Agriculture and Finance Committees gave me an unusual perspective. As a fiscal conservative, I believe that the best form of social justice is having a job in the private sector, with a real paycheck that isn't dependent on the whim of some congressional committee or vulnerable to shifts in a sluggish, overtaxed economy.

Let's face it, however: some people have nowhere to turn but to government. Much of my work on the Agriculture Committee revolved around the legitimate needs of these people. In Finance, the special pleaders are well heeled, well connected and wall to wall. Not so in Agriculture. There's no Poor PAC to remind us of all the fatherless families struggling to maintain their living without sacrificing their dignity. Poor people don't have lobbyists who take congressmen and their staffs to lunch on K Street.

In the closing months of 1982, bankers everywhere targeted me for an avalanche of postcards and personal appeals, all calling for repeal of 10 percent withholding on interest and dividends, appeals that I resisted. Old friends in the industry did everything but take back their toaster. It didn't matter so much for big banks: they had computers and personnel to comply with withholding requirements. Smaller financial institutions, by contrast, found the additional cost and paperwork burdensome.

The issue came to a head for me early in 1983, at a meeting of the Kansas Bankers Association in Dodge City. Waiting for me outside the room were two severely disabled young people with their parents. Tim was in a special wheelchair, unable to move anything except his eyes. Carla was only slightly more mobile. Both wanted to talk to me about help in gaining greater access to a more physically independent lifestyle. So often in politics, you're at the mercy of your schedulers. But sometimes instead of racing ahead to the next meeting, you need to slow down and talk with real people who have real problems.

On my way back to Washington I kept thinking about Tim

and Carla. What they faced was far more serious than the loss of a few tenths of one percent of compound interest. Back home, I sat in our bedroom and told Elizabeth how deeply moved I had been by this encounter. "I've been meaning for years to start a foundation for disabled persons," I said, "and I haven't done it. This is the time."

Since then, the Dole Foundation has raised over $7 million to address issues like job training and placement for disabled workers. One of the foundation's grants has assisted New York City's National Theater Workshop for the Handicapped teach its members advanced communications skills. In Kentucky, a challenge grant paved the way for a fast-food restaurant that employs the mentally retarded. Exceptional children in Virginia are being helped to adjust to the working world. Seattle students are being taught campground-management skills. Two dozen epileptics once thought of as unemployable have been trained for work through the Epilepsy Foundation of Ohio.

In the end, bank withholding was largely repealed. But I didn't lose, because out of that fight came the impetus for the Dole Foundation, which, through the generous support of thousands of donors, has invested in the most precious capital of all —human potential.

ELIZABETH

Congressmen weren't the only ones who liked the 1981 tax cuts better than their 1982 sequel. Part of my job at Public Liaison was to convince businessmen that the ultimate bottom line was a sound national economy. And it wasn't easy getting captains of industry to embrace a package whose benefits, unlike its costs, were theoretical.

Jack Albertine was an exception. As head of the American Business Conference, Albertine represented some of the country's most dynamic firms—tomorrow's IBMs.

"Jack," I told him, "we need a leader."

"Well, Elizabeth, it's not as if we were talking about cutting taxes."

"No, Jack, we're not. But you know as well as I do that we've got to get the deficit under control. The only way to convince the markets we mean business is by removing some of the Christmas-tree ornaments. If we don't do it now, interest rates will stay up. And you can forget about a growth economy."

Albertine paused for a moment. "But, Elizabeth, I haven't even seen the full bill."

"If it's any consolation," I said, "I haven't seen it either. But I will. And soon. And then I'm going to need you to lead the charge."

"Oh, what the heck, Elizabeth," sighed Albertine. "Count me in."

I also signed on Prudential's Bob Beck. Beck joined us even though he'd been warned that TEFRA might cost his company as much as $200 million. Reporters asked him why.

"It's good for America," said Beck, "and whatever is good for America will be good for Prudential."

Throughout this period, I worked to pave an avenue of trust between the White House and the business world. Loyalty, after all, is a two-way street. And the Prompt Pay Act of 1982 gave me a chance to return the support of businesses much smaller than Prudential.

For years, vendors doing business with the federal government often waited six months or more for payment. Once the 1981–82 recession hit, cash flow became a life-and-death matter for thousands of small and medium-sized firms. A drive was launched on Capitol Hill to require Uncle Sam to reimburse vendors on time or pay an interest penalty like any other customer. I supported the legislation as an exercise in elemental fairness and argued the points within the councils of government.

To say that not everyone in the Administration shared my logic is an understatement. Don Regan claimed it would cost too much. So did the Office of Management and Budget, the Pentagon and practically every agency that had ever bought goods and services with taxpayer dollars.

I arranged a meeting for Mike McKevitt of the National

Federation of Independent Business with the President. The session was held in the Roosevelt Room, a few steps from the Oval Office. Besides the President, McKevitt and myself, those around the table included Don Regan, Dave Stockman and Stockman's deputy at OMB, Ed Harper.

McKevitt came right to the point. "Mr. President," he said, "we have a problem. As a businessman, I have to pay my bills on time. As a citizen, I *certainly* have to pay my taxes on time. [Don Regan was starting to squirm in his chair.] But, Mr. President, when the federal government owes me money, it can pay whenever it feels like. And there's not a thing I can do about it."

"That's wrong," the President said. "I came here to change things like that."

"Mr. President," said McKevitt, "I know a perfect way you can do just that. We have legislation pending on the Hill that would take care of the problem once and for all."

"I can't imagine any reason why we wouldn't support it," said Reagan.

I glanced over at the Secretary of the Treasury, who looked as though he were about to detonate. Regan cleared his throat.

"Mr. President," he said, "there are some technical problems with the bill—"

Reagan cut him off. "I'm sure we can work them out, Don. The important thing is that we support the concept. We certainly don't want people calling Uncle Sam a deadbeat. Do we?"

Heads nodded all around. The Prompt Payment Bill was on its way to prompt enactment.

Coming on top of our other victories, this latest skirmish enhanced Public Liaison's credibility at both ends of Pennsylvania Avenue. I now felt able to offer bolder counsel at senior staff meetings. Like pressing presidential pollster Richard Wirthlin to sample public reaction on two fronts where the Administration seemed vulnerable. One was fairness. Administration budget cuts were widely portrayed as the thin end of a wedge dividing the poor—especially poor women—from the rest of society. The other issue haunting Republicans was the gender gap. Wirthlin's surveys subsequently confirmed that many Americans saw a White House tilt toward affluent white males. Left unaddressed, fairness and the gender gap could constitute a one-two punch against every GOP candidate in the upcoming elections.

In the 1980 campaign, President Reagan had gone out of his way to assure women voters that although he opposed the Equal Rights Amendment, he was committed to rooting out vestiges of discrimination in the legal code. Carrying out a campaign promise, the Reagan Administration established a Legal Equity Task Force, followed by the Fifty States Project—both intended to uncover discriminatory language in federal and state statutes.

Clearly, more had to be done. In August 1982 I was made head of a White House Coordinating Council on Women which was charged with increasing opportunities for women both within the Administration and in the country at large, the latter through presidential initiatives, directives and specific legislative proposals. The Administration also sponsored legislation that would make it easier for mothers to collect billions in court-ordered child-support payments. And Social Security laws were redrawn to equalize benefits for widows and widowers.

When Bob Dole introduced his own package of pension-law reforms, it revived the talk about the two of us working as some kind of political tag team. These people didn't realize how little time we had to compare notes. Nor did they understand how we can compartmentalize the issues we're working on. At one point during the negotiations over the 1983 budget, Bob said to me one evening, "Elizabeth, I'm not going to be able to talk to you about what I'm doing."

And he didn't. But then, he wasn't the only one of us with official secrets.

Early in his presidency, Ronald Reagan told me about the strains he had felt as governor of California. "Each morning began with someone standing before my desk describing yet another disaster," he said. "The feeling of stress became almost unbearable. I had the urge to look over my shoulder for someone I could pass the problem to. One day it came to me that I was looking in the wrong direction. I looked up instead of back. I'm still looking up. I couldn't face one more day in this office if I didn't know I could ask God's help and it would be given."

My own spiritual journey began many years ago, in a Carolina home where Sunday was the Lord's Day, reserved for acts of mercy and my grandmother's unforgettable Bible stories. Mom Cathey was such a perfect role model it was only natural that I should want to follow in her footsteps.

From an early age I was active in the church. But as we move along, how often in our busy lives something seems to get in the way of a more than ritualistic faith. It may be money, or power, or prestige. In my case, it was career. More specifically, the Holy Grail of public service became very nearly all-consuming. I was satisfied with nothing less than my best. Understandable enough but, as you can imagine, it becomes pretty demanding when you're trying to foresee every difficulty and realize every opportunity. It's even harder on those around you. My work left little time to be a friend to friends, let alone to the friendless.

Ironically, this form of perfectionism, so different from my grandmother's selfless spirituality, began crowding out what Mom Cathey had taught me were life's most important objectives. Sunday had become just another day of the week. Gradually, over a period of years, I realized that though I was blessed with a beautiful marriage and a challenging career, my life was close to spiritual starvation.

I prayed about this and, no faster than I was ready, I believe God led me to the people and the experiences that would transform my life. Mine has not been a road-to-Damascus experience, but a continuing search for guidance and the true perspective that comes with the strengthening of faith.

Growing up in Salisbury, I had cherished the ties that bind a permanent congregation. It was a feeling I missed in the non-denominational atmosphere at Duke and Harvard. Then, at the Foundry Methodist Church on Washington's Sixteenth Street, I found a pastor who urged me to join a spiritual-growth group that tried to relate personal faith to everyday experience. Each Monday night I left the White House and went to a church near Dupont Circle. I climbed a flight of stairs to a second-floor room sparsely furnished with an old couch and some chairs. The nine members of the group ranged in age from thirty to sixty-six. Our occupations and our politics were eclectic.

Soon I was sharing feelings that I would never have expressed to White House colleagues. We all felt a common need to stretch spiritually. Each of us was looking for answers, and depending on the others for help in phrasing the right questions. During these Monday-night meetings, for example, I came face to face with a compulsion to do things right, and the companion drive to constantly please. Gradually, I began to redefine perfectionism the way my grandmother had taught it. Some people define strength as independence, self-reliance and resourcefulness, but I have learned that real strength, inner strength, comes from a dependence on the one source who can replenish life with the power that comes from above.

I've also discovered that Sundays *can* be set aside for spiritual and personal rejuvenation without disastrous effects on your work week. With our frenetic schedules, Sunday is more precious than ever to Bob and me. In the morning we go to church services. Later we might have brunch with friends or just relax with the Sunday papers and a good book.

I'm a long way from where I want to be. At times I have even wondered whether I am trying to tackle spiritual growth with that same perfectionist zeal that prompts a man to pray, "Please, Lord, give me patience—and I need it right now!" One of my most cherished possessions is Mom Cathey's Bible. I love to read notes she wrote in its margins when she couldn't sleep some nights, including this notation next to Psalm 139: "May 22, 1952, 1:00 A.M.—my prayer: 'Search me, O God, and know my heart—try me, and know my thoughts. See if there be any wicked way in me, and lead me in the way everlasting.' "

My grandmother has never exerted more influence than she does today, when I am reminded that what we do on our own matters little—what counts is what God chooses to do through us. Life is more than a few years spent on self-indulgence or career advancement. It's a privilege, a responsibility and a stewardship to be met according to His calling.

This came home to me with special force in early January 1983, when President Reagan invited me to join his Cabinet as Secretary of Transportation. I didn't go to political advisers for counsel. I talked it over with the Monday-night group. Jenna

Dorn, who then worked for Senator Mark Hatfield and would later become my strong right arm at DOT, DOL and the American Red Cross, said I had no choice but to accept. "Think what it would mean for women!" she exclaimed.

When earlier rumors about a Cabinet appointment reached us, Bob and I had talked it over. He said it was a natural progression, and encouraged me, even though it might cause occasional conflicts with his Senate agenda or his prospects as a candidate for national office.

Since I knew he would approve, I decided to surprise him. But Jim Baker leaked the news to Bob, whispering in his ear at a meeting of the presidential commission on Social Security, "You might want to turn on the TV at eight o'clock tonight. I have a hunch you'll be interested in what the President has to say."

I went straight from the presidential press conference where my appointment was announced to my Public Liaison office. For the next two hours I called associates in the business, labor and other constituent communities with whom I had worked in the past and whose cooperation I would need at DOT. For most of the evening, Bob sat nearby, enjoying my excitement and the whirlwind of activity.

My confirmation hearing was set for January 16, 1983. Bob introduced me to members of the Senate Commerce Committee. As for himself, he said that he could identify with Nathan Hale. "I only regret that I have but one wife to give for my country's infrastructure."

BOB

You know what leadership is? It is the ability to get men to do what they don't want to do and like it.

—HARRY S. TRUMAN

The pace of American democracy is often likened to the tortoise, but popular government resembles the turtle in another way. The only way to make progress is by sticking your neck out. That's what I did on Social Security throughout Ronald Reagan's first term. For my efforts I almost got my head chopped off.

In the spring of 1981, the Reagan Administration proposed a scaling back of Social Security provisions dealing with student benefits and burial payments. The Administration also called for substantial penalties on early retirement, a thorough review of disability cases and the elimination of a $122-a-month minimum benefit going to three million recipients.

The sweeping changes produced near-panic on Capitol Hill, where almost no one wanted to confront the subject. I instructed staff members to quietly devise a long-range plan anyway, one that could satisfy both the retirees who received Social Security benefits and the wage earners who paid for them.

When Spencer Rich of the *Washington Post* wrote a front-page story detailing the staff's work, any chance we had for an early rescue attempt went out the window. In September 1981 Reagan backtracked on the issue of minimum benefits. He invited leaders of both parties to join him in "removing Social Security once and for all from politics." To begin the progress, Reagan appointed a national commission to examine the system's weaknesses and report its findings back within twelve months.

The blue-ribbon panel is a staple of modern government, one that Reagan would employ to win backing for his Central American policies and the MX missile. It is also an acknowledgment of political gridlock by representatives who are unable to make representative government work.

I was one of seven lawmakers named to the National Commission on Social Security Reform. The chairman was Alan Greenspan, Gerald Ford's favorite economist and now chairman of the Federal Reserve Board. On the other side, to watch out for labor's interests, was AFL-CIO president Lane Kirkland. Tip O'Neill was represented by former Social Security Commissioner Robert Ball, and the ageless Representative Claude Pepper of Florida carried the banner for the organized elderly. Rounding out the roster were emissaries from the business world led by Prudential's Robert Beck.

Tip O'Neill had his own solution to the Social Security

crisis: eliminate Republicans from Congress. Commission members paid less attention to party standings than to a different set of numbers. Social Security would soon go broke. According to demographers, when the baby-boom generation reached its peak earning power in the 1990s, the system would be in good health—but next month was another story. Social Security was paying out $30,000 more a minute than it took in, forcing it, late in 1982, to dip into reserves for $17 billion.

Raise taxes. Cut benefits. We had to find a compromise in there someplace.

The Reagan Administration properly refused to accept new payroll taxes. Republican commissioners reminded those across the table that under the Carter Administration in 1977 a scheduled series of payroll-tax increases that added up to the largest tax bill in U.S. history had been enacted to rescue the system—and here we were, five years later, trying to stave off total collapse. The problem could not be solved by taking $100 billion out of general revenues, as some suggested. We didn't *have* any general revenues—only a general debt. Politically and financially, however, there was no way to raise the $150 to $175 billion required to put the system on a sound footing through benefit cuts alone.

As the December 31 deadline neared, the commission was stalemated. Reagan reluctantly extended its life by two weeks. But neither the White House nor Tip O'Neill was anxious to embrace a compromise that had something in it to offend nearly everyone. So long as the President and the Speaker stayed aloof from the negotiations, commissioners resembled a pair of ball teams that had the talent to win but lacked a star pitcher.

What happened next bears little resemblance to the orderly processes described in civics books. The Ninety-eighth Congress convened for the first time on January 3, 1983. That morning, Daniel Patrick Moynihan came up to me on the Senate floor. He had read an article I'd written on Social Security for the *Washington Post* and had been encouraged by its description of "relatively modest steps" needed to save the system.

"Are we going to let this commission go down the tubes without giving it one more try?" asked Moynihan.

"Let's talk," I said. "Let's get ahold of Ball." Robert Ball was O'Neill's representative.

The next day, Ball, Moynihan and I met in a Finance Committee hideaway office. The results were promising enough for me to alert Alan Greenspan, and Moynihan invited Republican Congressman Barber B. Conable of New York. Our major stumbling blocks were payroll-tax increases and corresponding benefit cuts. Ball's solution to the first was to move up the already scheduled tax increases, which he would offset with tax credits for employers. When Claude Pepper showed flexibility on cost-of-living adjustments, the way was cleared to overcome the second hurdle.

Forty-eight hours later, we brought the White House into the negotiations. On the evening of January 5, Jim Baker convened the Gang of Seven—the original nucleus, plus Dave Stockman and himself—at his Foxhall Road home in northwest Washington. It was the start of an eleven-day marathon, conducted without staffers and under strict security. One morning I spotted in my rearview mirror a posse of reporters hot on my trail, but I managed to ditch them.

There was no way to blunt press curiosity about what was going on at Baker's house. Few people at the time caught the irony that a commission created because Congress wished to delegate its decision-making power had now delegated its authority to the Gang of Seven. Such are the birth pangs of public policy.

On January 13, in a San Francisco speech, Baker floated a trial balloon based on our talks. He said Reagan might accept some acceleration of already scheduled payroll taxes as long as they were balanced by spending reforms. The Administration pulled back from its opposition to taxing Social Security benefits of upper-income recipients. The logjam was breaking.

On Saturday, January 15, 1983, the Gang of Seven reassembled at Blair House. Bob Ball served as go-between with Tip O'Neill, who was playing in a West Coast golf tournament. While Ball talked by phone with O'Neill and others, I crossed Pennsylvania Avenue to have lunch with Jim Baker and the commission's trio of business representatives. Over a bowl of chili in the White House mess, Bob Beck and his colleagues agreed to give a little to save a lot.

Later that day, Ball, Greenspan, Moynihan and I worked out the final settlement in an hour. A light snow was falling when we left Blair House. Reagan and O'Neill had both indicated they would accept whatever we came up with, just as long as it was adopted by a large majority.

Greenspan explained the details of the compromise to the rest of the commission. No one was ecstatic over a package that would postpone cost-of-living increases due July 1, 1983, would accelerate the schedule of payroll taxes, and would give a tax credit for workers and employers to help offset any economic dislocation caused by the change. The retirement age would gradually be raised from sixty-five to sixty-seven. Upper-income retirees would pay income tax on half their Social Security benefits.

Still, it was the best a democratic government could do. The final vote was twelve in favor, three opposed. Greenspan called Baker at the White House, and Ball telephoned O'Neill. By nightfall, the President and the Speaker were in agreement for the first time.

The *Los Angeles Times* said it best: "The commission's job was to save the system by showing how its books could be balanced without hurting the 36 million retired Americans who depend on its checks each month. It has done that job well. It is now up to Congress to show the same political maturity in implementing the proposals that the commission showed in shaping them."

In March, Congress accepted the *Times*'s challenge. Reagan signed the bill into law on April 20.

I received a letter from Claude Pepper: "We could never have produced the solution without your skill and sincerest desire to see that our Commission make a meaningful contribution to the saving of Social Security. You never lost hope and faith in our accomplishing the immeasurable task of saving Social Security as a sound and solvent institution for the next seventy-five years."

• • •

In the midst of Social Security bailout negotiations, I accepted an invitation to speak at the capital's annual Gridiron Dinner. It seemed a good time to place Washington's breathless self-obsession in perspective, so I quoted words Justice Oliver Wendell Holmes had used half a century earlier: "We are the leaders of the whole stream of life. We lead it in the same sense that small boys lead a circus parade when they march ahead of it. But if they turn down a side street, the parade goes on."

Turning to President Reagan, I congratulated him for leading the country well and for avoiding policy side streets. "And I take heart from the knowledge that whatever you or I or any one of us may do, the American parade will go on, propelled by a vision two centuries old—the dream of an inclusive society, where individual rights are wedded to social responsibilities, and freedom to choose means obligation to serve."

The biggest laugh of the evening came at the end of my remarks. I flatly stated that under no circumstances would Dole be a candidate for President in 1984.

Elizabeth jumped to her feet.

"Speak for yourself, sweetheart," she said.

CHAPTER NINE

Mr. Leader, Madam Secretary

ELIZABETH

On February 7, 1983, I became the newest member of President Reagan's Cabinet. Bob assured reporters that there'd be no problem distinguishing our professional roles: as Finance Committee chairman, he was in charge of loopholes; as Secretary of Transportation, I was in charge of potholes.

Potholes would be the least of my concerns. Among its many responsibilities, the Department of Transportation channels highway funds to the states, regulates the movement of hazardous materials and inspects commercial and private aircraft. It wages war on illicit drugs at sea through the Coast Guard and campaigns against drunk drivers on land. Promoting commercial development of outer space, DOT is one branch of government for which the sky is no limit.

Drew Lewis, my predecessor, left some very large shoes to fill. Besides the administrative challenges that come with 100,000 employees and a $27 billion budget, there were conflicting demands from auto executives, railroad unions and congressional chairmen, for whom Cabinet officers come and go while the seniority system is forever. Finally, my years as Secretary would coincide with a dramatic period of transition, as industries accustomed to four decades of Washington's economic oversight were forced to adjust to a freer, more competitive climate.

222

My first week in office provided a taste of crisis management when independent truckers went on strike over heavy-vehicle taxes. By the time long-distance haulers were back on the road, I had identified $70 million to restore Washington's venerable Union Station, closed for five years due to congressional mismanagement. When reopened in 1988, this historic landmark soon became a magnet for tourists and Washington residents alike, housing dozens of shops, restaurants, and theaters, as well as a first-class transportation center. I would also need to implement complex congressional legislation doubling federal funds that assist states in repairing highways and transit systems.

In developing a broader policy agenda, I contacted former Secretaries and other respected members of the transportation fraternity. One of them cautioned me to stay away from public-safety issues, which he thought would only bring political trouble. Whenever there's a disaster in the air or on the ground, you can count on emotional media coverage, he said, and everyone will turn to the Transportation Secretary for explanations. Good news, on the other hand, barely gets yawning respect.

I didn't take the advice. In the limited time I'd have to serve, I could think of no greater satisfaction than knowing that my efforts might contribute to the saving of lives. Safety across all modes of transportation would be a dominant theme of my tenure. First, I asked to review what was on the drawing boards and in the research labs. One promising highway safety idea was an additional brake light to be mounted at the base of a car's rear window. The new light had been through five years of successful tests on taxis and police cars, so I took it off the shelf and made it standard equipment for 1986 vehicles. The device cost consumers less than twenty dollars a car, but studies that reached my desk estimated that when all cars are equipped with the tiny lamp we can eliminate some 900,000 rear-end crashes annually.

A much more difficult challenge arose from a long-standing dispute between government officials and leaders of the auto and insurance industries over air bags and other passive restraints in new cars. The passive-restraint requirement, known as Rule 208, had been promulgated by the Carter Administration, rescinded in the early months of the Reagan presidency, and appealed all the way to the Supreme Court. In the summer of 1983 the Court remanded 208 with specific instructions for additional departmental review. It was time once and for all to settle the issue. For nearly twenty years, while the lawyers argued and the politicians debated, people had been dying on the highways.

We knew from previous tests that air bags alone wouldn't stop the carnage. Although they provide excellent protection in front and front-angular crashes, they are not designed to deploy in a rear-end collision or a rollover. They were also expensive, but even when prices came down, it would still take a decade or more to equip the entire American automotive fleet with air bags. And since virtually no air bag–equipped cars were on the road, many consumers thought wrongly that the air bags would inflate when you crossed the railroad tracks! Safety belts, on the other hand, were proven lifesavers and already standard equipment. So at the same time that I arranged for five hundred government vehicles outfitted with air bags to continue testing, I also attempted to involve the American people themselves in the decision-making process through their state legislators.

Working for Rule 208 was the toughest policy issue I have ever encountered. Our goal: to save as many lives as possible, as quickly as possible, and break the long stalemate with a sound regulation that would stand up on appeal in the courts. That meant providing incentives for use of safety belts and the production of air bags. Therefore, the rule was designed to spawn a vigorous competition between proponents of state safety-belt laws and those advocating air bags and passive belts, thereby obtaining both the legislation and the new safety features.

Under the plan we devised, unless by 1986 two thirds of the population was covered by state safety-belt laws that met strict federal criteria, manufacturers would have to install either air bags or passive belts in at least 10 percent of all '87-model cars. This figure would rise over four years until it reached 100 percent in model-year 1990.

Statistics prove the rule worked just as designed. Since my plan was announced in the summer of 1984, forty-nine states and the District of Columbia have enacted belt-use laws. Safety-belt use has risen from 12 percent when I became Secretary of Transportation to 68 percent today. From 1982 through 1994, an estimated 65,290 lives were saved by safety belts, and more than 1.5 million moderate to critical injuries prevented.

In 1984, there were only a handful of air bag–equipped cars on the road. That number now stands at 40 million. Detroit understands that safety sells, and all model-year 1998 cars will have driver and passenger air bags, as will 1999-model light trucks. Air bags have saved more than 1,500 lives to date.

The lives saved and injuries prevented by increased use of safety belts and air bags have, in turn, allowed us to save literally billions of dollars through reduced health insurance costs and increased productivity.

It's a bleak truism that tragedy often precedes reform. A drunk driver snuffs out the life of a child—and public outrage leads to tougher laws and stiffer sentencing. Take it from one who lost an uncle to a drunk driver: the human costs can scar a family for generations.

Of the more than forty thousand Americans who die each year on the nation's highways, four out of every ten lose their lives in alcohol-related crashes. Almost 300,000 people are seriously injured, many maimed for life. While you can't begin to calculate the grief and suffering experienced by crash victims and their loved ones, taxpayers fork up billions of dollars annually to pay the medical expenses and rehabilitation costs of these victims. Medical costs alone add up to more than $5 billion each year.

Ordinarily, the state governments set traffic law. But when there's no uniform minimum drinking age, teenagers are tempted to drive across state lines to take advantage of more liberal laws next door. These in effect become "blood borders," inducements to drink and drive. The problem was serious enough that in 1984 President Reagan and I championed legislation encouraging states to raise their drinking age to twenty-one. Today, all fifty states have this law on their books, and the number of young people who die in crashes involving a young intoxicated driver has dropped by more than 60 percent.

I used the bully pulpit to wage my own war on drunk driving, insisting we would continue to fight until we got every drunk driver off the American road. Citizen activists like Mothers Against Drunk Driving (MADD) raised the national consciousness, and it was my privilege to join them in their efforts. We have made substantial progress in the fight to change both the laws and attitudes that tolerated drunk driving, but now is not the time to rest on our laurels.

In all my efforts to promote safer transportation, I tried to respect individual choice. But what happens when an individual's behavior becomes a public menace? In January 1987 an Amtrak train carrying passengers from Washington to Boston derailed outside Baltimore. Sixteen bodies were pulled from the twisted wreckage. Blood tests of the brakeman and the engineer of the Conrail train involved in the accident revealed traces of marijuana. If the rail unions had had their way, those tests would not have been permitted. For twelve years the unions had stalled efforts to test workers for alcohol or drug abuse. Then, eleven months before Amtrak's Colonial went off the tracks, we succeeded in implementing the first drug-testing procedure of its kind in railroad history.

It came none too soon. Of the first eight hundred employees tested after accidents, 5.1 percent showed alcohol or drugs in their system. This was more than enough to convince me that DOT should be the first civilian department to undertake the most effective deterrent, random drug testing. Not surprisingly, the decision didn't make me the most popular person around.

Public safety is a public trust. If you work in a cockpit or an engine room, you are responsible for the lives of your passengers. There is no escaping that responsibility. As Secretary of Transportation, I had to be able to look people in the eye and assure them that I'd done everything possible to give them what they expect and deserve—a drug-free transportation system.

Random testing is a sensitive issue, to be handled with maximum regard for individual dignity and privacy. Under our rules, tests had to be confirmed by a method that is virtually foolproof, and even then we asked a doctor to tell us whether there could be *any* reason to throw out a positive reading.

I believe that the most compassionate way to help an employee with a problem is rehabilitation. The idea wasn't to fire employees but rather to help those with a drug-abuse problem break free of their dependence. What could be more sensitive? My senior staff and I were among the thirty thousand DOT employees to be tested. The rest were in safety- or security-related positions—air traffic controllers and railroad inspectors, for example. I moved next to extend testing to those we regulated, such as pilots, maintenance crews, truckers, rail engineers and brakemen.

When I arrived at DOT, early in 1983, the economy was just coming out of recession. Later that year, as the President's tax and budget policies took hold, fuel costs dropped and airline deregulation belatedly realized its promise. Even the aviation industry was surprised by the surge in passenger traffic. Millions of people who never thought they would have the money to fly were taking advantage of lower fares. A Brookings Institution study at that time revealed that the combination of lower fares and more frequent flights has resulted in consumer savings of at least $6 billion annually.

Success can bring problems of its own, however. In this case, they included undeniable strains on the air traffic system. In essence, we had an aviation industry that was on the verge of explosive growth, surprised by this rapid surge, and hobbled by the ball and chain of a federal bureaucracy, the FAA, that was ill prepared to stay ahead of the growth curve. The challenge we faced was to get that bureaucracy to respond to a dynamic market while also making the world's safest air system still safer. It was a task of the highest order, one that I knew would require the vigilance of future Secretaries of Transportation.

One of my first actions as Secretary was to immediately order fourteen thousand "white glove" inspections affecting 374 separate airlines—inspections over and above those already scheduled. Next came a comprehensive eighteen-month probe of general aviation and a vigorous examination of the FAA.

I then established a panel of technical experts and program

analysts, a Safety Review Task Force. As it embarked on its first of a series of investigations across the transport spectrum, I delivered these simple marching orders: Tell us what we need to do differently; what we can do better. Skeptics who expected us to give an official whitewash of the FAA were surprised by the panel's first report, and the shake-up that followed. One of the first recommendations was a massive overhaul of the FAA's system of inspecting aircraft.

Astonishing as it sounds, we discovered that the FAA inspector handbooks hadn't been changed in twenty-eight years. So we rewrote the handbooks, and before long we rewrote the rule books, as part of a complete overhaul of FAA inspection procedures. Inspectors would now be reassigned periodically to prevent a buddy system from growing up between them and the inspected carriers. Methods of hiring and training personnel were updated, and the entire inspector workforce was increased 60 percent. We levied the largest fines in history, including $9.5 million against one carrier.

This was just the start of the FAA's makeover. Over the next three years the number of air traffic controllers grew by 24 percent, with an additional 860 hirings called for in my final budget request. While overall funding for DOT actually shrank during my tenure, I secured a 50 percent increase in money for the FAA. Even during a time of fiscal austerity, I was able to persuade OMB to accept a $1 billion shot in the arm in fiscal year 1988, only to see accounts for vital equipment and salaries cut by the House of Representatives. I was very proud that my final three years as Secretary of Transportation were the safest in aviation history.

One thing I learned very quickly in official Washington was that nothing happens as fast as you want it to. There are all sorts of procedural roadblocks. For example, it took months to issue a simple requirement that pilots of small aircraft must turn on their transponder, an identifying device that informs ground controllers of a plane's presence in the area. We first had to draft a proposed rule in the FAA bureaucracy; then we had to contend with cost-benefit analysis necessary to ensure the rule's survival in court, OMB reviews and a lengthy public comment period.

Before I proposed several measures to ensure that small aircraft do not cross paths with commercial airlines over the nation's busiest airports, cautious members of my staff warned me that some aviation interest groups would come off the wall. And, sure enough, the letters poured in, encouraged by full-page newspaper ads paid for by special interests alarmed over changes in the status quo. It was pretty much what I had come to expect. You take tough action, you get a reaction. All in a day's work.

A different kind of turmoil was brewing on the nation's runways, among weary travelers waiting for flights and baggage. I was a frequent flyer myself and had experienced my share of canceled flights, misplaced garment bags and nervous checking of my watch. One of the worst hours of my life was spent at Dulles Airport, trying to figure out some way to get to Philadelphia in time to attend the funeral of Virginia Knauer's son. I got there just as Virginia was leaving for the cemetery.

At such times, it's little consolation that weather is responsible for 70 percent of all delays. There's not much we could do about that, but we could and did move on a number of fronts to ease airport angst. By adding a dozen more flight paths, the FAA reduced delays in the congested skies around New York City by 40 percent. "Tiger teams" were sent out by the agency to visit individual airports and come up with measures suitable to each site. We couldn't wait for the NAS and other budget increases to address long-range problems. The problem existed *now,* when airlines were scheduling more flights during popular times of the day than air facilities could possibly accommodate.

I asked rival carriers to voluntarily adjust their schedules, suspending antitrust provisions long enough to get more than a thousand flights spaced out to consumer advantage. After hearing repeated complaints of delays, cancelations and lost baggage, we slapped one airline with a $250,000 fine. Still other investigations led to tough settlement agreements at numerous airports and to a new rule requiring airlines to inform travelers of their on-time performance and baggage complaints. The information made available under this "truth in scheduling" provision let consumers see which airlines had the best records, and by their choices they encouraged better service.

. . .

Transportation has always been a largely masculine domain. There aren't many female faces among the truckers, ship captains, railroad engineers and highway construction crews who made up my department's natural constituency. Ironically, since the Coast Guard dropped anchor in DOT waters, I was the first woman ever to head a branch of the U.S. armed forces.

At first, this took a little getting used to on both sides. Before I visited a ship, my staff would be peppered with questions by admirals wanting to know whether I objected to being helped from my car, and how I felt about the ritual boarding ceremony.

Old salts must have been a bit shaken (I know I was) when an unscheduled visit to a Coast Guard cutter was added to a Florida schedule and I found myself precariously climbing a gangplank in my three-inch-high heels. There was no choice but to hand my pocketbook to a saluting officer of the deck as I hoisted myself up one ramp across the water and down another. "Here," I said to him, "please hold this." After being piped aboard, I made things even worse by referring to topside as "upstairs."

Back on land, it was revealed that only 19 percent of the DOT workforce was female. What had it been in 1967, when the department was established? I asked. The answer: 18.5 percent. Minority workers had also been overlooked. I told a departmental women's breakfast that some changes would be made. Having heard similar vows in the past, employees had learned not to put much credence in them.

To counter the skeptics, I asked DOT women themselves to help us find ways to boost midlevel employees into senior management positions, and to give women in secretarial and clerical slots a chance to broaden their professional horizons. The result was a ten-point program that attracted the attention of other Cabinet members and even the Canadian government. It has boosted by several percentage points the number of females in a 100,000-member work force. Of equal importance, it has raised the confidence and the job prospects of thousands of women, many of them in the air traffic control system. I'll always remember the day a pilot told me that in his approach to a major U.S. airport he had heard three distinct voices over the air traffic control system. Women's voices. And DOT is proud to be one of the first in government to operate a day care center for the benefit of working mothers.*

We've taken some giant strides in the quarter century since a few Nixon Administration female appointees established a support system called Executive Women in Government. In those days the first question most bosses asked was "Can you type?" Today, many of the bosses are women and some of the typists are men. Diversity is the hallmark of the modern American woman. We wear the robes of a judge, the face mask of a surgeon, the pinstripes of a banker. We teach on campuses, peer through lab microscopes, design buildings and run businesses. Some of us write the laws that other women enforce. Some build rockets for others to ride into space. The most energetic of all run a home and raise a family. No role is superior to another.

Never having had children myself, I'm lucky to have Robin, who is much more than a stepdaughter, and a pair of nephews close enough to be like sons. John, a young minister, works in the Senate on issues of international religious liberty, and Jody works for Campus Crusade for Christ.

Given the predominance of two-income couples in today's society, there is nothing about the division of labor in the Dole household that isn't repeated in millions of American homes every night of the week. Just ask the makers of Lean Cuisine. Fortunately, I have the soul of a short-order cook, as well as a small library of thirty-minute-meal cookbooks. "Don't spend all that time in the kitchen," Bob tells me whenever I propose to cook him a full-course meal. "Let's go out so we can talk."

Thinking back, I can't recall precisely when I first had the feeling that outside forces were taking control of my life. It wasn't just the frantic schedule—the 8 A.M. appointments at the hairdresser, complete with phone calls taken under the dryer.

---

* We came a long way when I was at DOT, but I was reminded there was a long way to go when a stewardess approached me on a plane and whispered into my ear the comment put to her by a male passenger a few rows back: "I hear that Secretary Dole's wife is on board."

And how many nights I'd have eagerly traded dinner in a hotel ballroom with a couple thousand people for an evening at home with my husband, or the chance to watch television and use the treadmill that's set up in our small apartment.

Did I say *small*? When first married, we put off looking for a house. There'd be time for that later, we told ourselves. Twenty years have passed, and I'm still yearning for a fireplace and for a little backyard in which to commune with nature.

My advice to any dual-career couple is to have as many special times as you can, and not allow work to crowd out the really important things in life. Bob and I don't get to travel together as much as we would like, but we look for every opportunity. When Bob's on the road, he sometimes sends me flowers. He follows my schedule as closely as his own. Before I left town, he's been known to call my staff and ask what kind of plane I'd be using, to make sure it had two engines and two pilots, and to check up on weather conditions.

Whenever we're apart, we burn up the telephone wires. At home, we write lots of messages. I remember one time when Bob flew into town late at night, long after I was asleep. I had addressed the White House Conference on Small Business earlier in the day. On my way out the door the next morning for an early TV show while he still slept, I remembered that he was to speak to the same audience that day. Hurrying back inside, I left a note on the bathroom mirror: "Don't use the joke about making the bed—I already used it."

The bed joke is part of the very public private life that we lead. *People* magazine had included with its profile of Bob and me a photo of us making the bed together in our Watergate apartment. A few days after the magazine hit the newsstands, Bob got a letter from an irate California Republican. The man said he had nothing against a female Cabinet officer. His complaint was strictly personal. "Senator Dole," he wrote, "my wife saw that picture of you making the bed, and now she has *me* helping make the bed. Please, Senator, you've got to stop doing all that work around the house. You're causing problems for men all across America."

"You don't know the half of it," Bob wrote back. "The

only reason she was helping make the bed was because they were taking pictures."

I got my chance to return the ribbing when I was invited to match wits with former trade ambassador and Middle East negotiator Robert Strauss at the 1984 Gridiron Dinner. I was uniquely qualified to pass judgment on air bags, I reminded the audience; after all, I'd been driving around with one for years. I also recalled a recent interview in which a reporter had asked Bob whether being married to a powerful woman ever made him feel a bit emasculated.

"Hold it, cupcake," I had interrupted. "I'll take this one."

Bob laughed harder than anyone else.

BOB

If you would test a man's character, then give him power.

—ABRAHAM LINCOLN

Like most conservatives, I put great stock in self-reliance, but experience has shown me that there's no such thing as an entirely self-made man or woman. A government program called the GI Bill of Rights allowed me to complete college, the only one of four children in my family to do so. Without the encouragement of a Washburn law librarian who didn't even belong to my party, I might not have entered politics. And if it weren't for Hampar Kelikian, my life would have been very different indeed.

Everyone wants to make it on his own, but not everyone can. Maybe there aren't enough jobs where a person lives. Maybe the schools aren't as good, or he hasn't had the breaks you or I have. Homeless people didn't just show up yesterday on the grates of America's cities. As Russell County attorney, I used to get called in the middle of the night when some poor guy had been found off the side of the highway, sleeping in a car with his entire family. Saddest of all, the local welfare office often paid just enough to move the family on to the next town.

Conservatism means different things to different people. To me, it's a creed of opportunity, rooted in the ability of seemingly ordinary people to achieve extraordinary things. This explains my support for civil-rights legislation, as well as the 1983 bill making the late Dr. Martin Luther King, Jr.'s, birthday a federal holiday. I'm a conservative Republican, King was a liberal Democrat, but the ideals I defended in the mountains of Italy forty years ago included the rights for which King fought on the streets of Birmingham and Selma.

Opponents of the bill said King was too controversial, or claimed that a new federal holiday would be too expensive. As the bill's floor manager, I took a different stand in leading off final debate on October 3, 1983:

"A nation defines itself in many ways; in the promises it makes and the programs it enacts, the dreams it enshrines or the doors it slams shut. . . . Thanks to Dr. King . . . America . . . wrote new laws to strike down old barriers. She built bridges instead of walls. She invited the black man and woman into the mainstream of society—and in doing so, opened the way for women, the disabled, and other minorities who found their own voice in the civil-rights movement.

"There is nothing partisan about justice," I reminded my colleagues. "It is as conservative as the Constitution, as liberal as Lincoln, as radical as Jefferson's sweeping assertion that all of God's creation is equal in His eyes. . . ."

Ten days later, the Senate overwhelmingly approved the bill. The King holiday celebrates much more than one man's life. It reaffirms America's age-old commitment to human freedom. In our own time, freedom-loving people of both races have carried out one of history's great social revolutions. In doing so, they have reaffirmed America's status as the world's foremost developing nation. We are developing still, something we ought to think about every January 15.

Freedom is a gift from God, not government. It is indivisible. To have it for ourselves, we must demand it for others. That conviction, and our willingness to act upon it, has made America a beacon in the night of tyranny, and a source of inspiration to oppressed people everywhere: to boat people who fled Indochina after Communist rule turned that region into a vast

MR. LEADER, MADAM SECRETARY 235

prison camp; to Filipinos who poured into the streets of Manila demanding an end to Marcos' corruption and a return of political liberties; to Lech Walesa, Václav Havel, Boris Yeltsin and countless millions who helped to replace the false gods of Marxism with the sunshine of democracy.

Nowhere was America's commitment to freedom and pluralistic democracy put to a greater test than in Nicaragua. My own attitude to that unhappy land combined belief in the moral justification of U.S. aid to the contras resisting a Marxist regime, with frustration over the Reagan Administration's seeming inability to enlist popular support for the program.

Central America is in our geopolitical backyard, and was no place for a Soviet client state, let alone one sworn to subvert its democratic, peace-loving neighbors. The threat was real, the challenge undeniable. American credibility was on the line. If we believed our assertion that freedom was a universal right, I thought we had to break out of our natural insularity and reject the isolationism of those who would hide behind the Atlantic, the Pacific, and the Rio Grande.

Opponents of U.S. aid to the Nicaraguan resistance assumed a moral equivalence between the contras and the Sandinista regime in Managua. Just how wrong they were came home to me with dramatic force during a visit to Central America in August 1987. Along with four other Republican senators, I made the trip to sound out leaders in the region about prospects for a negotiated peace based on a plan initiated by Costa Rican President Oscar Arias and finally initialed by Nicaraguan strongman Daniel Ortega.

In between constructive talks with Honduran President José Azcona and would-be peacemaker Arias, we arrived in Managua August 31. None of us had any idea whether Ortega would even receive the delegation. But a short bus ride brought us to an old country club on the city's outskirts, its grounds lined with antiaircraft guns. There we cooled our heels for half an hour, before being ushered into a room full of media people.

I waited for the press to snap their pictures and leave, allowing Ortega and the rest of us to have a private discussion of the Arias plan and our concerns about Nicaraguan subversion in the region. Ortega had other ideas. With the media present and a nationwide audience listening in via Radio Managua, the "Comandante" began by ridiculing a recent broadcast to his country by the President of the United States. "And how are the contras doing after receiving President Reagan's radio message?" he asked sarcastically.

I interrupted Ortega's anti-American harangue by pointing out the military assistance his own regime was getting from the Soviet Union and its allies. According to Ortega, the Soviets, the Cubans and the Bulgarians were on hand to help the people of Nicaragua. "Well, we're helping the contras," I told him.

After further sparring over human-rights violations, I asked Ortega point blank, "Do you want to talk about the August seventh peace initiative or do you just want to have this pep rally?"

Democratic Congressman Peter Kostmayer, a last-minute addition to the meeting, jumped in to assure Ortega: "You have to do much less than you could imagine to stop contra aid." Ortega pricked up his ears as Kostmayer mentioned a few steps, like reopening the newspaper *La Prensa,* allowing the Catholic Church to resume uncensored radio broadcasts, and releasing some jailed opposition leaders.

"It'll take more than that," I interjected. "There's got to be a total democratization."

Ortega eventually calmed down enough to stop making speeches and start a dialogue. But it was obvious that there would be no agreement that afternoon. Ortega convinced me more than ever that he would never turn his back on his masters in Moscow and Havana or drop plans to export his revolution throughout Central America. Why else would a nation of 2.4 million people support a 150,000-man army? As for internal reforms, I had never known a Marxist to voluntarily relinquish power.

Yet everything I saw—the thumbs-up signs we got from average Nicaraguans on the streets of Managua, the spontaneous cries of "Freedom!" and the moral courage displayed by the editor of *La Prensa* and Cardinal Miguel Obando y Bravo—convinced me that in a free election Ortega would be voted out of office in a landslide.

What stood out most in memory about the trip wasn't Ortega, a man of limited charisma and predictable views; what I remember most clearly is the agony of refugees driven across the border into neighboring Honduras. A few hours before touching down in Managua, I had been to a United Nations–run camp housing six thousand people, forced from their homes and fearful of returning to Nicaragua as long as the Sandinistas held power. My heart went out to the little girls without shoes, the mothers without sons, the men who had farms confiscated and who now were forced to live in primitive huts—part of several hundred thousand Nicaraguans and Salvadorans made homeless by Marxist persecution. I tried to reassure the camp's inhabitants that the American people would never abandon them, nor permit a Soviet-backed regime to draw a totalitarian shade over Central America.

One of the biggest ovations at the Dallas convention that nominated Reagan for a second term in August 1984 went to United Nations Ambassador Jeane Kirkpatrick, who told delegates about an early conversation she had with some Third World diplomats in New York. They had asked her what separated Ronald Reagan's foreign policies from Jimmy Carter's. Kirkpatrick responded, "We have taken off our 'Kick Me' sign."

Kirkpatrick wasn't the only woman spotlighted in Dallas. Convention week gave me an idea what life must be like for Margaret Thatcher's husband. A prominent columnist asked me how I'd feel about a Bush-Dole ticket in 1988.

"I'm not sure," I answered. "To tell you the truth, I don't believe I'd really be interested."

"Good," he said, "because I wasn't thinking of *you*."

I decided it was a good omen that our Dallas hotel suite was numbered 1988. Then Howard Baker did a little checking. "That room isn't registered to Bob Dole," he informed the *Washington Post*. "It's registered to Elizabeth Dole."

But there are limits even to Elizabeth's name recognition, as we found out when a woman in the Kansas delegation overheard a pair of male delegates discussing upcoming events.

"What's on the program tonight?" one of the men inquired.

"I don't know," said his friend. "The Dole Brothers are going to speak."

There's no doubt which "Dole Brother" won the orator honors that evening. The best part of my speech was its conclusion: "A legacy is a gift to the future. I am fortunate to have one of my own, and I take great pride in presenting her to you now: the Secretary of the United States Department of Transportation."

Elizabeth promptly upstaged me. "The stature of women everywhere would be diminished if a candidate for national office were supported simply because she's a woman," she declared, a month after Democrat Geraldine Ferraro's nomination for Vice President. "The idea that an election could be won on the basis of gender insults our electoral process. We are thinking women. No platitudes will buy us. No party will inherit us. No candidate will own us." Elizabeth told the crowd exactly what it wanted to hear—and stole the show. I've never been prouder of her.

While Elizabeth and I are big supporters of each other in public, we observe a strict ban on speechmaking around the house. We also allow the other his or her indulgences. Because I'm a news junkie, Elizabeth surprised me one birthday with a cable-TV hookup. She doesn't complain about the round-the-clock headline service, and I don't complain—much—about her monopolizing the closet space, even if our dog has more room for his things than I do.

The dog is Leader, a miniature schnauzer Elizabeth found at a local Humane Society shelter. Harry Truman used to say that if you want a friend in Washington, get yourself a dog. We're both glad for the chance to get outdoors and think—or not think—that comes with walking Leader around the block. But not even canines, it turns out, are immune to controversy. After the press reported that Leader had allegedly ridden in a government car, the *Wall Street Journal* had a little fun with the pet-gets-chauffeured angle. A Hays, Kansas, newspaper ran a less amusing editorial, and Leader filed a protest: "I don't mind if you criticize my owner, as you occasionally do, but when you pick on me . . . that really gets under my flea collar! To compare me with Fala, FDR's best friend who was transported around the globe on a Navy vessel, is cynically unfair. Then again, just think what my critics would say if I drove myself!"

Next to a sense of humor, life in the political goldfish bowl demands nothing more than the ability to improvise. When I led a senatorial delegation on a trade mission to the Far East in the summer of 1985, Elizabeth wore three hats on the trip. As Secretary of Transportation, she conducted some tough aviation and maritime negotiations with her foreign counterparts. As wife of the delegation's chairman, and a Reagan Administration spokesman in her own right, she never knew in advance whether she would be called upon to give a toast to Deng Xiaoping or answer questions about U.S. railroads. And as host to senatorial spouses, she got in as much socializing as a crowded official itinerary would permit.

In some ways, the journey was a metaphor of our lives together. Not exactly relaxing, but full of memorable experiences. One Sunday morning Elizabeth slipped away at seven o'clock with Pat Moynihan and Pete Domenici to attend services in a Beijing cathedral. It was a special moment for her, finding a church overflowing with worshipers despite a torrential rainstorm, in the capital of Mao Tse-tung's officially godless state.

Closer to home, one of Elizabeth's most meaningful birthdays was spent with some of Washington's large homeless population. A friend had told her about Sarah's Circle, a church-sponsored organization that ministers to and houses street people. She decided that instead of a traditional birthday party, with people giving her gifts, she would reverse the process.

Since our birthdays are a week apart, I went in with her on decorating a local coffeehouse and choosing presents for each of the residents of Sarah's Circle. During lunch we heard from a woman named Beulah. According to her, before finding Sarah's Circle she had spent her time sitting on street corners. Now Beulah collects old clothing from area churches and sells it on the weekend to raise money for Sarah's Circle. She takes nothing for herself. "If I had some money," she explained, "I'd only want more."

At one point Beulah said she never thought she would be

sitting next to a United States senator. The honor was all mine, I told her.

Two political contests were decided in November 1984. Three weeks after Ronald Reagan's forty-nine-state sweep, Republican senators met to decide on Howard Baker's replacement as Majority Leader. In the weeks leading up to the caucus, I knocked on more doors than a Fuller Brush man. In one office, I got a blank stare from a receptionist who didn't know me. Luckily, she wasn't voting.

When the fifty-three senators filed into the restored Old Senate Chamber on the morning of November 29, it was Alaska's Ted Stevens against a field that included Richard G. Lugar of Indiana, Pete Domenici of New Mexico, James A. McClure of Idaho and myself. Stevens had earned high marks as a vote-counter during his four years as Baker's deputy, but, in this campaign, preelection polls were meaningless. There was no way to predict the outcome. After four secret ballots, Stevens and I were tied with twenty votes apiece. At the end of the fifth round, Howard Greene, secretary to the Senate majority, flashed me a thumbs-up sign. A few minutes later, the official count confirmed Greene's gesture: for Dole, 28; for Stevens, 25.

I had no illusions about the Majority Leader's position or the clout it carried within the Senate. Howard Baker once confided to me that there were days when he was sure he had the best job in Washington, but there were other times when trying to make the Senate function was like pushing a wet noodle. Personally, I think the job ought to be renamed Majority Pleader.

Unfortunately, tools of persuasion that were razor sharp in Lyndon Johnson's hands have long since been dulled. Old power bases formed on geographical or institutional allegiances have dissolved. Along with them has gone the ability of a few senior committee chairmen ("herd bulls," LBJ called them) to impose their will on deferential juniors. In this age of weakened party loyalties, any Majority Leader is part ringmaster and part traffic cop. He is an architect, building a legislative house brick by brick, commitment by commitment. Most of all, he's a juggler, keeping half a dozen balls in the air while looking down the road to see where vectors of policy and politics converge.

Despite the modern Senate's fragmentation of power, the Leader still has a few arrows in his quiver. A well-placed word from his office can help move a stalled bill through committee, or keep an unwanted one bottled up. He can assist colleagues by turning the media spotlight their way, scheduling their bills on the floor, raising campaign funds or wangling White House invitations.

A President in crafting his legislative agenda is obliged to consider the Majority Leader's reading of the political temperature on Capitol Hill. My own priorities for the Ninety-ninth Congress were spelled out plainly: to do something about the federal deficit and to write a new farm bill that would make U.S. agriculture more competitive in the world market.

I knew that each of these issues would demand more than the usual political courage from lawmakers. But the way I see it, voters send us to Washington to make things happen. Granted, when talking to most audiences about attacking the deficit I'm never sure whether all those heads out front are nodding in agreement or dropping off to sleep. But the problem is real. The deficit won't go away, or *grow* away, even with a robust economy.

Beginning in January 1985, Senate Republicans were determined to do more than nickel-and-dime the deficit. For weeks, Pete Domenici and others on the Budget Committee struggled to come up with a plan acceptable to the White House. But when the President's men dug in their heels on the issue of military spending, the ball was back in our court.

As a rule, I don't like meetings. Half of the people show up late; the other half never come at all. You're lucky to get a meeting of minds without a knocking together of heads. But I'd rather play the game than umpire, so that spring I turned my office into Budget Central. More than a hundred meetings produced a deficit-reduction package with teeth.

We hoped to realize $135 billion in savings over three years by freezing most government outlays at current levels, limiting the Pentagon to an increase covering only inflation, and deferring for one year scheduled cost-of-living adjustments on entitlement programs. No one on Social Security would forfeit any current benefits. Instead the ax would fall on fourteen federal programs that had outlived their usefulness.

It was a bold plan, affecting virtually every American and containing something to offend just about every senator. Passage hung on the vote of Pete Wilson, a freshman Republican from California (who is now, of course, the Golden State's two-term governor) who was taken to the hospital and operated on for an emergency appendectomy thirty-six hours before the final vote. Had it been anyone but Wilson, a former marine, I would have accused him of not being sick at all, just hiding out.

President Reagan couldn't give us much help, either, but for entirely different reasons. He was five thousand miles away, visiting European allies. That left Vice President Bush, who returned from a trip out West after being advised by White House chief of staff Don Regan that the Republican plan had the President's approval. Bush would be on hand to break a tie. Problem was, to get a tie we needed Pete Wilson.

On the morning of May 9, with Wilson in a recovery room at Bethesda, I called his doctors. Could he physically withstand a trip to Capitol Hill? I asked them. If the answer was yes, then how long could he remain in the Capitol? Was he sedated or sufficiently clear-minded to take part in a roll-call vote?

Wilson's doctors didn't want their patient jostled over the six miles of road from Bethesda to Capitol Hill. The Senator overrode their objections. Pete Wilson may have lost an appendix, but obviously he'd kept his backbone.

Late that Thursday night, Republicans met in S-230 to see where we stood. I knew we would lose at least four, maybe five from our ranks. Partly to compensate, we had Nebraska Democrat Edward Zorinsky, who was bucking his party's leadership with the same courage Wilson displayed in leaving his hospital bed. Assuming Zorinsky held firm and we suffered no more GOP defections, we'd have our tie.

"We'll give it a shot," I said.

Outside the Capitol, an ambulance siren announced Pete Wilson's arrival. Clad in pajamas and a robe, and hooked up to an IV tube, Wilson was taken out on a stretcher, then transferred to a wheelchair for the short tide to an anteroom off the Senate floor. It was nearly two in the morning when the junior Senator from California was wheeled into a hushed Senate Chamber, to be greeted by a bipartisan standing ovation. The cheers turned to appreciative laughter when Wilson jokingly asked the presiding officer, "Now, Mr. President, what was the pending question?" and then without waiting for an answer cast his aye vote.

At the end of the roll call, the Vice President in his traditional role broke the tie. In a moment for the record books the Senate demonstrated its capacity to govern. We didn't appoint a study commission. We didn't buck the decision to future Congresses, or to future generations.

"We had a pretty close call, Mr. President," I informed Reagan in a predawn transatlantic phone conversation. "But I think you'll agree, $135 billion is worth staying up all night for."

Unfortunately, the story didn't end there. Whenever you bite a bullet you run the risk of having it explode in your face. That's what happened to me a few weeks later when the White House cut a separate deal with some House Republicans and Tip O'Neill. Together, they decided to play it safe by going ahead with the cost-of-living increase in federal entitlement programs. In doing so, the Administration not only scuttled the Senate's package but also destroyed any prospect for significant action on the deficit. And it left most Senate Republicans standing on a trap door.

Our efforts weren't a complete waste, though. The momentum that was built up in the spring of 1985 led Congress later to adopt the Gramm-Rudman-Hollings formula designed by its authors to eliminate the deficit by 1991. Time has shown that it will take more than Gramm-Rudman or reforms of the budget process to do the trick. The problem isn't procedural, it's political. Quite simply, are we willing to curb our appetite for government benefits? Can America's leaders develop policies based on her future needs rather than on a reading of the latest polls?

I leave the question to you.

• • •

"Those who labor in the earth are the chosen people of God," wrote Thomas Jefferson.

Americans have always had a love affair with the land. For much of our history we have made our living as an agrarian nation. Long after the farmer and the rancher won the West, the life of sun and seed and soil still has a strong hold on our collective imagination. City folks dream of owning a little house in the country, and politicians since Jefferson have praised the self-reliant farmer as the backbone of an independent, land-owning citizenry.

As a senator from Kansas, my concern for agriculture goes hand in hand with representing the interests of my constituency. There's more to it than that, though. Growing up in Russell, I learned that if you take the farmer out of a rural community you might as well roll up Main Street. He's the one who comes into town to spend money and create jobs. And when the farmer has a bad year, so does just about everyone else.

For nearly fifty years, my father depended for his income on farmers who sold him their sour cream, grain and eggs. Today's food chain creates an even longer job chain than in Dad's time. Just over two million farmers are responsible for nearly nineteen million jobs in grain elevators, farm implement factories, processing plants and export houses.

If you don't eat, you don't need to worry about the farmer. Otherwise, his problems are at least in part your problems, too. Thanks to the productivity and efficiency of this country's farmers, Americans spend less of their disposable income on food than the people of any other Western nation. There are those who object to federal efforts aimed at stabilizing farm income in a fluctuating world market. When a farmer gets a check from the government, they call it a subsidy. In reality, it's an indirect subsidy to the American consumer, who has the best food bargain in the world.

Why should the farm economy be the center of national attention? The simplest answer is that agriculture is America's most basic industry, indispensable to our standard of living and economic growth. We *must* have a reliable food supply. We *need* to export large quantities of wheat, feed grains, soybeans and other agricultural products to help balance U.S. trade with the rest of the world.

Farming also isn't like other businesses. A farm family can work themselves ragged and then have their crops wiped out in thirty minutes by hailstorms or floods. Even with all the advances of twentieth-century technology, we can't completely protect against the threat of disease, insects and weather.

As if the farmer didn't have enough to worry about from nature, he also has to deal with the whims of Congress. Having spent twenty-seven years on the House and Senate Agriculture Committees, I can tell you there isn't a more popular vote for some on Capitol Hill than the one cast against a farm bill. To urban congressmen it's a chance to score points with consumers at the expense of farmers, and latter-day populists see almost any proposal as open season on the family farm.

Things weren't so bad during the 1970s, when a boom in farm exports kept prices and income levels high. Then came Jimmy Carter's 1980 embargo on grain sales to the Soviet Union, bracketed by double-digit inflation and crippling interest rates. Foreign markets shrank as a strong dollar and stiff competition from Argentina, Australia and much of Western Europe threatened to do to the American farmer what Japanese workers have done to the American electronics industry.

By the early eighties, rural America was reeling, with many farmers forced to abandon their livelihood, and young people in search of job opportunities compelled to look elsewhere. Against this backdrop, taxpayers and lawmakers alike were increasingly upset over federal farm programs whose costs had quadrupled in less than a decade to $18 billion in 1985. As Congress deliberated over a new farm bill early that year, I had to contend with two diametrically opposed schools of thought.

The White House sought substantial, immediate cuts in farm income and price supports. Essentially, the Administration wanted to go the free-market route overnight. In an ideal world, one in which other countries don't subsidize their farmers, we could all compete on a level playing field. American productivity and know-how would triumph. And the Administration's theories would be vindicated.

But as long as other nations refuse to play the game by free-market rules, it is unrealistic and unfair to pull the rug out from under U.S. farmers. Recognizing this fact, most farm-state legislators assailed the Administration's 1985 plan and argued instead for a four-year freeze of income-support payments at existing levels. A few went even further, calling for a return to mandatory controls over farm production—a modern variant on former Secretary of Agriculture Henry Wallace's planned scarcity of Dust Bowl days.

In my view, neither idea addressed the underlying need to restore the competitiveness of U.S. agriculture, so that farmers could earn more from the market than from the government. We burned the midnight oil in search of a workable compromise, one that would satisfy White House cost concerns and still achieve both these objectives. It took eleven months and countless hours of debate, but the final product was worth the effort. Weighing in at thirteen pounds, the 1985 farm bill included a two-year freeze on federal target price supports, followed by gradual annual reductions. This combination would help us cushion farm income during the ensuing transition period.

I looked at the 1985 farm bill as a high point of "getting things done." It wasn't a perfect piece of legislation. Perfect bills don't get written, except by columnists and economists. But if politics is the art of the possible, the 1985 farm bill was a real achievement—and so, too, was the historic farm bill of 1996, which built on the progress we made a decade earlier, and which will transition America's farmers into the twenty-first century without disrupting the farm economy or land values. Farmers will finally plant for the market and not the government. The government is getting out of the supply control business.

Over two centuries ago, George Washington wrote, "I know of no pursuit in which more real and important services can be rendered to any country than by improving its agriculture." Throughout my years in Congress, I have kept Washington's words in mind, and I am proud to be known as a champion of America's farm families. In my book, it is they who are the true champions.

ELIZABETH

At the age of eighty-eight, Oliver Wendell Holmes took a train trip. Unable to locate his ticket, Holmes searched his pockets as a conductor looked on.

"Don't worry, Justice Holmes," the conductor reassured him. "You don't need a ticket. You'll probably find it when you get off the train, and I'm sure the Pennsylvania Railroad will trust you to mail it back later."

"My dear man," Holmes replied, with some irritation, "that isn't the problem at all. The question is not, where is my ticket? The question is, where am I going?"

Before 1980, U.S. railroads were going nowhere. They were victims of declining patronage, poor management and stiff competition from the trucking industry. Adding to their problems was excessive government regulation. The Interstate Commerce Commission denied individual carriers the right to tailor services to specific shippers' needs. It was a policy of uniformity at the expense of economic dynamism, and as a result the world's largest rail system was on its knees, with a quarter of all U.S. track in bankruptcy.

Too many rules meant too much risk of companies unable to earn the capital to maintain aging tracks and cars. You could end up with service that was unsafe as well as unreliable. Congress recognized the problem in 1980, when it passed the Staggers Act, which partially deregulated the rails. Eight years later, rail shippers have signed over fifty thousand individualized contracts, agreements formerly prohibited under regulation. Increased competition has cut shipping costs and improved on-time deliveries. Railroads have become more profitable. And 1986 was the safest year in rail history. The industry's accident rate had declined from over 10,000 a year in the late seventies to 2,760 in 1986—the lowest ever.

The trucking industry has also been partially deregulated.

What used to be a closed market has been thrown open, and crazy-quilt rules—permitting some rigs to carry milk, for example, but not ice cream—have been thrown out. To graphically illustrate the absurdity of government regulation, I once testified before a Senate committee in support of legislation to complete trucking deregulation with a bowl of Orville Redenbacher's popcorn on my left and a bowl of Jiffy Pop on my right. Why, I asked committee members, did the ICC require truckers to file rates with the government for one brand but not the other?

The implications go far beyond the price of popcorn. Since transportation on average accounts for roughly 25 percent of a delivered product's cost, and government regulation tacks on another 20 to 40 percent, it's obvious that further deregulation will help U.S. businesses in their struggle to remain competitive.

Government deregulation is an acknowledgment of the superiority of individual enterprise and ingenuity. Remember the thrilling flight of the Voyager aircraft? The world held its breath in November 1986 as pilots Dick Rutan and Jenna Yaeger rode the tail winds of a Pacific typhoon and kept a watchful eye on their seventeen fuel tanks as they circled the world nonstop.

Voyager was not created by government experts. It began as a doodle on a restaurant napkin and was built with the life savings of its crew. In the deregulated, entrepreneurial climate of the Reagan years, the plane's creators had to fill out only two pieces of government papers: an application for airworthiness and a request for a tail number.

I began my government career promoting the rights of American consumers and arguing for economic deregulation. Twenty years later, those themes have been picked up by advocates in both major parties and in countless institutions, public as well as private. I hope that any temporary difficulties that may affect an economy in transition will not prompt lawmakers to pine for the imagined glories of reregulation.

A democracy—especially an economic democracy—cannot stand still. Anyone hoping to turn the clock back might just as well stop the world from spinning or the human mind from pursuing its quest for transportation that is faster, safer and more affordable. It's as simple as that.

"Deregulation" is a long word for a simple process. So is

"privatization." By putting business back into the hands of the people, privatization reverses a century of collectivism and centralized planning by the state. As former British Prime Minister Margaret Thatcher has said, "The wealth of a country is the efforts of its people, and effort depends on incentives."

During my years at DOT, the flagship of privatization was Conrail, the federally chartered railroad fashioned from the wreckage of Penn Central and a half dozen other Northeastern lines. Long before Penn Central's 1970 bankruptcy, structural changes in the region's economy, not to mention the Interstate Highway System and the eighteen-wheel trucks that use it, had sharply diminished rail traffic by traditional clients like steel, auto makers and coal shippers.

Reversing all this was a bit like ordering an avalanche uphill. Congress tried anyway, establishing the passenger railroad Amtrak in 1971 and Conrail five years later. Having racked up $1.6 billion in red ink during its first four years, Conrail was given a fresh round of concessions in 1981, including exemption from state taxes and an easing of the way toward abandoning unprofitable routes and commuter services. The line was also granted a federal bailout on its labor-protection costs, worth $325 million in the first year alone.

For all this, and despite the new deregulated climate of the eighties, Drew Lewis could see Conrail's fragility. By breaking up the company, Lewis hoped to get back at least some of the taxpayers' multibillion-dollar investment. Opposing him was the railroad's chairman, L. Stanley Crane, a rail industry veteran who was just as determined to keep intact what he liked to call "my railroad."

By the time I replaced Lewis, Congress had ordered DOT to begin a process leading to Conrail's sale, without specifying its own preference between a public stock offering and merger with another company. One might easily question the depth of Congress' commitment, since few if any governments in recorded history have voluntarily reduced their size or their authority, and the return of Conrail to private ownership would slice off a considerable chunk of federal turf.

When I arrived in 1983, the New York investment banking firm of Goldman, Sachs had already been selected to advise the department. I ordered the financial experts to work closely with Federal Railroad Administrator John Riley in an aggressive campaign to market Conrail. More than a hundred corporations were approached.

Throughout the summer and fall of 1984, we narrowed the list of fifteen bidders to six and then to three. I wanted a good up-front price, of course, but to assure Conrail's long-range viability and make certain the federal government didn't find a destitute railroad back on its doorstep in a few years, I also insisted on a series of protective covenants.

One of the requirements was that the line's new owners invest heavily in capital improvements over a five-year period. Another placed strict limits on dividend payments. A third would insulate Conrail from the effects of any sudden economic downturn by maintaining half a billion dollars in cash reserves.

In February 1985 I accepted the best offer, which came from the Norfolk Southern Corporation. In addition to $1.2 billion in cash, the company promised to buy out employee-owned stock and to restore wage cuts imposed by Stanley Crane as part of his corporate down-sizing efforts. Most important of all, Norfolk Southern committed itself to the protective covenants. To blunt criticism of the deal on competitive grounds, NS also accepted in principle a Justice Department plan to divest some of its current holdings and thereby allow rival railroads to break out of their regional isolation.

When a snag developed, it came in one of the most unlikely places. To schedule a Senate vote on the Norfolk Southern proposal, I went to the Majority Leader. You think it was an advantage being married to the Leader? Think again. Had Howard Baker still occupied S-230, I could have easily called him and said, "Howard, this one's important. I want my bill up now." But Baker was never questioned about his wife's role in determining the Senate calendar. Bob Dole was, and it was enough to make him cautious.

"Bob," I said one evening, "you're bending over backward to be fair. And that's fine. But, my gosh, you're bending over so far you're about to fall off the chart. Meanwhile, I can't get even one issue up for consideration on the floor."

Not until December 1985 did the Conrail bill finally reach the full Senate, where it promptly ran into a filibuster. Opponents of the Norfolk Southern deal warned of the consequences of a rail merger. But they aimed most of their fire at another merger—mine and Bob's.

"The fix is in," Michigan Democrat Don Riegle declared. "It has been for a long time."

Riegle didn't know what he was talking about. John Chaffee leaped to my defense, denying, as he put it, "that the Secretary of Transportation has a grip on us."

"I wish she did," interjected Democrat Fritz Hollings of South Carolina.

The Senate finally approved the deal, 53 to 39, a margin sufficient to move the bill to the House but not large enough to impress John D. Dingell, the powerful chairman of the House Energy and Commerce Committee. With typical candor, Dingell opposed the sale of Conrail to Norfolk Southern because of the threat he believed it posed to rivals of a merged railroad. Given the industry's history, and the nineteenth-century railroad oligopolies that once set prices and defined service, Dingell's concern had a surface validity. But Commodore Vanderbilt was in his grave. In the modern rail era, the danger is less one of monopoly than of extinction. By divesting some of its own lines and strengthening Conrail's long-range prospects, Norfolk Southern would enhance, not diminish, rail competition. For the first time in decades, two long-haul railroads would be competing from the Midwest to the East Coast.

The most outspoken opponents of the deal didn't care about the divestitures and disliked the protective covenants. At heart, they didn't want to sell the railroad, especially not in the summer of 1986. Dingell in particular knew that if Democrats managed to regain the Senate in November, he might get a more favorable hearing for his plan to reregulate the railroads. So critics of Norfolk Southern dug in their heels. With the advantages of seniority and entrenched positions in the House hierarchy, the opposition was confident it could stop the deal dead in its tracks.

If everyone in Washington allowed political differences to

get in the way of personal friendships, this would be a pretty lonely town. When reporters began writing of a Dole-Dingell feud, I called up the Congressman, whose love of the outdoors was legendary, and invited myself to go fishing with him while I was out in his home state, Michigan, on a speaking engagement. At first taken aback by the request, Dingell promised to check his schedule. He later begged off, claiming that the muskies weren't biting just then. (Dingell doesn't know how grateful he made my staff. Aware of my fondness for all living things, they weren't looking forward to taking me down to the Potomac and teaching me how to bait a hook.)

Before long, anti–Norfolk Southern forces in Congress moved to take matters into their own hands. NS chairman Robert Claytor was summoned to a private Capitol Hill meeting, where he was handed a prewritten press release announcing the company's withdrawal from the Conrail bidding. The congressmen misjudged the businessman. Instead of pulling out, Claytor came straight over to DOT and a hastily assembled war council of NS officials, investment bankers and departmental experts. After listening to ten minutes of talk that was going nowhere, I pulled Claytor out of the room and took him next door. When we came out fifteen minutes later, Claytor had agreed to ask his board to consider raising Norfolk Southern's offer to $1.9 billion.

I wasn't the only one taking heat on the proposed sale. Norfolk Southern critics in the House came under pressure from restive congressmen, among them Subcommittee Chairman James J. Florio of New Jersey. Florio had questions of his own about Norfolk Southern. But he also had vivid memories of Penn Central's final hours, when the dying company continued paying dividends out of an empty cash box. Knowing that the protective covenants I had in mind were intended to spare Conrail from a similar fate, Florio kept an open mind on the Norfolk Southern offer.

Then, suddenly, a couple of seemingly unrelated legislative actions transformed the atmosphere on Capitol Hill. Passage of the Gramm-Rudman Act caused everyone in Washington to look around for ways to whittle down the federal deficit. And a sweeping overhaul of the nation's tax laws led Norfolk Southern to withdraw. The next-best plan was a public offering of Conrail stock. This was acceptable to me, as long as the protective covenants were intact and not linked to railroad reregulation.

The climactic vote came on September 17, 1986, in an Energy and Public Works Committee room packed with lobbyists and reporters. Prowling on the edge of the crowd was DOT's Capitol Hill liaison, Rebecca Range, whose persuasive gifts had earned her the title "that woman" from some resentful committee members. Resourceful as ever, Rebecca latched on to a key congressman and steered him into an adjoining room for a last-minute telephone conversation with me. DOT's position prevailed by a single vote—"that woman" had done her job brilliantly.

Six months later, I stood on the floor of the New York Stock Exchange as frenzied bidders snapped up sixty million shares in the largest first-time industrial stock offering in U.S. history. Seventeen years and billions of dollars after its bailout by the American taxpayer, Conrail was again in private hands, assured of long-term viability and the option to merge with another company in as little as twelve months. And the federal deficit was reduced by almost $2 billion.

Our success on Conrail prompted a public thank-you from hundreds of private-sector groups that had banded together to form the Coalition for Privatization. At the Washington dinner held to salute DOT's efforts on the sale, there were generous speeches and toasts. Best of all, the dinner produced a scholarship allowing a student from Hine Junior High School in an inner-city neighborhood to attend George Mason University.

DOT had already "adopted" Hine, tutoring students, taking them on board Coast Guard cutters, and inviting them to departmental functions. I delivered the commencement address at their graduation ceremony. How appropriate it was that when Conrail went private, free-market advocates showed their gratitude by funding a youngster from a neglected neighborhood to study privatization and other economic issues. An evening like that makes all the hassles of policy-making worthwhile. It's enough to demonstrate you *can* make a positive difference in the lives of others. And that's a feeling of satisfaction hard to describe.

Sometimes public policy is made in the most private places. My next effort to get the federal government out of business, so to speak, started with a bit of pillow talk between Bob and me. Why should Uncle Sam operate a pair of airports, Washington National and Dulles International? Why subject a local, nonpolitical function like airport management to congressional oversight?

Bob quickly brought me down to earth. His Capitol Hill colleagues had personal reasons for opposing any transfer, he pointed out. For one thing, they appreciated National's proximity to downtown Washington—just ten minutes from committee room to boarding ramp. Did I really expect Congress to surrender control of both airports in return for vague assurances of future improvements? The idea was a nonstarter.

Bob rolled over and went to sleep. As far as I was concerned, the gauntlet had been thrown down. I reached for a bedside notepad and began sketching the outlines of a strategy to prove him wrong. Certainly Bob had history on his side. Administrations of both parties had attempted eight times since 1949 to move National and Dulles Airports out of federal control, without winning in either house of Congress. What made me think I could succeed where they had failed?

Three reasons: Deregulation. Decay. Deficits.

Because of the increase in air travel brought on by airline deregulation, Dulles International had become America's fastest-growing airport. To accommodate still heavier passenger traffic in the future, money was needed to implement a host of changes. To the south, National Airport was an embarrassingly shabby gateway to the capital of the free world. Dulles' awkward sister was badly in need of repairs. But in a period when federal deficits were causing a general belt-tightening, that kind of money—$700 million—simply wasn't available.

Finding an alternative source of cash involved a three-year process of persuasion, during which I mingled appeals to reason with old-fashioned horse-trading. We wouldn't get anywhere without support from airport users, key congressmen and the three government jurisdictions affected—Virginia, Maryland and the District of Columbia. To get it, I appointed an advisory commission, chaired by former Virginia Governor Linwood Holton. At the group's first organizational meeting I delivered some bluntly worded instructions: "Don't tell me whether to transfer these airports. Tell me how."

In the second week of June 1986, the Senate adopted the commission's plan to create an independent regional authority to run and rehabilitate both facilities. As with Conrail, the strongest resistance to change came in the House, whose members thought of Dulles and National—especially National—as *their* airports. I could go up to the Hill and talk myself blue in the face about why it was a philosophical contradiction for Congress to supervise an airport. It didn't matter: Adam Smith had never been stuck in rush-hour traffic while trying to make a plane that was taxiing down a runway thirty miles from his office.

A few congressmen who had were astonishingly candid. "I don't care about the merits of your case," one member told me. "I don't really care very much what you think is right. What's it going to do to my flight back home?"

By the time a final vote was scheduled, two weeks beyond Congress' original adjournment date, I was already booked into an extensive campaign tour for House and Senate candidates. Over the weekend, with the help of White House operators, I tracked down dozens of congressmen, including one in a hospital where his wife had just given birth to a baby boy. To California's Ed Zschau, locked in a tight race with Senator Alan Cranston, I said I'd do an extra West Coast event for him if he would round up votes for the airport bill back in Washington. Zschau readily agreed, as did several other candidates for whom I was scheduled to campaign out West.

On the night of October 15, I spoke at a Las Vegas temple with Senate candidate James Santini. Upon returning to my hotel room at eleven-fifteen, I found an urgent message: the House was about to take a final vote. On the other end of the telephone hookup was my deputy, Jim Burnley, who kept a running tally. "We need 218 to win," Burnley said. "One ninety ...205 ... 210 ... 215 ..." As we went over the top, there were cheers and shouts on both ends of the line. It was after midnight, Las Vegas time. A new day had dawned, in more ways than one.

The Cabinet is often called the President's official family, and like most families it has its disagreements. Ronald Reagan encouraged open debate among his Cabinet members, the more candid the better. During Reagan's first term a proliferation of Cabinet councils made it difficult for members to participate in a meaningful way. I myself was on seven of the eight panels. For the second term, the number of these sub-Cabinet decision groups was slashed to just two—Economic Policy and Domestic Policy. Even so, Cabinet members had to be prepared several times a week to discuss issues outside their bailiwick.

Secretary of Commerce Malcolm Baldrige was a warm, unpretentious Yankee from Connecticut. He was my seatmate at Cabinet meetings until his tragic death in a rodeo accident in July 1987. I used to look over Mac's shoulder as he doodled away. His mind was as active as his hands were restless. He was particularly forceful in pressing the Administration to take a tougher stance on foreign nations that were guilty of unfair trade practices.

I lined up with Mac on that one, but later I found myself in competition with him. The issue was which of our departments would oversee the development of a private U.S. space industry based on expendable launch vehicles (ELV's), rocket boosters used only once to send satellites into space. Mac and I went head to head. After we made separate presentations to the Cabinet, the President concluded that DOT was the logical partner to work with the private sector in commercializing space. With his usual professionalism, Mac closed ranks and argued just as loudly as I against NASA's space monopoly and its 40 percent subsidy to users of the space shuttle, an incentive which effectively crippled the development of a private industry.

One day I went to the Commerce Department for a strategy

session. Mac had just received a new lariat, and he was happy as a kid on Christmas morning.

"Hold on, Elizabeth," he said when I was ten feet from his desk. "I'll bet I can lasso you from here."

He did exactly that, with the grace and enthusiasm of a natural cowboy. Afterward, we huddled over ways to do a little bureaucratic lassoing, by convincing NASA to surrender its control over the launching of routine commercial satellites.

We argued for three years—at Cabinet meetings, in the National Security Council and with members of Congress—that America could not afford to put all her eggs into one basket by relying on the shuttle alone. Instead of launching satellites for private businesses, NASA should be free to perform more exotic missions like a space station and planetary exploration. I emphasized that private industry, eager to tap a growing market, was far better equipped than government to build and launch satellites at competitive prices.

The debate became quite intense. Satellite customers who received government discount fares weren't that eager to pay open-market prices, while some NASA officials regarded the vastness of space as their bureaucratic private property.

Then, in January 1986, seven of the nation's most daring explorers lost their lives when the space shuttle *Challenger* crashed into the sea off Cape Kennedy. The *Challenger* tragedy left the United States with no ready access to space. It stranded dozens of NASA customers with unlaunched payloads. Foreign rivals moved in: Europe's Ariane, China's Long March; even the Soviets hoped to get a piece of the action with their massive Proton rocket.

In the aftermath of the *Challenger* disaster, officials saw with new eyes the wisdom of space diversification. We had nothing to lose and everything to gain by moving routine commercial satellites off the shuttle and onto expendable launch vehicles. All that private manufacturers needed was a signal from Washington. The skies were already filled with satellites that improved our telecommunications, weather and crop forecasting, and search-and-rescue capabilities. From there it was only a short leap of the imagination for me to envision a high-flying utopia in which privately launched satellites gave us additional breakthroughs, locating fuels, detecting pollution and manufacturing space-based pharmaceuticals.

With all that potential, who would have expected that among DOT's first launch applications was one giving a whole new twist to the idea of cradle-to-grave government? Literally. Space Services, Inc., wanted to turn the heavens into a celestial cemetery. That is, they proposed to send aloft individual capsules full of cremated human remains ("cremains," in high-tech talk). The pitch to earthbound mourners was that they could look up and see Aunt Tilly whenever they wanted. Through all eternity, presumably. Environmentalists objected that Aunt Tilly and her companions would clutter up space. The media adopted an approach to the whole scheme that was anything but funereal. "Orbit for the Departed" ran the *New York Times* headline.

Eventually I gave the go-ahead for Aunt Tilly to rest in space. More important, in August 1986 President Reagan gave the green light to private manufacturers ready to enter the commercial launch market. Even as the President ordered a new orbiter to replace the ill-fated *Challenger,* he invited free enterprise to help relieve the taxpayer and meet the challenge of foreign competition.

"We must always set our sights on tomorrow," the President said in announcing his decision. "NASA will keep America on the leading edge of change; the private sector will take over from there. Together, they will ensure that our country has a robust, balanced, and safe space program."

Almost exactly a year later, I witnessed the initial signing of contracts and gave preliminary government approval for the first private-sector launch in the nation's history.

We must always set our sights on tomorrow. For the girl from South Fulton Street whose mother once rode in a horse-drawn rig courtesy of the Cathey Buggy Company, it was like coming full circle.

BOB

Nineteen eighty-six will be remembered as the Year of Tax Reform. Before revising the tax code, the Senate adopted a not unrelated change in how it conducts its business. For years Howard Baker had argued that we should follow the House and allow television cameras to broadcast our deliberations. I picked up where he left off, with the result that tax reform hit the Senate floor at about the same time TV technicians hit their lights.

The ensuing debates over IRA's—individual retirement accounts—and sales-tax deductibility posed no ratings threat to *General Hospital,* but they did give millions of viewers a first-hand look at Congress in action. Television also nationalized the issue, making lawmakers think twice before delaying or amending the bill simply to satisfy local demands.

Television coverage may have been historic, but not the speeches it has spawned. Like it or not, the days when Webster, Calhoun and Clay filled the halls of Congress with great oratory have gone the way of spittoons and snuffboxes. Americans today prefer their eloquence in thirty-second sound bites. Even so, millions of people are tuning in to the Senate—quorum calls, filibusters and all.

Shortly after coverage began, a faithful viewer in Boise, Idaho, approached me and said she was a bit uncertain about my exact role in the daily drama. "But you must be good," she added. "They call on you a lot."

She had plenty to watch before the Ninety-ninth Congress passed into history. In addition to tax reform, the Republican Senate confirmed President Reagan's Supreme Court nominations of William H. Rehnquist and Antonin Scalia, thereby extending the Reagan legacy long after the sun sets over Rancho del Cielo. We passed a tough new immigration law that increased control over our borders. Antidrug legislation was enacted to attack both problems of supply and demand. The Superfund that pays for cleaning up the nation's toxic-waste sites was renewed for five years at five times the previous level of funding.

Thirty-seven years after it was first submitted, a treaty to outlaw genocide was finally approved. So were the MX missile and $100 million in aid to democratic resistance forces in Nicaragua. After the April 1986 bombing raid on Qaddafi's Libya, I suggested changes in the War Powers Act to make it easier for a President to move against state-sponsored terrorism. Congress can criticize foreign policy, but only the President can create it. After all, how many businesses could survive a management structure that required the front office to consult with 535 directors on every decision?

In the atrium of the Hart Senate Office Building there is an enormous sculpture by Alexander Calder. Rearing up from the marble floor is a jagged metal mountain; overhead revolves a bank of stylized clouds. Passing by the work nearly every day, I used to wonder why the artist had made his clouds so black. On November 4, 1986, I found out.

Nationwide, GOP Senate candidates that day actually improved upon the party's aggregate vote compared with the 1980 landslide. But the distribution of support followed a different pattern. Six years earlier, we had won almost every close contest. In 1986, we lost enough of these to ensure that at the start of the One Hundredth Congress Minority Leader Robert Byrd and I would switch places.

We had no excuses, and no need for any. In six short years we had rewritten the Washington rule book, redefined the role of American government and ended the national identity crisis rooted in our Vietnam involvement. Thirteen million new jobs had been created, rekindling the spirit of American enterprise.

Political majorities ebb and flow. Chairmanships change hands. Offices rotate. But history will record that it was a Republican President and Senate who reversed America's decline and dispelled any doubts about the GOP's ability to govern. Beginning January 1987, I had fewer soldiers on my side of the aisle. We weren't going to win every fight, but we sure wouldn't duck any.

According to Elizabeth, living with a senator takes a certain amount of forbearance. "Ask him to take the trash out, and you get a filibuster." On the other hand, being married to a Cabinet officer has its own set of demands. One difference between the executive and legislative branches is that Elizabeth had a bigger organization than I. Besides that, her organization usually did what she told it to.

On the last day of March 1987, I went to the White House for a regularly scheduled meeting between the President and Republican congressional leaders. The Secretary of Transportation was already there—on hand, I discovered, to reinforce Reagan's appeal for votes to sustain his veto of an $87.5 billion highway bill.

Under the circumstances, my range of options was limited.

"This is what you call being caught between a rock and a hard place," I remarked to Reagan, who quickly corrected me.

"I may be the hard place," he said, "but Elizabeth's a gemstone."

When the Founding Fathers gave Congress oversight responsibilities, they must have had something other than potholes and parking lots in mind. I like roads as much as anyone, but, coming from Kansas, I can smell pork a mile away. I've never seen a better case for the line-item veto, giving Presidents the same budgetary authority now enjoyed by forty-three state governors. But that's another fight. Just then my hands were full trying to round up enough Republicans to sustain the President's veto.

On April 1 the Senate did exactly that, with one vote to spare. Bob Byrd got his chance to shout April Fool when he dug into parliamentary procedure and came up with a second roll call the next day. This gave Byrd and others in the Democratic cloakroom twenty-four hours to lobby North Carolina freshman Terry Sanford, whose defection had provided Reagan with his original margin of victory. When Sanford switched his vote under the harsh glare of the national media, it sealed the fate of the veto—unless one of thirteen Republicans who had defied the White House underwent a similar change of heart.

The chances of that happening were remote, I told the President on the morning of April 2; at best, one in ten. It didn't matter. Reagan had his Irish up. In a combative mood, he personally came to Capitol Hill for a hastily called meeting of GOP senators.

When the President arrived at the Old Senate Chamber, a few minutes after noon, he got a standing ovation. Unfortunately, that's all he got. At a second meeting in my office, I raised the possibility of all thirteen switching their votes as a bloc. Half a dozen members were willing to walk the plank, but no one wanted to be pushed.

"You're not going to get a vote out of here," someone finally called out.

He was right. On the final roll call, precisely two thirds of the Senate rejected the Reagan position. Pundits were quick to describe the outcome as a personal setback for the President. In his seventh year in office, they were still making the mistake of underestimating Ronald Reagan. Reagan may have lost on the highway bill, but the bigger loss would have been to do nothing. There are times when confrontation is better than capitulation, and this was one of them.

In rolling the dice that morning on Capitol Hill, Reagan had exercised the classic presidential leadership envisioned by James Madison's political system that was based on "countervailing interests." According to the Father of the Constitution, America was a land of conflicting groups and factions. "Ambition must be made to counter ambition," wrote Madison. Congress is the public arena where society's contentious fragments can thrash out their differences. But only a President can articulate and defend the national interest. That's what Reagan was doing in challenging the odds on the highway bill. Like any true leader, he knew that success is never final, nor defeat fatal, as long as you have the courage to act on principle and take the heat.

CHAPTER TEN

New Challenges, New Missions

BOB

As President Reagan's second term approached its halfway point, I wasn't alone in considering who could best build upon his legacy. And the more I thought about it, the closer I came to a decision to run for President in 1988. As chairman of the Finance Committee, and then as Senate Majority Leader, I had served on the front lines of the Reagan Revolution, day in and day out, fighting for the policies that restored America's economic, military and moral strength.

To his adversaries and even a few of his supporters, Ronald Reagan appeared the most uncomplicated of men. The same was said of Franklin Roosevelt, Reagan's boyhood hero, with whom he shared a sunny temperament and an elusive personality. Roosevelt, however, was a great improviser, who often appeared to be making up his New Deal as he went along. Reagan, by contrast, came to the presidency firmly wedded to a set of beliefs developed over a lifetime. Behind his amiable smile was an executive who could be immovable where basic convictions were concerned.

In other ways, Reagan and Roosevelt had much in common. Both were strong leaders, with a genius for going over the heads of special interests and making their case directly to the American people. Both changed the way Americans see themselves, and how they relate to their government. FDR was the patrician with a common touch; Reagan, an Everyman from Tampico, Illinois, a small town not unlike Russell, Kansas, restored elegance to the White House and moral grandeur to the presidency. Roosevelt went into office hoping to cut federal expenditures 25 percent. Reagan had no greater success in controlling the federal spending machine—although by the time he left Washington, the deficit largely run up by a spendthrift Democratic Congress had itself become a drag on runaway spending.

Historians who celebrate the "strong presidency" when it enlarges the functions of government were perplexed or contemptuous of the strongest leader of modern times—and his conservative agenda. They never understood Reagan, any more than most Washington journalists could, if only because he fit none of their existing models. Why did Reagan defy conventional analysis? Because he was the most unconventional politician ever to occupy the White House.

Long after storming the citadels of the Washington establishment, President Reagan continued to think like an outsider. Equally important, he thought of himself as an outsider. This enabled him to leapfrog orthodox economics and the incremental approach favored by foreign policy graybeards.

A more conventional leader than Reagan would have yielded to State Department bureaucrats who warned him against calling the Soviet Union an "evil empire," or demanding that Mikhail Gorbachev prove his reformist credentials by coming to Berlin and tearing down the obscene wall which for nearly thirty years had symbolized East-West divisions.

A more conventional leader would have been content to restrain the nuclear arms race, rather than ending it altogether, and on terms favorable to the West.

A more conventional leader would never doubt the officially sanctioned lunacy of Mutual Assured Destruction, under which the United States and Soviet Union confronted each other, in Reagan's words, like a pair of gunslingers with their hands on their holsters.

And more conventional leaders would have accepted the

establishment view of the Cold War as a geopolitical fixture, as permanent a part of the world scene as the welfare state was at home.

Most unconventional of all (especially in Washington, D.C.) was Reagan's genuine modesty, symbolized by a sign the President kept on his White House desk declaring that there was no limit to what a man can accomplish if he doesn't mind who gets the credit. In the short run, this allowed Reagan's critics to portray him as a passive bystander to his own presidency. With the passage of time, however, it is obvious that Reagan's achievements dwarf those of any American President since FDR.

Certainly, Reagan was anything but passive in questioning Washington's accepted wisdom. This, in turn, enabled him to tame record inflation, slash crippling interest rates in half and create eighteen million new jobs between 1983 and 1989.

Moreover, it took much more than 4 x 6 cards to win the Cold War, dispel the nuclear nightmare and put down democratic roots in the previously barren soil of the Third World. Reagan remade the federal judiciary to reflect common-sense conservatism. He recast the allegiance of young voters, setting the stage for an enduring realignment of American politics. He rebuilt a weakened military in a campaign that was controversial at the time, but that would look prophetic, indeed, with every "smart bomb" that found its way to an Iraqi target during the Gulf War.

Along the way, Reagan won support from many who disapproved of his policies, because he was so obviously a man of conviction. Voters were naturally impressed by a leader who never had to hoist a wet finger in the breeze of public opinion to find his core beliefs. Yet Ronald Reagan was a very practical idealist. More than once I heard him express puzzlement over those in his own ranks who were unsatisfied with anything less than total victory.

"If I can get 90 percent of what I want," said Reagan, "I'd call that a pretty good deal." It was an attitude dating to his years spent negotiating on behalf of the Screen Actors Guild. And it served him well in obtaining, if not 90 percent of his objectives, then vastly more than Washington's pundits had predicted at the start of his presidency.

All of which should make for caution in forecasting future presidential performance, or accepting snap judgments by revisionist historians for whom the only "imperial" Presidents are conservative Republicans.

Reagan's unconventional way of seeing the world around him extended far beyond politics. In July 1985, he underwent surgery for the removal of two feet of his large intestine. Speaking to reporters afterward, the chief surgeon announced, "The President has cancer." The patient, however, had not been consulted. He took vigorous exception to the professional's diagnosis.

"I didn't have cancer," Ronald Reagan insisted with the same willful optimism that so baffled his political opponents. "I had something inside of me that had cancer in it, and it was removed."

When, a decade later, former President Reagan wrote his now famous letter to the American people revealing that he was suffering from Alzheimer's disease, he chose to emphasize the positive. For Ronald Reagan, it will always be morning in America. Sustained by his beloved Nancy and the abiding affection of his countrymen, he could face the future with a serenity born of faith in God. Few men could hope for more.

Thanks to President Reagan, America had made a remarkable comeback in the 1980s. Just because the Reagan Administration was drawing to a close did not mean that the priorities —much less the values—espoused by the President were being consigned to the history books. Far from it. The contest for the 1988 Republican presidential nomination was essentially all about who could consolidate and build upon the Reagan record. I felt that I could protect what President Reagan had begun against the furious counterassault sure to be launched by Democrats on Capitol Hill and special interests whose professed love of democracy never quite extended to accepting the legitimacy of Ronald Reagan's two landslide victories.

I knew from the beginning that the race for the Republican nomination would be uphill all the way. George Bush, after serving loyally for eight years as Ronald Reagan's Vice President, was thought by many Republicans to have earned our party's nomination. A majority of the GOP establishment— governors, members of Congress, senators and major financial contributors—had already signed up with the Bush campaign by the time I returned to Russell on November 9, 1987, to officially enter the race.

By the end of 1987, the roster of Republican presidential candidates included Vice President Bush, myself, Congressman Jack Kemp, former Delaware Governor Pete du Pont, former Secretary of State Al Haig, and Pat Robertson, president of the Christian Broadcasting Network. Another possible candidate, my good friend Howard Baker, had removed himself from the race when he signed on as White House chief of staff to help the Reagan Administration recover from the Iran-contra affair.

George Bush and I had sat through countless meetings together during our careers in Washington, but we didn't really know each other on a personal basis. Given the difference in our backgrounds, I had long felt we had little in common. Perhaps it was those differences, combined with our competing political aspirations, that led to what had been a slightly awkward relationship in the 1980s—a relationship made even more tense by the pressure of a presidential campaign.

Given the Vice President's early advantage in terms of money, endorsements and organization, I knew that without an early victory, my campaign would be over quickly. Fortunately for me, the campaign began in Iowa.

"He's one of us," was my theme in Iowa, and it fit. Iowans are a lot like Kansans, and as I campaigned across the state, I could talk easily with voters about the price of corn, or the common-sense rural values which we shared. With the help of Iowa Senator Chuck Grassley, I put together a Hawkeye State organization with an eagle eye for recruiting volunteers and supporters. Our hard work paid off on February 8, when Iowa Republicans sent a political shock wave across America.

There were two headlines that day. The first was that I had won with 37.4 percent of the vote. And the second was that Pat Robertson, mobilizing citizens who had never before been active in the political process, came in second with 24.6 percent. Vice President Bush limped home third, with 18.6 percent.

There were now eight days until the New Hampshire primary. I knew that if I could win the Granite State—a tall order, given New Hampshire Governor John Sununu's all-out support for Bush—I would be well on the way to the nomination. It is said that there are three M's in presidential politics: momentum, money and media attention. My victory in Iowa gave me momentum, and brought in some additional money. But the media were another matter. For most of the attention usually reserved for Iowa's victor was diverted to Robertson's surprising showing.

Still, a week before New Hampshire, my campaign pollster raised expectations by publicly predicting victory. He wasn't just "whistling Dixie." In fact, he walked into my hotel room whistling "Hail to the Chief." Then he told me flat out that I would be the next President. Years later, I joked that I haven't seen that pollster since—and I haven't paid him either.

In any event, I didn't stop campaigning to write an inaugural address. In the days before the primary, I could feel my lead —if I ever had one—slipping away. A huge snowstorm hit New Hampshire, and the Vice President was all over the state, shoveling snow, driving plows and engaging in other telegenic activities. Thanks to Sununu's organization, "George Bush" signs blanketed the state like the snow, and with more lasting effect. There was another factor contributing to my growing uneasiness. The Bush campaign was running misleading commercials questioning my opposition to tax increases. Given the fact that as chairman of the Senate Finance Committee I had made President Reagan's tax cuts a reality, the advertisements struck me as disingenuous.

But the issue—always a critical one in New Hampshire, which has no state income tax—wouldn't go away. It arose dramatically in a televised debate the Sunday before the primary. Pete du Pont, violating the "no props" rule to which all candidates had agreed, handed me a piece of paper, said it was a no-tax pledge and challenged me to sign it. I believed the pledge was written in such a way that it would prohibit even the closing of unfair tax loopholes. I knew as well that no matter what a possible President Dole said on a New Hampshire television station, a Democrat Congress—where all tax bills originate—would be pushing for a tax increase. Having learned early in life not to make promises you might not be able to keep, I didn't sign the pledge.

Forty-eight hours later, I was conceding defeat in the primary. If I had to do it all over again, would I sign the pledge waved in my face in February 1988? No. Leading is more important than misleading, and stunts are not to be confused with statesmanship. I *did* sign a revised antitax pledge in 1996, one changed to allow the closing of loopholes. By then, too, I also knew that a *Republican* Congress would share a President Dole's staunch opposition to tax increases.

Is there anything else about my New Hampshire campaigning I would have done differently? In retrospect, agreeing to a live televised interview with NBC's Tom Brokaw as the primary results came in was not a stroke of genius.

I had just suffered a defeat which I knew might well end my campaign. I had endured weeks of television ads which distorted my record. I had the flu. Truth be told, I was angry with myself, for wanting to believe the rosy predictions of campaign staffers against my better judgment, and for not responding to the first wave of negative commercials rolling over the New Hampshire electorate. New Hampshire was a "slam-dunk" which had bounced off the rim.

Put yourself in my place. Sitting in a dark room, unaware that George Bush was simultaneously on-screen. Suddenly, I heard Brokaw's voice in my earpiece. Did I have anything to say to the Vice President. My response—"Tell him to stop lying about my record"—was anything but cheerful.

It wasn't the most diplomatic moment in my career, but at least it was *real*. I regretted it instantly, and the next day pundits gleefully compared my performance to Richard Nixon's famous 1962 press conference at which the defeated gubernatorial candidate declared, "You won't have Nixon to kick around anymore."

The jury's still out on whether Nixon or the press had the

last laugh over that one. Actually, you'd be surprised how many average voters over the next few days applauded my display of honest emotion. Like Harry Truman and Dwight Eisenhower, whose portraits I had proposed hanging in the White House Cabinet Room if I ever occupied the Oval Office next door, I am a plainspoken man, with a Midwestern preference for candor over concealment. In the climate of today's political campaigns, when so much of what a candidate says is artificially scripted, when Rose Garden ceremonies and cool blue backdrops supplant grass-roots democracy, and much of the press is reduced to playing Trivial Pursuit or front-page "gotcha," I'm not alone in wondering whether a peppery Truman or a tongue-tied Eisenhower could reach the White House.

Don't get me wrong. I'm not advocating public displays of anger. What I am saying is that we can't have it both ways— lamenting the synthetic gestures and empty theatrics of so much of modern politics, *and* lambasting a candidate who refuses to be homogenized by handlers. Presidents and, yes, would-be Presidents should set an example of civility and self-restraint. But they should also be themselves. In addition to the usual criteria cited by presidential scholars and voters alike, I'd add authenticity to the list. Which is just another word for knowing who you are, and never pretending to be something you aren't.

Meanwhile, my post–New Hampshire campaign temporarily righted itself a week later with victories in South Dakota and Minnesota. At the same time, I knew that Lee Atwater, President Bush's brilliant political strategist, had built a massive firewall in the Super Tuesday Southern primaries. There were seventeen separate contests that day, and although I came close in some, the Vice President won them all. I was out of the race before the end of March.

ELIZABETH

While Bob was nearing a decision to run for President in 1987, I faced one of my own: when to leave a challenging job I loved in President Reagan's Cabinet to campaign for my husband on a full-time basis.

By then, I had served four and a half years—longer than any-one else—as Secretary of Transportation. Remaining until the end of the Reagan Administration would be a great honor, but I could not imagine saying to Bob "Good-bye, good luck and I'll see you when it's over." I would be missing the opportunity to play a significant part in the drama of national politics, and the chance to talk with Americans about the man who I believed should be the leader of the free world.

I would face a similar choice in 1995, although there was one big difference: One cannot take a leave of absence from the Cabinet. And so I made the decision to resign.

I had spent the better part of a lifetime arguing that women should be able to define our own contributions to society. And during the course of my years in Washington, I had seen a transformation in the role played by men as well as women in American politics. It came as no surprise, then, when some people, men as well as women, questioned my decision to leave DOT. Why should I have to quit my job, they asked, just be-cause my husband was running for President?

I didn't see it that way at all. The decision was mine and mine alone, and I made the decision that was right for me—just as I would in 1995. Not because I *had* to, but because I *wanted* to. And isn't that what we women have fought for all these years—the right to make our own decisions about our careers and our families?

As I traveled the nation on Bob's behalf, it soon became clear that my decision was the right one. I enjoyed meeting new people, listening and responding to their thoughts on the future of our country, taking their concerns to my husband and de-scribing to them a leader who drew his strength from a lifetime spent overcoming adversity, and whose compassion for others comes from a deep well of human sympathy.

Like Bob, my hopes were raised by his victory in Iowa, only to be dashed a week later in New Hampshire. My sadness at Bob's defeat quickly gave way to incredible pride. Having seen his dream come to an end, it would have been easy for Bob to "take his marbles and go home." Or, he could have used the delegates he had won in the primaries to make demands on the Bush campaign. He did neither.

"We need a Republican President," he said. "And if it can't be me, then it will be George Bush." Within days of his withdrawal, Bob was on the road, traveling to twenty-two state Republican conventions, calling for party unity, and doing all he could to ensure the Vice President's victory in November. His efforts did not go unnoticed. George Bush valued loyalty as a sign of character. Of Bob he remarked, "Nobody could ask the man to do more than he's done for me."

I was also proud to travel the country on behalf of George Bush: Our elation at his landslide victory was tempered only by the fact that the Senate remained in Democratic hands.

Christmas 1988 found me where I always spend part of the holidays—with my mother in Salisbury. In between shopping for gifts and visiting family and friends, I was also thinking about my future. I had devoted twenty-three years of my life to government service. Perhaps now was the time, I thought, to try and make a difference somewhere else.

I had always been inspired by the extraordinary willingness of Americans to give freely of their time, talent and treasure to causes larger than themselves. But like most people, I was surprised to learn that, on average, Americans gave less than 2 percent of their incomes to charity. Convinced that my fellow citizens were prepared to do more, I had begun to envision an organization that would promote and increase charitable giving and volunteer time. Just a 1 percent increase in the overall amount given to charity would mean an additional $62 billion for those in need. It was a point worth making, and I hoped to make it by uniting churches, philanthropies and leaders from the worlds of government, advertising, business, sports and entertainment.

Two days before Christmas, however, President-elect Bush reached me at my mother's home, and asked if I would serve as Secretary of Labor. I had neither sought nor expected a Cabinet position. Although flattered by the offer, I asked the President-elect if I could think it over for a day or two. I wasn't being cagey. Before putting my plans on hold, I wanted to determine if I would feel a similar sense of mission as Secretary of Labor.

It didn't take me long to decide that the Department of

Labor offered a wealth of opportunities to affect people's lives for the better. By way of illustration, there is a story told about the late George Meany, the longtime president of the AFL-CIO. It seemed that Meany called a particular Cabinet officer to ask about a problem that had crossed his mind. The Cabinet secretary said, "George, what the blazes has that got to do with labor?"

"Sonny boy," Meany replied, "everything that happens today has to do with labor."

As I studied the portfolio I would inherit as Secretary of Labor, Meany's remarks seemed prophetic. Originally founded in 1913, the Labor Department was meant to be a voice for America's workingmen and women. Its many responsibilities included workforce training, workplace safety, promotion of good labor-management relations and oversight of pension plans. Here was an invitation, I believed, to help young Americans just entering the workplace, adult Americans already in the workforce and Americans seeking security in their golden years.

One of the first calls I made after accepting the President-elect's offer was to Lane Kirkland, George Meany's AFL-CIO successor. Some past Republican labor secretaries had adversarial relationships with America's union leaders, and I wanted to ensure that that did not happen on my watch.

"Lane," I said, "I know we'll have to agree to disagree on most issues, but I want you to know that my door and the department's lines of communication will always be open to you. America's workforce has some big challenges—and they are challenges that we won't meet if we don't trust one another." I repeated that message to the AFL-CIO executive council soon after taking office. The open relationship I maintained with union leaders remains a source of satisfaction.

From my first day at the Labor Department, I left no doubt that improving the skills of America's current and future workforce would be a top priority. The reason for that was simple. In the final years of the twentieth century, America's workforce was in turmoil because America's workplace was undergoing revolutionary changes.

Across the board, employers were insisting on higher skills

and a better educated workforce. Half the jobs in our economy, experts told me, would soon require schooling beyond the twelfth grade. Assembly-line jobs that had once required only hand-eye coordination now demanded the ability to read complex manuals, operate computers, analyze data, organize information and make difficult judgments.

Meanwhile, I was hearing from employers that the preparation students received in our classrooms was inadequate to meet the needs of our workplace. Twenty-five percent of our young people were dropping out of high school. Seventy percent of those who did graduate couldn't write a basic letter seeking employment. From one corporate leader I learned that four out of every five job applicants in his company had recently flunked entry-level employment exams requiring seventh-grade English and fifth-grade math skills. I knew that if changes were not made, then America's success in a complex and competitive world market would be in doubt, and we would also be sentencing countless young Americans to a future of little hope.

A ten-day, ten-city tour of Department of Labor offices and programs during my first month on the job introduced me to my talented DOL family, and to hundreds of young men and women whose lives had been literally turned around from the most negative behavior by our job-training classes. In heart-wrenching terms, they described childhoods darkened by abuse, gangs, crime and drugs. They told me that besides job skills, our training programs had given them self-respect and a way out of poverty. I brought several of these young people to Washington to testify at congressional hearings. What powerful testimony it was. Their street stories evoked tears and waves of applause from many Capitol Hill veterans. Hopefully, it would also lead to increased congressional support for our efforts to improve and modernize the skills of our workforce.

In the next year and a half, those efforts would include: the appointment of a blue-ribbon commission, chaired by former Secretary of Labor Bill Brock, charged with developing national competency guidelines that reflect work readiness and which can be used by schools for curriculum development; sponsorship of the first-ever national conference on the "school-to-work" population (youth who enter the job market directly out of high school); expansion of work-based training along the principles of apprenticeship, which is so successful in the construction industry; and refocusing of the Job Training Partnership Act on the least skilled and most economically disadvantaged Americans, providing not just training for a job, but basic skills, literacy and remedial education.

These efforts did not require new federal programs or a massive influx of dollars. They were the best examples of using the federal government as leader, convener and catalyst of our citizens. They succeeded then—and continue to succeed today —because they are run and managed by our schools, employers and unions, not by a remote bureaucracy.

During those early months at the Labor Department, I put together a first-rate team of public servants who would work with me. Once the appointments were made, I looked around the conference table where we met most mornings, and noted that nearly two thirds of my senior staff were women or minorities. I hadn't set out to send a message. I simply selected the best people for the jobs. But I was hoping that corporate America took note, as one of my objectives at Labor was to serve as a catalyst for change in removing every last vestige of discrimination from the workplace, and ensuring that women and minorities had equal access to senior management employment opportunities.

Frances Perkins, who as Franklin Roosevelt's Secretary of Labor was the first female Cabinet officer, was once asked if being a woman posed a disadvantage in public life. "Only," she said, "when I am climbing trees." A lot of women and minorities were discovering that as they rose up the "corporate tree," the highest branches were often out of reach. As Secretary, I initiated an examination of what has come to be known as the "glass ceiling," the invisible but impenetrable barrier that seemed to prevent women and minorities from reaching the top levels of corporate America.

We studied training, rotational assignments, developmental programs and reward structures—all indicators of upward mobility in corporate America—to determine if qualified women and minorities were included. The results were disturbing. Of the nearly 4,500 executive-level managerial positions in the nine corporations we reviewed, only 6.6 percent were held by women, and 2.6 percent by minorities. In other words, women and minorities—who account for half the workforce—comprised less than 10 percent of top managerial positions.

I oppose quotas of any kind, but I did want to use the Labor Department as a "bully pulpit," to tell business in no uncertain terms that if they effectively block half of their employees from reaching their full potential, then they were only hurting themselves.

Bob was sending the same message in the Senate, with his sponsorship of legislation that established a National Commission on the Glass Ceiling. It's worth noting that Bob does more than just talk about opening doors for women, he has backed up his words with action.

As chairman of the Republican party, he appointed the first woman in history to serve as deputy chairman. As Senate Republican Leader, he appointed the first woman in history to serve as Secretary of the Senate—the chief administrative officer of the Senate. He was also the first Senate Leader in history—Republican or Democrat—to have a woman as chief of staff.

In his leadership office, his top advisers on policy issues like health care, taxes, the environment and foreign policy are all women. And at the Dole for President campaign, his finance director and his political director are just two of the many women who play leadership roles.

Both Bob and I hope for a future where the glass ceiling meets the same fate as the Berlin Wall.

BOB

In his inaugural address on January 20, 1989, President Bush said the American people "didn't send us here to bicker," and he extended a hand of friendship to the new Senate Majority Leader, George Mitchell of Maine, and to Jim Wright of Texas, the Speaker of the House of Representatives. It was a genuine offer, and it was one that the Democrat Congress refused nearly every day for the next four years.

While congressional Democrats almost always refused to work with President Bush, our partnership—and our friendship—became very strong. Some White House staff members had trouble forgetting that I had run against their boss in 1988. But not George Bush. Years of competition dissolved almost overnight. My respect for Ronald Reagan's successor grew each day of his presidency. It would later extend to Bush's sons Jeb and George Jr., both sharing their father's integrity and each having a bright future in the Republican party.

There were times where I disagreed with the President, and I told him so, believing that I owed him my candor and my judgment, as well as my vote. But I also owed him my loyalty. I knew from day one that my job as Senate Republican Leader in the Bush Administration was the same as it had been during the Reagan presidency—to do everything possible to support the man in the Oval Office.

He needed all the support he could get, as an increasingly partisan Democrat Congress looked for battles wherever they could be incited. The first confrontation between Congress and President Bush was over John Tower's confirmation as Secretary of Defense. During his nearly thirty years in the Senate, including a distinguished stint as chairman of the Armed Services Committee, Tower had earned a reputation as one of America's leading voices on military and national security issues.

To some minds, he had also earned a reputation for activities outside the Senate. Having served his country in World War II, and chaired the Tower Commission, which reprimanded the Reagan White House for its conduct in the Iran-contra affair, Tower was reduced to fighting an entirely different kind of battle against rumor and innuendo. It was a classic Washington ambush, culminating in Tower's defeat on March 9, 1989. The vote against his confirmation was 53–47.

John Tower was not perfect. But no one could deny his impressive qualifications to serve as Secretary of Defense. He was not the first presidential nominee to be defeated by the Senate. Nor was he the last. Something very disturbing took place during the twelve years of the Reagan and Bush Administrations, as Senate Democrats turned the confirmation process into an inquisition.

When Republicans returned to the Senate majority in 1995, some of my colleagues urged me to accord President Clinton the same treatment. Turnabout may be fair play, but it is rarely good government. Elections are about choices. And when the voters choose a President, they also choose the men and women who will serve that President. I have always believed that Presidents—whatever their party—are, banning something extraordinary, entitled to choose the men and women they want to serve at their side.

President Clinton's nominees are much too liberal for my taste, but most were also qualified to occupy the positions for which they were nominated. And I did not fight their confirmations. By restoring some civility to the confirmation process, I hope we can encourage outstanding Americans to consider government service.

Far from Washington, the world's attention in 1989 was focused on the remarkable events occurring in Eastern Europe, where the Iron Curtain was vanishing like a late-season snowdrift. That August, when Elizabeth and I traveled to Poland, we became eyewitnesses to history. We arrived in Warsaw the very August afternoon the Polish Parliament elected Solidarity leader Tadeusz Mazowiecki as his country's first non-Communist Prime Minister in more than forty years. Soon after the vote, we attended a caucus of Solidarity members of the Parliament. It is hard to describe the emotions we saw and felt in that room. Poland had been reborn, with faith in democracy that no regime could hope to suppress.

Following our emotional meeting with the Parliament, Elizabeth and I met with the Communist President of Poland, General Wojciech Jaruzelski, the same man who had jailed Mazowiecki in 1981. We were impressed by the General's frankness, and heartened by his acknowledgment that the tide of democracy would not and could not be stopped in Poland.

The joy and optimism we saw in Poland was in stark contrast to the horror we witnessed en route to Warsaw, in the shattered nation of Armenia. Because of Dr. Kelikian, I have long felt a special connection with Armenians. As it happened, President Bush was interested in knowing how Armenia was recovering from a devastating earthquake months earlier. Elizabeth and I arrived carrying $50,000 worth of relief supplies destined for Project Hope, an American relief agency working in Armenia. One didn't have to look far to realize that much more help would be needed.

More than 25,000 Armenians had been killed in the earthquake, and five times that number injured. Half a million were homeless, with a brutal winter fast approaching. Incredible as those statistics are, they can hardly prepare you for the human tragedy behind the numbers. No statistics can gauge the anguish of the mothers in the city of Leninakan, where four hundred children were lost when their school collapsed. While we were being briefed by the city leader of Spitak, someone whispered in my ear that this same man lost his wife and every one of his twelve children in the earthquake. Before leaving, we went to a hillside covered with eight thousand still-fresh graves, each marked by a tombstone bearing the etched face of an individual quake victim.

In the face of such overwhelming loss, Elizabeth and I were deeply moved by the determination, optimism and genuine humanity we encountered in the Armenian people. Such a spirit guided Hampar Kelikian throughout his life, and inspires me still. Whenever a President takes office, attention is paid to the first foreign country the new chief executive chooses to visit. I can think of no land to which I would rather make one of my first overseas trips than Armenia.

ELIZABETH

Our journey to Armenia and Poland was full of memories that will last a lifetime. For me, the most enduring were of the day we walked through the shipyards of Gdansk with Lech Walesa, the Polish electrician and Solidarity union leader who would eventually succeed General Jaruzelski as President.

Walesa told me then that the metaphor for a Communist economic enterprise was "a hundred workers standing around a single shovel." "What Poland needs now," he said, "is a hundred shovels."

While the Department of Labor did not provide shovels, I

made clear in a return visit to Poland in December 1989 that we could provide an impressive array of advice and technical assistance to help Poland in its historic transformation from a Marxist, centrally controlled economy to a free-market economy.

Perhaps the most innovative of our programs was the creation of a construction training center in the Praga district of Warsaw. One of the vestiges of central planning under Communism was a housing shortage—a shortage so severe that Polish families hoping to move faced waits of up to twenty-five years. Needless to say, this would be a drag on a vital private-sector economy, dependent upon the ability of workers to move where jobs are created.

With the assistance of the AFL-CIO, which had provided invaluable support to Solidarity during the Communist regime, American plumbers, pipefitters, carpenters, electricians, bricklayers and ironworkers all traveled to Warsaw to train Polish workers. The Praga center proved so successful that another was opened in Gdansk.

Flying home from Poland a few weeks before Christmas 1989, I saw my usual holiday plans turned upside down by one of the most divisive labor disputes in recent American history. I was no stranger to the controversy. The previous April, the United Mine Workers struck the Pittston Company and by early fall the company and the union were locked in a bitter confrontation. Throughout that period I had monitored the situation, speaking separately with Paul Douglas, the head of Pittston, and Rich Trumka, then president of the UMW, as well as with the federal Mediation and Conciliation Service, which was trying to resolve the dispute. Old animosities die hard in the coal mines, however. After several months of fruitless negotiations the parties were still meeting in separate rooms, and no solution was in sight.

I decided to take a firsthand look at the situation in mid-October, by visiting southwest Virginia where the divisions were as deep as the mines. I saw a community torn apart, and met with families who had one member walking the picket lines, and another in management. In that tense atmosphere, many feared that widespread violence was unavoidable.

I sensed that the impasse might be broken if I took a more active role and tried to bring the company and the union together. At the same time, however, I knew that as Secretary of Labor I should respect the collective bargaining process and not try to force an agreement.

The day after my trip to the mines, I asked Douglas and Trumka to come to my office, in the hope that they would agree that I could help. My strategy was to get the two men in the same room to see if there was a prospect for progress. If there was, then I had a lunch prepared in an adjoining room, where we could break bread and continue discussions. My guests arrived shortly before noon, and each left their lawyers outside with my staff so that the three of us could meet privately. As our meeting began, both expressed frustration with the deadlock, and both agreed that they would appreciate any suggestions I might have. When Rich asked for a second cup of coffee, I made my move. "I assume that you haven't had lunch yet," I said. "Why don't we have a quick bite to eat?"

As we talked over lunch, the ice between Douglas and Trumka really began to melt. By the end of our meal, both had agreed that my appointment of a "supermediator" would be a welcome step, and I led them in toasting the resolution of the strike. My next challenge was to select a supermediator acceptable to both parties. In former Labor Secretary Bill Usery, whose negotiating skills rivaled Henry Kissinger's, I found exactly the right person. The acting head of the Federal Mediation and Conciliation Service also knew Bill well, and he readily agreed to my request that his agency support Bill in this difficult task.

Bill later told me that of the more than eight hundred disputes he had mediated or negotiated in his career, Pittston was the toughest. Around-the-clock negotiating sessions—one lasting ninety-six straight hours—extended into the holiday season. I remained in my office night after night as Bill reported to me on the slow progress, and as Bob awaited my arrival in Florida for a brief vacation. Finally, on December 31, a settlement was reached. And on January 1, 1990, while millions of Americans watched football on television, I joined Bill Usery, Paul Douglas and Rich Trumka at a press conference to announce our victory.

BOB

In February of 1990 democracy came to Nicaragua. Bowing to outside demands, Daniel Ortega had finally agreed to hold a free election. It was less of a conversion than met the eye. Believing his own propaganda, Ortega was supremely confident of victory. To make certain that Marxism would retain its grip over Nicaragua, however, he took election-rigging steps worthy of Tammany Hall and the Soviet Politburo combined.

A funny thing about freedom: It's unpredictable, as Ortega would discover much to his dismay. On election day, the Nicaraguan people turned to Violeta Chamorro—the courageous widow of a crusading newspaperman murdered during the long Nicaraguan struggle for freedom. Frustrated in his search for ways to retain power, Ortega at last did what he should have done long ago, releasing his death grip over Nicaragua and allowing peace to come to that sorely troubled land.

While the Bush Administration pressed the case for freedom abroad, at home another kind of liberation was won by the 43 million Americans who happen to have a disability. One of the most rewarding days of my life came on July 26, 1990, when President Bush signed the Americans with Disabilities Act into law.

I suppose there were some that day who saw only a White House lawn covered with wheelchairs and guide dogs. But that just goes to show who in our society is truly limited. My own perspective was very different. As I looked around, I saw Americans possessed with amazing gifts, who could finally contribute to a nation much in need of their skills and insights.

ELIZABETH

A few months after I became Secretary of Labor, Dick Schubert came to my office for a meeting. Dick was a former deputy secretary of labor, and a top executive of Bethlehem Steel. At the time he was serving as president of the American Red Cross. The two of us discussed workforce training issues.

We also spoke of our mutual interest in reaching out to those in dire need of help.

"Elizabeth," Dick told me, "if you want to help those in need on a full-time basis then the Red Cross is the place for you." He also revealed that he would soon be leaving the presidency of the Red Cross, and asked if I would be interested in succeeding him. The suggestion surprised and intrigued me, but since my Department of Labor agenda was still in its infancy, changing jobs just then was out of the question.

The Red Cross did enter my DOL agenda a few months later, when through the Occupational Safety and Health Administration I proposed a new regulation to protect 5.4 million workers against blood-borne pathogens, such as AIDS and Hepatitis B. It was the first time in history that OSHA had proposed rules to deal with a biological hazard or infectious disease.

In the late summer of 1990, I received a phone call from Marian Andersen, a civic leader in Omaha, Nebraska, and a member of the American Red Cross board of governors. With characteristic directness, Marian came right to the point. After a year's search, the board of governors had still not found the person they wanted to run the Red Cross. Would I be willing to throw my hat in the ring? And, by the way, she needed an answer soon, as the board was committed to announcing a new president at its meeting that October.

Unlike a year earlier, Marian's request was well timed. I had enjoyed my service as Secretary of Labor. I felt as if we had made substantial progress in improving the skills of America's workforce, increasing health and safety in the workplace, and ensuring security for retired Americans. Yet the Red Cross offered an opportunity to devote all my time to an organization whose exclusive mission is to help society's victims. This time, I accepted the offer.

On a trip to a North Carolina political event aboard Air Force One, I told President Bush of my plans to leave the Labor Department. He was, as always, gracious and understanding. We agreed to delay public announcement of my departure for a while so he would have ample time to consider a replacement. Eventually, however, the President had to let his staff in on our secret, and, as always happens in Washington, word leaked out faster than you can say "hold the presses."

During the week of Thanksgiving 1990, my final days at the Labor Department were devoted to packing boxes and thanking the dedicated DOL employees. My thoughts, however, were with Bob, who was spending the holiday visiting the brave soldiers called upon to stop Saddam Hussein from carving up Kuwait.

BOB

In April 1990, a bipartisan delegation of four other Senators and I had journeyed to Egypt, Israel and Syria to lend our support to the delicate peace process, then generating new hope under the surefooted leadership of President Bush and Secretary of State James Baker. One of the region's wild cards was Saddam Hussein, the Iraqi dictator, who was growing increasingly bellicose in his threats. Egyptian President Hosni Mubarak offered to set up a meeting between our delegation and Hussein, and with the approval of President Bush, one was quickly arranged.

When we arrived in Baghdad, we were met by Iraqi officials who told us that the meeting would be held in the northern town of Mosul. Arriving there, we presented Iraq's leader with a letter signed by the entire delegation, delivering a stern warning that his efforts to develop nuclear, chemical and biological weapons capability jeopardized, rather than enhanced, his security. We also urged him to become actively and constructively engaged in the peace process.

At one point in the discussion, I gestured to my right arm. It was a daily reminder to me that we must all work for peace, I said. Our host might have read our letter and heard my words, but that didn't mean he took them to heart. Early in August we got our answer. Iraq invaded the tiny, practically defenseless nation of Kuwait.

Three months later, I joined President Bush and a bipartisan delegation of congressional leaders in spending Thanksgiving with some of our 500,000 troops then in the Gulf. You couldn't talk with those young Americans, assigned a difficult and possibly deadly task far from home, and not be impressed by their ardor and professionalism.

President Bush had been spectacularly successful in building an international coalition to remove Saddam Hussein's troops from Kuwait if he didn't leave voluntarily. The home-front was a different story. Many Americans were divided. I knew we could not afford another war like Vietnam that split the nation, and I resolved that if war was to come, it must enjoy the support of the American people, and the explicit approval of Congress.

As the weeks went by and Iraqi troops remained in Kuwait, the United Nations Security Council drew a line in the sand. Saddam was to get out of Kuwait by January 15, or risk war.

In the days leading up to that deadline, Congress engaged in an extraordinary debate. We had two choices. One was to support a resolution sponsored by Democratic Senator Sam Nunn of Georgia, chairman of the Armed Services Committee. It would have denied congressional authorization for military action by our troops, forcing the President to rely for a longer period of time on economic sanctions. The other resolution was sponsored by Virginia Senator John Warner and myself. It would give congressional support to whatever decision was made by President Bush if Saddam did not obey the UN deadline.

Nobody in the Senate wanted war—least of all those of us who had fought one. But I also knew that passage of the Nunn resolution would be a disaster of historic proportions. Economic sanctions had been in place for months, and Iraq's occupation of Kuwait had continued without any sign of a letup. If Congress refused to authorize the use of military force, then Hussein would know that his attack on Kuwait just might succeed.

Saddam could presumably count the planes and other weapons arrayed against him. He had to know that if shooting started, he was going to lose. I believe he remained in Kuwait as long as he did because he underestimated American will. He doubted our staying power, not our firepower. He questioned our unity. And Saddam's strategy almost paid off because the U.S. Congress came uncomfortably close to making one of the biggest mistakes in American history.

When the roll was called, every member of the House and Senate Democratic congressional leadership—Speaker of the House Tom Foley, House Majority Leader Dick Gephardt, Senate Majority Leader George Mitchell and Senate Majority Whip Wendell Ford—were counted in opposition to the Dole-Warner resolution. In the course of the debate, many Democrats harshly attacked President Bush. They predicted that any fighting would be a "tremendous blunder," costing fifty thousand American lives.

Given the united opposition of the Democrat leadership and the 57–43 Democratic majority in the Senate, we had little margin for error. Our margin grew even smaller when two Republicans—Chuck Grassley of Iowa and Oregon's Mark Hatfield—told me they could not vote for war. Fortunately, eleven Democrats, led by the highly respected Joe Lieberman of Connecticut, broke from their leadership. Their votes, combined with those of forty-one Republicans, gave the Dole-Warner resolution a 52–47 margin.

Immediately following the Senate action, I asked the Iraqi ambassador to the United States to come to my office and meet with a bipartisan delegation of Senators. I came right to the point. "America and the Senate are standing with President Bush," I said. "Tell Saddam Hussein to get out now, or be ready to get kicked out." It wasn't exactly diplomatic language, but it was what the situation called for.

The January 15 deadline came and went. Iraqi troops remained in Kuwait. Late in the afternoon of the next day, the congressional leadership gathered around my desk for a briefing by CIA Director Robert Gates. He told us that American planes were already in the air, and that the bombing of Iraq would begin that evening.

Senate Republican Whip Alan Simpson joined me at 9 P.M. to watch President Bush's eloquent address to the American people. And then, like millions of Americans, we watched as the Persian Gulf War became the first conflict broadcast live on television.

After a month and a half of aerial bombing, and a brilliantly conceived and executed ground assault lasting just a hundred hours, the war was over. One hundred forty-six American lives were lost in action. One death is too many, but our losses were far fewer than the Vietnam-like casualties predicted in advance by some congressional Democrats. My state of Kansas shared in the tragic loss of brave soldiers and airmen. Michael Daniels, Marty Davis, Jeff Middleton, Gary Streeter, George Swartzendruber and William Gimm died serving the cause of freedom. My Kansas colleague, Nancy Kassebaum, and I attended many of their funerals and memorial services—the least we could do to show our respect for their sacrifice and heroism.

President Bush's leadership in the Persian Gulf War earned him the highest public opinion approval ratings in history. Ironically, however, the war may also have played a role in the events that would lead to his reelection defeat. With his attention focused on the Persian Gulf in the fall of 1990, the President yielded to the Democrats' insistence on a budget that included a tax increase. In the process he broke his most celebrated campaign promise of 1988.

More than a few Republicans, including Congressman Newt Gingrich, were outraged by the President's action. Given the fact that President Bush had employed the "no new taxes" pledge to defeat me in New Hampshire, they told me that I should be equally upset. I have always said, however, that leadership comes with a price. My role as Republican Leader was to support the President. And that's precisely what I did.

The Bush Administration and I did agree to disagree over events in the Soviet Union, then in the process of disintegration. I had visited Moscow in 1990, meeting with both President Mikhail Gorbachev and Boris Yeltsin, who would later become President of Russia, the first Soviet republic to declare its independence.

While I admired much of what Gorbachev had accomplished, I also thought the Bush Administration was wrong to put all its eggs in one basket, and should have acknowledged democratic reformers like Yeltsin. In 1991, Majority Leader George Mitchell and I invited Yeltsin to visit the United States. When his plane landed at Andrews Air Force Base in mid-June,

I was there to greet him—joined only by a lower-level State Department official.

A year later, Yeltsin received a much more elaborate greeting when he returned to the United States. By then, he had earned the world's admiration for standing atop a tank and rallying the forces of democracy against the gray apparatchiks trying to depose Gorbachev in a coup. Like any good politician, Yeltsin remembered who had stood with him in his time of trial. Breaking away from Washington's pomp and circumstance, President and Mrs. Yeltsin joined Elizabeth and me for a summer's day in Kansas. Yetsin met with a group of college students at Wichita State University, impressing them with his quick wit. I also brought him to a family farm and a meat-packing plant. One of the plant employees presented Yeltsin with a company windbreaker. In return, Yeltsin took off his suit jacket and presented it to the stunned Kansan. Détente never had it so good.

ELIZABETH

February 1, 1991, was my first day on the job as president of the world's leading humanitarian organization. Hundreds of American Red Cross staffers and volunteers gathered at the beautiful national headquarters building to bid me welcome.

In remarks that morning, I recalled how often, during the preceding months, I had been approached by people who wanted me to know how Red Cross assistance had changed their lives after a disaster, how we had delivered important messages to a loved one in the armed services, how they had learned to swim in one of our classes, or how blood collected, tested, processed and distributed by the Red Cross had made a life-or-death difference for them or a loved one.

I don't have to tell you that we live in a time when few institutions enjoy automatic popular confidence. The Red Cross was and is an exception. What struck me most during these conversations was the absolute trust placed in an organization founded over a century before by Clara Barton. People trust the Red Cross to always be there when needed, and to do what is right. From my standpoint, this tradition of trust was—and is —the organization's most valuable asset. To protect and strengthen this tradition would be my overriding goal as president.

On my first day, I also announced a decision I had reached weeks earlier: I would not accept a salary during my first year as president. What better way was there, I had concluded, to let the army of one and a half million volunteers know that they are the heart and soul of the Red Cross?

As we gathered that day, our thoughts were with the 156 Red Crossers stationed alongside our troops in Saudi Arabia. There, they continued our century-long commitment to America's servicemen and women by providing an oasis of reassurance in a distant and hostile desert land. Already, Red Cross staffers were delivering eight thousand emergency messages from home daily to Desert Storm personnel. On a more sobering note, I knew that the Red Cross was also poised to ship as many as seven thousand units of blood per week to the Persian Gulf, should they be needed.

Shortly after the war's end, I was on my way to the Persian Gulf to thank our courageous staffers, and to deliver the first sixty-six tons of relief supplies to the people of Kuwait. At the same time, I wanted to conduct a firsthand examination of what was needed, and to learn if there were other ways in which the Red Cross could help.

My questions were answered during a visit to an institution for physically and mentally handicapped children in Kuwait City. The conditions could only be described as nightmarish. During those terrible months of occupation, three hundred children had been cared for by only twenty-two nurses. An additional 170 children had died. Many of the staff had fled the country. The hospital had been riddled with gunfire, much of it passing directly over the beds where children often lay in the dark since there was only intermittent power or water.

No one could see the suffering of these innocent children and not be deeply moved. On the spot, I pledged that the American Red Cross would send fifty nurses, doctors and physical therapists to the institution. Some Red Cross staffers who specialized in international affairs gasped at this. They reminded me that since I was new in the job, I might not know that such projects were the province of the International Red Cross Federation, and that our sponsorship of such a project might break a few rules of protocol. Making pledges like the one I had just delivered so impulsively, they told me, was not the way we did things.

"It is now," I said. And within weeks, we were able to meet that pledge, as courageous nurses and doctors from across the nation answered our call for help. Many gave up paid jobs. All left their friends and families to travel halfway across the world to accept a hardship assignment. The generosity of the American people could also be seen in the more than $26 million we raised in contributions and in-kind gifts to underwrite Red Cross services in the Gulf.

Shortly after accepting the presidency of the Red Cross, I was reminded by my mother of her own service as a Red Cross volunteer during World War II. "Elizabeth," she said, "Nothing I ever did made me feel so important." Flying home from Kuwait, only one month into my job, I knew that Mother was right. I had found a job that filled me with a sense of mission like I had never known.

In May 1991, Red Crossers from across the nation convened in San Diego for our annual convention. These gatherings offer a good opportunity for staffers and volunteers to exchange ideas, to learn about new programs, and to plan for the future. Not the sort of things that make national news. But this convention was different. For it was in San Diego where I announced the most ambitious project in Red Cross history.

As it happened, my first month at the Red Cross coincided with the fiftieth anniversary of our blood services program. Since its inception in World War II, the program had grown to the point where we collected, processed and distributed more than half of America's blood supply. Nothing could be more important to our tradition of trust than to ensure that that supply was as safe as we could possibly make it.

For many years, the Red Cross had performed two tests for infectious disease on each unit of donated blood. By 1991, with the advent of HIV/AIDS and medical advances that made the presence of certain diseases detectable, we were performing eight tests on every unit of blood. Overall, the Red Cross conducted 100 million more blood tests in the second half of the 1980s than in the previous five years.

As new tests and new quality-assurance procedures were added, the Red Cross Blood Services infrastructure, already overburdened, became more and more weighed down. I knew that if we were to continue our involvement in blood services, bold action was required—not an incremental change, but a complete and total overhaul. And so as Red Crossers gathered in San Diego, I announced what ultimately would be a $162 million project to transform the Red Cross blood operations into a state-of-the-art system that would quickly incorporate medical advances and new technology as they evolve.

When I began my leave of absence in October 1995, the transformation was 80 percent complete. It included creation of the world's largest blood information database, establishment of an unsurpassed quality-assurance system, replacement of fifty-three aging and semi-independent regional labs with nine cutting-edge national testing laboratories that are unquestionably the best in the world, replacement of twenty-eight different computer systems with a single next-generation computer linking all Red Cross blood operations, and the founding of the Charles Drew Biomedical Institute, a technology-based education and training center that will deliver the latest in techniques and tools to Red Cross personnel. The institute was hailed by FDA Commissioner David Kessler as "exceptionally well suited for seeking and achieving the highest standards."

All of these improvements led Secretary of Health and Human Services Donna Shalala to recently tell a congressional committee that we had made "an extraordinary effort to upgrade the quality of management and of blood safety procedures." "I can't say enough good about what the Red Cross has done," she continued. "They have made a huge investment in improving the quality of their own oversight and of the blood supply. Mrs. Dole has been very tough-minded about raising the standards." Needless to say, that was music to my ears.

It is worth noting that all of the improvements we have made will be useless if Americans don't donate the blood which provides life to so many. No matter what time of the year, some areas occasionally experience blood shortages. The next time you have a few free minutes on your hands, call your local Red Cross, and ask how you can donate blood. It is absolutely safe and virtually painless. Men, women and children you may never know will have reason to thank you for the gift of life.

BOB

While Elizabeth was immersing herself in the technicalities of blood services, she and I found ourselves researching a topic which had unexpectedly entered my life—prostate cancer.

In the summer of 1991, I noticed I was getting up more frequently at night. I mentioned this to my doctor during my annual medical exam that July, and he gave me a PSA blood test —a simple procedure that detects the presence of prostate-specific antigens. PSA readings of 0 to 4 are considered normal. Anything above indicates the possible presence of cancer. My PSA was 4.1. My doctor recommended a follow-up test a few weeks later. This time, the PSA was slightly higher. A biopsy provided the final confirmation.

In fact, it was a classic bad news/good news situation. Given the relatively low PSA numbers, my doctor believed the cancer had been caught in its earliest stages, and that because of my otherwise excellent health, a complete recovery was likely. Naturally, I hoped he was right.

Elizabeth and I began to educate ourselves about a disease we knew next to nothing about. What we learned surprised us. Prostate cancer was one of the most commonly diagnosed cancers in America. In 1985 alone 85,000 men were diagnosed with the disease. And the American Cancer Society estimates that this year 317,000 American men will be told they have prostate cancer.

One of the chief reasons for that dramatic increase is that more and more men are now being tested for the disease. I would like to think that I played a role in increasing public awareness, testing and early detection.

Many men don't like to talk about their physical disorders, and some are embarrassed to use the word "prostate" in public. In fact, prostate cancer was so little understood that once my diagnosis became common knowledge, my office received calls from a number of women, wondering how they should be tested.

There are a variety of treatment options, and I studied several before choosing surgery. A three-hour procedure on December 18, 1991, at Walter Reed Hospital confirmed my doctor's optimism. The cancer had not spread, and the surgeons were able to successfully remove it all. Sixteen days later, I was back on the Senate floor. And nearly five years after surgery, my PSA level is holding steady at zero.

Because I was fortunate in having my cancer detected early, I decided to do whatever I could to let other men know of the benefits of early detection. For a while, I joked I had become the "prostate poster boy." I attended meetings of other prostate cancer survivors. I talked about the importance of PSA tests in nearly every speech and television interview I gave. I even sponsored PSA testing booths at the Kansas State Fair and at the 1992 Republican National Convention.

In the past few years, more and more men—among them General Norman Schwarzkopf, Alabama Senator Richard Shelby and Buffalo Bills football coach Marv Levy—have gone public with their own successful battles against prostate cancer. For those who are reading this and who may have questions, I urge you to call the Us Too organization at 1–800–808–7866.

ELIZABETH

Bob never ceases to amaze me. Like most men of his generation, he is a private person, uncomfortable talking about himself; yet he could not have been more candid in sharing the details of intimate medical matters. While he says he "likes to think" he is partially responsible for increased public awareness of prostate cancer, I *know* he is. The reason is that I have read hundreds and hundreds of letters Bob has received from men who underwent a PSA test because of his urging, and who were cured because of early detection. This is just one more example of Bob's desire to make life better for people—whether on the battlefield, the Senate floor or in private life.

BOB

Having received a clean bill of health, I turned my attention to a decision I had delayed until after the surgery—whether to run for another term in the Senate in 1992. I loved my work, but, to be honest, there had been times when I thought it might be best to move on. At the White House one afternoon, I mentioned the possibility of retirement to President Bush, who immediately took me into a small private office just off of the Oval Office. After saying he hoped I was joking, he asked me to run again. I could help him in his second term, he told me. The subsequent debate over the Persian Gulf War reinforced the President's generous words. More than anything else, it convinced me I could still make a difference.

And so it was on January 24, 1992, that I gave what has been billed as the shortest reelection announcement ever. At a press conference in Topeka, in response to a reporter's question as to whether I was going to run that year, I replied, "Yes." End of speech. I *told* you the Dole men are laconic.

While I never take any election for granted, I felt confident that Kansans would keep me in the Senate. About President Bush's chances for reelection, however, I was far less certain. After the Persian Gulf War, I had urged the White House staff to take advantage of the President's high approval ratings, and to seize the initiative with an ambitious domestic agenda. Although Republicans were outnumbered in the House and Senate, the President's leadership in the Gulf had established an almost mythic aura about his White House. As long as the afterglow of victory lingered, I believed we could get enough Democrat votes to pass whatever the President sent up to us.

For two years, Senate Majority Leader Mitchell had prevented a number of Bush proposals—including a reduction in the capital gains tax rate—from becoming law. Could Mitchell have enjoyed similar success against the victor of the Gulf War? The question answered itself. Or it should have, if the White House staff had ever raised it. But from the other end of Pennsylvania Avenue, word leaked out that as far as the President's inner circle was concerned, Congress could do nothing for the rest of the year.

Within a few months, the war was receding from popular memory, and the perception began to take hold that the remarkable economic expansion of the Reagan and Bush years had stalled. Americans looking for action were soon demanding change. I had never met Arkansas Governor Bill Clinton, the man nominated in July 1992 to be the President's Democratic opponent. While bothered about the actions Clinton had taken to avoid the draft during the Vietnam era, and his apparent lack of candor about this issue, I never underestimated his formidable abilities as a campaigner.

I did know Ross Perot. I had met with him several times over the years on a variety of matters, chiefly our mutual commitment to ensuring a full accounting from North Vietnam of all Americans listed as prisoners of war or missing in action. Perot had also made a generous charitable donation to the Dole Foundation, helping it to expand programs promoting the employment of disabled Americans.

Knowing Ross Perot is not the same as understanding him. And I never did understand why he was running for President in 1992. I believed his candidacy drew more votes away from President Bush than from Governor Clinton, thereby helping to ensure the victory of a very liberal candidate with whom he had little, if anything, in common.

During election night television interviews, as the Clinton victory became more and more apparent, I tried to let Republicans know all was not lost, despite the fact that for the first time since 1980 Democrats would control the White House, as well as both houses of Congress. I pointed out that 57 percent of Americans voted for someone other than Bill Clinton. And my intention was to represent that 57 percent on the floor of the Senate.

"Obviously, we'll cooperate with the Clinton Administration when it advances the best interests of America," I said at a press conference the next morning. "But we will also stand up against bad policy, and offer common-sense alternatives on the most important issues confronting our nation, whether it's health care, the deficit, or jobs." I couldn't resist a good news/bad news line of my own. "The good news is that Bill Clinton is getting a honeymoon in Washington. The bad news is that Bob Dole will be his chaperon."

Several weeks later, President-elect Clinton came to my office for our first meeting. The two of us spoke privately for about thirty minutes. It was entirely cordial. I assured him that there were a number of issues on which we could work together. The deficit was one; Clinton said it would be a top priority for him, too. Bosnia was another. I had tried unsuccessfully to convince the Bush Administration to lift an arms embargo in the region, and to allow the Bosnians to defend themselves from bloody attacks by Serb aggressors.

I knew the year ahead would be a busy one, but over Christmas my thoughts of the future were pushed aside by the death of John Diamantakou, a talented member of my Capitol Hill staff. John was only twenty-six when he succumbed to a previously undetected congenital heart ailment. John was from a very close family of Greek heritage. Each time he visited his family in Massachusetts, he would return to the office with a supply of Greek pastries, baked by his mother.

John was typical of the young men and women I have been privileged to have on my staff over the years—bright, hardworking, personable and totally committed to serving their country. I can't help but think how much John would have enjoyed the 1996 campaign—and how much I would have enjoyed having him around.

Bill Clinton ran for President as a self-proclaimed "New Democrat" vowing to create a "New Covenant" between Washington, D.C., and the American people. On the campaign trail he fell into the very traditional habit of promising more than he could deliver. By the time November rolled around, he had pledged to attack the deficit, cut taxes for middle-class Americans, reform welfare, and work to shift power out of Washington and return it to the states.

Few of these promises would survive past inauguration day. Within a month of taking office, the new President announced that he would be seeking congressional approval of a $16.3 billion "emergency" economic stimulus package. This was about as new as the New Deal. Some of the money would be spent on worthy needs like highway improvement. But much of it was pure pork. Quite apart from the merits of the Clinton spending plan was the fact that none of what the President proposed to spend would be paid for by offsetting cuts in other government bureaucracies. Instead, the $16.3 billion would simply be tacked onto the deficit, leaving our children and grandchildren to pay the tab. In other words, business as usual.

I was determined that we would not saddle future generations with still more debt. Though we were outnumbered in the Senate 57–43, our rules required the majority to obtain sixty votes to end debate and bring the package to the floor. As always, the Senate Republican caucus contained members of diverse philosophical stripes—conservatives, moderates and liberals. Could I unite forty-one of these individualists in opposition to Bill Clinton's spending spree? The answer came at a meeting of all Senate Republicans, at which moderate John Danforth of Missouri said that if we didn't stand against mindless spending now, we might as well pack up and go home.

Not one Republican disagreed. Four unsuccessful efforts to bring the package to the floor later, President Clinton and Senate Majority Leader Mitchell gave up. In between these votes, I made clear to the President our willingness to work with him. We proposed a smaller spending package—one that was completely paid for through reductions in government programs. Our offer was refused. It was either the President's package or nothing.

It would not be the only instance where the President's failure to reach out to Republicans harmed him and his program unnecessarily. Unaccustomed to a two-party system as Governor of Arkansas, where he dealt with just a handful of Republican state legislators, the President appeared to have concluded that since Democrats had a majority in the House and Senate, he didn't need us. Whatever his reason, the President's refusal to involve Republicans in the legislative process was a serious mistake—one that would be repeated throughout the first two years of the Clinton presidency.

Preventing another $16.3 billion from being tacked onto the deficit was good policy. But it also turned out to be good politics. Following withdrawal of the Clinton package, I heard from Republicans, Democrats and Perot supporters who were glad we stood on principle; they were willing to take another look at the Republican party as a result of our action.

In August 1993, there was another, even more dramatic example of the differences between President Clinton and congressional Republicans. After promising in the campaign to get tough with the federal deficit and give "middle-class" Americans a tax cut, the President proposed a budget containing a staggering $265 billion in additional taxes. Yet the largest tax increase in history was not enough to control the deficit. The real problem, of course, was the Administration's spending habits. They were beyond control.

The most outrageous part of the President's plan was that it increased taxes retroactively to January 1, 1993—before President Clinton's inauguration. In short, the President was telling millions of individuals and small businesses who had been paying their income taxes that they hadn't been paying enough. They had to pay more. A lot more. In some cases, 67 percent more.

Remember the old saying that the only sure things in life are death and taxes? President Clinton managed to combine both in his retroactive tax increase. Under his plan, Americans who passed away earlier in the year would be survived by family members forced to pay higher inheritance taxes. The plan gave a whole new meaning to the expression "You can't take it with you."

And while tax increases were made retroactive, 80 percent

of the spending cuts called for in the President's plan were put off for at least three years.

In a nationally televised address on August 3, 1993, I suggested that Americans ask themselves four questions about the Clinton plan: Does it raise taxes? Does it reduce spending? Does it create jobs? And does it solve the deficit problem? The first question could only be answered "yes," and all the others "no." Taking a page out of Ronald Reagan's book, I also suggested that viewers might want to register their opinion of the President's proposal by calling their senators and representatives. I also gave out the Capitol phone number, so they could do just that.

The next day, the Capitol switchboard operators were buried in an avalanche of calls—the overwhelming majority of which opposed the President's budget. In the Senate, six Democrats joined all forty-four Republicans in voting against the plan. Nebraska's Bob Kerrey came close to voting with us, before White House arm-twisting brought him and other wavering Democrats back in line. With the vote deadlocked at 50–50, Vice President Gore was brought in to break the tie. An identical one-vote margin carried the plan in the House of Representatives. As in the Senate, every Republican House member opposed the package of tax increases and phantom budget cuts.

That fall, I hit the campaign trail on behalf of Republican candidates in November's off-year elections. George Allen, Jr., was running for Governor of Virginia. In New Jersey, Christie Whitman was up against another big tax increaser, incumbent Governor Jim Florio. Rudy Giuliani was trying to bring his tough-as-tacks approach to New York City's mayoralty. All three began as underdogs, but come election day, they produced a Republican trifecta, all winning offices that had been held by Democrats. These victories, combined with Paul Coverdell's victory in a run-off election in Georgia several weeks after election day and Kay Bailey Hutchison's victory in early 1993 in the race for the Texas Senate seat left open when Lloyd Bentsen became Secretary of the Treasury, made it clear that I wasn't alone in questioning the direction the Clinton Administration was taking.

As I traveled across the country on behalf of other Republicans, a number of people called out, "Dole for President." Since Elizabeth already was a president, I assumed they were talking about me. I had little time to think about 1996, however, as the budget battle gave way to the momentous debate over the future of America's health care system.

Soon after taking office, President Clinton announced that his wife would be in charge of health care reform. When Mrs. Clinton came to Capitol Hill for her first round of meetings, I made the point that a number of Republicans—myself included —had been involved in the issue for a long time, and that there was bipartisan agreement on the need to make our health care system both more accessible and more affordable. I assumed our meeting was just the first of many such discussions between the White House and congressional Republicans. Guess again.

Mrs. Clinton soon surrounded herself with a team of self-proclaimed health care experts, and began to write a plan. Republicans weren't the only ones excluded from their closed-door meetings. Doctors, nurses, hospital administrators, pharmaceutical companies and seemingly anyone else with experience was shut out, too. After many months of delay, the Clinton plan was finally announced on October 27, 1993. Rube Goldberg would have been proud. Instead of trying to fix parts of the health care system that needed fixing, the Clinton proposal threw out the entire system, and turned health care in America over to the federal government.

The following January, President Clinton boosted the plan in his State of the Union address. My own nationally televised response followed. You may not recall what I said, but many Americans still remember the chart I brought with me. It had been prepared by a young staffer for Senator Arlen Specter of Pennsylvania. (A staffer who had voted for President Clinton, by the way.) She made the chart in order to show what our health care system would look like under the Clinton plan.

The results weren't pretty. There were 207 boxes on the chart—each representing a current, expanded or new bureaucracy. There was a box for a "National Health Board." A box for an "Advisory Commission on Regional Variations of Health

Expenditures." And a box for something called the "National Institute for Health Care Workforce Development." Way down on the bottom of the chart, buried beneath a mountain of red tape and federal regulations, were "we the people."

The President's plan was written in such a way that many believed it would actually bar Americans from receiving care from a specialist or a clinic outside of their own state—unless they received government permission. "Big Brother" were two words that came quickly to mind.

As I saw it, we could fix our most pressing problems—and there *were* problems—without performing the equivalent of a triple bypass operation on our existing health care system. We could fix them without the estimated trillion-dollar budget shortfall the Clinton plan would create. We could do so *immediately* by passing a series of common-sense reforms that already enjoyed wide bipartisan support and that would assist those who are denied health insurance because of a pre-existing condition, or who lost coverage when they changed jobs.

Unfortunately, President and Mrs. Clinton refused to budge. For months, they traveled the country, campaigning for their plan and attacking Republican opposition. The more they spoke, however, the more they dissipated public support. The problem wasn't in the sales pitch. The problem was in the product. It was a lemon, and the American people knew it.

In the end, the tragedy was not that the Clinton plan to federalize health care was defeated. The tragedy was that the President's refusal to consider any plan but his own denied many Americans improvements that would have increased accessibility and reduced health care costs for them and their families. (In April 1996, the Republican Senate would remedy the situation by unanimously passing health care reform legislation containing many of the provisions blocked by President Clinton in 1994.)

When Bill Clinton ran for the White House, he said little about foreign policy. About the only statements he made were ones criticizing President Bush for spending too much time dealing with the world beyond our shores. Once in office, however, the world has a way of intruding on the best-laid plans of Presidents. Events in Somalia, Bosnia and Haiti, to cite but three hot spots, quickly demonstrated the need of having a President experienced in global affairs. Within months of Bill Clinton's inauguration, even the President's friends were using words like "confusing" and "indecisive" to describe his foreign policy.

I was especially frustrated with the President's policy—or lack of one—with regard to Bosnia. Along with Senators like Joe Lieberman, I had urged the Bush Administration to take decisive action on Bosnia—and earlier on Croatia. In the 1992 campaign, candidate Clinton stated that he would lift the arms embargo against Bosnia, thereby allowing the people of this small, independent country to defend themselves in the face of bloodthirsty aggression by neighboring Serbia. But after his election, President Clinton did nothing. Meanwhile, the slaughter continued, and the world first heard the hateful euphemism "ethnic cleansing." It was just another word for genocide, as far as I was concerned. Yet, Clinton seemed willing to subjugate American leadership in the former Yugoslavia to that of the United Nations, which had adopted a policy of "managing" genocide—feeding Bosnians, but not protecting them from artillery shells—and denying the Bosnians the means to defend themselves.

Late in 1995, of course, American "peacekeeping" troops were on their way to Bosnia. By that time, the Congress had already voted overwhelmingly to lift the arms embargo. Would American troops have been needed had President Clinton not rejected our earlier efforts? I don't believe so.

Many Americans urged me to lead the fight against the President's deployment of troops in the Balkans. Poll numbers suggested that it would have been a popular action to take. My conscience told me it also would have been the wrong action. For while I disagreed with the President's decision to commit troops, I could not deny that, as Commander-in-Chief, he had the Constitutional power to deploy those forces—and he had already done so, as hundreds of American soldiers were in Bosnia, and thousands more were on the way.

Still others, mindful that Congress has the "power of the

purse," urged us to pull the plug on American troops by cutting off all funds for their deployment. Shades of the 1970s. In Senate debate, I reminded my colleagues of those turbulent times, recalling that while American soldiers were fighting and dying in Vietnam, and while heroes like Arizona Senator John McCain were being held prisoner, Congress had repeatedly debated similar draconian measures to cut funding for our troops. If such a course was horribly wrong then—and it was—then what made it any less objectionable in Bosnia? American soldiers were on the ground, following orders and risking their lives. The duty of Congress was clear: to support our troops in the field.

In the long term, the President's deployment of troops only makes sense if the Bosnian people can resume a normal life, if Bosnia survives as a democratic and unified state, and if the Bosnians can defend themselves in the future. Arming and training the Bosnian forces is therefore a top priority. If this is not accomplished before NATO forces leave, then our commitment will have been for naught.

In April 1996, Congress and the American public were shocked to learn that while the Clinton Administration was publicly leading the fight against lifting the arms embargo, it had privately decided to allow Iran to provide arms to the Bosnians. This duplicitous policy not only seriously damaged our credibility with our allies, it also allowed the Iranian camel to get its nose under the European tent. The presence of Iranian military forces and intelligence officials in Bosnia may yet pose a threat to our armed forces, to the peace process and to the future of Bosnia as a multi-ethnic democracy.

The health care fiasco, higher taxes, a confusing foreign policy and a general sense that America was headed in the wrong direction all combined to keep the Clinton Administration on the defensive through much of 1994. As the November elections approached, I felt cautiously optimistic that I might soon change my job title—from Minority Leader to Majority Leader.

To do so, Republicans would need to pick up seven seats. Our motto, naturally, was "Seven more in '94." Early in the year, I thought it was a tall order, but as the months passed, and as I toured the country for GOP candidates, I could feel things breaking our way. In 1992, Americans had voted for change, hopefully for the better. What they got was Washington's version of "Back to the Future," a repeat of yesterday's failed liberal policies. The best way to change the status quo, I told audiences that fall, was to change the party that had controlled Congress for the past forty years.

The point I made on the campaign trail that fall was that the complaint "there isn't a dime's worth of difference between Democrats and Republicans" is wrong. In fact, there are hundreds of billions of dollars' worth of differences. Americans who want a balanced budget should vote Republican. If they want a tax cut, they should vote Republican. If they want welfare reform, regulatory reform, a coherent foreign policy, they should vote Republican.

Led by Haley Barbour, the energetic chairman of the Republican National Committee, the GOP was united as never before. Everywhere I went I heard federal, state and local candidates hitting the same themes. In that sense, Bill Clinton had proved to be a great unifier.

By midafternoon on election day, my office got wind of early exit poll numbers in a number of states. They were even better, far better, than I had hoped for. Not only did we appear to be on our way to a Senate majority, but the emerging landslide just might give control of the House of Representatives to Republicans for the first time since 1954.

I have learned over the years to not always believe polls—exit or otherwise. This time I was overly cautious. As Elizabeth and I watched the returns come in that evening, we saw the biggest Republican landslide in half a century. Not one incumbent Republican governor, senator or member of Congress seeking reelection was defeated. In the Senate, two Democratic incumbents lost their seats, and all nine seats where no incumbent was running went Republican. As a result, the Senate would switch from a 54–46 Democratic majority to a 52–48 Republican majority.

Republican ranks grew to fifty-three when Alabama Senator Richard Shelby switched parties the day after the election. (They would reach fifty-four with Colorado's Ben Nighthorse Campbell's conversion in March 1995.)

Against all predictions, the voters had given Republicans a majority in the House of Representatives. For the first time since Americans liked Ike and loved Lucy—and only the third time since 1930—the Democrats would not be calling the shots on Capitol Hill. As I received and made congratulatory calls on election night, I couldn't help but think how much I would have enjoyed talking to President Nixon, whose death six months earlier had ended one of the most extraordinary careers in American politics. In the years preceding his death, I had made a special effort to keep in touch with Nixon, who possessed one of the best political and foreign-policy minds in America—an opinion reinforced each time we spoke.

In January 1994, for example, I hosted a lunch in the Capitol marking the twenty-fifth anniversary of Nixon's first inauguration as President. More than a hundred senators and representatives, Democrats and Republicans alike, set aside past differences and gathered to honor the thirty-seventh President. When the lunch ended, President Nixon stood and delivered one of the most compelling speeches I had ever heard, and without a note in his hand. It's not often that a hundred politicians can keep quiet for twenty minutes. But you could have heard a pin drop as Nixon took us on a round-the-world tour, analyzing the global situation as only he could, before sharing his inspiring vision of America's future in an era increasingly reflective of American values.

Afterward, President Nixon rested in my office before leaving the Capitol. Only he got very little rest. For the place was filled to the rafters with young Hill staffers, members of the Capitol police and others hoping to shake his hand, get an autograph or simply express their best wishes. And he didn't disappoint one of them.

It was the last time I was to see my combative friend. Three months later, President Nixon waged a final fight against an opponent that not even he could overcome. The popular reaction to his passing amazed many of his critics, who lost no time in reminding us of the circumstances surrounding Nixon's departure from the White House. But Nixon wouldn't have given these adversaries a second thought. In fact, in an especially rough time in his life, his wife, Pat, asked him how he managed to get out of bed every day. The former President replied, "I just get up each morning to confound my enemies."

The line came back to me as I prepared a eulogy at the invitation of Tricia Nixon Cox and Julie Nixon Eisenhower, who are President and Mrs. Nixon's best memorials. It was an honor I will always remember, along with the remarkable and controversial patriot who never gave up. President Nixon's final book, published several weeks after his death, was entitled *Beyond Peace*. Had its author in his later years found for himself what his Quaker ancestors called "peace at the center"? I think he had.

I recall the day in June 1993 when Pat Nixon was buried in Yorba Linda, a stone's throw from the gleaming presidential museum and library. After the formal ceremony in the magnificent gardens that reflect Pat's love of flowers, a composed if obviously grieving widower appeared in the lobby of the library to thank his fellow mourners for coming to honor Pat.

Then he did an amazing thing. For the next ten minutes or so, Richard Nixon delivered his own, intensely personal, tribute to the woman whose strength of character had more than once saved his life. He described the joys of grandparenting, and the time his first granddaughter, Jennie Eisenhower, had asked Pat what she wished to be called.

Mrs. Nixon thought "Grandmother" too formal, and "Grandma" a bit old for her liking. So as a compromise Pat suggested the little girl call her "Ma."

Jennie next posed the same question to her grandfather.

"Oh, you can call me anything," Richard Nixon told the little girl, "because I've been called everything."

As laughter swept the room, I struggled to control my emotions. So did George McGovern, Nixon's 1972 opponent, who had flown out to Yorba Linda in response to my invitation. As Nixon spoke, George dabbed at his eyes with a handkerchief. Later in the day, asked by a reporter why he should honor the wife of the man whose alleged dirty tricks had kept him out of the White House, McGovern replied, "You can't keep on campaigning forever."

In a day full of emotion, McGovern may have given the most powerful—and certainly the classiest—eulogy of all.

ELIZABETH

When I began my leave of absence from the Red Cross, I expressed the wistful hope that "Mother Nature" would do the same. In fact, my years at the Red Cross have coincided with a record number of the most destructive, most expensive disasters in America's history.

It's a depressing litany: Hurricanes Andrew and Iniki in 1992. The Midwest floods of 1993. The Los Angeles earthquake, California wildfires, Tropical Storm Alberto and the Greater Houston floods of 1994. In 1995, there were terrible hurricanes with deceptively graceful names like Marilyn and Opal. The list goes on at heartbreaking length. Yet, each new catastrophe added to our storehouse of knowledge even as it demonstrated the grit and resiliency of the human spirit. The most important thing I have learned while at the Red Cross was that no matter how strong the forces of mother nature, the forces of human nature are much stronger still.

On a quiet Sunday afternoon, August 23, 1992, the week following the Republican National Convention in Houston, I was in the kitchen of our apartment preparing dinner for Bob and me when the phone rang. It was a call alerting me that Hurricane Andrew was expected to hit south Florida in the next eighteen hours and that the Red Cross in the threatened area was mobilizing disaster relief teams and equipment as never before.

Wanting to personally assess our relief activities in Florida and lend support to the storm's victims, I told Bob dinner would be ready in two hours and I hoped he and Leader would enjoy it. I quickly packed a bag, rushed to the airport and headed south. So severe had the winds been in the southern half of the state that all airports south of Melbourne were already closed. A Red Cross staffer and I did manage to get the last flight to arrive in that city before its airport shut down.

That night, shrieking gales hit the side of my hotel room. It sounded as if the windows would be sucked out of the wall at any moment. Early the next morning, we rented a car and started for Miami. I was shocked at what I encountered along the way, and later, south of Miami. Sides of buildings gone, cars overturned like matchsticks, fragments of homes everywhere— it looked like a war zone. Eventually, I made my way to our Red Cross Disaster Services command post located in a generously donated union hall. Following a quick briefing, I headed further south to the Homestead area—a portion of Dade County that had received the full brunt of Andrew's wrath.

En route, I visited several Red Cross shelters—accompanied by President Bush, honorary Red Cross chairman, who had arrived that afternoon to survey the damage.

The Red Cross had opened 230 shelters throughout the area, providing food, clothing, shelter and medical supplies. Red Cross relief teams, many of whom were themselves storm victims, worked tirelessly day and night. At one shelter, I remember a little boy about five years old. He looked up at me with tears in his eyes and said, "My house is broken. My house is broken. The roof is gone, where Santa Claus comes." I assured him the house would be repaired, and that Santa would indeed find him at Christmas.

Nightfall came as we left Homestead for points north. With no electricity, there were no house lights or streetlights, and the streets were pitch black and deserted, since the Governor had declared a curfew. Nearly every traffic sign had been blown away by the storm, causing us to become thoroughly lost. We wanted to check in with local Red Cross staffers, but the cellular phone we had with us didn't work; neither did the pay phones we tried. Finally, the car's headlights pointed out two teenage girls who had somehow located the only working telephone for miles. As they chatted away, we waited . . . and waited . . . and waited to use the phone (an experience with which I'm sure countless parents of teenagers are familiar). Eventually, a policeman investigating curfew violators drove up, and good thing, too. Not only was I spared arrest for violating curfew, but the helpful officer even shared his soda pop and cookies with a very hungry lady.

A few minutes later, we were joined at the phone booth by a news crew from ABC's *Good Morning America,* who reminded me I was scheduled to discuss Red Cross relief efforts on their program at seven the next morning. And the following day the Army National Guard offered me a seat on one of their Blackhawk helicopters. With windows and doors removed from the helicopter, I caught a bird's-eye view of the destruction on the ground.

While many people evacuate from impending storms, the Red Cross does just the opposite—we move in. This time, it was Louisiana—Andrew's next target. I flew into New Orleans just ahead of the monster in the Gulf, and again witnessed the inspiring work of the Red Cross and others bracing for the worst. Fortunately, by the time Andrew reached Louisiana, the storm's winds had lessened somewhat, and the state was spared much of the devastation visited upon Florida.

From epic disasters like Hurricane Andrew that wreak havoc on millions, to house fires affecting individual families, the Red Cross responds to more than 68,000 disasters a year with compassion and efficiency. We are able to do so because of people like Frank Sauer.

I met Frank in 1993 when I was helping to stack sandbags along the banks of the rampaging Mississippi River. Frank's cabin had been completely flooded, and he told me he wanted to become a Red Cross volunteer. I thought to myself that he would probably need to wait until he recovered from his losses. But Frank was too worried about his neighbors to consider his own plight. As the waters continued to rise, he undertook immediate training, and soon after we talked he was riding one of our emergency-response vehicles, assisting other victims, touching other hearts.

The spirit exhibited by Frank Sauer and countless other Red Cross volunteers was perhaps best expressed by the words of the mayor of a small California town hit by the October 1989 Loma Prieta earthquake. Said the mayor, "After our homes were knocked off their foundations, our water and gas lines destroyed, we all looked around to see where the Red Cross was, and then we realized that *we* were the Red Cross." What he meant, of course, is that Red Cross assistance is not something delivered by strangers or faceless bureaucrats. Rather, it's provided by friends and neighbors whose response is classically American.

When we see others hurting, we hurt, too. We hurt and then we help. Whether the aid comes from a small-town chapter operated out of somebody's kitchen, or big-city chapters with million-dollar budgets, the motive is the same. The Red Cross patch can be found on the arm of the Main Street merchant, the union official or the retired teacher two houses down.

For all their talents, Red Cross staffers and volunteers are not prophets. None of us can predict where the next natural disaster will hit, only that it will occur. One of my goals as the organization's president was to ensure that future responses would be even faster and more efficient than in the past.

This was especially crucial in light of the criticism the Red Cross Disaster Services had received after Hurricane Hugo and the Loma Prieta earthquake occurred within weeks of each other in the fall of 1989. While I was still at the Department of Labor at the time, I had read the statements of those who thought the Red Cross response was too slow, and who believed that our relief teams should reflect the diversity of the areas they served.

My response was to launch a multimillion-dollar Disaster Services revitalization effort, which included the opening of our version of a war room—a National Disaster Operations Center open twenty-four hours a day, 365 days a year, where we can monitor ongoing disasters and impending threats, mobilize relief efforts, and move our people and equipment wherever they are needed. We also quadrupled to sixteen thousand the number of those trained to handle national catastrophic disasters, and positioned millions of dollars' worth of state-of-the-art communications equipment and resources in strategic locations most vulnerable to the ravages of nature.

Yet nature is nothing if not fickle. The unprecedented series of natural disasters that began in 1990 challenged more than our manpower. They also tested our finances. Back when I worked for Uncle Sam, my "fund-raising" activities consisted of making requests to the Office of Management and Budget, and then traveling up to Capitol Hill and fighting for my agency's budget before the appropriate congressional committees. The Red Cross, however, is not funded by the government. Instead, we depend upon the voluntary contributions of the American people—who have responded with great generosity, donating more than $360 million for disaster relief in my years as president. Indeed, when I arrived at the Red Cross, a $30 million shortfall was projected for our Disaster Reserve Fund. By the time I began my leave of absence, there was nearly $100 million in that fund to provide relief for future disasters.

In return for their generosity, I believe that the American Red Cross—like every other philanthropic organization—must be held to the strictest standards of fiscal accountability, integrity and plain good sense when it comes to spending each and every dime.

Soon after coming on board, I instituted a series of strict financial controls aimed at making donations to the Red Cross go further. As a result, we were able to achieve a $20 million reduction in overhead at the national level. These economies in turn allowed me to reduce local chapter dues by 20 percent. Nearly 93 cents of every Red Cross dollar is spent on programs and services. I am very proud that we have received the highest possible rating from the American Institute of Philanthropy, the National Charities Information Bureau, the Council of Better Business Bureaus' Philanthropic Advisory Service and numerous other charity watchdog organizations.

By far the most wrenching moments of my Red Cross career have been spent in foreign countries. As a member of the International Federation of Red Cross and Red Crescent Societies, and the International Committee of the Red Cross, we provide humanitarian and relief services to victims of natural and man-made disasters. We also assist refugees fleeing zones of conflict.

We operate under principles of neutrality, impartiality and independence—meaning we do not take positions on issues having political, racial, religious or ideological overtones, and we serve *all* victims according to need. It is these rules that allow the Red Cross to operate successfully in such treacherous theaters as Somalia, Croatia and Bosnia.

My visit to Somalia over four years ago left cruelly vivid images that will haunt me the rest of my life. In Baidoa, I came upon a little boy lying under a sack. I thought he was dead. His brother sat him up, and I could see that he was severely diseased and malnourished. I asked for camel's milk to feed him, and as I raised the cup to his mouth, I put my arm around his back. The feeling of the little bones almost piercing through his flesh is something I will never forget. That is when the horror of starvation becomes real—when you can touch it.

In Bardera, I found a bloody shirt on the stairs of the Red Cross headquarters. A religious leader had been shot the night before, when looters had broken into his home. A Red Cross doctor himself had operated for hours under flashlights, only to lose his patient. Now, the doctor feared retribution. Meanwhile, in our little field hospital, I saw four severely malnourished Somalis with gunshot wounds inflicted by looters who had burst into our Red Cross feeding station for the severely malnourished to steal food from people who had next to nothing.

Horror of an even greater scale greeted me two years later in the refugee camps of Goma, Zaire, where the Red Cross was assisting over one million Rwandan refugees. These people had fled their country literally overnight to avoid the ghastly civil war destroying their homeland. In Rwanda, the Red Cross was the only humanitarian organization still operating in the area—all others had left in the wake of the bloodshed. One of the courageous Red Crossers on duty was Dr. John Sundin, a Connecticut native, who was the only surgeon for miles around, and fighting was continuing all around him. Hundreds upon hundreds of Rwandans were being brought to him each day with gunshot and machete wounds. When I spoke with him later, he said, "Mrs. Dole, I almost lost it. There was no way I could operate on all those in need—even though I worked around the clock. I had to decide which ones had the best chance of living and turn my back on the rest."

To compound the ongoing tragedy, nature herself seemed in conspiracy against humanitarian efforts at the Goma refugee camps. Water, a source of life, was now contaminated and an instrument of death. Bodies were simply piled by the roadside, as lava rock from nearby volcanoes made the ground too hard to dig latrines or graves. Cholera and dysentery were rampant. Still, for the refugees, fear of returning home was far greater than the fear of dying in a strange land.

To this day, I can close my eyes and see a boy sitting all by himself on a mound of African dirt. He was probably thirteen or fourteen—all arms and legs and feet, as most boys are at that age. His face was covered with dust, and he was crying. The tears left little paths down both his cheeks. I sat beside him to try to comfort him, but there was no reaction. Nothing moved except for his tears. He was traumatized.

Outside one of the tents, a semiconscious woman lay dying of cholera. At her side, a child cried piteously for milk and comfort its mother could not give. As I walked through the camp, another child, about six years old, came up to me and took my hand. He followed me wherever I went.

I wonder where he is now. What kind of future is there for him? What kind of future is there for seventy thousand Rwandan children whose parents had been lost in the mass exodus or killed—often before their eyes? No parents, no home, no food, no clothes, no hope. No future—nothing but the Red Cross to try to fill their needs.

As I pray for these children, I continue to reflect on just how fortunate we are to live in this great land. Not that we are immune from disasters, natural or man-made—as I witnessed when I visited Oklahoma City the day of the tragic April 1995 bombing there. But all things considered, we Americans have been blessed to be a blessing . . . we have received that we might give.

· · ·

Somalia and Rwanda certainly had no monopoly on human misery. War-torn Bosnia had been in the headlines for several years when I traveled to the Croatian-Bosnian border to visit a Red Cross center assisting Bosnians released from Serb prisons.

This facility offered a first taste of freedom for many who had known unspeakable torture and beatings. Through a translator, I spoke with several men who had somehow managed to survive their ordeal. It was late at night, and the electricity was out. By the flickering light of candles, I heard tales of horror and heroism.

I especially remember one young man. It was almost too painful for him to talk about what happened. And no wonder. Just a few months earlier, he and his family had been eating breakfast, when men entered his home and beat him in front of his wife and two young daughters. Then, he had been taken to a soccer stadium where several people from his town, including a cousin, were lined up and shot.

"This will happen to you if you don't cooperate," he was told. He was then imprisoned in a detention camp, where the Red Cross was allowed in to verify that prisoners were receiving humane treatment. I asked what happened when the Red Cross left. In tears, the man responded that the guards told him, "You will cry for this." And in fact, everything Red Cross had given the prisoners was taken away, and three men in his barracks were shot that night.

As he related his story, despondent over the fate of his family, the man gazed at the cigarette in his hand. "This cigarette is worth more than my life," he remarked.

The tragic situation in the Balkans has been called a "second Holocaust." Perhaps it will surprise you to learn that more than forty years after World War II, the work of the Red Cross includes helping Holocaust survivors and their families. In 1990, in cooperation with our central Maryland chapter, we established a Holocaust and War Victims Tracing and Information Center in Baltimore. Initially, the work was frustrating. Essential records were either destroyed or kept under lock and key by foreign governments.

Then came the collapse of the Iron Curtain, which brought with it the lifting of the shroud of secrecy in Eastern Europe. Still greater amounts of information came to light when our own National Archives released documents containing the names of 300,000 or more Holocaust victims. These files, originally collected as evidence for prosecuting Nazi war criminals after World War II, revealed transport lists, ship manifests of refugees and concentration camp records from Buchenwald, Auschwitz and other camps of death.

The existence of these invaluable documents had been known for some time. Yet, because they were used primarily by historians and academic researchers, their humanitarian value was only imperfectly realized. It didn't take the Red Cross long to make up for lost time. Within forty-eight hours, our Tracing and Information Center had received and responded to nearly eight hundred telephone inquiries. Through these records, one lady I met with was at least able to learn the fate of the parents she had left behind in Vienna in 1939.

"In the back of my mind," she told me, "I was always in doubt about what really happened to them. Of so many millions of people, they were like a needle in a haystack, but the Red Cross found them. . . . They were together to the end." She couldn't bring her parents back, but in the midst of so much anguish, she could feel at least a semblance of peace of mind.

Some of our inquiries produced small miracles, uniting relatives who had completely lost touch with one another. During a Polish family's journey to a Nazi labor camp, the then-six-year-old son became ill, and was placed in a hospital. His mother and sister were forced to go on without him. His mother never returned. His sister somehow survived, and she began a forty-year quest for her brother.

After decades of frustration, she turned to the Polish Red Cross, which confirmed that her brother had been sent to the United States in 1952. From that small scrap of information, our Tracing Center was able to discover that the boy had settled in a small Iowa community and become a U.S. citizen in 1960. We contacted the local Red Cross chapter, who learned that he was still there. The news that he had a living sister was delivered to him by Red Cross officials. Prior to that visit, all he had known of his family was that his mother's name was Ana.

"I can't believe I have somebody," he stammered in amazement.

In the wake of natural disasters, and in places of unimaginable tragedy like Somalia, Rwanda and Bosnia, the Red Cross is that somebody. I have been asked many times how Red Crossers can continue to work day after day amidst death and terror and misery without yielding to despair. To be sure, no matter how many people we are able to help, we know there are others we will never reach.

But in times of the greatest distress, I remember the words of that living saint—Mother Teresa of Calcutta. Each day for decades she has risen and labored in the ghettos of India. When asked how she could do such heartbreaking work day after day, with no end in sight, Mother Teresa said, "God did not call me to be successful, he called me to be faithful."

However overpowering the forces of nature or the cruelty of man to man, I can guarantee you that the grand old organization that is the American Red Cross will always be faithful.

CHAPTER ELEVEN

Fighting for the Future

BOB

Soon after Ronald Reagan assumed the presidency, he related a story about the great baseball manager Frankie Frisch and the time he sent a rookie out to play center field. The new guy promptly dropped the first ball hit to him. On the next play he let a grounder go between his feet. When he finally retrieved the ball, he threw it to the wrong base. At this point, Frankie stormed out of the dugout, took away the rookie's glove and said angrily, "I'll show you how to play this position."

The next batter slammed a line drive right over second base. Frankie came in fast and missed the ball completely. Falling down, he threw away his glove and yelled at the rookie, "You've got center field so screwed up *nobody* can play it."

As usual, President Reagan wasn't telling a story just to get a laugh. He was also making a point. Given the mess he inherited after four years of the Carter Administration, it would have been tempting to govern by blaming all the nation's difficulties on past mistakes. But, with authority goes responsibility. Far more than criticizing the past, true leadership means providing solutions for the future.

It was a point I kept in mind in January 1995, as Republicans took the reins of Congress for the first time since Dwight Eisenhower occupied the White House. There were times when I wanted to ask the American public for patience. The "new management" on Capitol Hill could hardly expect overnight to eliminate the Democrats' forty-year legacy of big government, reckless spending and higher taxes. But I knew from my own experience that public sentiment can shift like a prairie breeze. And so I told my Republican colleagues that we should act as if we had only a two-year lease on Capitol Hill.

On January 4, 1995, I temporarily recessed the Senate so my fellow lawmakers and I could walk across the Capitol to personally witness a sight many had given up hope of ever seeing—the swearing in of a Republican Speaker of the House.

Newt Gingrich and I had known of each other since he came to Congress in 1979, but we didn't really know each other on a personal basis. As a member of a House minority rendered virtually powerless by a majority that was anything but democratic, Newt had a different set of priorities. He didn't have to worry about getting legislation passed. That was my concern as Republican Leader. By the same token, Newt had also been free to disagree with Republican Presidents whenever he felt they were in the wrong. As a result, some in the media reported there was "bad blood" between us. The same prophets of doom speculated, with more hope than accuracy, that we would have at best a rocky relationship in trying to run the first Republican Congress in four decades.

The theories were proven wrong from the start of the 104th Congress. Naturally, there were times when the Speaker and I differed. Neither one of us was notably reticent about forming strong views on the legislative process. But we are in complete agreement that Americans knew what they were doing when they elected a Republican Congress. Like the voters themselves, we both wanted a government defined by its limits and not by its reach.

Throughout the 1994 campaign, Republicans had promised to fight for fundamental change: for an honestly balanced budget, sweeping welfare reform, tax relief for working families, an end to the double standards Congress applied to itself and a historic return of power from Washington to the ultimate source of that power—our states, our communities and the

American people themselves. Day after day, week after week, the Republican Congress has done everything possible to deliver on those promises.

We got off to a fast start in our efforts to restore credibility to a badly tattered Congress. It was no accident that the first bill enacted by the new Republican majority ensured that, henceforth, lawmakers on Capitol Hill would live under the same laws they imposed on everyone else. This was a revolutionary change. For as long as they had been in power, Democrats in Congress had routinely practiced a double standard, exempting themselves from laws covering civil rights, antidiscrimination, workplace safety and a variety of other rules and regulations applied to the rest of the citizenry.

Before the 104th Congress was two weeks old, we ended the practice—for good. It would take a little longer to make other much needed reforms. But we passed legislation shining additional light on the lobbying process. We slashed Congress' own budget by the largest amount in forty years. And we dramatically curtailed the federal government's ability to impose costly mandates on our states and cities.

Important as these victories were, we understood that the most critical battle lay ahead.

A few years ago, I met with a group of one hundred high-school seniors—one boy and one girl from each state. During our meeting, one young man stood up and said, "Senator, it seems like every group of Americans is represented in Washington. Everyone has somebody who speaks for them. But who speaks for us?" he asked me. "Who speaks for the future?"

For far too long, the answer to that young man's question was "No one." Had it been otherwise, we never would have mortgaged our children's America for short-term political advantage. There's plenty of blame—and red ink—to go around. Every child born in 1995 already owes $18,500 as his or her share of the national debt. That same child can also anticipate paying $187,150 in taxes during his or her working life just to pay interest on the unwelcome gift prepared by previous generations.

Republicans, in drafting a balanced budget, were guided by far more than actuarial principles. More than an administrative blueprint, the budget is an exercise in national self-definition. Our own views represented a sharp break from a half century during which Washington came to regard taxpayers, not as clients to be served, but as cash cows to be milked dry.

In a time of mass anxiety, individual citizens desire nothing so much as control of their own lives. Yet their government careens along, pretending it has no obligation to them or their children. Bankruptcy, I would remind you, is measured in moral as well as financial terms.

Those who don't want to see what's coming take refuge in a neatly packaged set of platitudes, crafted to placate every interest group at Washington's table, and tied up with soaring rhetoric. No surprise here; making speeches is a lot easier than making choices. But words will not stop the aging of America or repeal the inexorable laws of demographics.

We all know, for instance, that the next few years will generate even greater demands on existing entitlement programs. In recent years entitlement programs have swollen to the point where they consume 51 percent of the federal budget. Another 15 percent goes to cover interest on the debt.

All those numbers can be intimidating. Look at it this way: According to the Concord Coalition, the debt and continued deficit spending have together lowered the average income of American families by $15,000 a year—from $50,000 to $35,000. On the other hand, once we achieve a balanced budget, interest rates will drop significantly. For the typical home-owning family, that means a monthly savings of $500 on the mortgage bill. A family that buys a $100,000 house in 2002—when Republicans propose to eliminate the deficit once and for all—can expect to save nearly $65,000 over the life of a thirty-year mortgage. Those who take out college and auto loans will receive similarly dramatic savings.

The best job-creation program the government can provide is a balanced budget. According to the Congressional Budget Office, each percentage point of economic growth translates into 600,000 new jobs. Using that formula, the New York Federal Reserve Bank estimates that deficit spending between 1978 and 1988 cost the economy three million jobs. In a broader sense, there is little mystery as to what it will take to make personal incomes grow at a faster rate than they have in recent years. Essentially, we need to foster greater investment and less consumption. In eliminating the deficit, we redirect the economy from government spending—much of it wasteful or politically motivated—to private savings and investment.

If we do nothing, in a few short years merely servicing the interest on the debt will consume half of all discretionary spending. Already, interest payments are squeezing money from social programs. Meanwhile, if the status quo goes unchallenged and present trends continue, the children of today's "Generation X" can expect to pay 82 percent of their wages to the tax man.

And what about the elderly? They stand to benefit the most from an end to fiscal irresponsibility. For they will undoubtedly suffer the most if Medicare is left to its fate, or inflation reignites to ravage Social Security and other fixed incomes. Balance the budget by 2002, says the General Accounting Office, and the average American will have real-income growth of 36 percent by 2020.

None of this fits neatly into a network sound bite. But such were the motivations prompting Republicans in Congress to fight for a balanced budget. To many Americans, no doubt, all the wrangling over rival spending plans sounded like so much Washington hot air. Forget the posturing; there was more at stake than dollars and cents. What is the proper role of government in an era of down-sized industries, privatization and increased personal responsibility? How can we free future generations from the ball and chain of debt, and restore the birthright of all American children to rise as far and as fast as their talents take them, unburdened by the fiscal irresponsibility of their ancestors?

No one ever said that imposing fiscal discipline would be easy. It would be harder still for Washington to relinquish voluntarily any of the authority it has so jealously hoarded for much of this century. Both moves would entail tough decisions, sacrificing some personal popularity, alienating some old friends. But what else is leadership? And if we weren't willing to lead, then what was the point of the 1994 Republican mandate?

The battle to make a balanced budget a reality was waged on two fronts. The first involved amending the Constitution to require Congress to live within its means. On March 2, 1995, having already passed the House by the required greater than two-thirds majority, the proposed balanced-budget amendment reached the floor of the Senate. Sixty-seven votes were needed to send it on to state legislatures for adoption. Initially, I was optimistic about success. Certainly there was never any doubt where the public stood on the issue.

But then, President Clinton began to lean on Democratic senators to deny Republicans what would have been a historic victory. In the end, six Democrats who had voted for the amendment in the past buckled under White House pressure. Fourteen other Democrats said they would stand with me. That meant we would need all fifty-three Republicans to win. We were on the brink of success when Senator Mark Hatfield of Oregon confided his opposition to me.

In a tense meeting hours before the vote, I urged Hatfield to change his mind. Instead, he offered to resign. Hatfield knew that with his resignation, the Senate would have only ninety-nine members. And sixty-six out of ninety-nine would give supporters the requisite majority to send the amendment on to the states. I rejected Hatfield's offer on principle. While I disagreed with his position, I would also fight for his right as a United States Senator to vote his conscience.

Whether by one vote or a million votes, it hurts to lose an issue of such importance. But the fight was just beginning. It goes on today. Having come so close in the face of a hostile White House, I have little doubt what a supportive President—especially if his name is Bob Dole—could do to secure passage of the Constitutional amendment. As President, I would govern as if we *had* won and *were* required by law to do what virtually every governor, mayor and American family does as a matter of course.

Some who opposed the Constitutional balanced-budget

amendment said it was a gimmick. If Congress wanted to balance the budget, they argued, it should have the courage to do so without amending the Constitution. Taking the critics at their word, I gave the Budget Committees a new charge. I told committee members I wanted no "smoke and mirrors." No fudging the numbers. No rosy scenarios. Just an honest plan that would put America on a path to a seven-year balanced budget. New Mexico's Pete Domenici in the Senate, and Ohio's John Kasich in the House, led the Budget Committees in producing exactly that.

Not that the President hadn't proposed a budget of his own. He had. It was something less than a profile in courage. The President's vision for the American future promised $200 to $300 billion deficits well into the next century. Spending cuts were put off until after the 1996 presidential election. When put to a vote, it was defeated 99–0.

This was not by any means the President's last proposal on the subject. In fact, as the lengthy budget process unfolded— some would say unraveled—it was hard to determine just what he did stand for. In his 1992 presidential campaign, candidate Clinton had promised on the *Larry King Live* television program to balance the budget in five years. On May 20, 1995, he said he could do it in less than ten years. On June 13, 1995, he said it would take all of those ten years. On October 19, 1995, he said he could do it in either seven, eight, or nine years. Unfortunately, numbers were not his strong suit, unless they were polling numbers.

While the President danced around the issue, Congress took action. By the fall, both houses had passed historic proposals that would put America on the road to a balanced budget for the first time in a quarter century.

Within our balanced budget, we reduced taxes by $245 billion through a variety of provisions, including a $500 per child tax credit and reductions in the capital gains tax and "marriage penalty" tax. We replaced a failed welfare system with one based on the principles of work, family and personal responsibility. We did not shy away from the politically explosive issue of Medicare. The Medicare trustees—three of whom were members of the President's Cabinet—had issued a report plainly stating that, unless reformed, Medicare would go bankrupt in seven years. To avert that disaster, we took steps to reduce the program's rate of growth while broadening health care options available to recipients, thereby ensuring its survival.

If visions are about the future, what is more visionary than ensuring that Medicare will be there when today's workers need it—just as we did when we saved Social Security in 1983? And what is more short-sighted than exploiting the fears of seniors for a couple points in the Gallup Poll?

From the start of the 104th Congress, I had hoped that the White House and congressional Republicans would be allies in innovation, not merely rivals for power. For a time, I truly believed that President Clinton would sign the budget we sent him. Certainly I urged him both publicly and privately to do so. It would have been consistent with his 1992 campaign promises to restrain federal spending, cut taxes for the middle class and put an end to welfare as we knew it. Signing the budget would keep faith with the American people in an era of disenchantment with political figures whose promises were written in disappearing ink.

Most of all, signing the budget would have been the right thing to do for America's future. In the end, however, the self-proclaimed agent of change took his stand behind the barricades of the status quo. Clinton's veto of the bill was coupled with a propaganda blitz as cynical as it was (temporarily) successful.

Throughout the summer and fall of 1995, the President traveled the country, attacking the Republican budget. Wherever he went, he said it would "slash" spending. According to the President, it would throw the poor into the streets. Our family-friendly tax cuts would favor the business community. Our Medicare plan would leave America's seniors destitute. Indeed, Michael McCurry, the White House press secretary, made the astonishing claim at one point that what Republicans really wanted was for senior citizens to die.

Some of these statements were contemptible. All of them were false—and the President knew it. Our budget did not cut overall spending—it allowed for growth of 22 percent over seven years. Our budget did not cut programs to the needy—it expanded them by 34 percent over seven years. Seventy-three percent of the tax cuts in our budget went to America's families. And our Medicare proposal—one very similar to a plan advocated by President and Mrs. Clinton in 1993—actually increased average spending per beneficiary from $4,800 this year to $6,700 over seven years.

Those are the facts. And "facts," as Honest John Adams liked to say, are "stubborn things." Some in the media—among them the editorial page of the *Washington Post,* not usually known as a Republican cheerleader—called the President's rhetoric "Medigoguery." But the vast majority of the media—especially the television networks—transmitted the President's rhetoric day after day, without bothering to inquire whether his statements bore any relation to the truth.

While the media for the most part let President Clinton's misrepresentations go unchallenged, the President's rhetoric was reinforced by a massive advertising campaign by the Democratic National Committee. Americans couldn't turn on their televisions without seeing commercials trumpeting the President's "balanced budget," or repeating the now familiar claim that Republicans wanted to slash Medicare.

These professionally made commercials were replete with catchy music and charming pictures. There was only one problem: not a word of them was true. The President had never submitted a balanced budget. And the Republican plan increased Medicare spending. Unfortunately, many Americans accepted the President's rhetoric as reality.

The *Wall Street Journal* published the results of one national survey, in which participants were asked, "As you may know, average Medicare spending per person is $4,800 each year. From what you have seen, read, or heard in the press, do you think the Republican Medicare proposal would:

    A. Cut spending to below $4,000.
    B. Keep it the same.
    C. Increase spending to $6,700.
    D. Don't know or not sure."

The correct answer was "C," a fact that every Republican in Congress had been repeating for months. But in an example of the power of the White House to dominate media coverage, that was not the answer given by the majority of Americans.

In fact, 27 percent of those questioned said that the Republican Medicare proposal would cut spending to below $4,000. Twenty-four percent said it would keep spending the same. Twenty-five percent said they did not know or weren't sure. Only 22 percent—only slightly over one in five Americans—knew the correct answer of $6,700.

By now you've gathered my unhappiness when public policy takes a backseat to public relations. To be fair, however, let it be said that the Republicans didn't stumble over the budget battle solely because of the President's rhetoric or his verbal agility. We provided him with a little help ourselves.

In the midst of the budget battle came the tragic assassination of Israeli Prime Minister Yitzhak Rabin, by an extremist opposed to the Prime Minister's peace plans. Just a few weeks earlier, I had sat beside Rabin at a ceremony in the Capitol Rotunda marking the three-thousandth anniversary of the City of Jerusalem. We spoke that day of our mutual hope for peace in the Middle East. Frankly, I had a special reason to admire Rabin. On the surface a gruff, uncharismatic soldier, he was no "Great Communicator." But he was one of this century's towering leaders. He kept his eyes on the stars, while at the same time keeping his feet planted firmly on the ground. He was the most practical visionary I've ever known.

On learning of Rabin's death, I broke off a campaign swing to travel to Israel for his funeral. I went as part of a large delegation of congressional and Jewish community leaders accompanying the President aboard Air Force One. As we departed Jerusalem for our lengthy return flight, Speaker Gingrich and I wondered if President Clinton might take the opportunity to put aside his partisan rhetoric of recent days, and meet with congressional leaders of both parties in hopes of reconciling our differences over the budget and other issues. At the time, a number of appropriation bills funding government agencies were in limbo because of the President's threatened veto. If agreement on these measures eluded us much longer, then at least some portions of the government would face a shutdown.

Adding to the somber mood aboard Air Force One was a sadly uneventful return flight. I believed then, and still believe, that the President missed an opportunity for productive discussions that could have helped avert a crisis. He was the host, I was the guest, and it was certainly his decision to make. But Newt Gingrich was hardly the only member of Congress who returned to Washington convinced that the Clinton White House wanted nothing more than a highly publicized confrontation, deliberately and cynically staged to make the President look like a forceful leader.

Unfortunately, Gingrich, who had grown increasingly frustrated with the President's misleading statements, let his emotions get the better of him. Shortly after our return, he publicly lamented the airborne discussions that never were. Worse, he complained about having to exit the plane from the rear.

Congressional Democrats, unwilling to debate the substantive elements of our budget plan, seized upon the Speaker's words to change the subject. As the appropriations deadline approached, they offered the Speaker's faux pas as proof that Republicans were willing to shut down the government solely out of pique over one man's hurt feelings. It was phony as a three-dollar bill, but it worked, and it continued to work when the government did indeed shut down. The incident showed yet again how trivialized our politics have become, and how easy it is to manipulate the media, for whom the intricacies of budget reform paled in comparison with the prospect of a fight between the President of the United States and the Speaker of the House.

While I spent my weeks trying to fulfill promises made in the 1994 campaign, my weekends were aimed at 1996. On April 10, 1995, I officially announced my presidential candidacy in Topeka. I can't say that it came as much of a surprise. A few weeks earlier, I had "leaked" my decision to David Letterman, and the millions of Americans who watch his nightly television program. I also brought along my own version of Letterman's "Top 10 List." (Since Republicans were cutting everything by 30 percent, I brought along a list reduced to the "Top 7 Ways to Reduce Government Spending." My personal favorite was to reduce government ink expenditures by switching the "William Jefferson Clinton" signature to the much shorter "Bob Dole.")

Letterman and I got along well. We're both Midwesterners, impatient with pretense, and with a sometimes cranky sense of humor. On the other hand, many in the entertainment industry took the strongest possible exception to what I had to say about Hollywood and its impact on popular culture.

On May 31, 1995, I traveled to Los Angeles to share some thoughts that had been on my mind, and—judging from the avalanche of mail I received following the speech—on the mind of many of America's parents, as well.

"One of the greatest threats to American family values is the way our popular culture ridicules them," I said before an audience of several hundred. "Our music, movies, television and advertising regularly push the limits of decency, bombarding our children with destructive messages of casual violence and even more casual sex. . . . We must hold Hollywood and the entire entertainment industry accountable for putting profit ahead of common decency. . . .

"I am not saying that our growing social problems are entirely Hollywood's fault," I continued. "They are not. People are responsible for their actions. Movies and music do not make children into murderers. But a numbing exposure to graphic violence and immorality does steal away innocence, smothering our instinct for outrage. We have reached the point where our popular culture threatens to undermine our character as a nation."

My speech ignited a national conversation, much as former Vice President Dan Quayle inspired the reexamination of the American family with his comments about Murphy Brown. Time has proven just how right he was. For my own part, I intend to continue speaking out about popular culture during the current campaign and beyond.

The vast majority of Americans still hold fast to the values that make ours the greatest land on earth—not because of its military might, but because of its moral strength. Today it's not enough to sit in silence as movies and music, television and advertising mock what we hold most dear. We must preach what we practice, braving the ridicule of cultural elites, if necessary, naming names and calling to account those merchants of sleaze whose products pollute the airwaves, movie theaters and billboards of America.

Individually and collectively, values count. The economy will never be strong enough to transform a neighborhood where 80 percent of children lack a father, and legitimate jobs are dismissed out of hand as "chump change." Nor will there ever be enough programs or police to enforce order in our society if there is rampant disorder in our souls.

It's a lot harder to rise out of poverty when the popular culture denigrates the values that make individual success possible. Likewise, it's much harder for society to control crime when "role models" glorify violence and women are degraded by "artists" whose sole talent is for exploiting the media's preoccupation with hype and vulgarity.

By the fall of 1995 I was facing other candidates for the Republican nomination: Texas Senator Phil Gramm, commentator Pat Buchanan, millionaire publisher Malcolm "Steve" Forbes, Jr., former Tennessee Governor Lamar Alexander, Indiana Senator Dick Lugar, Congressman Bob Dornan, former Ambassador Alan Keyes and businessman Morry Taylor. I thought the field was a little crowded. Some in the media thought it wasn't crowded enough. Their attention was focused on someone who was not a candidate, and whose political affiliation was still an open question—General Colin Powell, former Chairman of the Joint Chiefs of Staff.

I had met with General Powell on numerous occasions during his years of White House and Pentagon service. Like anyone who dealt with him, I was deeply impressed by his patriotism and his leadership skills. He had—and has—star quality to spare, combined with an inspiring personal story embodying the American Dream at its noblest. Still, some believed that statements made by General Powell in interviews surrounding the publication of his autobiography indicated he was not a Republican.

I disagreed. Throughout my career, I have fought to expand the GOP. Now that we were finally America's majority party, it was no time to raise philosophical litmus tests as a requirement for party membership. At a press conference on November 8, 1995, General Powell made two announcements: one, that he would not run for President and two, that he was a Republican. I spoke with him that afternoon, and welcomed him to the party. I am confident that this true American hero will play an important role in our country and our party for many years to come.

After a seemingly endless stream of debates, joint appearances and straw polls, the nomination battle was joined in Iowa. Given my special connection to the state, I had long been regarded as the favorite. Early poll numbers from the Hawkeye State showed me with approval ratings in the unheard-of range of 80 percent. Then the Forbes campaign opened its wallet, producing and airing millions of dollars of negative advertisements attacking me and my record. By the time Iowans went to caucus meetings on the evening of February 12, my once sky-high approval rating had been sliced nearly in half.

I had been the target of negative ads before, and thought I had a pretty thick skin. But these misrepresentations were so chillingly effective that I observed if the charges they made were true, even I wouldn't vote for Bob Dole.

In the final analysis, while the commercials damaged me— I won narrowly in Iowa with only 26 percent of the vote— they may have inflicted more lasting damage on Forbes himself. Instead of turning out voters for his candidacy, the relentless attacks turned voters off. To his credit, Forbes said he would stop airing negative ads after Iowa. By then, however, his commercials had been saturating New Hampshire for months.

On February 20, I learned again why New Hampshire is called the Granite State—because it's tough to crack. Some political pundits declared that Pat Buchanan's narrow victory in the primary guaranteed a long, drawn-out struggle for the GOP nomination. My instincts told me otherwise. By then, I had withstood millions of dollars of negative ads in Iowa and New Hampshire and emerged with a first- and a second-place showing. With eight primaries on March 5, and seven more on March 12, none of the other candidates could focus all their efforts on one state, as they had in Iowa and New Hampshire. After a big victory in South Carolina on March 2, signs began appearing at campaign rallies hailing me as "The Comeback Adult."

I went on to win all fifteen primaries held on Junior Tuesday and Super Tuesday. Two weeks later, I returned to Russell to claim victory.

ELIZABETH

Bob and I have been blessed with challenging and fulfilling careers. But I hope you don't get the impression that our lives are an endless string of memos and meetings. No matter how busy our schedules, the priority will always be friends, family and one another.

Those who think Washington, D.C., is one endless social whirl might be pretty surprised when they look at our life. Our favorite evening engagement is a dinner at home or at a favorite or new restaurant. Weekends are time for church, brunch with Robin and my nephew John Hanford, walking Leader, exercising on the treadmill, listening to music and watching movies.

We also still delight in trying to surprise one another. December 6, 1995, marked our twentieth wedding anniversary. As that day drew closer, it became clear that the Senate would be in session late into that evening. When I was invited to speak at an event in Iowa, we quickly decided to postpone our anniversary celebration until the coming weekend.

Bob, however, had a few surprises up his sleeve. First he organized a group of eight friends and supporters who were part of the campaign in Iowa, and invited them to a dinner that evening. Then he called Iowa Senator Chuck Grassley and asked him to recommend a restaurant in Iowa, where I was staying.

Then he called the manager of the restaurant—The Boat House —put together a menu, and arranged for dinner for nine to be served. Then he called the florist and arranged for a delivery of roses. And while I enjoyed my surprise dinner party, he called me at the restaurant.

The rest sounds like an O. Henry story. Having no idea what he was up to, I had arranged for a dinner from one of Bob's favorite restaurants to be delivered to his office, along with his favorite dessert—a hot fudge sundae.

In our phone call that evening, I said, "Bob, you know something? We're just as much in love now as we were the day we were married." "No," Bob corrected me. "We're more in love."

CHAPTER TWELVE

The Next American Century

BOB

On May 15, 1996, I announced my resignation from the U.S. Senate. This announcement caught by surprise some who believed that Congress was my life. With all due respect to Congress, *America* has been my life. And my decision to leave the Senate was an expression of my belief that as a presidential candidate I owe America my full attention, everything I can give, everything I have. And that is what America shall receive from me.

A presidential campaign is a national conversation conducted over millions of back fences. Between now and November 5, Americans will look themselves in the mirror and ask where we are going as a nation and whether we are satisfied with the course we are on. Contrary to media hype, choosing a President is not to be confused with running a race. It is not about *who* is ahead this week, but about *what* lies ahead next year, or next decade, and how we can make the future our friend.

My presidential campaign is about telling the truth. It's about doing what is right. I will not shy away from speaking my mind about the failings of government at a time when millions of Americans have become alienated from their leaders and apprehensive about the future.

333

AN ECONOMY OF HOPE

Fear in the 1990s wears a very human face. It is a father of four who has lost his job and can barely support those he loves. It is a mother of two who worries her job may be the next to go. It is a breadwinner nearing the end of his career who is concerned about losing his health insurance. And it is millions of parents convinced that their children will be relegated to a lower standard of living.

The Clinton Administration makes light of such apprehensions. It says the economy is doing quite well, thank you—certainly better than most people think. It boasts of creating some 8.5 million jobs over the last three and a half years.

What it doesn't tell you is how anemic the current economic recovery is compared with others in recent years. Let me put it in perspective. Had we merely duplicated the same rate of job growth seen in the last three economic recoveries, we could have created almost twelve million jobs since January 1993. In other words, Americans are suffering from a job deficit of more than three million.

The Clinton Administration says that two thirds of the new jobs pay high wages. On closer examination, one finds the claim applies exclusively to those holding full-time jobs. It has no relevance to the millions of part-time positions people have taken on in order to make ends meet. And it says nothing about comparable wages for those who manage somehow to find employment after being laid off. As it happens, those rehired workers can expect to earn 10 percent less than they did in their former positions.

Since Bill Clinton took office, Americans are working more and earning less. In the last two years—years of economic growth as measured by the White House—American productivity rose by 2 percent, yet wages declined by more than 2 percent. The Clinton Labor Department reports a 17 percent increase in the number of workers holding two or more jobs since January 1994. As a result, today's Americans are caught in a "Clinton Crunch" between higher taxes and stagnant wages. According to a study by the Heritage Foundation, the President's $265 billion tax increase in 1993 cost the economy more than one million jobs, $264 billion in real personal disposable income, and $138 billion in personal savings.

In the ten years before President Clinton took office, the economy averaged 3.2 percent annual growth. In fact, in 1992, when America was experiencing economic growth of 2.7 percent, candidate Clinton derided President Bush for presiding over what he termed "the worst economic performance in fifty years." Yet the President congratulates himself on an economy that has grown at an annual rate of only 2.4 percent during his first three years in office. Apparently he thinks this represents the outer limit of America's economic potential.

Unfortunately, President Clinton and his Democrat allies "distrust the market, preach government as the answer to our problems, preferring the bureaucrat they know to the consumer they can't control."

I didn't say that. Democrat Senator Bill Bradley did in announcing his retirement in the fall of 1995.

The fact is that more government will not create more jobs. Only more freedom will. As President, I will move aggressively to ensure that Americans are free from deficits, free from unreasonable taxation, free from excessive regulations, and that they have the freedom to compete in a fair global marketplace.

I've already outlined some of the economic benefits flowing out of a balanced budget. The *Washington Post* has reported that last year's Republican plan to eliminate federal red ink over seven years would have saved $60 billion in annual interest payments. That's $60 billion that could have been invested in new-job creation or returned to taxpayers. Even now, some will tell you it is impossible to balance the budget and still protect Social Security. Well, don't believe them. Because Republicans did it. And Bill Clinton killed it.

For three years, President Clinton has failed to propose any dramatic changes in the American tax code—with the exception of his $265 billion tax increase—the biggest in history. Add the surcharges included in the Clinton tax package, and the top federal tax rate now stands at almost 40 percent. Throw in state and local taxes, and Social Security taxes, and many Americans find themselves paying over half their income for the privilege of supporting a government grown fat and happy on their hard-earned dollars. Indeed, according to the Tax Foundation, the typical American family *pays more in total taxes—federal, state, and local—than it spends on food, clothing and shelter combined.*

Americans fought a revolution fueled by the belief that taxation without representation is tyranny. Two centuries later, taxation with representation isn't much better. Since 1992, individual taxes have soared 33 percent. This year, Tax Freedom Day—the day when the average American stops working for the government, and starts working for him- or herself—fell on May 7, the latest ever. It was April 30 when President Clinton took office.

This means that in just three years, the Clinton Administration has condemned Americans to work seven more days each year for the government. I would like to be the President who liberates American workers to enjoy more of the fruits of their labor, and who pushes Tax Freedom Day earlier in the calendar.

As President, I will stop using tax policy to feed the federal bureaucracy. I will propose a new tax code with lower, flatter, fairer rates. To be fair, such a system should not penalize success. Rather, it should reward people for working harder, saving more and investing wisely.

A fair tax system would relieve the burden on working families. I believe a family of four earning $25,000 to $30,000 per year should pay little or no federal income tax. I also believe that our tax code should be revised to recognize that a family's most important responsibility is raising children, not supporting Washington—that's the concept driving the Republican effort for a $500 per child tax credit.

A fair tax system would stop taxing capital twice: first as income, then as capital gains, thereby reducing the return on investment and discouraging risk-takers from creating new jobs. Today, the United States has the highest capital gains tax of any major industrial country. When it comes to competing with countries like Germany and Japan—who hardly tax capital gains at all—we're tying the hands of the most productive, innovative people in our economy.

I would cut tax rules as well as tax rates. That means ending the IRS as we know it. It's estimated that last year alone individual taxpayers spent 1.8 billion hours filling out their tax forms. Businesses spent twice as much time sending the IRS over one billion reports. Uncle Sam boasts that it should take taxpayers "only" 2 hours and 42 minutes to complete a 1040 EZ. I don't know about you, but it takes that long for me to make sense out of the thirty-six pages of instructions that accompany that form.

The IRS was never meant to be an intrusive, oppressive presence in American life. But as the tax code has grown ever more complex, as the agency has swelled to more than 100,000 people, costing taxpayers nearly $10 billion a year, tax collectors have grown more aggressive and more arrogant. Today, there are more investigators working for the IRS than for the Drug Enforcement Administration. Compliance costs run to hundreds of billions of dollars, and it is not unusual for some companies to file tax forms that resemble the tax code itself in their length and complexity.

With a fairer, flatter, simpler tax system, the 1040 form would go the way of the Iron Curtain. Americans could file the tax return on a postcard, or electronically, without paper at all. And thousands of IRS investigators, accountants and tax lawyers would be able to utilize their talents in more productive ways.

To ensure that Congress doesn't turn a flatter tax system into a political football, I would insist on amending the Constitution to require a "super majority" vote of three fifths before Congress can raise your income-tax rates. This would guard our reforms, hold Congress accountable and do more than anything else to keep Washington out of our wallets. Such an amendment would protect taxpayers from the shifting political winds. And it would allow business leaders to make decisions based on market opportunities, not the advice of their tax lawyer.

According to estimates by the National Association of Manufacturers, the millions of words in the federal regulatory code cost a typical American family nearly $6,000 a year.

As Senate Majority Leader, I have fought hard for the most sweeping regulatory reforms in history. But President Clinton has convinced liberal Senate Democrats to stand in the way of their enactment. If I were in his place, I would, on my first day in office, direct every federal department and agency to raise the following questions before imposing any new regulations on American citizens: Is there a need for this regulation? Do the costs outweigh the benefits? Does this regulation make common sense? It's a simple test, yet one that millions of pages of current regulations would undoubtedly flunk.

Common sense is also needed in the trade arena. It goes without saying that we cannot wall out foreign goods without simultaneously walling in American ones. We cannot grow in isolation from the rest of the world. Those who would follow the siren song of protectionism have lost faith in the ability of the American worker to outperform the competition anywhere in the world.

Yet, I understand the frustrations that many workers feel. President Clinton's paper trail of 200 trade agreements have amounted to little more than surrender and sign on the dotted line. Last year, America imported $175 billion more in merchandise than we exported—the highest merchandise trade deficit in history. With China, the Clinton trade deficit has nearly doubled, hitting $34 billion in 1995 alone. And our merchandise trade deficit with Japan is $10 billion higher than the day President Clinton took office.

As bad as these numbers are, their implications for future policy are even worse. Trade mismanagement by the Clinton Administration provides fertile ground for those who would strangle the free flow of goods and services across national boundaries and around the globe. A Dole Administration will use the powerful market-opening tools Congress has given the President. In trade, as in other aspects of foreign policy, I will never shy away from asserting America's legitimate interests abroad.

Fairness should be the hallmark of economic competition inside, as well as outside, our borders. According to a study by the Congressional Research Service, there are more than 160 federal programs that grant preferences to individuals on the basis of race or gender. Instead of expanding opportunity, such programs divide Americans by race and gender, fostering suspicion and distrust.

If affirmative action means remedying proven past discrimination against specific individuals, then I'm all for it. If it means recruiting qualified women and minorities to give them an opportunity to compete, without guaranteeing the results, then I'm for that too. But when affirmative action means quotas, set-asides and other preferences that favor individuals simply because they happen to be a member of a certain group, then that's where I draw the line.

Affirmative action was never meant to be a permanent fixture in American society, but a source of transitional assistance, narrowly applied. Anything else flies in the face of a truly color-blind society. In America, merit, talent and individual efforts—not gender, ethnic background or skin color—should be the keys that unlock the doors of opportunity.

WHOM DO YOU TRUST?

Some officeholders excel at cutting ribbons and taking credit for road repairs. I'm more interested in repairing the two-way street of trust that runs between the American people and their government. Of all the factors which have combined to erode popular confidence in our government, none is more insidious than a lack of straight talk, matched by an abundance of political gamesmanship, on the part of our leaders.

Every four years we hear a lot of talk about "new ideas"—who has them, and who has the will and energy to implement them. The Clinton Administration would like you to think it has a patent pending on new ideas. Yet telling people what you think they want to hear just to win their votes is a very old idea, indeed.

In the words of President Clinton's assistant, George Stephanopoulos, "The President has kept the promises he meant to keep." Like me, many of you might be asking which promises did he *not* mean to keep? And which President is he talking about?

Is it the President who promised us a trillion-dollar health

plan run from Washington, D.C., or the born-again budget cutter who declared "the era of big government is over"?

Is it the President who delivers eloquent speeches about the
need for campaign reform, or the one who sits down to dinners
raising $10 million from campaign contributors, promising
them access to trade missions and Cabinet secretaries?

Is it the President who promised to "end welfare as we
know it"—or the one who maintained the status quo by twice
vetoing welfare reform?

Is it the public orator who pounds the podium and draws
the line at reductions in projected Medicare spending—or the
President who quietly submits a budget containing $124 billion
in such reductions in growth?

Is it the President who talks tough on drugs—or the one
who gutted the White House Office of National Drug Policy?

Is it the advocate of legal reform—or the President who
kills legislation restoring common sense to our justice system
because it offends powerful trial lawyers, the largest contributors to his campaign?

Is it the President whose Administration in February 1996
announces an end to the B-2 bomber program—or the one who
goes to California a month later and announces that another
B-2 will be built, adding $493 million to the local economy and,
coincidentally enough, a few points to his approval ratings?

So much for new ideas. There is another very old, very
cynical notion that holds: If you can't win on the merits of your
ideas, appropriate those of your opponents. For over a year,
President Clinton has done a masterful job of appearing to be
something that he isn't—a social and fiscal conservative. Hardly
a week goes by when the East Room or Rose Garden doesn't
serve as a backdrop to official pronouncements about everything from school uniforms and TV ratings to teen pregnancy
and corporate responsibility.

"It's a form of leadership that is tailored to the era of
divided government," said White House Communications Director Don Baer. "We put it in play, the media cover it, and
people respond."

Maybe. But at what cost to personal candor and public
trust?

I said trust was a two-way street. Why should people trust those in positions of responsibility when those they put there do not reciprocate? That sounds harsh. But stop and think of the great leaders of the past, people like Theodore and Franklin Roosevelt, Dwight Eisenhower, Harry Truman, Ronald Reagan. Whatever may have separated them ideologically, they understood that trust is the coin of the democratic realm.

The Clinton Administration has tarnished that coin.

It doesn't trust American parents to choose the best education for their children.

It doesn't trust American taxpayers to know how to spend their hard-earned dollars better than Washington bureaucrats.

It doesn't trust governors and mayors to administer programs closest to the people.

It doesn't trust small-business people—who create 80 percent of our jobs—to behave responsibly without bearing the staggering load of federal rules and regulations costing consumers $600 billion a year.

And it rejects the idea of limited government, the genius of America's founders, because it prefers to deal with governing elites rather than trusting "We the people."

In 1992, the Clinton campaign ran on the theme song "Don't Stop Thinking About Tomorrow." For the last three years, President Clinton has governed by the slogan "Don't Stop Thinking About the Next Election."

TWO AMERICAN VISIONS

Voters in November 1996 will be able to choose between two radically different visions of the American future. One vision defines that future as the next election. The other defines it as the next generation and beyond.

One relies on bureaucrats to manage the economy and to apportion equal shares of scarcity. The other places its confidence in individual Americans to generate new ideas and the jobs which follow.

One looks to Washington to solve America's problems; the other views Washington as a source of those problems.

One would dictate from the top down; the other would organize society from the bottom up.

One would nationalize health care, federalize education, and entrust both our culture and our character to bureaucrats; the other has faith in the average citizen's ability to choose his own health care, select the best school for his children and define and defend community standards of behavior.

One vision classifies Americans by their membership in groups, each competing for "its" share of the federal pie, each hooked on "its" federal program or subsidy. The other vision sees Americans as more than a warring bunch of special interests; it sees them as patriots whose most sacred possession is their individual, not their group, rights.

Thomas Jefferson told us, "The God who gave us life, gave us liberty at the same time." Jefferson and his contemporaries were perhaps the greatest visionaries of all time. Loving liberty as much as they hated tyranny, they believed—in defiance of the accepted wisdom of their day—that ordinary people are capable of extraordinary accomplishments, none more extraordinary than self-government. The Founders placed limits on government so that there would be no limits to individual achievement or social mobility.

Unfortunately, for much of this century, Jefferson's vision has been clouded by the uncontrolled growth of government. During this time Americans have ceded to Washington responsibilities traditionally assumed at the local and state level. Along the way, we have unwittingly given rise to many of the very institutions we now reject as too large, too expensive, too remote, too unresponsive, and, finally, too undemocratic to be genuinely representative of Americans at our best.

Conservatives distrust centralized bureaucracies, not just because they waste our money, but because they limit our options. Left to grow unchecked, they can undermine our national character, even as they destroy our already fragile sense of community. Thirty years after the Great Society, is anyone naive enough to believe that government can foster moral values or implant feelings of individual dignity and self-worth?

RESTORING AMERICAN VALUES

The anxieties which beset so many Americans on the eve of the twenty-first century involve more than economics. Taxpayers want value for their dollar, to be sure, but they also insist on a government that reflects their values. At the moment, they are getting neither.

Historically, Americans have regarded themselves as masters of destiny, not victims of fate. Today, sadly, millions of us feel as if we are no longer in control of anything. We are justifiably concerned by the rise of violent crime and the decline of civilized behavior. We are sickened by a coarse, tabloid culture. And we are baffled by leaders who seem to pay less attention to fighting crime in the streets than they do to banning prayer in the schools.

In the words of the Reverend Billy Graham, "America is not at a crossroads. America is a long way down the wrong road."

At one point in World War II, General George Marshall was asked whether the United States had a secret weapon in the war against Fascism.

"Yes," Marshall said. "Our secret weapon is the best darn kids in the world."

Not long ago, a *New York Times* correspondent put a very different question to a mother whose teenage son had just been arrested for taking part in a gang-rape. She was asked if her son was a good boy. You know what she replied? "There are no good boys anymore."

How have we, as a nation, gone from "the best darn kids in the world" to that mother's chilling lament for an entire generation?

Of course, she was wrong. Millions of young Americans are shining examples of good citizenship, good scholarship and good sportsmanship. Millions more would be the same if only challenged by leaders who agree with Reverend Graham that America's future lies down a road radically different from the one we have been traveling of late.

Former Secretary of Education William Bennett, in his

"Index of Leading Cultural Indicators," provides sobering confirmation of America's moral confusion. Bennett reports a 560 percent increase in violent crime since 1960. The same period has witnessed a more than 400 percent increase in illegitimate births, a tripling of teen suicides and an 80-point drop in SAT scores.

At times it feels as if American society is unraveling before our eyes. Today, nearly one in three American babies is born to an unwed mother. One in eight American students drops out of high school before obtaining a degree. Teenage boys—in or out of school—are more likely to die of gunshot wounds than from all natural causes combined. Meanwhile, the typical American youngster will be exposed to eight thousand murders and over one hundred thousand acts of violence on television *before finishing elementary school.*

Here, then, is the tragic detour which has taken us from Marshall's proud generation to the moral zombies who menace decent people on too many American street corners.

If we want a society that values life, honors character, rewards effort, cherishes its children, respects its elders, believes in justice and lives in peace with itself and with others, then Americans must make it our business to instill such values in our young people.

No one thinks it will be easy—the path of least resistance would be to withdraw into numbed indifference. Yet that would be the worst possible response from a nation which is never greater, never more true to its ideals, then when enlisted in a great moral cause. If you don't take General Marshall's word for this, there's always Bina Dole's admonition that "Can't never could do anything."

What can Americans do at the end of the twentieth century to reverse the bleak trends of social and cultural disintegration? We can begin by taking a long, hard look at government policies which have either created our problems or exacerbated them.

For example, crime in the 1990s is more random and more violent, yet our justice system seems unable to keep predators in jail. Our schools teach recycling but our kids can't add, can't identify George Washington, and certainly aren't allowed to pray in the classroom. Illegitimacy is epidemic, but our tax code penalizes marriage, while a decrepit welfare system drives away fathers. Programs designed to eliminate poverty have only perpetuated it, creating a seemingly permanent underclass of citizens whose suffering and isolation are a reproach to every caring American.

THE PURSUIT OF COMMUNITY

In earlier days, Americans came together amid the adversity of economic hardship and global war. More recently, our unity has been shattered by moral and cultural relativism. Noble concepts like duty and sacrifice have been crowded out by a mindless pursuit of additional entitlements for special-interest groups.

Doctrines of political correctness now dominate our school's curricula, assigning equal value to all cultures and lifestyles. In celebrating what makes us different from each other, we have come dangerously close to discarding whatever might bind us as one people.

Today there are more laws on the books, and less respect for authority, than ever before. Substance abuse, abortion, rampant crime, youthful despair—these are the depressing road signs which confirm Reverend Graham's diagnosis that the highway of the 1990s leads to the loss of faith, the destruction of families, the squandering of trust and the end of the old American belief in ourselves as a people who do and dare greatly.

But there is another road beckoning to us—it leads straight to the next American century.

If you've read this far, you know that I have never espoused the barren philosophy of every man for himself. Growing up, I was taught to put my trust in God, not government, and never to confuse the two. I learned the hard way that while self-reliance is an essential part of the American character, so is that generous spirit that reaches out to those wounded in body and soul. This is part of my legacy from Russell.

When I went off to war, it was to defend a community of values unique to all the world. I came back sustained by the love and support of neighbors who quickly renewed my sense of life's possibilities. In Russell, we never doubted that our neighbors were looking out for us, or that they would be there to help in case of emergency. At the same time, they were not the only ones to care for me after World War II. Army doctors aided my recovery. And when I attended college, I owed my education to the GI Bill of Rights.

Maybe all this explains my tendency to see government's proper role as that of a neighbor and not a warden. Government should be willing to provide help as a last resort. But it should also know when to leave us alone. It should keep its hands out of our pockets and its nose out of places where it doesn't belong.

Is all this an exercise in nostalgia? I don't think so. I think it's a formula for national renewal. Of all the challenges confronting America at the end of the twentieth century—whether it's combating crime or providing jobs for the future or fashioning an educational system better suited for the age of computer chips than Mr. Chips—nothing is more important than regenerating the proud belief that each American is part of a worthy enterprise, larger than any one individual.

Early in the century, the journalist Walter Lippmann wrote that the true function of democratic government was "not to direct the affairs of the community but to harmonize the direction a community gives its affairs."

It will take a very different kind of President to harmonize instead of direct. It will take a leader who is willing to rethink the stale and limiting conventions of interest-group politics. For example, conservatives must be more imaginative in reaching out to African Americans, with whom we share so many values, especially when it comes to strengthening the family and fighting crime.

Baby-boomers have been characterized in the media as materialistic and self-absorbed. That's not what I find as I travel the country. I find more and more of the postwar generation concerned about personal responsibility and fiscal integrity—the very qualities most conspicuously lacking in today's "buy now, pay later" government.

I also find that it is the youngest voters who are the most realistic about the limits of government in the twenty-first century. My generation shares an interest with "twenty-something" Americans in guaranteeing the viability of programs like Social Security and Medicare. Having said that, is it not reasonable to expect my contemporaries, so accustomed to sacrificing for the larger good, to resolve now to avoid burdening our grandchildren with a crushing debt not of their making?

Pollsters detect a "gender gap," which pundits enlarge, often at the expense of the facts. I think it's the worst kind of patronization to talk about "women's issues" as if they existed in a political or cultural vacuum. *All* issues are women's issues. Women-owned businesses are the fastest-growing sector of the American economy, employing more people than all the Fortune 500 companies combined. Certainly women, no less than men, want lower taxes and fewer regulations, as well as safer streets, better schools and a strong America.

Because I believe a President gets his strength from the American people, I want to be the President who builds bridges, not walls, between Americans of all races and generations. As President, I would speak out often, urging Americans to overcome the shrill and artificial divisions of modern life. I would ask all Americans to stop thinking of our fellow citizens as mere labels, and start looking for ways to be reunited in mutual respect and common purpose.

My presidency would be guided by the 10th Amendment of the Constitution, which reads: "The powers not delegated to the United States by the Constitution, nor prohibited by it to the states, are reserved to the states . . . or to the people." The language may sound dry, but its implications are profound. Democracy, after all, is measured by the dispersal of authority, and the belief that true leadership resides in the many, not the few. This idea was radical when first put forth over two hundred years ago. It is, if anything, even more radical as we approach the millennium.

What makes it so revolutionary is the philosophy of human freedom it encapsulates—expressed through trust in the American people to do for themselves what the federal government cannot do as well.

The Constitution is quite specific about federal powers. The 10th Amendment is equally clear about the limitations of those powers.

Over the years, however, federalism has given way to Washington-style paternalism, with disastrous results. Even today, there are many in our nation's capital who refuse to accept the ability of our states, cities and citizens to govern themselves.

HOLDING WASHINGTON ACCOUNTABLE

The time is long overdue for us to return to first principles. As President, I would govern in the conviction that accountability is most direct at levels of government the people can touch for themselves. I would begin by applying a means test to the entire federal establishment. From Amtrak to zoological studies, I would ask: Is this program a basic function of a limited government, or is it an example of how government has lost faith in the judgments of our people and the potential of our markets?

Are we really serious about reforming American government? If we are, then the best place to begin is with four of Washington's most ineffective, burdensome and meddlesome departments: Education, Housing and Urban Development, Energy, and Commerce. Together, they spend over $74 billion each year and employ more than seventy-four thousand workers.

Let's close down the Education Department and spend the money we save where it will do the most good—fostering innovation and excellence in our classrooms instead of perpetuating the stranglehold of the National Education Association.

President Clinton says he wants to put a computer in every classroom. Fine. But we'd be even better off putting parents in every classroom. Unfortunately, we'll never empower parents or promote imaginative education alternatives like charter schools until we break the grip of yesterday's thinking.

HUD has become a cash cow for well-connected developers and big-city political bosses. We should privatize the Federal Housing Authority, and have the Department of Health and Human Services oversee homeless assistance. The Justice Department can enforce fair-housing laws. Above all, we should give housing vouchers to those in need, and, along with them, the independence and self-respect that accompany home ownership.

The Department of Energy, in its current form—or formlessness—is a confused and costly muddle that spends almost two thirds of its budget on defense and defense-related environmental cleanup. These functions should be returned to where they belong—the Department of Defense. The remaining functions should either be eliminated, privatized or redirected to other agencies that can truly address this country's energy needs.

The environment, let me say, is as precious to conservatives as to anyone else. Indeed, the essence of conservatism is the conserving of the best in nature, society and the individual. There is absolutely no reason why twenty-first-century Americans should have to choose between a healthy economy and a pristine environment. The current debate is not over *whether* to protect our environment, but what is the best way of doing so.

In pursuing a cleaner, safer and healthier environment, I would trust those who live in affected communities. Right now, this country can boast of the most advanced technology and the best scientists on earth. Unfortunately, we are not using the best science. The current Superfund program, designed to undo the environmental damage of earlier generations, is bogged down, not because Congress or the President is withholding funds, but because we're wasting billions of dollars on litigation that is clogging American courts. As a result, the only ones cleaning up are the trial lawyers.

The recent tragic death of Commerce Secretary Ron Brown should not blind us to the shortcomings of a department he led with vigor and flair. More than half of what the Commerce Department does is unrelated to commerce or trade. It is duplicated by seventy-one other governmental departments, agencies and offices. Typical of the problems with Commerce is the badly outmoded National Oceanic and Atmospheric Administration, labeled "technologically obsolete" by the General Accounting Office.

Worse, the fastest-growing section of Commerce is something called the Advanced Technology Program, commonly dubbed ATP, which is a fancy name for a billion dollars a year in corporate welfare. Uncle Sam has no business and no competence in picking and choosing among technological contenders. I could think of no better tribute to the free enterprise system than to abolish the woefully misnamed Department of Commerce.

Downsizing the Washington bureaucracy is a good start at restoring common sense to American government. But it's only a start. Washington must also tap into the imaginative leadership of America's talented mayors and governors who are making our cities and states more efficient and responsive to the taxpayer.

PARTNERSHIP NOT PATERNALISM

It stands to reason that fifty laboratories, each of them pursuing a different path toward medical breakthroughs, will produce a greater range of solutions than a single institution hobbled by tradition or ensnared in red tape. That common-sense view holds just as true for America's states which, now more than ever, serve as dynamic incubators of economic growth, education and welfare reform, the strengthening of family and community structures, and environmental cleanup.

As President, I would insist that Washington recognize and learn from what the states have to teach us. At the same time, I would promote home-grown innovation and local flexibility through block grants rather than the traditional "Washington knows best" federal mandate. One size *does not* fit all. The 1994 crime bill is a case in point. Contrary to what President Clinton's TV ads may suggest, there exists broad bipartisan agreement on the need for more cops on America's streets.

But consensus does not mean unanimity, and federalism is not to be confused with federal dictation. The right kind of anticrime legislation gives states and localities maximum flexibility to fight criminals on their streets and not as statistics in a national trend. Some local leaders will choose to spend the money to increase the police presence in their communities. Others will choose a mixed approach, investing in improved technology or adding squad cars as well as the men and women in blue who ride in them. The point is, that *they*, and not Washington, should make the choice.

If federalism is to propel the next American Century, it will be because we have a President genuinely committed to replacing the old paternalism with a new sense of partnership. I don't want governors to have to come to Washington on bended knees, seeking waivers every time they want to pursue a fresh way of problem solving. As President, I don't want to give them *permission,* I want to give them *power.*

Besides eliminating four useless and expensive Cabinet departments, I would establish two new offices to institutionalize the federal-state partnership. The first would be an Office of Governmental Reform, a sort of permanent Hoover Commission, enlisting the best minds in state and local government to identify what Washington does well and what the states, cities or private businesses might do better.

The second would be a bipartisan Council of American Governors, modeled after the Council of Economic Advisors, designed to infuse the federal establishment with the same energy, creativity and common sense that so many of today's governors bring to their task.

Already the states are far ahead of Washington in fashioning creative alternatives to the dead-end welfare programs enshrined by the Great Society. Liberals fear such experimentation, in part because it may work, but also because any acknowledgment of local responsibility is a dagger aimed at the heart of the welfare lobby. In my experience, welfare bureaucrats love the status quo a whole lot more than they love the prospect of their clientele escaping to independence.

Candidate Clinton promised to end welfare as we know it. But President Clinton got cold feet when Congress sent him legislation that contained deep cuts in the welfare bureaucracy, required single teen parents receiving assistance to stay in school and live under adult supervision, encouraged work by placing a five-year limit on welfare payments, and offered financial incentives to states that reduce out-of-wedlock births without increasing the number of abortions.

Through his inaction at the federal level, the President has inadvertently spurred state and local efforts combining educational and financial incentives to break the vicious cycle that now robs too many American youngsters of their childhood, and saddles too many taxpayers with the bill for youthful irresponsibility.

By all means, let's continue to encourage grass-roots solutions to the welfare crisis. But this does not excuse Washington from enacting sweeping reforms at the federal level, ending welfare as a right and substituting in its place community-based alternatives that encourage welfare recipients to take their own destinies in hand.

CHOOSING BETTER SCHOOLS

On the brink of a new century, it is obvious that the empires of tomorrow will not be built on battlefields or under the chandeliers of diplomatic reception rooms, but in America's classrooms and science labs. Once, our public schools were a source of limitless hope and opportunity. Today, too many of them are dangerous, demoralizing places.

The problem isn't one of financial commitment. The United States spends more on public education and achieves less for it than virtually any of the world's leading industrial powers. In 1993, Congress passed a $65 billion education bill. One thousand pages long, it was brimming with new regulations on how our schools should discipline students and what parents and teachers should discuss in their conferences.

Still, many in Washington cry out for more money and more mandates. By the way, the National Taxpayers Union Foundation recently estimated that if all the programs on the National Education Association's wish list were enacted, they would cost an additional $702 billion—that's $10,544 a year in additional taxes for every American family.

Education, historically the single greatest force for constructive change in society, instead has become a bloated monument to political influence and the status quo. Things aren't likely to get any better as long as Washington insists on playing the role of hall monitor.

Americans know how to build a world-class education system. We built one once. It rested upon a solid foundation of parents and teachers who exercised direct control over school budgets, curricula and hiring practices.

We need that system back again. A first step would be to return to local school districts decisions and dollars now channeled through Washington. As President, I would support and encourage policies that would assist parents—especially those living in areas where schools fall far short of meeting the educational or safety needs of students—in educating their children in the school of their choice.

In contrast, President Clinton and Congressional Democrats killed a proposal that would, with the approval of the Washington, D.C., City Council, give parents of poor children in the nation's capital vouchers worth up to $3,000 to send their child to the public or private school of their choice.

The point Republicans made with this innovative proposal is worth repeating: It is not the children of the Washington elite who are trapped in a failing public school system. They attend the many fine private and parochial schools in the area. Why shouldn't the less-advantaged children of D.C. have the same opportunity?

History is on our side. Remember the GI Bill of Rights, long praised as a shining example of educational democracy and inclusiveness. Under its provisions, a student is free to use his or her government funding to attend any school—state, private or church affiliated. That includes Notre Dame, Brigham Young and Yeshiva University.

We should encourage our teachers to teach without Washington looking over their shoulders. And we should expect our schools to reflect once more the values of America, instructing our children in the glories as well as the shortcomings of American culture.

I want a society in which many cultures are respected. Yet diversity, while important, is not more important than unity.

We must remember that our children's embrace of the

American idea is not automatic. They must come to value freedom as dearly as every refugee fleeing persecution who sailed, swam or scrambled here to find it; as much as every soldier who fought and died to preserve it. America must be in their hearts as well as their heads. Because it takes only a single generation for a nation to forget the idea from which it draws inspiration and the history which can inspire even greater achievements.

PARTNERS AGAINST CRIME

Crime fighting is another area in which the federal government must develop a more creative partnership with states and localities. Recent statistics out of Washington point to an alarming dichotomy. While the overall crime rate in some categories has fallen slightly, the decline masks a frightening rise in violent activities among the young. No one suffers more than America's minority communities. The Justice Department estimates that one out of every twenty-one African American men will be murdered. That's two times the casualty rate of American soldiers during World War II.

If, in fact, there is a war now being waged on the streets of America, the forces of law and order are fighting it with rubber bullets. Today, a criminal who commits a serious offense has less than a 10 percent chance of going to jail. If he is locked up, the odds are overwhelming that he will serve only a fraction of his sentence. Nearly 40 percent of the murders in this country are committed by predators taking advantage of probation, parole and bail. Remember Polly Klaas? Remember James Jordan, Michael Jordan's father? Both were murdered by convicted criminals who left jail long before their original terms were up.

Americans don't have to surrender our streets, or throw up our hands in despair. There are things a civilized society can do to restrain and punish the uncivilized.

First, we must bridge the gap between crime and punishment. We can start by encouraging states to abolish parole for violent offenders, as has been done at the federal level. A fifteen-year sentence should mean just that—fifteen years, not five or ten.

Second, criminals in prison should not be clogging our courts with frivolous lawsuits. In 1994, some forty thousand of these suits were filed. They involved such "grievances" as insufficient storage-locker space, "defective" haircuts by a prison barber and—I'm not making this up—being served "creamy" peanut butter instead of the "chunky" variety. In the words of a popular diet author, it's time to stop the insanity. Congress has already passed legislation I authored to remedy this madness. As President, I would regard this legislation as a start and not a conclusion.

The third element of my anticrime agenda recognizes that Americans are sitting on a time bomb. As today's five-year-olds become tomorrow's adolescents, we face a wave of what some experts call "super predators," morally deadened youngsters who are capable of committing the most vicious acts for the most trivial of reasons. A pair of sneakers. A football jersey. A misplaced glance that is mistaken for disrespect.

These children—however morally impoverished they may be—happen to be citizens of our country. They were not dropped here from some alien world. They were born here, they have lived here, and chances are they will steal, maim and kill here.

This brutal fact is a source of sadness for everyone. But sadness must be matched with resolve to prepare ourselves for the coming danger. For this reason I believe we should shift the focus of the current juvenile justice system from rehabilitation to punishment. Teenage thugs must understand that every act of violence has a consequence. This consequence is called imprisonment. Teenagers who commit murder, rape and other violent crimes should be prosecuted as adults. They should receive sentences equal to the danger they pose to society. If you are old enough to do the crime, you're old enough to do the time.

Fourth, we must rededicate ourselves to the war on drugs. Crime and drug use go hand in hand. Wherever there is a drive-by shooting or a school-yard knifing, you can bet that drugs are somehow involved.

Until recently, the Clinton Administration's most memorable voice on the issue was that of a Surgeon General who believed the best way to fight illegal drugs was to legalize them.

When polls revealed the extent of American concern over the drug threat, the President began to pay more attention. This election-year conversion, welcome as it is, cannot make up for three years of neglect, inaction and the short rations provided those on the front line of the war against drugs.

Such neglect by the Clinton Administration has moved New York Democratic Congressman Charles Rangel—one of America's most respected antidrug advocates—to say: "I have been in Congress for over two decades, and I have never, never, never found any administration that has been so silent on this great challenge to the American people."

We are reaping a shameful harvest for this silence. Survey after survey reveals that today's children are smoking more dope, snorting more cocaine and shooting up more heroin than any time in recent memory.

To get back on track, we must strengthen the federal government's interdiction efforts—to stop drugs before they reach our shores. We must tell those countries who supply these poisons that trade with and economic aid from the United States will depend on their own demonstrated efforts to halt the flow of drugs. But our most effective weapon in the war on drugs is not a Coast Guard cutter or even a prison cell. It is the culture itself.

Liberals like to say that the root cause of crime is economic poverty. I say the root cause of crime is moral poverty.

We will never weaken the grip of drugs on America's youngsters until we strengthen the cultural stigma associated with drug taking. In some quarters, it may be fashionable to minimize the effectiveness of Nancy Reagan's "Just Say No" crusade. But Mrs. Reagan deserves enormous credit for having alerted millions of Americans—of all ages—to the deadly menace of drugs and the moral urgency of fighting them. Today, everyone in positions of authority—parents, teachers, coaches, religious leaders and yes, politicians—must be willing to tell our kids that drug use is wrong and that drugs kill. Our children will listen to this message, but they must hear it first.

And as President, I will make the point that they must hear it from our entertainment industry. Surveys suggest that our kids regard what they see on television entertainment programs as much more influential than what they hear in antidrug education classes. A message that drugs are harmless fun—a message that has been seen in television and movies and heard in popular music on an increasing basis—is a message we should not and must not tolerate.

Finally, we can hardly hope to combat crime and drugs in America if we entrust justice to men and women in our courts who are more interested in rewriting than upholding the Constitution. A generation later, Americans are still paying the price for the Warren Court's unparalleled activism, which expanded the rights of criminal defendants, while tragically curtailing the ability of police to protect the law-abiding public.

I'm not one to make a lot of promises, but I can promise you this: In a Dole Administration, the only judges appointed will be ones who are tough on crime and tougher on criminals. They will protect the victims of crime against the victimizers. Because they, like myself, will be less interested in rationalizing crime than in punishing it.

RESTORING AMERICAN CREDIBILITY

Government's first obligation, whether in mean streets at home or international trouble spots, is to provide for the common defense. The American people are not isolationists. They have never shirked their global responsibilities, because they have never lost their confident belief in America as a place apart, a beacon of liberty in a world all too often darkened by oppression.

But in accepting the price of leadership, they naturally expect their own leaders to speak in one voice, to be clear, consistent and farsighted in designing a foreign policy that protects American interests in a dangerous world. Over the years, such leadership rebuilt Europe after World War II. It defended freedom in places like Korea and Vietnam. It stood guard in Europe and throughout the world as long as the Cold War divided the free from the oppressed. And if there is to be peace in the

Middle East, it will only come about through American leadership—just as it required a strong, experienced American President to keep Saddam Hussein's fingerprints off the world's oil supply.

It goes without saying that Americans wish tyrants would retire from the field, and that no young man or woman would ever again have to confront a dictator in the desert or a terrorist with access to nuclear weapons. But wishful thinking is no substitute for national will. Sure, the Cold War is over. At the same time, I find it amusing to hear members of the Clinton Administration sounding almost nostalgic for the "clarifying" issues of U.S.–Soviet rivalry. These days, it seems as if everyone was a Cold Warrior—even those who were consistently wrong about the Soviet threat, whether in Central America, Grenada or elsewhere.

Today, the Soviet Union is no more. But the dark impulses behind Soviet expansionism linger on. Missiles once controlled by the "Evil Empire" exist in a volatile, unpredictable region. Notwithstanding our protests, Russia is selling nuclear reactors and technology to Iran. Iraq is manufacturing gruesome biological and chemical weapons. North Korea may well join the nuclear family by the end of the century. China is arming Pakistan with nuclear missiles, while just across their contested border, India already has them.

The world remains a dangerous place. Make no mistake about it, the United States is the only superpower in the neighborhood. Nobody wants us to be the world's policeman. Yet we can't just turn off the porch light, lock our door, cross our fingers and hope everyone behaves.

"Some are tired of leadership," said Richard Nixon not long before his death. "They say [America] carried that burden long enough. But if we do not provide leadership, who will? The Germans? The Japanese? The Russians? The Chinese? Only the United States has the potential . . . to lead in the era beyond peace. It is a great challenge for a great people."

What kind of leadership are we providing to a world just getting accustomed to freedom? All too often, the Clinton Administration's approach to foreign policy has resembled Dr.

Dolittle's mythical beast the Pushme-Pullyou—a creature that wants to go in two directions at once, and, consequently, winds up going nowhere.

All over the world, we've been all over the lot: trying to rebuild nations like Somalia that weren't nations to begin with; making open-ended promises to police war zones like Bosnia; pursuing a zigzag course toward China; and, incredibly, responding with a wink and a nod when the Iranian government sent arms shipments to Bosnia. The last misstep has created an Iranian presence in Bosnia, one that could threaten the security of American troops stationed there, as well as the future of Bosnia as a unified democratic and multiethnic state. Moreover, it has virtually destroyed U.S. credibility in any attempt to isolate the terrorist regime in Tehran.

From a sham agreement with North Korea that may well allow that paranoid island of Stalinism to develop nuclear weapons, to chronic indecision about defending a democratic ally like Taiwan against Chinese aggression, to the humiliation visited upon the U.S. Sixth Fleet when a bunch of dockside bullies frightened Uncle Sam out of the harbor of Port-au-Prince, this Administration has stumbled from crisis to crisis, learning little and leading less.

Indeed, until his hand was recently forced by Congress, the President had no intention of standing up to a weakened and isolated Fidel Castro—even after his Communist regime murdered American citizens in cold blood.

Under President Clinton, the American defense budget has been slashed, and American soldiers have been delegated to serve under UN command. The last time I read the Constitution, the President of the United States was Commander in Chief, not Boutros Boutros-Ghali and the bureaucrats of the United Nations.

All too often the Clinton foreign policy is a mere offshoot of domestic political considerations. We intervene in Haiti in pursuit of political and not strategic interests. We place all our eggs in the basket of personal diplomacy. Whatever the fate of Boris Yeltsin, we should think twice before personalizing a country as vast and complex and changeable as Russia, because the will of the voters has a way of superseding presidential friendships.

As you can tell, there are substantial differences—both conceptual and operational—in how Bill Clinton and I approach American foreign policy. Yet, as my support of the President's authority to deploy U.S. troops in Bosnia suggests, I have never been reluctant to put the national interests ahead of short-term political gain. In that spirit, I would appeal to President Clinton and his party to reconsider a real and growing danger to the United States posed by ballistic missiles fired from half a world away.

Polls suggest that most Americans believe that our country could defend itself against such an attack. But that is not the case. In fact, today we would not be able to destroy a single incoming enemy missile. This isn't because we lack the technical know-how to shield ourselves against such an attack. It's because we lack presidential leadership that is truly visionary.

In 1995, Congress passed and sent to the White House legislation committing this country to a national missile defense system by the year 2003. The next American century, we resolved, would not be held hostage to nuclear blackmail of the kind which darkened half of the twentieth century.

The President vetoed the bill, thereby leaving the United States cruelly exposed. Perhaps this is because the President and his advisers are themselves prisoners of history, trapped by Cold War–era arms-control thinking which placed a greater priority on preserving the 1972 Anti-Ballistic Missile Treaty than on protecting the American people. The realities of today are that countries like Russia, China and North Korea subcontract terror by shipping missile components and lethal technologies to some twenty-five countries around the globe.

As I write this, the North Koreans are developing a ballistic missile capable of threatening Alaska and Hawaii early in the next century. In response, the Clinton Administration has adopted a "What, me worry?" policy toward the proliferation of ballistic-missile technology. It says the threat is years away.

Well, isn't it the responsibility of leaders to anticipate and counter future threats? Certainly history shows, with unmistak-

second term on November 5, neither his instincts nor his ideo-

able conviction, that the rate of scientific advance cannot be safely predicted. In 1949, the CIA released its annual report on the Soviet atomic program, confidently predicting that a Soviet atomic test was unlikely before mid-1953 at the earliest. A few weeks after that report's release, the Soviets joined the nuclear fraternity.

The choice is ours. We can leave America undefended and hope for the best. Or we can deploy the finest minds and the world's most advanced science to ensure that Americans a century from now will have reason to thank us for extending a protective shield over posterity.

I've seen more than enough of war to know that you can't take chances with American security. Peace through strength is more than a slogan; it is the blueprint for American survival in a world bristling with dangers. In modernizing our military forces and sharpening our technological edge, our goal is not just sufficient strength to turn back a threat. No, America must be so strong that no tyrant is ever tempted to threaten us at all.

HOPE, FAITH AND THE FUTURE

Over the years, I've watched Presidents of both parties strive to do what they thought was best for America. For all my criticisms of his administration, I'm sure Bill Clinton is trying to do no less.

For whatever reason, however, the President has cast himself as the rear guard of big government. Oh, sure, between now and election day, he will hijack a few Republican flags and employ his verbal skills to depict himself as a moderate or a conservative. But if you strip away all the rhetoric, what you find is a very genial apologist for the liberal status quo.

Can anyone deny that it took a Republican Congress to drag Bill Clinton, kicking and screaming, toward theoretical acceptance of a balanced budget? But the President has yet to implement that theory, and it's a safe bet that, should he win a second term on November 5, neither his instincts nor his ideological soulmates will permit it.

Come November 6, the New Democrat would revert to form. With no need to face the voters again, a reelected Bill Clinton would be free to revive a Washington takeover of health care. He would be liberated to raise taxes, to pack our courts with liberal judges, to take another whack at American defense and to quietly shelve any possibility of rethinking education or genuinely reinventing government.

You have it within your power to change America this November. Bill Clinton won't, or can't, do it. But I can.

You want less government and more freedom. So do I.

You want a positive alternative to a bankrupt government and a creaky welfare state. So do I.

You want pro-growth policies that will create and sustain jobs worthy of the next century. So do I.

You believe you're entitled to lower taxes and more take-home pay. So do I.

You want a balanced federal budget and the lower interest rates sure to follow. So do I.

You want real welfare reform. So do I.

You want schools that work and students prepared for an economy in which change is the only constant. So do I.

You want Social Security to be strong and secure for this and future generations. So do I.

You want Medicare to be around when today's young working families have need of its protection. So do I.

You want judges who will put criminals in jail and keep them there. So do I.

You want a society that will not stand silently by and tolerate a gruesome procedure where babies are partially removed from the womb in the ninth month of pregnancy and then aborted. So do I.

You want a strong defense in a dangerous world and a foreign policy dictated by principle, not polling data. So do I.

You want a country whose citizens have both access to affordable medical care and the right to choose their own doctor, hospital and insurance policy. So do I.

You are anxious about the future. I know something about anxiety, of a kind few people will ever experience. For there once was a time when I too, doubted the future. There were moments when I thought I would spend the rest of my life on the sidelines, maybe selling pencils or eking out a meager existence.

That's when I learned the validity of my state's motto, "To the stars through difficulties." And that's when I discovered that the only limit to a man's future is self-imposed.

The same holds true for America. For all our challenges, this remains the freest, most generous, most imaginative nation on earth. There is nothing we can't do, no obstacle we can't overcome, no dream we can't realize. I want to be President, not merely to soothe some temporary anxieties, but to help the American people realize their hopes in a new century of limitless possibility.

All this summer, Americans are following the progress of the Olympic Torch as it is carried across the continent in a series of relays. The presidency is a sort of relay into the future, with the torch of responsibility passed from one Commander-in-Chief to another. It has been run for two centuries now, and the world looks on in mingled admiration and envy.

This fall, Americans must ask themselves: Are we satisfied with the way the flame has been tended these last four years? Does it burn as brightly as it should for young and not-so-young Americans? Does the flame light the way to a better life for ourselves and our children? Are we taking it along the right path to a freer, fairer, nobler America?

Or should the torch be passed to a new President, one who knows a better way, and who will carry it on a steady course to a higher destination before passing it on to other hands?

I believe the torch should be passed in 1996, and I am prepared to receive it. I understand America's anxieties, but I am motivated by America's hopes.

At the end of what has been called "The American Century," I stand ready to work with the American people to renew our prospects by returning to the principles and values which made us unique in the family of nations.

I am prepared to restrain a runaway government and to lift restraints placed on the spirit and enterprise of individual

Americans. I am moved to reassert America's rightful place as a light to guide the nations. I do so mindful of the words of another plain-spoken Midwesterner.

"America was not built on fear," said Harry Truman. "America was built on courage, on imagination, and on an unbeatable determination to do the job at hand."

Bob Dole's America is a land strong of courage, rich in imagination and united in an unbeatable determination to meet the challenges of the next American Century.

Acknowledgments

Writing an autobiography is as much a group endeavor as running for office or crafting public policy. Along with the friends and colleagues who helped in the original 1988 publication of *Unlimited Partners,* we are indebted to the following, whose memories helped us recapture the past eight years: Marcie Adler, Sheila Burke, Roy Clason, Bob Davis, Jenna Dorn, Phil Hasseltine, John Heubusch, Clarkson Hine, Roberts Jones, Tom Korologos, Carol Scott and Cindi Williams.

We are grateful to Alice Mayhew, our original editor at Simon and Schuster, and to Trish Todd, who has shepherded this new edition through the publishing process with speed and skill. Thanks, as well, to Aviva Goode and Theresa Horner, who are part of Simon and Schuster's talented team.

Richard Norton Smith—Rick to his friends, and we are fortunate to be among them—has been much more than a collaborator over the years. A highly respected biographer and historian, Rick was the guiding force behind the original publication of *Unlimited Partners.*

For the past seven years, Kerry Tymchuk has worked for one of us—or, more often than not, for both of us. We appreciate his devoting his own time to this project, and we value this talented Oregonian's writing skills, political acumen and friendship.

Index